Surveillance, Law and the Humanities

Surveillance, Law and the Humanities

Edited by Anne Brunon-Ernst,
Jelena Gligorijević,
Desmond Manderson and
Claire Wrobel

EDINBURGH
University Press

Edinburgh University Press is one of the leading university presses in the UK. We publish academic books and journals in our selected subject areas across the humanities and social sciences, combining cutting-edge scholarship with high editorial and production values to produce academic works of lasting importance. For more information visit our website: edinburghuniversitypress.com

Grateful acknowledgement is made to the sources listed in the List of Figures for permission to reproduce material previously published elsewhere. Every effort has been made to trace the copyright holders, but if any have been inadvertently overlooked, the publisher will be pleased to make the necessary arrangements at the first opportunity.

Edinburgh University Press Ltd
13 Infirmary Street, Edinburgh, EH1 1LT

First published in hardback by Edinburgh University Press 2023

Typeset in 11/13 Adobe Garamond Pro by
IDSUK (DataConnection) Ltd

A CIP record for this book is available from the British Library

ISBN 978 1 3995 0508 6 (hardback)
ISBN 978 1 3995 0509 3 (paperback)
ISBN 978 1 3995 0510 9 (webready PDF)
ISBN 978 1 3995 0511 6 (epub)

This work was supported by a grant from the Australian French Association for Research and Innovation (AFRAN). We also thank the Law and Humanities research group (CERSA, Paris-Panthéon-Assas University), and the Centre for Law, Arts and the Humanities (The Australian National University).

Contents

Figures

Contributors

Georgiana Banita (University of Bamberg)

Anne Brunon-Ernst (CERSA (Paris-Panthéon-Assas University) and Centre Bentham (Sciences Po School of Law))

Lucie Cluzel-Métayer (Paris-Nanterre University, Research Centre of Public Law (CRDP) and Administrative Science Research Center (CERSA-CNRS))

Jelena Gligorijević (College of Law, The Australian National University)

Peter Grabosky (School of Regulation and Global Governance (RegNet), The Australian National University)

Rachel Joy (Australian College of Applied Professions)

Desmond Manderson (Centre for Law, Arts, and the Humanities, The Australian National University)

Yves Poullet (Emeritus Professor at the Faculty of Law of Namur and Co-president of the NADI Institute, Associate Professor at UC-Lille, Member of the Royal Academy of Belgium)

Yvonne-Marie Rogez (Université Paris-Panthéon-Assas)

Philippe Sabot (Lille University)

Alexis Tadié (Sorbonne-Université)

Gregor Urbas (School of Regulation and Global Governance (RegNet), The Australian National University)

Aliette Ventéjoux (Saint-Étienne University)

Claire Wrobel (Université Paris-Panthéon-Assas and VALE (Sorbonne Université))

1

Introduction: Watcher, Watching, Watched

Anne Brunon-Ernst, Desmond Manderson,
Jelena Gligorijević and Claire Wrobel

Figure 1.1 Banksy, *Mobile Lovers* (Bristol Youth Club, 2014). Photograph by Ben Birchall, courtesy of PA Images/Alamy.

I. Contemporary Surveillance

The con-temporary, Giorgio Agamben argues, is not simply another word for the present. 'Those who are truly contemporary, who truly belong to their time, are those who neither perfectly coincide with it nor adjust themselves to its demands.'[1] To see ourselves truly in *relation* to our own time demands that we look past the repetitive aphasia of our condition. Images of darkness and light pulse through his text and account for its metaphorical richness.

[1] Agamben, 'What is the Contemporary?', 40.

It is a matter of struggling 'to perceive not its light, but rather its darkness'.[2] And again:

> The ones who can call themselves contemporary are only those who do not allow themselves to be blinded by the lights of the century, and so manage to get a glimpse of the shadows in those lights, of their intimate obscurity.[3]

If this is Agamben's metaphor for contemporary critique, it is doubly apt for a collection of essays about the protean forms of contemporary surveillance. For what is surveillance itself but a play of light and shadows? In Michel Foucault's celebrated terms, we have witnessed a shift from a society organised around power as a spotlight designed to 'render accessible to a multitude of men the inspection of a small number of objects', to one in which power is a searchlight intended to make visible 'for a small number, or even for a single individual, the instantaneous view of a great multitude'.[4] The searchlight is exactly that which lights us up, exposes our position, individually and collectively, for the benefit of various interrogators, investigators, invigilators and night watchmen. It is not just that *they* are hidden in the shadows but that *we* are 'blinded', as Agamben says, 'by the lights of the century'. The glaring light of our exposure is what makes it so hard to see what's going on around us. We suffer from miosis.[5]

Surveillance is a notoriously elusive concept and many authors opt for safely short definitions such as 'the systematic monitoring of people or groups in order to regulate or govern their behavior';[6] 'the monitoring of human activities for the purposes of anticipating or influencing future events';[7] or 'processes in which special note is taken of certain human behaviours that go well beyond idle curiosity'.[8] This collection aspires to something a little more specific. *Law, Surveillance and the Humanities* borrows its definition of surveillance from the report on 'The Surveillance Society' prepared by David Murakami Wood and colleagues for the United Kingdom's Information Commissioner. In that document, surveillance is defined as 'purposeful, routine, systematic and focused attention paid to personal details, for the sake of control, entitlement, management, influence, or protection'.[9] It is further

---

[2] Ibid., 44.
[3] Ibid., 45.
[4] Foucault, *Discipline & Punish*, 216–17.
[5] A contraction of the pupil, typically brought on by excessive exposure to bright light.
[6] Monahan, 'Surveillance as Cultural Practice', 498, original emphasis.
[7] Rosen and Santesso, *Watchman in Pieces*, 10.
[8] Lyon, *Surveillance Studies*, 13.
[9] Murakami Wood, *Report on the Surveillance Society*, 4.

emphasised that 'surveillance is also systematic; it is planned and carried out according to a schedule that is rational, not merely random'. This definition offers several key points. First, it de-dramatises surveillance (as opposed to the way it may be represented in sci-fi thrillers, for instance) and reminds us that it is carried out in a 'routine' way as part of our everyday life. The social field invested by surveillance is not limited to policies of crime control or prison environments.[10] While our volume touches on such questions, it aims to encompass a far wider range of practices. Second, the definition above is a reminder that surveillance does not act on its own; it is the product of policy, the embodiment of a rational 'schedule'. Third, it also highlights the ambivalence of surveillance, on a spectrum ranging from control to protection, implicitly raising the question of how surveillance applies, is experienced, or is valued differently depending on whom it targets.

This collection understands surveillance as an activity enhanced by, but not dependent on, state-of-the-art technological innovations. Indeed, it is necessary and fruitful to draw on past reflections and representations to try to understand the present,[11] rather than treat surveillance as an altogether new phenomenon. Nonetheless, the rise in technological tools is so critical that the phrase 'digital modernity' is used to describe its impact on society.[12] In this new era, both the way surveillance is carried out (what is monitored, how, when and where) and its pervasiveness have been revolutionised, not only in terms of its incidence but also its acceptability in society and by individuals. Governments, and particularly intelligence and police agencies, are of course the prime beneficiaries of these developments. But at the same time, as many scholars have catalogued – most notably Shoshana Zuboff – practices of surveillance have transformed not only media and social media, but capitalism[13] and human subjectivity itself.[14] COVID-19 has only made more apparent the grip of state and corporate surveillance on human beings. In a matter of months, the majority of human activity went online, making it possible comprehensively to monitor mankind on a global scale.

Law, Surveillance and the Humanities takes stock of surveillance's long history, but also of these recent shifts. Surveillance is here also understood as a multidirectional rather than a top-down process. Citizens are not only

[10] See Christie, *Crime Control as Industry.*
[11] Particularly given the instrumentality of surveillance in past imperial endeavours, not least through the implementation of coercive colonial laws, whether by one-directional surveillance of the colonised communities or unwitting cooperation of those communities with the colonial enforcement project: Neti, *Colonial Law in India*, 125, and 142, in particular.
[12] Lyon, 'Surveillance Culture', 1–18.
[13] Zuboff, *Age of Surveillance Capitalism.*
[14] Munar, 'Digital Exhibitionism'; Eichhorn, *End of Forgetting.*

its passive subjects. They take part in it in a variety of ways ranging from the willing to the unwitting. And, although speaking of 'surveillance' in general terms seems to invite universalising statements, this book also draws attention to the ways it is experienced differentially, especially in contexts where power relations are most obvious – and most unequal.

II. The Turn to the Humanities

Ironically, this book represents the fruit of an intercontinental alliance that was not weakened by COVID-related restrictions – and its attendant rise in surveillance capabilities – but strengthened by it: a *pièce de résistance* in its own right. In the limbo that was 2020, we convened seven panel discussions on a wide range of perspectives. Our discussions were interdisciplinary, comparative and critical. We drew on and responded to literature that has plumbed the ubiquity, extent and power of surveillance from diverse disciplines at the intersection of law, society, culture and technology. We examined the transformation and implications of changing practices of surveillance in security, intelligence, the digital economy, and on social media.[15]

The notable features of this collection are its interdisciplinary approach and its commitment to the humanities. Our work draws on and further develops broader interests in control, governance and subjectivity manifested by recent scholarship in the field of law and literature,[16] while further sharpening its focus to the specific question of practices and consequences of surveillance in the modern world. As David Rosen and Aaron Santesso note, such studies continue to be dominated by political science, communication theory, sociology and legal studies, and do not sufficiently draw on the humanities.[17] Of course the distinction is often far from clear-cut, and we can see in important work such as Shoshana Zuboff's *Surveillance Capitalism* and Nicholas Mirzoeff's *The Right to Look* an impressive mastery of many disciplinary perspectives.[18] Yet in broad outline, what distinguishes the disciplines of the humanities is their focus on individual subjectivity and experience, on singularities of voices, narratives and expression, and on the role of culture and representation in how those unique subjects and experiences are understood and remembered.[19] The humanities are less interested in populations or

---

[15] Douzinas, 'Humanities of Resistance', 49.
[16] For examples, see Barter, 'Encrypted Citations'; Neti, *Colonial Law in India*; Nicolazzo, *Vagrant Figures*.
[17] 'The distinctive and necessary contribution of the humanities as such to this conversation has largely gone unarticulated', in Rosen and Santesso, *Watchman in Pieces*, 3.
[18] Zuboff, *Surveillance Capitalism*; Mirzoeff, *Right to Look*.
[19] Manderson and Yachnin, 'Treating HPHD Disorder'.

forces than in stories and identities, subjective experiences and perspectives, individual lives and mentalities. The universal – as Jacques Derrida said on the subject of literature – is *in* the particular;[20] the devil – as someone else said on the subject of governance – is *in* the detail.

In public and political discourse generally, the humanities is sometimes thought to be less relevant to the social problems of the modern world than social science, science or technology.[21] We beg to differ. In this, of course, we are far from alone. This collection aims to participate in what might be called surveillance studies' 'cultural turn', including notable contributions by Frank Pasquale[22] and David Lyon, as well as the approaches grounded in law and literature adverted to elsewhere. Witness the title of Lyon's latest book (*The Culture of Surveillance: Watching as a Way of Life*) or a special issue of *The Sociological Quarterly*, dedicated to 'Surveillance as a Cultural Practice'.[23] What is studied are 'forms of life'[24] or a 'way of life' which consists in 'not only being watched but watching itself, meaning that the contribution of "ordinary people" to surveillance is put under scrutiny'.[25] The phrases 'surveillance state' or 'surveillance society' may no longer seem adequate – if they ever were – because of their exclusively repressive connotations. A 'surveillance culture', on the other hand, is made up of 'the participation and engagement of [both] surveilled and surveilling subjects'.[26] Lyon continues: 'While acknowledging what goes on in our organizational surveillance, it turns the spotlight on all our very varied roles in relation to surveillance.'[27] Torin Monahan likewise describes surveillance as 'embedded within, brought about by, and generative of social practices in specific cultural contexts'.[28]

This cultural turn entails a shift in perspective. Gary T. Marx defines surveillance as 'the operations and experiences of gathering and analysing personal data for influence, entitlement and management'.[29] The inclusion of the word 'experiences' is telling. As Marx puts it, 'surveillance technology is

[20] Derrida, 'Before the Law', 213.
[21] Note that in recent years the Australian federal government has rejected humanities-based grant applications recommended for funding according to the stringent selection criteria of the Australian Research Council, its peak expert advisory body, precisely on the grounds that such research is not sufficiently for 'the public benefit'. Whether this habit of mind will change under a new government remains to be seen.
[22] Pasquale, *Black Box Society*; Pasquale, *New Laws of Robotics*.
[23] Monahan, Torin, ed., 'Surveillance as Cultural Practice,' *The Sociological Quarterly*.
[24] Monahan, 'Surveillance as Cultural Practice', 499.
[25] Lyon, *Culture of Surveillance*, 2.
[26] Ibid., 16.
[27] Ibid., 7.
[28] Monahan, 'Surveillance as Cultural Practice', 496.
[29] Gary T. Marx , qtd in Lyon, *Culture of Surveillance*, 6.

not simply applied; it is also *experienced* by subjects, agents and audiences who define, judge and have feelings about being watched or a watcher'.[30] While for a long time the focus was on institutional-level power dynamics with surveillance being exercised from the top down, social studies of surveillance centre on 'individuals in local contexts'.[31] The change consists in adopting the perspective from below, from the watched, but also in studying the latter's possible agency, which ranges from active participation to resistance. Pasquale identifies human accountability as key to resistance.[32] Simone Browne adapts Steve Mann's definition of sousveillance as 'active inversion of the power relations that surveillance entails' to the specific context of race-based surveillance practices. 'Dark sousveillance' then refers to a form of counter-surveillance in which the racialised targets of surveillance challenge the gaze they are under.[33]

In keeping with these approaches, Philippe Sabot, in his contribution to the present collection, addresses the contradictory desires of social media users for exposition and protection; elsewhere, Grabosky and Urbas explore similar motivations amongst non-state investigators. In a sense, at least in liberal democracies, fighting COVID-19 with surveillance requires the approval and active participation of the watched,[34] for instance by encouraging them to download tracking apps, one of the tools mentioned by Yves Poullet here. Surveillance is not a monolithic tool of the state. Rather, the essays collected here illustrate the extent to which it is multifaceted, multidirectional and dynamic. *Law, Surveillance and the Humanities* covers and confronts the perspectives and indeed the responses of those engaged in surveillance, subjected to it, and using it, noting that one individual is not restricted to occupying one position only.

As to the specific contribution of the humanities to these projects, Torin Monahan argues that '[j]ust like all technologies [. . .] surveillance systems attain presence as negotiated components of culture and accrete meaning by tapping a culture's immense symbolic reservoirs, which can include narrative, media, and art, among other things.'[35] This suggests a range of possible lines of inquiry, all of which are pursued here. In the first place, the work

---

[30] Marx, *Windows into the Soul*, 173.
[31] Monahan, 'Surveillance as Cultural Practice', 496.
[32] Pasquale, *Black Box Society*, 213: 'Accountability requires human judgment, and only humans can perform the critical function of making sure that, as our social relations become ever more automated, domination and discrimination aren't built invisibly into their code.'
[33] Browne, *Dark Matters*, 18–19, 21. See also Mann, Nolan, and Wellman, 'Sousveillance'.
[34] Not dissimilar to the 'unwitting cooperation' of colonised communities in former empires, which, though not liberal democracies, also relied on compliance and complicity for effective control over the populace: Neti, *Colonial Law in India*, 125.
[35] Monahan, 'Surveillance as Cultural Practice', 499.

of writers and artists can provide us with a focus and an image capable of distilling and clarifying our anxieties, 'provid[ing] imaginative resources that oftentimes channel latent concerns and anticipate future worlds'.[36] Consider for a brief moment a work by Banksy (Figure 0.1) which likewise plays on the relationship between dark and light, between the seen and the unseen.[37] Sheltered in a doorway on a dark city street, a couple embrace, lit up by the glow of the mobile phones to which their attention is in fact directed. What are they so anxious about missing? What in their own relationship, or in the city from which they seem to be in retreat, does their anxiety cause them to miss? Who, we may ask, is watching whom – and with what consequences for our personal and our public lives? What is correlative about their mutual exposure, illumination and blindness? In what ways is the image of something as mundane as the light of a mobile phone suggestive not just of the banality of modern technological data and communication, but of practices of surveillance in which it is sometimes difficult to tell the watchers and the watched apart? And with what effect on our contemporary affective lives?

Second, thinking on surveillance may benefit from literary analysis and literary history. Any such discussion stands in the shadow of D. A. Miller's path-breaking work in *The Novel and the Police*. Miller perceived in the triumph of the form's social realism and its psychological interiority during the nineteenth century a powerfully conventional normativity and a radical extension of Foucauldian discipline.[38] Yet there is an important distinction to be made here. Miller, and others such as John Bender who have developed similar arguments, see literature as a form of internal self-surveillance, complicit with modern governance.[39] Without denying the force of this argument, others – including the authors assembled in the current volume – are alive to literature's potential to illuminate the social forces operative in our society, and indeed to ignite a spark of resistance. In *The Electronic Eye: The Rise of Surveillance Society*, David Lyon warned against resorting exclusively to Orwell's *Nineteen Eighty-Four* or Foucault's version of Bentham's Panopticon and pointed instead to Franz Kafka's *The Castle* or Margaret Atwood's *The Handmaid's Tale* as potential sources of powerful metaphors.[40] He went on to include films like *Brazil*, *Blade Runner*, *The Truman Show*, *Minority Report*,[41] and, most recently, David Eggers' 2013 novel *The Circle*.[42] Others

[36] Ibid., 501.
[37] O'Brien, 'Banksy's Latest Works'.
[38] Miller, *The Novel and the Police*.
[39] Bender, *Imagining the Penitentiary*; Purdon, *Modernist Informatics*.
[40] Lyon, *Electronic Eye*, 78–9.
[41] Lyon, *Surveillance Studies*.
[42] Lyon, *Culture of Surveillance*, 149–72.

have taken as their point of departure the 'laws of robotics' first adumbrated by Isaac Asimov in 1942.[43]

In this volume, Alexis Tadié's account of eighteenth-century British literature reminds us that neither surveillance nor its discontents were inventions of the twentieth century. Peter Marks, in his book on surveillance and literary utopias, takes us back to Thomas More's *Utopia* (1516).[44] David Rosen and Aaron Santesso begin their survey in the Renaissance.[45] Sal Nicolazzo starts her study of vagrancy, which 'offered a legal and tropological model for police as a mode of governance', with the Settlement Act of 1662, which legally defined parish settlement.[46] One might even go back to the Domesday Book compiled for William the Conqueror in 1086. This volume further widens the literary pool with analyses of Margaret Atwood's novels by Claire Wrobel, and by Aliette Ventéjoux of Jonathan Raban's 2006 novel *Surveillance* – the beginning, perhaps of a distinctive genre.[47]

Contemporary fiction does not only provide heuristic metaphors. It makes systematic use of the mechanisms already apparent in eighteenth-century fiction, that is, it uses the distance induced by genres such as dystopia or, more generally, speculative fiction to hold a satirical mirror to society, crystallising with biting clarity surveillance phenomena which we perceive confusedly. The variety of tones and registers it resorts to enriches our cultural response to surveillance. Moreover, the literature that foregrounds surveillance may perform a didactic function. As Peter Marks suggests, literature may 'offer vicarious experiences of surveillance' by 'provid[ing] us with scenarios, narratives and characters through which we can imagine surveillance worlds similar to, or intriguingly different from, our own, and in which we see individuals, groups and societies responding to the existence or development of surveillance regimes, technologies and protocols'.[48] Nor do our cultural metaphors come only from literature. Foucault's controversial, strategic interpretation of Bentham's plan for a model prison has turned the late eighteenth-century fantasy into a key figure of social analysis. As Anne Brunon-Ernst's chapter explains, although the relevance of the Panopticon has been called into question, it retains an alluring cultural significance.

Conversely, awareness of surveillance and of its techniques may be changing the very way stories are told.[49] CCTV does not speak by itself. Not only

[43] Pasquale, *New Laws of Robotics*, 2.
[44] Marks, *Imagining Surveillance*, 40–3.
[45] Rosen and Santesso, *Watchman in Pieces*.
[46] Nicolazzo, *Vagrant Figures*, 3.
[47] Nellis, 'Since *Nineteen Eighty Four*', 197.
[48] Marks, *Imagining Surveillance*, 3.
[49] See Wasihun, 'Resisting Authority'.

do CCTV images only make sense when inserted within the framework of a narrative, but such images have also become cultural material themselves.[50] Shaping and controlling narrative is central to criminal policy, as the chapter by Georgiana Banita illustrates. On the one hand, then, our critical literacy about surveillance can be furthered by the 'metacognitive capacities' developed through the practice of literary analysis.[51] On the other hand, however, the authors in this collection are vigilant in situating their analyses within longer cultural histories and practices of surveillance of people occupying the margins of society[52] – including not least practices of fiction writing and their political appropriation which have as often mystified the experiences and processes of slavery or colonialism (for example) as illuminated them.[53]

Third, if generalising statements about surveillance have sometimes leant on images of abstract, automatic, anonymous systems, this collection reminds us that, from the perspective of the humanities, individual agency remains central to the discussion. Surveillance is inherently ambiguous – its spectrum ranges from care to control,[54] from empathy to coercion.[55] In such a context, motives, principles, and our practices of 'ethical assessment' surely matter as much as a purely instrumental analysis.[56] Nicolazzo ends her study of Equiano's *Interesting Narrative* (1789) by noting how 'the aesthetic history of the police is in fact a history [. . . which includes] improvisation, creativity, narrative idiosyncrasy, loquaciousness, humor, terror, and more'.[57] Such remarks call for a nuanced analysis of the functioning of surveillance which is at odds with presumptions of panoptic uniformity and requires literary awareness of tones and registers. As Rosen and Santesso suggest, '[t]o the extent that both the initiators and the targets of surveillance remain human, the human arts will remain relevant to understanding the stakes in any surveillance situation.'[58] Furthermore, as they go on to explain, '[t]he complex dialectical struggle between surveillance and selfhood is one that the study of literature, with its close interrogation of character, and philosophy, with its

---

[50] See Falkenhayner, *Media, Surveillance and Affect*.

[51] Rosen and Santesso, *Watchman in Pieces*, 278.

[52] See for example Ellis, *Race War and Surveillance*; Purdon, *Modernist Informatics*; Mirzoeff, *Right to Look*; Barter, 'Encrypted Citations'.

[53] Rinehart, 'The Man that Was a Thing'; Neti, *Colonial Law in India*; Nicolazzo, *Vagrant Figures*; Barter, 'Encrypted Citations'.

[54] Monahan, 'Surveillance as Cultural Practice', 497.

[55] Rosen and Santesso define empathy as 'surveillance for the purposes of understanding and anticipation' and coercion as 'surveillance as an attempt to change behaviour through applied pressure' in *Watchman in Pieces*, 225.

[56] Lyon, *Culture of Surveillance*, 17.

[57] Nicolazzo, *Vagrant Figures*, 236.

[58] Rosen and Santesso, *Watchman in Pieces*, 277.

central interest in the thinking subject, are well positioned to tackle.'[59] Thus, as the chapters by Jelena Gligorijević and Lucie Cluzel-Métayer forcefully demonstrate, the centrality of concepts of agency, privacy and personhood to our self-understanding marks a point of convergence between law and the humanities.

Finally, then, the humanities invite us to take a step back from 'the lights of the century', to understand better its underlying structures and normative assumptions; and a step forward, into the sinews and signs of everyday life. Foucault's appropriation of Bentham's Panopticon has long been a vital point of reference in surveillance studies.[60] But Foucault's work equally sets the standard for understanding powerful historical transformations through their literary, aesthetic and cultural avatars as much as through developments in science and technology. In that vein, while the present volume is attuned to technological developments in the field of surveillance, from online crime and e-health to algorithms and artificial intelligence, we continue to interpret them through an interdisciplinary and humanistic tradition that makes it possible to explore how surveillance relates to ourselves, to others and to institutions; and that connects the world in which we live to its representations and to its effects on individuals and communities.

III. Foundations, Spaces and Critique

Part 1 of this collection considers the *foundational* concepts and literatures that form the necessary background to any discussion of surveillance in the twenty-first century. These texts focus on identity, privacy and surveillance, as these concepts have been refracted and represented through key works at the heart of our intellectual tradition, including in philosophy, legal theory, history and literature. In 'Surveillance and its Ambiguities', Philippe Sabot examines contemporary forms of surveillance by focusing on the normative ambiguities they contain. Recent developments, particularly in the context of online behaviours and the use of social networks, reveal a tension between a society of *surveillance* and a society of *exposition*. The growing desire of individuals for self-exposure appears at odds with certain ways of thinking about surveillance as an unwelcome intrusion on private individual life. But, Sabot argues, this desire itself may be related to a paradoxical need for protection: the exposition of oneself, of private life as well as personal data, may increase our desire for security, as if what was to be monitored is the very possibility of a limitless exposition. As he writes, 'the desire for control and the control of desire are folded back onto each other, shaping new forms of subjectivity and redrawing the contours of freedom and security'. This

---

[59] Ibid., 4.
[60] Foucault, *Discipline and Punish*, part 3, ch. 3.

way of delegating to external systems the control and regulation of our private lives gains new salience in the context of the public health crisis of the 2020s, in which the desire for biological security and the desire for individual freedom appear increasingly on a collision course. Drawing specifically on practices illuminated and refined during the present pandemic, Sabot shows how contemporary surveillance *dispositifs* arise from contradictory desires and the ambiguous divisions they establish between private and public, freedom and security, intimate and healthy living. Indeed, in a redolent turn of phrase, Sabot suggests that it is only those at risk of spreading disease who are, through mechanisms of digital surveillance, to be 'vaccinated' against their own dangerousness.

The contradictions highlighted by Sabot, particularly the tension between ideal and critical depictions of social control, have a long history. In 'Surveillance, Utopia and Satire in Eighteenth-Century British Literature', Alexis Tadié takes us back to a much earlier period, drawing our attention to the surprising roots of modern ideas of surveillance in utopian fantasies. Tadié's work therefore participates in a line of work that situates a history of surveillance within a history of literature.[61] But his approach takes a different and ultimately more optimistic approach to the lessons to be drawn from surveillance's literary antecedents. He takes as his starting point Francis Bacon's *New Atlantis*, a thought experiment about a society whose scientific principles are rigidly policed by a regime of strict surveillance. These utopian arrangements become key moments in Jonathan Swift's *Gulliver's Travels*. From the beginning, when Gulliver lands in Lilliput and undermines its inhabitants' attempts at controlling him, to the end when he submits willingly to the will and power of the Houyhnhnms, Gulliver is confronted with issues of surveillance, control, obedience and rebellion. The satirical approach to such issues finds a different expression in Pope's *Dunciad*, but the conclusion is the same. In a manner quite distinct from, for example, Miller's critique of the history of the novel, Tadié impresses on us both the long connection between the idealisation of surveillance in utopian literatures and the equally long prescription of laughter as the best vaccine with which to develop resistance to it.[62] The current debates, which Sabot situates for us and to which Poullet offers a legal background and Gligorijević a jurisprudential framework, are

---

[61] Miller, *The Novel and the Police*; Bender, *Imagining the Penitentiary*; Purdon, *Modernist Informatics*; Neti, *Colonial Law in India*.

[62] In this respect Tadié's argument has something in common with, for example, the work of Faith Barter, who has recently demonstrated how encryption, or the concealed testimony of unfree individuals (paradigmatically, slaves), may form a way of resisting the brutalising and oppressing dogma apparent on the face of the law itself and in its dominant social narratives. Just as Tadié in this collection reveals the importance of satire to resistance, Barter's contention is that this literary device is likewise an important tool of emancipation: Barter 'Encrypted Citations'.

not unique to the contemporary world; on the contrary, their literary origins and their social anxieties go back hundreds of years. Double-edged tropes of surveillance, isolation, vision and self-control haunt figures as varied – and as significant for Western literary history – as Bacon, Gulliver and Crusoe. So too, as Tadié makes clear, literary techniques from narrative and satire to close reading are essential weapons in the toolkit of our response. Indeed, as he argues, the hardest challenge for satire is to allow the reader to admit to their own complicity in the structures thus satirised.

If laughter is a form of resistance, so also, as our next two contributors insist, is the law. In his contribution to this volume, the eminent Belgian jurist Yves Poullet offers a *tour d'horizon* of legal structures and issues around the use of surveillance in the European context, using Belgium as his case study. Poullet draws our attention to foundational principles that are still capable of holding the exercise of power to account and insists on their continuing relevance. But at the same time and paying particular attention to legal and governmental developments prompted by the COVID-19 pandemic, he observes how partially these protections operate and how quickly the language of emergency and necessity can obtain a more extensive remit than a close reading of the various legislative instruments might suggest. The restrictive measures adopted over the past two years, in particular through the use of digital surveillance technologies, go well beyond mere temporary inconveniences imposed on European citizens, whether in Belgium, France or elsewhere; rather, they represent a serious challenge to our legal foundations. The language of emergency, the experience of crisis, and rapid developments in technology, Poullet reminds us, are by no means strangers to overarching legal principles and structures. On the contrary, we would do well to recall their continuing applicability – and their intellectual rigour.

With this appeal to the demanding rigour of the law, Gligorijević would be in whole-hearted agreement. In 'Privacy as Liberty and Security: Implications for the Legitimacy of Governmental Surveillance' she drills down into one of the core values that permeate not only Poullet's discussion but each and every essay in this volume. Although writing from the perspective of the common law, rather than the civil law orientation of the previous chapter, her argument nevertheless demonstrates the foundational legal and moral principles shared by both. Privacy provides a vital way of exposing and resisting governmental surveillance policies and practices, even when they are promoted as necessary for the public good. Gligorijević finds appeals to collective security, which so often underscore arguments for the legitimacy of governmental surveillance even in cases that intrude upon individual privacy, unconvincing. Security, alongside liberty, is normatively embedded in the concept of privacy. It is the very reason why privacy is cherished and protected. Indeed, Gligorijević argues that, at heart, privacy, security and liberty articulate necessarily interrelated aspects of human identity. We cannot simplistically imagine, therefore, that we can use one to override the others. But Gligorijević's contribution here, while analytically rigorous, is by no means merely conceptual. She provides a cogent and compassionate argument for the kind of harm that surveillance does – to our personhood, our dignity, our well-being. She draws on a wealth of empirical, social and psychological examples of that harm, grounding her discussion in details and emotions echoed and paralleled throughout the rest of this book.

Each of the chapters that comprise Part 1 attempts to give us a thick description of a core set of cultural resources – foundations deployed, in various ways, throughout the book and throughout, indeed, the literature on surveillance. For Sabot, those foundations are social and political. For Tadié, they are historical and literary. For Poullet and Gligorijević, legal, ethical and jurisprudential. For Brunon-Ernst, as the first chapter of the next part makes clear, they are architectural.

Part 2, *Spaces*, turns from the foundations of critiques of surveillance to a more detailed consideration of the dimensions and spheres of its operation in contemporary society. Current health policies, on the one hand, and initiatives directed against transnational and international terrorism, on the other, provide high-profile instances of the expansion and development of such measures, but only make newly visible what has long been taking place in other spaces – virtual and real, cyber and urban, personal and global. Contemporary mechanisms of surveillance exploit and amplify these spatial fields in complex ways.

In this respect, Anne Brunon-Ernst's analysis of Foucault's treatment of Bentham's Panopticon provides the ideal bridge between the first and second parts of the book. On the one hand, as a form, an image or an idea, the Panopticon is a starting point and foundation for all the literature on surveillance to follow. Foucault's discussion unites, in a single figure, historical, literary, legal *and* conceptual lodestars for our thinking about surveillance and constitutes, therefore, a pivotal intellectual nexus for present discussions. On the other hand, what is the Panopticon if not the best-known and most influential representation of surveillance as an actual space? – a physical and material architectural form that, across multiple iterations and diverse interpretations, has helped us understand the past, present and future of surveillance.

Brunon-Ernst's analysis of Foucault's seminal treatment not only enriches the use made of his work in, for example, the discussions by Sabot and Gligorijević in this collection. It draws out precisely the ambivalence nestled within the idea of surveillance that Tadié already finds in eighteenth-century literary treatments: that is, their utopian and dystopian aspects. Several recent scholars have concluded that this model is out of date. But Brunon-Ernst argues that its very longevity, spanning from an eighteenth-century image to nineteenth-century efforts at implementation, twentieth-century social and legal theories, and twenty-first-century works of fiction, demonstrates an astonishing fecundity across diverse fields of knowledge. The extent to which the Panopticon remains a fitting descriptive tool in relation to contemporary surveillance may be debatable, but the image of the Panopticon continues to tap into our collective psyche – a spectre that captures our primal fears about the dissolution of our liberties and ourselves. Thus Brunon-Ernst's rich discussion of the continuing reception of Foucault's imaginative reading, not just in the work of scholars of surveillance but in works of fiction, argues that it is precisely through the lens of the humanities that it can best be understood and indeed can best be critiqued and resisted. A vital claim to which much else in this collection undoubtedly attests.

In 'Online Undercover Investigations and the Role of Private Third Parties', Peter Grabosky and Gregor Urbas turn to more specific developments in crime-prevention surveillance. They focus primarily on online child exploitation, highlighting the potential for abuse by state agencies, and questioning the adequacy of remedies available to its targets. They then turn to non-state investigators, including NGOs, vigilantes and even TV shows, noting that their targets have even less protection. Significantly, Grabosky and Urbas position their critique not simply in relation to the growing power that governments have ceded to surveillance activities, but to the fundamental legal principles that might be thought to mark their limit. While they give due recognition to the avenues of legal resistance explored by other writers, they are at pains to point out their inadequacy given the protean forms that contemporary surveillance takes, and the culture of toleration that surrounds it. As Gligorijević argues in a broader context, in a climate of high anxiety about certain sorts of criminal conduct the law has apparently made its peace with the use of exceptional and intrusive countermeasures. The long-term implications of these zealous responses have not always been adequately considered. Above all, Grabosky and Urbas astutely demonstrate the link between surveillance activities carried out by the state and those of non-state actors. Indeed, as they note, in the twenty-first century the line between the two is sometimes illusory. As others in this collection, such as Sabot, have observed, the logic, practice and legitimation of digital surveillance is a global and social phenomenon; a language of rights – or for that matter, a legal regime – which focuses exclusively on government action without considering this broader context will miss the point.

The next two chapters bring these concerns with law and policing back to everyday life, as it is experienced and as it is lived. Each draws in different ways on Pasquale's main argument in *The Black Box Society* that knowledge asymmetries in the world of data (banking and Internet) are the basis of power relations.[63] Aliette Ventéjoux's study of Jonathan Raban's 2006 novel *Surveillance* translates what we might call the conflation of spatial jurisdictions, and the disorientation it produces, into the intimate and subjective realm of literature. The novel depicts a world riven by fear, where the interconnected methods of government-sponsored and peer-to-peer surveillance generate suspicion and paranoia. Raban examines the impacts of surveillance, not just on personal identity but on a global scale, and moreover highlights how such practices destabilise the distinctions between them, intensifying and exploiting the very insecurity they are allegedly meant to assuage. As Ventéjoux writes, surveillance is rhizomic, creeping 'like branches [. . .] into every corner of public and private space'. On the one hand, the 'enhanced surveillance procedures' of the Patriot Act (2001) form the political background to the novel. On the other hand, as Raban states, 'we're all data miners now': surveillance is a game in which we are all willing or unwilling participants. In fact, as she observes of Raban's book, the promise of surveillance is largely an illusion: it fails to predict, it fails to prevent. It is rather at the level of the fragmentation of personal space and the production of anxiety that it excels. In a world where technology allows the sharing of information across borders and boundaries at the speed of light, Ventéjoux shows how literature can bring home the ways in which the dissolution of space – personal, psychological, social, political – is experienced and felt by subjects themselves.

Lucie Cluzel-Métayer's 'Safe Cities: The French Experience' picks up on Raban's urban and contemporary themes but parlays them in the register of everyday changes in police practice. Again, the logic is seductive – even utopian: in a context of tensions exacerbated by terrorist and health threats, the collecting, modelling and cross-referencing of Big Data on the circumstances and modalities of past crimes and misdemeanours allows the police to better predict and combat risks. That the utopian should so readily bleed into the dystopian will, to readers of this book, come as no surprise. As Cluzel-Métayer warns, these techno-police experiments pose serious risks to fundamental rights, combining and amplifying the power of disparate data, video surveillance, geolocation, biometrics, 'intelligent video surveillance' and facial recognition algorithms. Cluzel-Métayer provides fascinating details about the ways in which this disparate data can now be used to detect suspicious behaviour in real life, and even in some cases claiming to be able to

---

[63] Pasquale, *Black Box Society*.

predict the location of offences, enabling rapid and preventive police deployment – transforming Philip K. Dick's 'The Minority Report' (1956) from fiction to reality. In Cluzel-Métayer's view, these experiments will undoubtedly flourish given the security, health and corporate interests involved. We may see a rise in the power of private stakeholders, as well as growing engagement by the population, generating a form of co-production of security and a decline in the role of the state. The balance between police measures and individual freedoms has become fragile. Echoing arguments made by Sabot, Gligorijević, and Grabosky and Urbas amongst others in this collection, Cluzel-Métayer posits several reasons: the context of the terrorist threat, to which the health crisis must now be added, but also the transformation of our relationship to digital privacy, and the struggle for both regulatory regimes and enforcement mechanisms to keep up. Again, as Grabosky and Urbas have already observed, the line between police action and social attitudes cannot be clearly drawn. Neither, in the era of outsourced responsibilities, is the distinction between state and corporate interests meaningful any more. On the contrary, there is a 'co-production of security' at work in which corporations, police, governments and individual citizens are all implicated.

Above all, Cluzel-Métayer detects a deep emotional paradox which others in this volume, such as Ventéjoux, have already observed. Urban life is digital living: fuelling both our anxiety for safety and the 'omnipresent digital technology' that enables its surveillance and control. As she suggests, the rhetorical shift from 'Smart Cities' to 'Safe Cities' thus appeals to a heartfelt desire that the use of increasingly extensive surveillance tools at once affirms, addresses – and jeopardises. Cluzel-Métayer offers several examples in which the French legal system has resisted, with no little intestinal fortitude, the will of governments and businesses to further expand their data collection and surveillance of individuals – most notably in relation to measures introduced in response to the recent pandemic. But Cluzel-Métayer, like Poullet before her, remains unconvinced as to whether, in the long run, judicial intervention will be enough to roll back the vast technological and social transformations which she charts.

Part 3 engages in the traditional humanities practice of *Critique*. As Parts 1 and 2 of this book have surely shown us, surveillance affects us all; but it does not affect us all equally. Indeed, for all their ostensible novelty, contemporary forms of control and technologies of surveillance are inextricable from much older patterns of oppression based on race, class, ability, gender, sexual identity and age.[64] In giving voice to the perspectives of those who

---

[64] Kenner, 'Securing the Elderly Body', 252–69; Currah and Moore, '"We Won't Know Who You Are"', 113–35; Browne, 'Digital Epidermization', 131–50; Eubanks, *Digital Dead End*; Magnet, *When Biometrics Fail.*

experience these oppressions on a daily basis, and specifically in reconnecting practices of surveillance to their sublimated racial and colonial histories, we draw on the work of scholars such as Mirzoeff, working in critical and postcolonial theory, criminology, visual studies and comparative literature.[65] Thus Daniel Heller-Roazen, in *Absentees*, highlights an ethical duty to pay 'attention' to 'nonpersons', who 'deserve investigation' in their own right.[66] Among the three categories of 'nonpersons' he discusses – missing persons, diminished individuals and the deceased – the second one, which gathers the disenfranchised, is the most relevant to this section. As he writes, 'nonpersons are legion. [. . .] In every community, society, and assembly, nonpersons are lesser ones – where "lesser" points not to a quantity, but to a quality, which is intensely variable in kind.'[67] His cross-cultural study, which takes us back to ancient Greece and Rome, highlights how the law deals with and produces such nonpersons. The 'nonpersons' or 'lessened beings' of ancient times – 'women, children, foreigners, enemies, pirates, and slaves' – are the focus of the chapters in this section.[68] Far from being merely juxtaposed, these categories of 'nonpersons' are inextricably linked. So too, as Nicolazzo demonstrates, cast-off mistresses, children, slaves and unemployed Asian sailors could all come under the category of 'vagrants' established in the early modern period. They were regarded as 'waste' which, instead of imposing a burden for the parish, could be repurposed in the service of empire. Being labelled a vagrant was to be thrust into a capacious category that did not care for identity, and to enter in a relation to the law in which one was perceived proleptically as a potential threat.

In 'Black Futures Matter: Racial Foresight from the Slave Ship to Predictive Policing', Georgiana Banita offers a compelling 'archive' of the surveillance of Black Americans from slave ships to civil rights activists to broken windows theory, in line with Nicolazzo's study, which shows how English vagrancy laws were repurposed 'to manage the intensifying racialization of space and labor in the colonies' and ends by identifying a 'call for a return to an earlier model of policing that emphasises anticipatory prevention of threat rather than the investigation of crimes already committed' in Kelling and Wilson's article.[69] Banita's work, alongside Nicolazzo's, sustains the arguments

---

[65] See Mirzoeff, *Right to Look*; Mirzoeff, 'Artificial Vision'; Mirzoeff, 'The Sea and the Land'. See also Rinehart, 'The Man that Was a Thing'; Ellis, *Race War and Surveillance*.

[66] Heller-Roazen, *Absentees*, 88, 78.

[67] Ibid., 7.

[68] Ibid., 88.

[69] Nicolazzo, *Vagrant Figures*, 162, 247. See also Kelling and Wilson, 'Police and Neighborhood Safety'.

for the historical continuity of surveillance made in Part 1 of this book. At the same time, drawing in particular on the figure of the Panopticon, she rightly insists that surveillance is fundamentally visual in nature. This visuality, this obsessive watching of bodies marked by their visible difference, has always been animated by and inextricable from patterns of underlying racism. In particular, Banita argues that what is sought through surveillance is not the control of violence but the prevention, in advance, of its potential. As we have seen elsewhere in this collection, the fantasy of surveillance is ingrained in the past but fixated on the *future*. It is a dream of 'racial foresight'. Even the murder of an unarmed Black man like Amadou Diallo, in 1999, did little to prompt any questioning of police tactics. 'For the police, [he] was a broken window too, not a human being but a signal of disorder to come.'

Banita situates contemporary methods of surveillance aimed at *pre-empting* Black violence, from racial profiling and the chokehold to the use of predictive algorithms, within this oppressive history of watchfulness. Her chapter exposes the panoptic logic involved in, and the devastating consequences of, the social construction of Black futures, as always and presumptively dangerous. Thus, Banita separates herself from those, like Shoshana Zuboff, who treat 'surveillance capitalism' as a form of neo-colonialism enmeshing us all. On the contrary, domination continues to be highly differential and selective in its effects. It is Black futures that are now, as they have been for centuries, the singularly blighted.

Endemic racism forms the basis, motivation and origins of practices of surveillance in societies all over the world. Nevertheless, each historical experience is distinctive. Racism takes protean forms in numberless countries. The virulent racism that has marked Australia's settler colonial history is well known and worthy of particular attention, particularly in a collection which emerges out of a unique Franco-Australian collaboration. In 'Fear of the Dark: The Racialised Surveillance of Indigenous Peoples in Australia', Rachel Joy provides a critical analysis of how surveillance has been used by settlers against Indigenous populations, demonstrating on multiple levels the ways in which institutional and everyday practices of surveillance mark out spaces that 'Blacks cannot cross and whites cannot see'. A specific range of settler colonial atmospherics, they argue, can be seen to have produced the racialised lawscapes that negatively affect Black bodies, maintaining them under conditions of constant visibility, while scrupulously shielding from scrutiny the privileges of white bodies, and the interests of capital. Again then the paradox of visibility and invisibility, of precisely who is visible to whom, is central to this analysis. The surveillance of Indigenous communities and the biopolitics of controlling Aboriginal bodies emerge as central techniques of settler colonial governance, at every level: practices of hyper-incarceration (note that suggestive word, 'the watch house'), income management, racial profiling, sentencing practices, CCTV cameras that document abuse but do nothing to prevent it. This is not to mention the exceptional powers to intrude, to surveil and to monitor the lives of Aboriginal Australians authorised, with indecent alacrity, by the 2007 Northern Territory Intervention. Indigenous peoples live perforce in settler society; they are the object of an endless, anxious, obsessive watchfulness.

Joy is by no means the first to point out that Foucault's argument in *Discipline and Punish* failed adequately to consider the racial and colonial motives of these modes of surveillance. The work of Mirzoeff, for one, is exemplary on this score.[70] In Australia, Joy argues, governance by surveillance routinely undermines Indigenous self-determination, and enforces the vulnerable status of the hyper-visible. It turns communities into what Agamben calls 'the camp' – sites of violent spatial regulation, discipline and management that Achille Mbembe characterises as 'topographies of cruelty' or, in Loïc Wacquant's terminology, the 'carceral continuum'. Joy's chapter makes for grim reading. As with other contributors to this Part, they argue that contemporary surveillance is old wine in new bottles. It cannot be understood without paying proper attention to its socio-economic and socio-historical context, on the one hand, and the lived experience of its subjects, on the other. 'Right back to mission days', Joy writes, 'there was always some *whitefella* watching. Pastor, protector, policeman: watching, always watching.'

In a similar vein but through the lens of a very different social context, Yvonne-Marie Rogez turns our attention from race to poverty, although without for a moment gainsaying their relationship. 'Policing and Surveillance of the Margins: The Challenges of Homelessness in California' recalls the stark wealth disparities in one of America's wealthiest states, where more than 100,000 people sleep outdoors. Rogez provides a critical overview of the legislation, case law, and political issues and tensions raised by the need to deal with homelessness and its visibility in Californian cities. She focuses on the problematic implications of the surveillance technologies and practices of, and the ways in which they are deployed by, three different groups: government, street police forces and the general population, including homeless charities themselves. Drawing on work in legal studies, urban anthropology and theory, Rogez evaluates recent changes in surveillance practices brought on by the COVID-19 pandemic, particularly as they have exacerbated the very problems of homelessness they were intended to address.

---

[70] Mirzoeff, *Right to Look*; Mirzoeff, 'The Sea and the Land'. See also Ellis, *Race War and Surveillance*; Sonu, 'Making a Racial Difference', 1–15.

Rogez's discussion highlights and provides a remarkably apt contemporary example of a fundamental theme that runs through this collection. Surveillance operates as a mode of hyper-visibility but also operates as a way of enforcing *invisibility* on its subjects. It makes some of the most vulnerable in our society visible to those charged with their care and control, while at the same time endeavouring to remove them from places of public visibility where they are a source of anxiety and discomfort. This structure is by no means anomalous. As Joy has already said of Indigenous Australians, and as Wrobel will observe in relation to gender in the final chapter, marginalised communities experience an exclusion from public space alongside the denial of their private life. Surveillance technologies typically enforce the former (for example, by the use of CCTV or move-on powers) while expanding the latter (for example, by monitoring practices set up by charities, the police, and in shelters). In the case of the homeless, as Rogez so clearly shows, this question is all the more pressing given that the lack of any physical private space lies at the root of their vulnerability.

Claire Wrobel's chapter on gender and surveillance in the fiction of Margaret Atwood is a further contribution to scholarship which has seen science fiction and fantasy as key modes of dramatising problems of control, ideology and the state – from Thomas More and Jonathan Swift to Isaac Asimov.[71] She argues that the psychology, sociology and technology of gendered surveillance has been a *leitmotif* in Atwood's fiction both before and after the dystopian classic *The Handmaid's Tale*. Wrobel reinforces Banita's and Joy's argument on the treatment of race, and echoes Rogez's observation that surveillance operates in a paradoxical play of administrative visibility and social invisibility. She critiques the 'gender-blind' approach to surveillance studies, a blindness all the more surprising given feminism's long-standing theoretical interest in the gaze.[72] Like Banita, she insists that surveillance is essentially visual in its orientation and discriminatory in its operation. And like Cluzel-Métayer, she argues for the importance of literature in helping us affectively engage with the experience of living under this visual regime. The first novel studied here, *Bodily Harm*, shows how Atwood drew on feminist criticism of the male gaze, emphasising that the dyad of watching and being watched – the essential visual structure of surveillance – has always been and remains gendered. This gendering has immediate and everyday significance in how women live their lives. Atwood's increasingly ecofeminist novels make a direct connection between modern surveillance and murderous patriarchy.

[71] See the discussion in Tadié, Chapter 3 of this collection; Pasquale, *New Law of Robotics*.
[72] van der Meulen and Heynen, *Expanding the Gaze*.

They present exaggerated depictions of contemporary Western society, laying bare the processes which are relied on to screen, control, surveil and exclude.

In particular, Wrobel argues, Atwood makes it possible to study the full complexity of gendered surveillance. In *The Handmaid's Tale*, she dramatises the tension between internal and external control as well as the paradoxical situation of female subjects who are made – exactly as we saw in the previous chapter's discussion of the homeless – at once invisible *and* hyper-visible. The oppressive regime of 'the eye' is omnipresent; the paradox between the utopian and totalitarian sides of surveillance, which we have already on several occasions noted, is manifest. Atwood highlights the multiple mechanisms by which female 'docile bodies' are produced, from social sorting and biological monitoring to ideologies of improvement and self-regulation. As others, such as Sabot in this book, have argued, the psychological and the technological aspects of surveillance are intertwined. Like Banita, Wrobel's analysis of Atwood insists on the deep cultural and historical roots of gendered surveillance. Even the heavily caricatured corporate state of the *MaddAddam* trilogy is essentially patriarchal in nature. But at the same time, Atwood's fiction suggests that no surveillance technology, no matter how advanced, is inescapable. Throughout her body of work, minute, personal, and radically low-tech glimmers of subversion provide the critical fuel that fires Atwood's imagination and our own. Furthermore, as Wrobel writes avowing Tadié's defence of satire in a previous chapter, 'fiction both stages resistance and develops its own literary modes of subversion'. Atwood's novels explicitly join a literary tradition of impassioned counter-surveillance primers stretching back to *Gulliver's Travels* and *Robinson Crusoe*. So too recalling the force and longevity of this tradition brings the collection full circle.

IV. Keeping Perspective

Advances in technologies of surveillance, including 'dataveillance'[73] and 'Big Data',[74] have given rise to unprecedented capture, storage and analytical capabilities. But David Lyon points out that 'digital devices only increase the capacities of surveillance or, sometimes, help to foster particular kinds of surveillance or help to alter its character'.[75] The drive to observe, document and discipline – land, people or phenomena – and to collect information so as to exert control over them did not appear suddenly in the twentieth or twenty-first centuries. New surveillance technology has not 'rendered quaint' the ethics of critique

---

[73] Clarke, 'Information Technology', 498–512.
[74] Andrejevic and Gates, 'Big Data Surveillance', 185–96.
[75] Lyon, *Surveillance Studies*, 15.

and resistance at the heart of scholarship in the humanities: indeed, resistance in the pages of the present volume is articulated from a basis in critical theory rather than from the perspective of law and human resources,[76] although the approaches are surely complementary. Nor, as many of the chapters in the current collection attest, has it 'rendered obsolete' earlier technological forms.[77] CCTV cameras have not disappeared from our streets, and bags are still checked by security agents at airports. It seems more apt to describe the current situation as one in which surveillance technologies are combined and maybe hybridised, a concatenation which, this collection argues, we cannot make sense of without adequate historical, philosophical and critical depth.

Part 1 therefore grounds key concepts such as privacy and transparency in a legacy which goes back to the eighteenth century, an era which offered early literary representations of surveillance as well as influential concepts such as panopticism. So too the analysis of surveillance policies and practices, in Part 2, neither hyperbolises recent advances nor divorces them from deeper humanistic approaches. Throughout the book, we adopt a multidirectional approach, looking at who uses surveillance, against whom and where. In the process, our analyses demand that we extend our concern over the power and politics of surveillance from the state to encompass the actions of corporations and citizens themselves. In Part 3 our focus moves outward towards the entrenched furrows of power and discrimination that surveillance deepens but did not invent. Lyon writes, 'devices and data are not somehow morally neutral but are already implicated in activities and institutions that have to be judged on whether they promote or support good or evil'.[78] Surveillance is a tool for the consolidation and exertion of power. For that reason, it is never neutral but rather 'ever amenable to ethical assessment'.[79] Our focus on the dimensions of race, class, gender and sexual identity, only bears this out. But at the same time, by focusing on the particular embodied experiences of individuals, and striving to understand how they actually use and interact with the systems in which they find themselves, these critical contributions highlight continuing possibilities of resistance, escape or redefinition. Jonathan Swift was already imagining such possibilities three hundred years ago.

Walter Benjamin's last work, 'Theses on the Concept of History', was found in his suitcase after his untimely death in 1940. Benjamin uses the word *jetztzeit* – '*the now!*' – to describe the urgent potential of alterity that is latent

---

[76] See for example Pasquale, *Black Box Society.*
[77] The reference is to the notorious memo on interrogation in the age of terror: Alberto Gonzales, Counsel to the President, 25 January 2002.
[78] Lyon, *Culture of Surveillance*, 24.
[79] Ibid., 17.

but almost buried beneath history's teleological impetus and its technological detritus.[80] What, he asks, can we pull from the wreckage? It is his version of 'the contemporary', a moment of critique which is both deeply implicated in the present and yet which refuses to be immersed in it: untimely,[81] uncanny, unwelcome. Like his 'angel of history', a storm of progress is propelling us like a blast wave away from the pile-up of history we are nevertheless compelled to witness.[82] The question is, what does it really mean to watch? What responsibilities, what ethics, are required of us as critics – watching the watchers, watching the watched? Or is it just a case of *sauve qui peut*?

V. Bibliography

Agamben, Giorgio. 'What is the Contemporary?' In *What is an Apparatus? and Other Essays*, translated by David Kishik and Stefan Pedatella, 39–54. Stanford: Stanford University Press, 2009.

Andrejevic, Mark, and Kelly Gates. 'Big Data Surveillance: Introduction.' *Surveillance & Society* 12, no. 2 (2014): 185–96.

Barter, Faith. 'Encrypted Citations: *The Bondwoman's Narrative* and the Case of Jane Johnson.' *MELUS* 46, no. 1 (2021): 51–74.

Bender, John. *Imagining the Penitentiary: Fiction and the Architecture of Mind in Eighteenth-Century England.* Chicago: University of Chicago Press, 1987.

Benjamin, Walter. *Selected Writings: Volume 4, 1938–1940.* Translated by Edmund Jephcott. Edited by Howard Eiland and Michael Jennings. Cambridge, MA: Belknap Press, 2003.

Browne, Simone. *Dark Matters: On the Surveillance of Blackness.* Durham, NC: Duke University Press, 2015.

———. 'Digital Epidermization: Race, Identity and Biometrics.' *Critical Sociology* 36, no. 1 (2010): 131–50.

Christie, Nils. *Crime Control as Industry.* London: Routledge, 2000.

Clarke, Roger. 'Information Technology and Dataveillance.' *Communications of the ACM* 31, no. 5 (1988): 498–512.

Currah, Paisley, and Lisa Jean Moore. '"We Won't Know Who You Are": Contesting Sex Designations in New York City Birth Certificates.' *Hypatia* 24, no. 3 (2009): 113–35.

Derrida, Jacques. 'Before the Law.' In *Acts of Literature*, 181–220. London: Routledge, 2017.

Douzinas, Costas. 'A Humanities of Resistance: Fragments for a Legal History of Humanity.' In *Law and the Humanities: An Introduction*, edited by Austin Sarat, Matthew Anderson, and Catherine O. Frank, 40–72. Cambridge: Cambridge University Press, 2010.

---

[80] Benjamin, 'Theses on the Concept of History', in *Selected Writings*, § XIV, 395. See also Manderson, 'Here and Now', 175–90.

[81] Nietzsche, *Untimely Meditations*, 40.

[82] Benjamin, 'Theses on the Concept of History', in *Selected Writings*, § IX, 392.

Eichhorn, Kate. *The End of Forgetting: Growing Up with Social Media.* Cambridge, MA: Harvard University Press, 2019.

Ellis, Mark. *Race War and Surveillance.* Bloomington: Indiana University Press, 2001.

Eubanks, Virginia. *Digital Dead End: Fighting for Social Justice in the Information Age.* Cambridge, MA: MIT Press, 2011.

Falkenhayner, Nicole. *Media, Surveillance and Affect.* London: Routledge, 2019.

Foucault, Michel. *Discipline & Punish: The Birth of the Prison.* Translated by Alan Sheridan. New York: Random House, 1977.

Gonzales, Alberto. Memo of White House Counsel to the President, 25 January 2002. https://nsarchive2.gwu.edu/NSAEBB/NSAEBB127/02.01.25.pdf.

Heller-Roazen, Daniel. *Absentees: On Variously Missing Persons.* New York: Zone, 2021.

Kelling, George L., and James Q. Wilson. 'The Police and Neighborhood Safety.' *Atlantic Monthly* 249, no. 3 (March 1982): 29–38.

Kenner, Alison Marie. 'Securing the Elderly Body: Dementia, Surveillance, and the Politics of "Aging in Place".' *Surveillance & Society* 5, no. 3 (2008): 252–69.

Lyon, David. *The Culture of Surveillance: Watching as a Way of Life.* Cambridge: Polity, 2018.

———. *The Electronic Eye: The Rise of Surveillance Society.* Cambridge: Polity, 1994.

———. 'Surveillance Culture: Engagement, Exposure, and Ethics in Digital Modernity.' *International Journal of Communication* 11 (2017): 1–18.

———. *Surveillance Studies: An Overview.* Cambridge: Polity, 2007.

Magnet, Shoshana. *When Biometrics Fail: Gender, Race and the Technology of Identity.* Durham, NC: Duke University Press, 2011.

Manderson, Desmond. 'Here and Now: From "Aestheticizing Politics" to "Politicizing Art".' In *Sensing the Nation's Law: Historical Inquiries into the Aesthetics of Democratic Legitimacy*, edited by Stefan Huygebaert, Angela Condello, Sarah Marusek, and Mark Antaki, 175–90. Cham: Springer, 2018.

Manderson, Desmond, and Paul Yachnin. 'Treating HPHD Disorder—Shakespeare, Law, and Public Life.' *Cogent Arts & Humanities* 3, no. 1 (2016): 1239320.

Mann, Steve, Jason Nolan, and Barry Wellman. 'Sousveillance: Inventing and Using Wearable Computing Devices for Data Collection in Surveillance Environments.' *Surveillance & Society* 1, no. 3 (2003): 331–55.

Marks, Peter. *Imagining Surveillance: Eutopian and Dystopian Literature and Film.* Edinburgh: Edinburgh University Press, 2015.

Marx, Gary T. *Windows into the Soul: Surveillance and Society in an Age of High Technology.* Chicago: University of Chicago Press, 2016.

Miller, D. A. *The Novel and the Police.* Berkeley: University of California Press, 1988.

Mirzoeff, Nicholas. 'Artificial Vision, White Space and Racial Surveillance Capitalism.' *AI & Society* (2020): 1–11.

———. *The Right to Look.* Durham, NC: Duke University Press, 2011.

———. 'The Sea and the Land: Biopower and Visuality from Slavery to Katrina.' *Culture, Theory & Critique* 50, no. 2–3 (2009): 289–305.

Monahan, Torin. 'Surveillance as Cultural Practice.' *The Sociological Quarterly* 52 (2011): 495–508.

Munar, Ana Maria. 'Digital Exhibitionism: The Age of Exposure.' *Culture Unbound: Journal of Current Cultural Research* 2, no. 3 (2010): 401–22.

Murakami Wood, David, ed. *A Report on the Surveillance Society*. Wilmslow: Office of the Information Commissioner, 2006.

Nellis, Mike. 'Since *Nineteen Eighty Four*: Representations of Surveillance in Literary Fiction.' In *New Directions in Surveillance and Privacy*, edited by Benjamin J. Goold and Daniel Neyland, 178–204. Cullompton: Willan Publishing, 2009.

Neti, Leila. *Colonial Law in India and the Victorian Imagination*. Cambridge: Cambridge University Press, 2021.

Nicolazzo, Sal. *Vagrant Figures: Law, Literature, and the Origins of the Police*. New Haven, CT: Yale University Press, 2020.

Nietzsche, Friedrich. *Untimely Meditations*. Translated by R. J. Hollingdale. Cambridge: Cambridge University Press, 1997.

O'Brien, Terence. 'Banksy's Latest Works Tackle Technology, Surveillance, and Our Crumbling Humanity.' *Endgadget*, 14 April 2014.

Orrù, Elisa, Maria Grazia Porcedda, and Sebastian Weydner-Volkmann, eds. *Rethinking Surveillance and Control*. Baden-Baden: Nomos, 2017.

Pasquale, Frank. *The Black Box Society: The Secret Algorithms that Control Money and Information*. Cambridge, MA: Harvard University Press, 2015.

———. *New Laws of Robotics: Defending Human Expertise in the Age of AI*. Cambridge, MA: Harvard University Press, 2020.

Purdon, James. *Modernist Informatics: Literature, Information and the State*. Oxford: Oxford University Press, 2016.

Rinehart, Nicolas. 'The Man that Was a Thing: Reconsidering Human Commodification in Slavery', *Journal of Social History* 50, no. 1 (2016): 28–50.

Rosen, David, and Aaron Santesso. *The Watchman in Pieces: Surveillance, Literature, and Liberal Personhood*. New Haven, CT: Yale University Press, 2013.

Sarat, Austin, Matthew Anderson, and Catherine O. Frank, eds. *Law and the Humanities: An Introduction*. Cambridge: Cambridge University Press, 2010.

Sonu, Debbie. 'Making a Racial Difference: A Foucauldian Analysis of School Memories Told by Undergraduates of Color in the United States.' *Critical Studies in Education* (2020): 1–15.

van der Meulen, Emily, and Robert Heynen. *Expanding the Gaze: Gender and the Politics of Surveillance*. Toronto: University of Toronto Press, 2016.

Wasihun, Betiel, ed. *Narrating Surveillance – Überwachen erzählen*. Baden-Baden: Ergon, 2019.

———. 'Resisting Authority: Surveillance in Contemporary American and German Fiction.' In *Narrating Surveillance – Überwachen erzählen*, edited by Betiel Wasihun, 169–91. Baden-Baden: Ergon, 2019.

Zuboff, Shoshana. *The Age of Surveillance Capitalism: The Fight for a Human Future at the New Frontier of Power*. London: Profile Books, 2019.

Part 1

Foundations

2

Surveillance and its Ambiguities

Philippe Sabot

I. Introduction

This contribution aims to question some of the contemporary forms of surveillance by focusing on the major changes we are witnessing today and the ambiguities they contain. The most obvious ambiguity today concerns the articulation between the surveillance society and the expository society. This articulation reflects a recent evolution, linked in particular to the explosion of the Internet and social networks and to the evolution of surveillance itself, which finds a decisive relay and a new sophistication in the desire for self-exposure and virtual transparency of individuals. At another level, this desire may itself be linked to a paradoxical need for protection: the exposure of oneself, of one's private life as well as of one's personal data, may appear to be the expression of unlimited freedom; but it also increases our desire for security. These debates have found in the COVID-19 health crisis a particular topicality that concentrates and intensifies their stakes and ambiguities. In the following considerations, we will take up the thread of these contemporary debates and show how contemporary surveillance apparatuses are born out of these contradictory desires and the ambiguous divisions they establish between private and public, freedom and security, intimate and exposed life.

II. From Disciplinary Panopticon to Biopolitical Governmentality

The very idea of surveillance is full of contradictory meanings. This ambivalence resides, on the one hand, in our reticence in the face of the implementation of control procedures which have the effect of limiting our freedom in fact and sometimes in law, and, on the other hand, in a deep desire for security, which itself calls for the control of some acts, some behaviours, and even some populations said to be 'at risk' (whether ordinary offenders, radicalised people or even, in recent times, people infected with COVID-19).

This ambivalence may be seen as the correlate of an evolution which concerns both the modes of exercising surveillance and its supposed purposes.

Recall that from the mid-1970s, Foucault drew the contours of a disciplinary society and of a biopolitical governmentality based on 'apparatuses of security' (*dispositifs de sécurité*).[1] But in the twenty-first century, surveillance operations are changing and do not play the same role in either case.

The very notion of surveillance, as Foucault developed it in *Discipline and Punish*, is rooted in an 'anatomo-politics of the human body'.[2] It aims at shaping individuals through the development of control over their actions, over their distribution in space and time, and over their activities. What justifies this type of integral control of the life of individuals is the need, at the time of the rise of industrial capitalism, to make docile and useful subjects, whose activity is oriented towards the optimisation of gestures and inter-individual relations on a production line. As Brunon-Ernst elucidates so well in her chapter, for Foucault, the making of disciplined subjects extends throughout the entire social space.[3] In a lecture given in Rio in 1973 ('Truth and Juridical Forms'), he evokes in this sense a vast 'institutional network of sequestration'[4] which includes the factory, the school, the asylum, the hospital, the prison. And he questions the functions that such institutions fulfil by 'inserting' individuals into an 'apparatus of normalisation'.[5] Consequently, as early as 1973, one of the central themes of *Discipline and Punish*, capable of arousing both the interest and the anxiety of its first readers, was that the prison was only the most 'concentrated, exemplary, symbolic form of all the institutions of sequestration created in the nineteenth century'. As such, it participates in the 'great social panopticism, whose function is precisely that of transforming people's lives in productive force'.[6] The genealogy of prison as this particular institution of sequestration is thus put into perspective through a more global analysis of the modern form of social control and of what one is tempted to call a panoptic society. This panoptic society is the expression of a 'type of power that is applied to individuals in the form of continuous individual supervision, in the form of control, punishment, and compensation, and in the form of correction, that is, the moulding and transformation of individuals in terms of certain norms'.[7] Surveillance is thus part of a continuum of social control. As such, it is part of an effort to pay constant and close attention to deviances of all kinds and, at the same time, it constructs the knowledge that makes it

---

[1] Foucault, *Security, Territory, Population*, 19–35.
[2] Foucault, *History of Sexuality, Vol. I*, 139.
[3] See Brunon-Ernst, Chapter 6 of this collection.
[4] Foucault, 'Truth and Juridical Forms', 79.
[5] Ibid., 78.
[6] Ibid., 85.
[7] Ibid., 70.

possible effectively to correct these deviances by measuring them against a standard previously set and fixed in scholarly discourse, regulations and laws. Following this first approach, surveillance appears as the technological bias of a disciplinary society. And the type of control it allows is oriented towards correcting individual breaches of the standard.

Viewed in this way and projected onto our contemporary era, the control and standardisation of individuals could be construed as an attack on both the freedom and equality of citizens. Indeed, the inherent capacity of surveillance to interfere with privacy is, as Gligorijević argues in her chapter, one of the primary ways in which surveillance undermines individuals' liberty.[8] The economy of surveillance itself distinguishes between the useful and the useless; it leads to the distribution of subjects into good and bad subjects, the latter to be monitored more closely and, if necessary, corrected more fully. Surveillance is thus seen as the effect (but also as the model) of a centralising power that prioritises the standard to be attained or respected over the freedom of individuals. At the same time, it is thrifty in its agents: a minimum of control and direction for a maximum of targets. But it is also thrifty in its visibility insofar as it does not seek to emit 'the signs of its potency' or to impose 'its mark on its subjects': it is content to 'hold them in a mechanism of objectification'.[9] The strength and, in a sense, the legitimacy of this mode of total surveillance thus lies in the constant pressure of the norms of behaviour that it continuously disseminates to prevent errors, faults and crimes before they are committed. Indeed, this form of surveillance is not dissimilar to the predictive policing techniques described in Banita's chapter.[10] Self-surveillance, the application by the subjects to themselves of a certain number of behavioural models, minimises external controls and lightens the apparatus without reducing its efficacy.

None of this should blind us to the infringement of individual freedom represented by the panoptic model, or to its hierarchical disproportion and the lack of reciprocity between those who manage the instruments of surveillance and those who are its targets and who suffer its concrete effects. Nevertheless, the comprehensive and continuous mode of surveillance thus implemented can also be seen as a condition for the security of all. In order to understand this, another dimension of surveillance must be brought into play, which this time refers not to the individualising-normalising dimension of panoptic surveillance but rather to issues of the biopolitical management of populations and the governmentality of living beings; what Foucault calls 'apparatuses of security'.

---

[8] See Gligorijević, Chapter 5 of this collection.
[9] Foucault, *Discipline and Punish*, 187.
[10] See Banita, Chapter 10 of this collection.

In a certain way, in this new paradigm of power relations, it is still and always the capacities of standardisation and productive orientation of behaviours that are put forward. But the reference to norms is no longer a question of submission to an external command. It is made completely immanent to the behaviours themselves, in the form of a social habitus deployed on a population scale. While individuals may still be subject to surveillance, the transformation of the ways in which it is carried out goes hand in hand with the reorientation of its aims towards *securing* individual lives through their integral traceability, obtained through new identification and localisation techniques.[11] And it is precisely this positive appeal to securitisation which is deployed to justify such mass surveillance; as Gligorijević argues in her chapter, we should seek to disambiguate such security justifications and ensure we do not forget the harm to individual liberty which is inherent in surveillance.[12]

Indeed, Foucault gives an account of the ambivalence attached to the very principle of surveillance, articulating both the coercive side of a grip on individual freedom and the more ambiguous side of a securing of populations. In Foucault himself, we find the shift from one side to the other, corresponding to the introduction of the hypothesis of the 'biopolitics of the population',[13] from which the notion of 'governmentality' was to be introduced into the lectures *Security, Territory, Population* in 1978. What does this passage from disciplinary society to the government of the population mean? According to the logic of biopolitical governmentality, the exercise of surveillance is presented as free of any relation to constraint – whereas we have seen that discipline in no way excludes it. Disciplinary supervision remains linked to a 'social orthopaedics',[14] that is to say, under its corrective and even punitive aspect, to an effort of redress imposed on bodies that can be confined and reshaped, more or less violently, the better to ensure and verify their effects. Under the theme of governmentality and oriented towards populations as a whole, Foucault acknowledges that surveillance techniques are themselves transformed.

---

[11] Gros, *Security Principle*, 133–4.

[12] See Gligorijević, Chapter 5 of this collection.

[13] Foucault, *History of Sexuality, Vol. I*, 139.

[14] See Andry's engraving, 'Orthopaedics or the art of preventing and correcting deformities of the body in children' (Foucault, *Discipline and Punish*, 169). See also the back cover of the French edition of Foucault's book: 'Le XIXᵉ siècle, lui, était fier des forteresses qu'il construisait aux limites et parfois au cœur des villes. Ces murs, ces verrous, ces cellules figuraient toute une entreprise d'orthopédie sociale' (The nineteenth century was proud of the fortresses it built on the outskirts and sometimes in the heart of cities. These walls, these locks, these cells represented a whole enterprise of social orthopaedics).

The imposition of disciplinary rules on individuals is now combined with planning-regulation aimed at the large masses of the population. This regulation of populations actually proceeds from a completely different logic and no longer has any repressive character insofar as, in advance, it invests the totality of the collective existence envisaged in all its biological processes (fertility, mortality, morbidity, disease, hygiene). It is then these processes, and no longer individuals as such, that are subject to increased surveillance, not by watchers housed in the recesses of the panoptic architecture, but by experts and statisticians observing and analysing, for forecasting purposes, curves, diagrams and indicators expressing the health or general state of a given population. This is particularly evident in light of the current pandemic. The demand for biosafety and the correlative demand for biosurveillance are increasing, not only from individuals but also from public authorities. We *demand* surveillance that protects populations, setting up identification and monitoring systems that define their profile in order to determine who is 'at risk', either to themselves or to others. Yet preventive protection can quickly turn against those who claim it, restricting and tracing their freedom of movement (lockdown and quarantine). This protective surveillance finds its legitimacy in the dimension of social and public health, but nevertheless shifts its strategic point of application once more. While it still concerns populations, it will focus more precisely on epidemiological curves and on indicators that make it possible to define, in terms of risks, the foreseeable impact of the health crisis in order to regulate its medicosocial effects. What is then monitored is no longer directly individuals (by modifying their behaviour) or even populations (by tracking the biological processes that shape them). For example, in European countries during the pandemic, the purpose of surveillance by health authorities was clearly a relationship between health capacities and the development of the virus in a population. Surveillance in the era of biopolitics thus became the instrument for exercising and implementing a public health policy.

We can then understand the ambivalence directed towards these developments. The deployment of enhanced biosecurity apparatuses is feared and criticised inasmuch as they appear to jeopardise individual freedoms. At the same time, however, governments are being called upon to monitor the circulation of the virus and provide guarantees of an increased surveillance of its development. Contemporary biomonitoring modalities have not eliminated the disciplinary logic of the Panopticon but place their action at another level (the population) and for another purpose (security). Surveillance is thus becoming less and less centralised. It is no longer the exclusive operation of a central power that would implement it for the purpose of controlling and sanctioning deviant or risky behaviour. It covers the everyday acts of the entire population, from communication to consumption and travel, concentrating at the same time all our desires (desire to expose oneself and to exist in this virtual and interactive world) and all our fears (fear of being dispossessed of oneself, deprived of an opacity which forms the refuge of freedom).

III. Surveillance and Exposure: The Ambiguity of Societies of Control

This 'expository society'[15] forms the counterpart of what Gilles Deleuze referred to as 'control societies',[16] taking over from what Foucault had described as a disciplinary society. Control societies do not put an end to the surveillance mechanisms developed to respond to the objectives of disciplinary norms but rather develop them and reorient them towards new objectives, precisely of the order of regulatory control. How, then, can we characterise these control procedures and the type of surveillance that develops in them?

In the first place, they no longer function with the corrective sanction of behaviours according to norms set forth by legal and autonomous bodies according to a disciplinary grid of individuals and their actions. New forms of control continue to be exercised but they operate at a distance, through devices that address the motivation and participation of individuals themselves; all the more powerful as they are based on the desire to participate in this vast movement of self-exposure and to access a digital self. Instead of slackening, surveillance is thus strengthened by taking the form of continuous incentives and solicitations. Surveillance is monitoring the virtualities of problematic behaviours in order to secure the social body. Thus the refinement of a control society (and the corresponding crisis of disciplinary societies noted by Deleuze) is driven by a collective adherence to this virtualisation of individual existence. In each case, the desire to expose oneself in virtual space outweighs the fear of being watched. A new form of subjectivity is thus shaped by contemporary uses of digital technology, which make us increasingly transparent, blurring the boundaries of public and private, freedom and security. We become fully traceable, integrated into data networks that assign us a specific profile and induce targeted behaviours, based on identified desires, and which are available to both commercial companies and the apparatus of the security state. As Cluzel-Métayer explains in detail in her discussion in this book of Smart Cities, our movements are recorded without our knowledge, thanks to the GPS applications on smartphones, making it possible to define both preferences (if we move around in commercial areas) and locations (useful in

---

[15] Harcourt, *Exposed*.
[16] Deleuze, 'Postscript on the Societies of Control', 6.

the event of a police investigation and if we have to give an account of our actions).[17] This point is in line with an idea that Zuboff develops in her book *The Age of Surveillance Capitalism*. All of this data is therefore collected less from individuals, extracted from our behaviour to become the subject of a normalising power-knowledge, than it is provided by each of us ourselves during our purchases, our daily travels, our consultations on search engines, and therefore as our digital identity (as consumer) is constituted and deployed.

We thus arrive at a reformulation of the previous ambiguity. The new regime of surveillance is based on a desire for unlimited exposure that confers digital transparency on everyone. But this transparency must be seen as both the refuge of the greatest freedom and the most ardent desire (the desire to exist), as well as the vector of an increased vulnerability that forms its flip side: 'any police seeking intelligence have less need to spy on individuals secretly than they do to access their social networks on which they spontaneously present their photos, their relationships, their use of time and their concerns'.[18] We are witnessing a progressive deprivation of intimacy, which is less the deliberate effect of a certain exercise of power (and notably of centralised state power) than a new regime of truth in which contemporary subjects install themselves in order to exist: we are faced not so much with a 'surveillance state' as with a 'surveillance amalgam' or, in the words of John Gilliom and Torin Monahan, a 'surveillance society'.[19] We are not being watched: we are knowingly exposing ourselves to the protocols and apparatuses which monitor our digital traces,[20] even if we do not always measure its effects. Surrounded by digital technologies (from the Internet to the Internet of Things), we are becoming blind to the potential invasions of privacy that these technologies represent. The private is no longer what escapes the grip of possible surveillance, but what is exposed to the eyes of the greatest number and to the algorithms that target, profile and ultimately construct desires.

The desire for control and the control of desire are folded back onto each other,[21] shaping new forms of subjectivity and redrawing the contours of freedom and security. As Olivier Razac points out, GPS combines the desire for security (to locate and to be located), the desire for efficiency (to facilitate circulation), and the desire to intensify existence (as proposed by the products in the 'TrackME' range). At the crossroads of these three dimensions,

---

[17] See Cluzel-Métayer, Chapter 9 of this collection.
[18] Gros, *Security Principle*, 138–9.
[19] Gilliom and Monahan, *Supervision*, qtd in Harcourt, *Exposed*, 78.
[20] Harcourt, *Exposed*, 90.
[21] Razac, *Avec Foucault, après Foucault*, 61.

GPS secures movements (of people and goods) and seems to offer new spaces for virtual expression, beyond the constraints of matter and time.[22] If these participatory surveillance apparatuses raise questions as to personal freedom, they are so integrated into our lifestyles that it is rather their deprivation than their operation that is experienced as an infringement of rights. It is difficult in these conditions to protect citizens against themselves and to make them renounce modes of self-exposure that spontaneously give themselves up as the exact opposite of the logics of confinement and disciplinary surveillance, and that rather exalt the desire and freedom to be oneself.

As Frédéric Gros and Bernard E. Harcourt point out, the expository society obeys the logic of a neoliberal governmentality, based on the principle of a regulation of desires, as opposed to any constraint on wills. To regulate is not to subject unruly bodies directly to the panoptic gaze and the threat of disciplinary sanction, but indirectly to monitor and orient individual desires in order to encourage the investment of energy in a given direction, maximising the flow of information, goods or people with a view to optimising behaviour, costs and profits.[23] If everyone is free to bend or not to this soft injunction to be an exposed self, freedom remains conditioned by the place one wishes to occupy in the social order, or even by the fact of simply having a place in it. The cost of entry into this expository society is the transformation of our own private self into nothing but its digital avatar, 'a shifting space of negotiation where privacy is traded for products, better services or special deals'.[24]

IV. Surveillance at the Time of Virtualisation of Punitive Practices

A tacit contract links free self-expression to the transparency of one's digital life. So too we witness a convergence with the renewal of punitive practices that deploy digital forms of correctional control.[25] Free of the practices of confinement integral to Foucauldian discipline, modern control technologies appear preferable to incarceration. Razac analyses the development of the 'open environment' (*milieu ouvert*) as a method of sentence management. The 'open environment' permits certain prisoners to serve their sentence outside of a cell, for example by doing community service or by being placed under mobile electronic surveillance (by wearing an ankle tag):[26]

> Prison appeared human in the face of torment, just as today the open environment seems more humane than prison. For many petty crimes, prison seems unsuitable and disproportionate and alternative sentences are becoming

[22] Ibid., 54–7.
[23] Gros, *Security Principle*, 145–7.
[24] Haggerty and Ericson, 'Surveillant Assemblage', 616, qtd in Harcourt, *Exposed*, 166.
[25] Harcourt, *Exposed*, 236–7.
[26] Razac, *Avec Foucault, après Foucault*, 87.

unavoidable. But the open environment can be understood as an improvement of the prison system rather than as 'human' progress. For, each time, behind the softness, behind the claim of humanity, are hidden considerations of another order, economic, strategic and functional. This is why it is necessary to go beyond emotional impressions and affects to constantly remind ourselves that 'the most dangerous thing about violence is its rationality' (Foucault).[27]

Such rationality makes violence more acceptable *a priori*, giving it, for example, the appearance of freedom in the form of consent, exactly as in contemporary forms of self-exposure on the digital stage, which likewise present the extension of surveillance under the guise of consent.

The geospatial technology of an individual wearing an electronic ankle tag constitutes a virtualised social control in which the virtual does not mean the watering down of control or its relaxation but rather its precision and its reinforcement. In fact, the ankle tag exemplifies the logic of virtualisation at work in contemporary digital devices and especially of the limits or threats it represents when muted. In a sense, placing people under mobile electronic surveillance seems to completely dematerialise the delimitation of space characteristic of the prison. However, this delimitation remains assured by the awareness of the risk incurred in the event of a boundary being crossed. The risk is not avoided but internalised. The offender who wears the electronic bracelet is therefore in a virtually closed space (he has no total freedom of movement); the closure of this space is actually carried out at the level of his mind (which prevents the body from moving outside the limits assigned by the judge); and it is, as it were, reinforced by the surveillance technologies being used.

The ankle tag represents a transition from a logic of confinement and exclusion (linked to closed environments) to a logic of traceability (linked to open environments). But even more surely, it corresponds to a virtualised security technology that combines the three modalities of spatial delimitation distinguished by Foucault in his lecture of 11 January 1978, when he evokes the epidemics of leprosy (in the Middle Ages), plague (in the classical age) and smallpox (in the modern period). The connection between Foucault's analysis and the case of individuals placed in an open environment with an electronic bracelet may seem surprising. In reality, this comparison is instructive on two levels. First, it illustrates a historical evolution in the treatment of major epidemics as well as in the treatment of criminal offences, and this evolution corresponds to a 'history of technologies of security'.[28] With smallpox,

---

[27] Foucault, 'Foucault Examines Reason', 5–6.
[28] Foucault, *Security, Territory, Population*, 25.

says Foucault, the problem is no longer strictly a disciplinary problem but a security problem:

> The fundamental problem will not be the imposition of discipline, although discipline may be called on to help, so much as the problem of knowing how many people are infected with smallpox, at what age, with what effects, with what mortality rate, lesions or after effects, the risks of inoculation, the probability of an individual dying or being infected by smallpox despite inoculation, and the statistical effects on the population in general. In short, it will no longer be the problem of exclusion, as with leprosy, or of quarantine, as with the plague, but of epidemics and the medical campaigns that try to halt epidemic or endemic phenomena.[29]

This technology of security, correlative to the development of social medicine and public health programmes (along with vaccination campaigns), sheds light on the development of electronic surveillance. Here and there, we are dealing with the same 'spatial injunction' that reads: 'Tell us where you are going, insofar as your movements represent a risk, but you must still move.'[30] Yet, and this is the decisive point, this spatial injunction specific to security-sanitary technology does not erase the spatial injunctions relating to Foucault's other spatial modalities. It is indeed the 'securitary' correlation of law, discipline and control that defines the triple mode of spatialisation of the offender or its triple relationship to space. For there are places where this individual does not have the right to go, from which he is therefore excluded (like a leper pushed out of the city). And there are also prescribed zones to which he must go, and to which it is imperative that he goes: zones of inclusion that correspond to the activities and disciplinary environments (like family, work, compulsory meetings with officers) in which his possible reintegration is at stake. Finally, it is important to keep track of the person 'placed' in order to evaluate, with statistics and a computer map in support, the risks involved in his movements (for him as well as for the others).

Proscription, prescription, regulation: the contemporary condition of the 'placed' offender is played out in this triple dimension and in this triple relationship to space that a virtual control device now regulates remotely. We can see all the ambiguity of such a device. For it consists in locating individuals in order to protect them, and in particular to protect them from other individuals – this is how it becomes possible to place GPS beacons on children – but also, in the case of the 'placed' offenders, to protect them

---

[29] Ibid., 24–5.
[30] Razac, *Histoire politique du barbelé*, 234.

from themselves, by working and making them work on their reintegration, by 'vaccinating' them against their own dangerousness. But this device also extends the virtual reach of control almost without limit. Now everyone deserves to be located and 'placed' under surveillance (video, computer), tracked so that a curious and anxious 'social protection' can be organised and carried out, based on a desire for security that it has itself contributed to engendering by injecting us with a feeling of insecurity. As Razac writes, 'electronic surveillance or traceability does not replace confinement, it adds to prison forms and produces spatial limits where none existed before. Virtualisation allows an extension of prison space more than it replaces it.'[31] Doesn't this mean that the society of control itself constitutes an open-air prison, a space where control (which implies subtle forms of surveillance) takes over from punishment in order to reach, with a view to treating (as one treats information) behaviours, individualities (no longer just dangerous but exposed) that have hitherto escaped its grasp?

These considerations make it possible to underline once again the kind of convergence, identified by Harcourt, between the virtual transparency of the digital exhibition and the new figures of penality. The latter simply bring out more clearly the paradox attached to a surveillance that seems to be exercised all the more precisely and implacably as it tends to fade away. Thus, one has access to surveillance that is in principle unlimited, benefiting from the potential unlimited connections between surveillance operators and the dematerialisation of surveillance instances (individuals are replaced by data flow sensors).

The spectre of unlimited surveillance echoes what Antoinette Rouvroy calls the 'algorithmic governmentality' of a 'profiling' society.[32] A new articulation between control, security and freedom thus appears, which ensures the convergence between the generalised digitalisation of our contemporary lives and the entry of punitive practices into the virtual world of decision-making algorithms. On the basis of the analysis of an offender's profile, these algorithms can calculate the probability of recidivism and thus lead to a judicial recommendation concerning the nature of the sentence to be administered and its follow-up: in an open environment with an electronic bracelet for offenders likely to be reintegrated, or in a closed environment for those who are deemed to represent a lasting danger to society.[33] Algorithmic governmentality thus defines a new modality of decision support by integrating the probabilistic calculation of a risk into the judge's deliberation. However, it

[31] Razac, 'Le placement sous surveillance électronique mobile', 6.
[32] Rouvroy, 'De la surveillance au profilage', 62.
[33] Razac, *Avec Foucault, après Foucault*, 107–8.

is also clear that the profiling society tends to put our decisions (individual, legal, social) under surveillance, by deploying an insidious control of freedom and by reducing the complexity of individual trajectories to a combinatorial set of data offered to the anonymous calculation of a 'profiler' software program. As Banita argues in her chapter, police surveillance is therefore not only about directly addressing violence when it occurs.[34] It is also part of a preventive approach, which attempts to assess the risks that such violence may represent.

V. Conclusion: Escaping Surveillance?

In view of the ambiguities that affect the very exercise of surveillance today, it is difficult to determine the most appropriate formula to qualify our era – disciplinary society, surveillance society, control society, expository society? Perhaps surveillance remains a relevant paradigm, but under two conditions. First, it must be freed from reference to a single, central depositary (the state) in favour of multiple agencies and politico-economic groups (diffuse but powerful surveillance networks, like the mesh of social networks and GAMAMs that make them available to users eager to expose themselves[35]). Then, it is necessary to combine these three dimensions, that is to say, to understand surveillance itself from the paradoxical dimension of self-exhibition and from control modalities that, decentralised, are continuously exercised across social, economic and juridical space.

The blind spot in these analyses remains, however, the possibility of active and effective resistance. The difficulty is immense: how to flee from an anonymous power that follows us everywhere, and which is at one with the very development of our desires and our virtualised existence, which proposes an increased control of our lives by making us believe that this control anticipates our desires and fulfils even in advance our greatest desire, the desire for security? Perhaps in reality it is not reasonable to flee from this power but rather to confront it, by developing a form of collective vigilance with regard to devices intended precisely to put our vigilance to sleep, to silence our critical sense. Harcourt develops an opposition between a state of 'undervigilance' that characterises our digitised life and a new kind of 'surveillance' to be developed with regard to those who watch us, disposing of our freedom and betting on our submission: 'One approach is to turn the surveillance camera around: to aim the optic at those who are watching us.'[36] It is about

[34] See Banita, Chapter 10 of this collection.
[35] The acronym GAMAM refers to the five tech giants: Google, Amazon, Meta, Apple and Microsoft.
[36] Harcourt, *Exposed*, 275–6.

countering surveillance 'with even more surveillance'.[37] Increasingly repressive laws seek to thwart and even penalise such civic vigilance; examples include Article 24 of the French 'Loi de sécurité globale',[38] which limits filming law enforcement officials, the 'Wikileaks' case, or the Witness K prosecutions in Australia. The authorities are no doubt worried. Their concern is no doubt commensurate with the devastating effect that this counter-surveillance strategy could have, if it were capable of exposing the traps, dangers and opacity of the digital transparency regime to which, it must be acknowledged, we most often freely and passionately submit, as if our very lives depended on it. Finally, the question is: how much do we want to be watched; or rather, how much do we want *not* to be watched quite so much?

VI. Bibliography

Deleuze, Gilles. 'Postscript on the Societies of Control [1990].' *October* 59 (1992): 3–7.

Foucault, Michel. *Discipline and Punish: The Birth of the Prison*. 1975. Translated by Alan Sheridan. 2nd ed. New York: Vintage Books, 1995.

———. 'Foucault Examines Reason in Service of State Power.' *Campus Report* 6, no. 24 (October 1979): 5–6.

———. *The History of Sexuality: An Introduction. Volume I*. 1976. Translated by Robert Hurley. New York: Pantheon Books, 1978.

———. *Security, Territory, Population: Lectures at the Collège de France, 1977–1978*. 2004. Translated by Graham Burchell. New York: Palgrave Macmillan, 2007.

———. 'Truth and Juridical Forms.' In *Essential Works of Michel Foucault, 1954–1984. Vol. 3: Power*, 1974, edited by James D. Faubion, translated by Robert Hurley and others, 1–89. London: Penguin Books, 2001.

Gilliom, John, and Torin Monahan. *Supervision: An Introduction to the Surveillance Society*. Chicago: University of Chicago Press, 2012.

Gros, Frédéric. *The Security Principle: From Serenity to Regulation*. 2012. Translated by David Broder. London: Verso, 2019.

Haggerty, Kevin D., and Richard V. Ericson. 'The Surveillant Assemblage.' *British Journal of Sociology* 51, no. 4 (2000): 605–22.

Harcourt, Bernard E. *Exposed: Desire and Disobedience in the Digital Age*. Cambridge, MA: Harvard University Press, 2015.

Mann, Steve, Jason Nolan, and Barry Wellman. 'Sousveillance: Inventing and Using Wearable Computing Devices for Data Collection in Surveillance Environment.' *Surveillance & Society* 1, no. 3 (2003): 331–55.

---

[37] Ibid., 275. This inversion of surveillance against itself corresponds to the concept of 'sousveillance' as proposed by Mann, Nolan, and Wellman.

[38] In the first draft of the law, this section stated: 'It is punishable by one year's imprisonment and a fine of 45,000 euros to disseminate, by any means whatsoever and regardless of the medium, with the aim of harming his or her physical or psychological integrity, the image of the face or any other element of identification of an officer of the national police when he or she is acting in the context of a police operation.'

Razac, Olivier. *Avec Foucault, après Foucault: disséquer la société de contrôle.* Paris: L'Harmattan, 2008.

———. *Histoire politique du barbelé.* Paris: Flammarion, 2009.

———. 'Le placement sous surveillance électronique mobile: un nouveau modèle pénal?' *Rapport de l'École Nationale de l'Administration Pénitentiaire.* Agen: L'École Nationale de l'Administration Pénitentiaire, 2010.

Rouvroy, Antoinette. 'De la surveillance au profilage.' *Philosophie Magazine*, Hors série no. 36 (2018): 60–3.

Rouvroy, Antoinette, and Thomas Berns. 'Gouvernementalité algorithmique et perspectives d'émancipation. Le disparate comme condition d'individuation par la relation?' *Réseaux* 177 (2013): 163–96.

Zuboff, Shoshana. *The Age of Surveillance Capitalism: The Fight for a Human Future at the New Frontier of Power.* London: Profile Books, 2019.

3

Surveillance, Utopia and Satire in Eighteenth-Century British Literature

Alexis Tadié

I. Introduction

In book IV of *Gulliver's Travels*, Gulliver finds himself among the wise horses, the Houyhnhnms, and is taken by their rational approach to life, adopting their mode of life, as much as, shall we say, is humanly possible. Gulliver decides to submit to the rule of the Houyhnhnms, although the horses execrate Yahoos like himself and dream of exterminating them. In doing this, he separates himself willingly from human beings and becomes enslaved to the wise horses:

> I had not yet been a Year in this Country, before I contracted such a Love and Veneration for the Inhabitants, that I entered on a firm Resolution never to return to human Kind, but to pass the rest of my Life among these admirable *Houyhnhnms* in the Contemplation and Practice of every Virtue; where I could have no Example or Incitement to Vice.[1]

The passions (*Love, Veneration*) which Gulliver experiences determine his decision to remain among the horses, which is further justified by the promise of the contemplation of virtue and the absence of all vices. The structure of the episode suggests, on Gulliver's part, a willing submission to forces of control, an acquiescence to being ruled, a desire to be part of the Houyhnhnms' world. While at first Gulliver admits not to have felt the awe which characterises the Yahoos' relationship to the Houyhnhnms, it eventually grew upon him, 'and was mingled with a respectful Love and Gratitude, that they would condescend to distinguish me from the rest of my Species'.[2]

---

[1] Swift, *Gulliver's Travels*, 388.
[2] Ibid., 420.

In his portrayal of Gulliver's predicament among the Houyhnhnms, Swift foreshadows modern forms of control. The structure whereby our passions lead us into restraint, perhaps even to a *desire* for subjection, is characteristic of certain forms of domination. As Philippe Sabot notes in the previous chapter, Bernard Harcourt has argued that our desires and passions can enslave us.[3] Unlike what Orwell had described in *Nineteen Eighty-Four*, modern society has mastered individuals and populations by means of their passions and interests, and has ensnared them. We willingly deliver ourselves to surveillance technologies, in particular to the digital world, and we have come to accept forms of control exerted by powers over which we have no influence. Like Gulliver, we agree to certain types of surveillance which use our passions rather than attempt to suppress them. For the most part, Harcourt argues, and just like Gulliver, we surrender willingly. In *Gulliver's Travels*, though, Swift introduces further irony vis-à-vis the reader, who contemplates the narrator's fate from a position of apparent superiority. But the joke is also on the readers: like Gulliver we are Yahoos, like Gulliver we are willing to surrender ourselves, in the name of rationality, to the order advocated and implemented by the Houyhnhnms.

Beyond the predicament that we face when dealing with surveillance, this example shows the complex position in which satire can place us: we may find a certain pleasure (which does not preclude horror of course, and a host of other emotions) in a satirical take on surveillance; but this pleasure is cancelled, or perhaps enhanced, when we realise that, as readers or spectators, we are also included in the satire. As Swift himself wrote, 'Satyr is a sort of *Glass*, wherein Beholders do generally discover every body's Face but their Own; which is the chief Reason for that kind of Reception it meets in the World, and that so very few are offended with it.'[4] Which means in turn, as Swift was quick to acknowledge, that satire's most profound aim is to disturb and provoke rather than simply to offer lessons.

David Rosen and Aaron Santesso have argued in favour of a repositioning of surveillance studies to include the point of view of the humanities, thereby displacing and reformulating an argument which was elaborated in sociology, political science and legal studies. In their words, '[t]he complex dialectical struggle between surveillance and selfhood is one that the study of literature, with its close interrogation of character, and philosophy, with its central interest in the thinking subject, are well positioned to tackle.'[5] The inquiry into personal autonomy and selfhood which characterises the work of literature is in this respect essential to the study of surveillance. Their starting

---

[3] Harcourt, *Exposed*.
[4] Swift, *Tale of a Tub and Other Works*, 142.
[5] Rosen and Santesso, *Watchman in Pieces*, 3.

point is the individual, understood as an agent and not simply as the object of strategies of domination. The perspective they adopt confirms the centrality of concepts of agency, privacy and personhood to understanding our relation to surveillance, as evidenced by Jelena Gligorijević's and Lucie Cluzel-Métayer's chapters in this volume. In this respect, the power of instantiation of literature is invaluable. Rosen and Santesso's approach to, and understanding of, surveillance focuses on the contribution of literature to a history of surveillance, and, consequently, surveillance is analysed in the same way as one would tackle literary issues, summoning concepts such as narrative or readership, and of course interpretation, which are usually absent from the debate. In a reversal of standard Foucault-inspired analyses, they claim that 'power often lies in the control of narrative – a control frequently in the hands of the person under watch'.[6] Certainly, satire offers, if only symbolically, means of examining, interrogating and overthrowing dominant forces and modes of control.

This chapter will build on these insights in its examination of representations of surveillance in eighteenth-century literature. It will elaborate on the possibility for literature and philosophy to illuminate the workings of surveillance, suggesting that satire can be conceived as a mode of resistance, as an undermining of burgeoning practices of investigation and control of the individual. The genre of utopia, which will provide the starting point of this chapter, entertains connections with surveillance, not only because it suggests the possibility of creating a world in which such operations can be sketched or fleshed out, but also because it rests on a necessary connection with the future. This is of course the point of surveillance, the prediction and control of our moves, not to mention our mouse-clicks – we know that this is what is traded in our current age of 'surveillance capitalism'.[7] Just like the genre of utopia, surveillance seeks to control, change, and improve the future. It is in the genre of utopia, and more specifically in the satirical use of and response to utopia, that reflections on surveillance were elaborated.

This chapter charts a brief course through early modern literature, as the age in which reflections on the nature of surveillance began to surface (in a century which closed on Bentham's Panopticon). The chapter first reminds us of one of the most celebrated worlds where science and surveillance seem to walk hand in hand, that of Francis Bacon's philosophical tale, *New Atlantis* (1627). It then moves on to the ambiguities of utopia, to the island where Robinson Crusoe finds himself stranded for a number of years. Finally, it considers the satire of utopia enacted first by Swift, who, in book III of *Gulliver's Travels* (1726), seemed to be responding to Bacon's House of Salomon, and

[6] Ibid., 8.
[7] Zuboff, *Age of Surveillance Capitalism*.

then by Pope, who tries to open up the path to resistance to the world of surveillance that was slowly beginning to unfold.

II. Bacon's *New Atlantis*: Science and Surveillance

Bacon's posthumously published narrative has often been regarded as a blueprint for a science academy, as an ideal state of affairs where the progress of science will be organised along rational lines. The proposed scheme combines observation through the senses and interpretation of experiments, thanks to the hierarchical collaboration of scientists. Bacon's text is roughly divided into two parts. The first part narrates the arrival on the island of Bensalem of a group of fifty-one travellers on board a stray ship. They are welcomed by the inhabitants, who look after them. An officer conducts them to their residence, the 'Strangers' House'. There, they enter into conversation about the history of the island with one of the local dignitaries. The second and shorter part of *New Atlantis* describes the organisation of the local Academy of science, called 'Salomon's House'.

While the island of Bensalem and the scientific institution at its centre are built on the scientists' and natural philosophers' observations and deductions of the true nature of things, they also depend on secrecy, which the text suggests at every turn. As soon as they arrive, the travellers are, for instance, submitted to the 'laws of secrecy',[8] which are in force for foreigners. As the 'Father of the House of Salomon' enjoins, all experimenters need to take an 'oath of secrecy'[9] until decisions have been made as to which experiments should be advertised and which should not. This implies a system of surveillance.

Indeed, the paradoxical configuration of the island, both on the margins of the world and at the centre of things, rests on two principles. First, the Bensalemites rely on what we would now call an extreme form of protectionism: nine hundred years ago, their king 'did ordain the interdicts and prohibitions which we have touching entrance of strangers; which at that time [. . .] was frequent; doubting novelties, and commixture of manners'.[10] Forbidden interactions with foreigners, to which changes in maritime routes must be added, means that the Bensalemites have remained independent and out of sight. But this isolation goes hand in hand with, secondly, information gathering, which guarantees access to the knowledge developed in the rest of the world:

> every twelve years there should be set forth out of this kingdom two ships, appointed to several voyages; That in either of these ships there should be a

---

[8] Bacon, *New Atlantis*, 136.
[9] Ibid., 165.
[10] Ibid., 144.

mission of three of the Fellows or Brethren of Salomon's House; whose errand was only to give us knowledge of the affairs and state of those countries to which they were designed, and especially of the sciences, arts, manufactures, and inventions of all the world; and withal to bring unto us books, instruments, and patterns of every kind.[11]

Beyond secrecy, the Bensalemites do not hesitate to have recourse to confinement. Having installed themselves in the House of Strangers, the travellers are asked not to 'think [themselves] restrained' in spite of the fact that they have 'to keep within doors for three days', thereby introducing a form of quarantine, while the attendants 'have an eye upon [them]'.[12] Hence, from the beginning the narrative is placed under the sign of seclusion, which is described not as a form of imprisonment but as a moment of leisure, in language which will become familiar as the language of surveillance ('For these men that they have given us for attendance may withal have an eye upon us'[13]). This is further exemplified by the speech of the governor of the House, who comes to explain, 'The state hath given you licence to stay on land for the space of six weeks.'[14] This is both presented as a convenience, and indeed the visitors may enjoy the hospitality for longer should it be needed, but also as a restraint: 'Only this I must tell you, that none of you must go above a *karan*' (that is with them a mile and a half) 'from the walls of the city, without especial leave.'[15]

The principles of secrecy and surveillance in their different forms are again apparent in the functioning of the Academy.[16] Knowledge on the island is dependent on a strict hierarchy of tasks and of access. This is apparent at the beginning because information is imparted only by those who have the power to do so. It is made clearer in the presentation of the House of Salomon, where each and every individual is found at a specific place in the scientific hierarchical order. Certain men collect knowledge, others think out new experiments, others still carry them out, and so on, while at the top of the hierarchy the 'Interpreters of Nature', the most dignified philosophers, are to be found. The organisation of society suggested by Bacon ascribes to each individual a specific place, a role to be played, and

---

[11] Ibid., 146.
[12] Ibid., 133.
[13] Ibid., 134.
[14] Ibid., 135.
[15] Ibid. Similar dispositions applied in France during the COVID-related lockdown in 2020, the prescribed distance being one kilometre from one's home.
[16] This concern for secrecy has sometimes been seen as typical of magical adepts. See Henry, *Knowledge is Power*.

consequently reduces individuals to their social function. For the island is a theoretical construct, the embodiment of a world governed by experimental knowledge rather than a representation of a polity, a meditation on the desirable direction which science ought to follow.

It is therefore under these stringent circumstances that the centre of the island, Salomon's House, can grow and prosper. Secrecy and surveillance appear as conditions for science to develop; Bacon seems to recognise that they might be crucial to the advancement of learning. The House of Salomon itself, in its inner organisation and functioning, bears the marks of such concerns. First, the landscape described by the priest appears as bucolic with its lakes and ponds, spacious houses, baths, orchards and gardens. But all around, 'high towers' (the text indicates that they are half a mile in height, which is about the height of the current tallest building in the world) give structure to the whole landscape; they are further placed on high hills, suggesting that they organise the landscape (they are purported to be for storing, for astronomy, for observation of the weather). Among the very many operations which can be carried out in the Academy, beyond the dispensaries which remind us of the importance of medicine for Bacon, beyond the mechanical arts which are crucial to the advancement of natural philosophy, some have to do with vision. The organisation boasts 'perspective-houses' where various types of optical instruments can be found, such as laser beam-like concentrations of light 'which we carry to great distance, and make so sharp as to discern small points and lines'; telescopes, which are 'means of seeing objects afar off; as in the heaven and remote places'; 'helps for the sight, far above spectacles and glasses in use'; and magnifying glasses which seem to announce the microscope.[17] This emphasis on vision and on the mechanical aids to vision is compounded by the sound-houses where diverse experiments enable the circulation of sounds in unforeseen ways, the perception of sounds not usually audible, and of course modes of transforming the voice. The scientists' abilities are also manifest in the house of deceits of the senses, where they experiment on deception, but of which they do not make use because they 'hate all impostures and lies'.[18] The concentration and isolation of deceit in a specific house is reminiscent of the idols which, in Bacon's philosophy, are obstacles to the progress of knowledge, and which must be destroyed.

At the heart of the Academy therefore, one encounters experiments and mechanical operations which project the scientist's power beyond the immediate perimeter of the island. The coherence and life of the system rest in

[17] Bacon, *New Atlantis*, 161–2.
[18] Ibid., 164.

part on tools for observation and surveillance. This in turn suggests that a desirable model for the construction of knowledge would include secrecy, hierarchy and surveillance. In Bacon's blueprint, the organisation of this ideal polity, at all levels, is not separable from modes of control, neither in the functioning of the state, nor in the structuring of knowledge. While it purports to embody the advancement of learning at the beginning of the seventeenth century and looks forward to a future based on science and knowledge, it is also, perhaps above all, a thought experiment which enables Bacon and the reader to follow through the workings of the new science advocated by the author.[19] The progress of thought is enacted through the progress of the narrative, generating in the reader's mind the utopia of a society based on science and knowledge, but also on secrecy, surveillance and control

III. *Robinson Crusoe*: The Ambiguities of Utopia

The trope of the island, so important for the development of narratives of utopia since Thomas More,[20] is also essential for the novel, thereby suggesting perhaps links between the emerging narrative genre of the novel and the mode of utopia. In Bacon's tale, the island enables the development of a thought experiment. But while Bacon's perspective is that of the structure of the state, Defoe's novel *Robinson Crusoe* famously focuses on the emergence of the individual. The relationship between society, religion and autonomy is at the core of the novel, but equally important, as noted by Rosen and Santesso for instance, are the constraints exercised on the experiment.[21] The limitations are apparent in Crusoe's ignorance of the forces that drive him, in the authoritarian elements that surface through the construction of a generally liberal state, prompting Rosen and Santesso to describe the island as 'a perfect little surveillance state'[22] in which the interactions between personhood, autonomy and surveillance are not fully resolved. They rightly insist on the ways in which the text of *Robinson Crusoe* explores the possibility of a liberal state while being aware of, at the time, necessary constraints: 'the ends Defoe imagines are fully consistent with a liberal state (covenants, liberty of conscience, toleration), but the means to secure them are still authoritarian and inspired by fear'.[23]

But the ambivalence of *Robinson Crusoe* goes further. In the same way that *New Atlantis* was partially dependent on an underside of secrecy, control and hierarchy in order to develop its blueprint for the desired organisation of

[19] I have argued more fully this point in Tadié, *Francis Bacon. Le continent du savoir.*
[20] See Marin, *Utopiques.*
[21] Rosen and Santesso, *Watchman in Pieces*, 84–5.
[22] Ibid., 85.
[23] Ibid., 84.

science, and perhaps of the state, *Robinson Crusoe*'s investigation of personhood is dependent on an economic underside. Crusoe's stay on the island is made economically possible by the fact that his fortune prospers because of his investments in Brazil, in particular in a sugar plantation itself based on slavery. And the shipwreck occurs as Robinson Crusoe is on his way to Africa to acquire slaves. The story's experiment in the construction of personhood and society is in turn dependent on forms of colonial oppression and exploitation.[24]

Not unlike Bacon's *New Atlantis*, the island operates under the trope of observation. This starts with what is the first gesture of the castaway, the survey of the land so as to organise and appropriate space and defend it against possible intrusions ('My next Work was to view the Country, and seek a proper Place for my Habitation, and where to stow my Goods to secure them from whatever might happen'[25]). This trope of observation is apparent at every turn of Crusoe's wanderings on the island: there are about 150 occurrences of the verb 'see', to which must be added verbs denoting similar operations such as 'observe' or 'spy'. The discovery of the footprint, one of the most famous pages in Western literature, is for instance solely dependent on the senses, in particular hearing and sight:

> I stood like one Thunder-struck, or as if I had seen an Apparition; I listn'd, I look'd round me, I could hear nothing nor see any Thing [. . .] I could see no other Impression but that one, I went to it again to see if there were any more, and to observe if it might not be my Fancy.[26]

This brings about, in Robinson, 'Apprehensions of seeing a Man', and he is 'ready to sink into the Ground at but the Shadow or silent Appearance of a Man's having set his Foot in the Island'.[27] The silence which surrounds this quasi-apparition throws into relief the visual shock of observing the footprint, and suggests, ominously, a hidden presence, a concealed observer, a danger that lurks and spies. This adds to Robinson's sense of isolation, which characterises the first part of the novel, where he finds himself 'so absolutely miserable, so without Help abandonn'd, so entirely depress'd'.[28]

This feeling of isolation has two consequences. On the one hand it brings about introspection on the part of Robinson ('Now I look'd upon my past Life

---

[24] For a detailed analysis of these economic conditions, see Carey, 'Reading Contrapuntally', 105–36.

[25] Defoe, *Robinson Crusoe*, 46.

[26] Ibid., 130.

[27] Ibid., 133.

[28] Ibid., 54.

with such Horrour [. . .]'[29]), and contributes to the investigation of the self and the fashioning of personhood. On the other hand, isolation is conducive to building defences and fortifications, and erecting walls; after the sighting of the footstep, his abode becomes his 'castle',[30] leading him to build a second fortification. So that the landscape is reshaped by Crusoe, not only because he domesticates parts of it, but also because he structures it around the castle, to which he returns to seek safety at every opportunity. Both aspects, inner investigation and outer fortifications, are not unconnected, as suggested in John Bender's pioneering work on the penitentiary:[31] indeed, above the text looms the figure of the prison, through the narrative of confinement ('the Island was certainly a Prison to me'[32]), inducing, at the individual level, a metaphor of the prison as protection and reform. In Bender's words, 'Prison, now equated with solitary reflection, is first viewed as random, punitive, vengeful; but it slides into another thing entirely – something salubrious, beneficent, reformative, and productive of wealth and social integration.'[33] In tropes and forms of confinement, seclusion can sometimes turn into protection. The ambiguity and possible reversibility of these figures is a distinctive feature of the processes of surveillance from that day to this. It is already apparent in one of the formative *Bildungsromane* of Western literature.

The presence, in the text, of the language of surveillance, if not its tools and implements, suggests that the possibilities of utopia, opened up by Crusoe's isolation on the island, are inseparable from control and power. They extend the ambiguities of a text caught between, on the one hand, the establishment of a liberal persona in a state which appears to be built along Lockean lines of social contract, and, on the other hand, the presence of tropes and figures, such as prison, fortifications, absolute rule, which suggests the connections of the liberal state with a regime of surveillance and of domination, characteristic of autocracy. Before any other encounter, Robinson surveys the land with the feeling of pleasure at finding himself the 'King and Lord of all this country indefeasibly'.[34] He calls himself variously 'Lord of the Manor', 'King' or 'Emperor'.[35] And when the island starts being populated, he finds himself as 'absolute Lord and Law-giver'.[36] So that in spite of some possible references

---

[29] Ibid., 83.
[30] Ibid., 131.
[31] Bender, *Imagining the Penitentiary*.
[32] Defoe, *Robinson Crusoe*, 83.
[33] Bender, *Imagining the Penitentiary*, 55.
[34] Defoe, *Robinson Crusoe*, 85.
[35] Ibid., 109.
[36] Ibid., 203.

to a Lockean state of nature and ensuing social contract, the language of polity remains, at least ambiguously so, that of autocracy in the Stuart mould.[37]

This is perhaps best understood if one thinks of the legacy of *Robinson Crusoe*, where the text gave birth, roughly, to two different types of interpretations or rewritings. The benevolent, optimistic dimension of life on the island can be traced through such texts as Johann David Wyss's *Swiss Family Robinson* (1812) or R. M. Ballantyne's *Coral Island* (1857), which interpret the experience on the island as nurturing and formative. On the other hand, interventions such as H. G. Wells's *The Island of Dr Moreau* (1896), with its macabre scientific experiments, or William Golding's *Lord of the Flies* (1954), which dissolves the Lockean social contract into a Hobbesian state of nature, enhance, through their dystopic portrayals of life on the island, themes of tyranny, control and surveillance.

IV. *Gulliver's Travels*: Satire and Surveillance

Texts like Bacon's or Defoe's, therefore, while appearing to be a blueprint for a better science, or to investigate personhood and construction of the modern individual, reveal that such projects can be developed in different, darker ways, intricately linked with their proposals. Or perhaps that the investigation of a liberal, autonomous subject could not wholly part with the impulse to control. And it is precisely the role of satire to bring out this darker side and to make it apparent to readers.

The overarching metaphor of *Gulliver's Travels* is containment. From the multitude of ligatures that tie Gulliver to the ground when he wakes up in Lilliput, to his being paraded in a box in Brobdingnag, to his willing captivity among the Houyhnhnms, not to mention his choice of spending as much of his time as possible in the stables with his horses at the end, Gulliver appears to be battered from one structure of control to another. While Gulliver is the arch intruder into various lands and polities, while he is the arch observer of distant lands and unknown countries, he is also the arch prisoner, finding that (perhaps with the exception of book III) he constantly needs to extricate himself from the power that others attempt to exert over him. This builds in fascinating ways issues of surveillance into the text, and the dystopian regime of some parts of the narrative adds to the complexity of his position – and of the reader's.

As noted in Pat Rogers's essay, 'Gulliver's Glasses',[38] Gulliver's favoured mode of observation is, like Robinson's, the eye; the glasses which he keeps

---

[37] Rosen and Santesso, *Watchman in Pieces*, 71–3.
[38] Rogers, 'Gulliver's Glasses'.

with him at all times not only help his sight but protect him from the volley of arrows thrown at him by the Blefuscudians. When Gulliver is condemned for treason by the Lilliputians, they sentence him to 'put out' both his eyes, because it would be sufficient for him 'to see by the Eyes of the Ministers'.[39] Gulliver's glasses escape the attention of the Lilliputians, as does his pocket 'perspective' (that is to say, his telescope), which Gulliver ironically mentions as 'being of no Consequence to the Emperor, I did not think my self bound in Honour to discover'.[40]

Vision and exposure are also at the heart of Gulliver's adventures in Brobdingnag, with equally ambiguous effects. From the beginning of the episode, Gulliver, for fear of being trampled on by the giants, hides in the middle of a corn field. But as he is picked up by the farmer and then later finds a place at the court of the king, he becomes literally an object of curiosity. He is observed, but also paraded as an attraction – an activity of course not unfamiliar to the eighteenth century where natives from distant lands could be displayed in similar fashion.[41] The ambivalence of vision is further explored through Gulliver's vision at close quarters of the skin of the fine ladies of Brobdingnag or of the vermin in the beggars' clothes. Because of the dangers which surround Gulliver in Brobdingnag, because of his sudden diminutive size, he is not to be kept out of sight, which suggests once again the complex attractions of surveillance, both as protection and as control. This further materialises in the boxes which are built for Gulliver to live and to travel in. The box both shields him and displays him, both protects him and contains him, functions both as a space of seclusion and as a space of comfort, it is a prison but one from which he can emerge for fresh air. It constitutes finally his means of escape as he is caught by an eagle and dropped in the sea. Swift's text articulates here the very metaphor of surveillance, where control and domination can be appropriated, perhaps even undermined, by individuals who find ways of transforming them, its tools turned into protection and even freedom.

The place left to the individual in a political system, and, in Gulliver's case, his willing acceptance of the political order, lies at the heart of book IV of Swift's satire. Gulliver, in his last expedition, is confronted with the utopia of a world governed by the extreme rationality of the Houyhnhnms. The complexities of the episode, and of its possible interpretations, proceeds from the fact that the Yahoos, despicable beings kept at bay by the Houyhnhnms,

---

[39] Swift, *Gulliver's Travels*, 100.

[40] Ibid., 55.

[41] One famous example of such practice involved Omai, the Tahitian man who was brought to England in 1774 by Captain Cook.

embody humanity. In Swift's words to his friend Sheridan, 'expect no more from Man than such an Animal is capable of'.[42] The Houyhnhnms want to eradicate the Yahoos because of their nature. Gulliver is therefore caught between the aspiration to pure reason, embodied, literally, in the horses, and the impossibility of discarding his own humanity, which makes of him a Yahoo. But the Houyhnhnms themselves are ambiguous beings, and the topic discussed at one of their Assemblies, 'Whether the *Yahoos* should be exterminated from the Face of the Earth',[43] suggests, yet again, a darker use of reason. The Houyhnhnm who argues in favour of their eradication highlights, among other things, that the Yahoos are not originally from the land, they are not *Aborigines* in the language of the text, they are foreigners as we would say today. But Gulliver's master offers another option, following Gulliver's cue:

> among other Things, I mentioned a Custom we had of castrating *Houyhnhnms* when they were young, in order to render them tame; that the Operation was easy and safe; that it was no Shame to learn Wisdom from Brutes [. . .]; that this Invention might be practised upon the younger *Yahoos* here, which besides rendering them tractable and fitter for use, would in an Age put an End to the whole Species, without destroying Life.[44]

So that the utopian land, for which Gulliver feels love and veneration, is exposed through satire as a dark utopia, where control, submission and separation are also the organising principles, while potentially offering destruction and eradication of a species, ironically, 'without destroying Life'.[45]

Swift's treatment of the possibilities of utopia, of rational projects and managerial schemes, is therefore undermined by satire, which carries to their logical conclusion the principles on which such utopias rest. As noted by Jason Pearl, 'Gulliver travels, and satire travels with him, seeming to doom utopia wherever he sets foot.'[46] In Swift's *Gulliver's Travels*, utopias can no longer exist, and Gulliver can no longer inhabit them. In focusing on vision as both a favoured means of investigation of the world and as a definition of the satirical position, Swift ties together modes of surveillance, utopia, and satire. In doing this, he is also placing readers in the position of Gulliver. They

---

[42] Letter to Thomas Sheridan, 11 September 1725, in *The Correspondence of Jonathan Swift*, vol. 2, 595.

[43] Swift, *Gulliver's Travels*, 408.

[44] Ibid., 410–11.

[45] The satirical gesture of the proposal of castrating the Yahoos is reminiscent of Swift's proposal to feed the babies of Dublin to affluent people in *A Modest Proposal*.

[46] Pearl, *Utopian Geographies*, 126.

relate to his predicament, while necessarily seeking a distance – itself an illusion. The only utopias which are left are utopias of the mind: 'my Memory and Imaginations were perpetually filled with the Virtues and Ideas of those exalted *Houyhnhnms*'.[47]

V. *The Dunciad*: Sinking All Hope

> Lo! thy dread Empire, Chaos! is restor'd;
> Light dies before thy uncreating word:
> Thy hand, great Anarch! lets the curtain fall;
> And Universal Darkness buries All.[48]

The ambiguities and satire of the surveillance state are carried to an extreme in Pope's *Dunciad*. In this poem, the forces of darkness prevail and the last lines are a fitting tribute to the triumph of Dulness over the world. In foreshadowing the triumph of Dulness and chaos, Pope draws the consequences of the political and poetical transformations of literary life in England in the first half of the eighteenth century. Like Swift's exploration of the nature of the conflict between Ancients and Moderns in *The Battel of the Books*, Pope's intervention in the defining quarrel of the age is at once a description of a state of affairs, a stark warning against the consequences of a possible victory of the Moderns, and a literary detonation of the Republic of Letters. It creates a fiction in which 'The sick'ning stars fade off th'ethereal plain',[49] where '*Art* after *Art* goes out, and all is Night':[50] the triumph of Dulness has cancelled out any form of creation ('Light dies before thy uncreating word'). At the end of the poem Pope envisages a world in which the place of individuals, as manifested by their ability to create, has disappeared. But Pope sees the conditions for the victory of the Moderns as having been generated by the political world of the Hanoverian dynasty and above all by the ministry of Robert Walpole. Thus, the political and the poetical merge to offer a world where surveillance comes to reign supreme. While *The Dunciad* does not deal with privacy in the modern sense, it equates personhood with social persona and literary role, and expresses anxiety towards their possible dissolution in chaos and darkness. The triumph of the Moderns leads to their invasion of a public space from which all value and all bearings have disappeared. The places where poetry had once thrived have been taken over by the likes of Colley Cibber and his army of

---

[47] Swift, *Gulliver's Travels*, 434. See Pearl, *Utopian Geographies*, 126: 'He re-creates Houyhnhnmland as an internal state, an imaginary space to which he can return at will.'

[48] Pope, *The Dunciad*, 409, ll. 653–6.

[49] Ibid., l. 636.

[50] Ibid., 407, l. 640.

dunces. The individual, equated in Pope's poem with his social role, is a victim of the corruption of (the politics of) the Republic of Letters. While the 'old world' of the Republic of Letters was one where harmony and literary conversation were at the centre of proceedings, in the 'new world' the Moderns have crossed all barriers and fully appropriated the literary and political life, and its narrative. In this new world, creation, values and taste have been stifled under dominance, control, fear and surveillance. The Moderns, whose rule is embodied by Dulness, now reign over the literary world. Pope's satirical stance lies in both the display of this new world and in the scathing elaboration on its consequences for literary life. Satire allows Pope to attack the hegemony of the Moderns and to prompt (the reader's) laughter as a powerful tool to undermine this new order.

Pope's great satirical poem proceeds from a series of quarrels which involved Pope and a number of writers.[51] The early versions of *The Dunciad* proceeded from the enmity between Lewis Theobald and Pope over Shakespeare. Theobald, the author of *Shakespeare Restored* (1726), had attacked Pope's *Shakespeare* (1725) for providing an incorrect edition of Shakespeare, based on insufficient attention to detail. Pope of course held the opposite view, one where the sense of the whole rather than the microscopic focus on detail was crucial.[52] *The Dunciad* provides a satiric intervention in the quarrel, one which, by placing Theobald on the throne of the Dunces, aims at bringing the controversy to an end. Theobald, the hero of the poem, is busy, ready to 'crucify poor *Shakespear* once a week'.[53] A devotee of Dulness, he reclaims the text through his commentaries, and Dulness rewards him by placing him on the throne: 'I see a King! who leads my chosen sons / To lands, that flow with clenches and with puns.'[54] In its early incarnations, *The Dunciad* is the occasion for Pope of settling accounts, of provoking enmity, of responding to attacks. The satirical mode enables the poet to plunge his enemies into the 'disemboguing streams'[55] of oblivion while addressing the political and poetical corruption of the world. With the last version of 1743, in four books, Pope articulates further the form of the satire and the numerous individual quarrels in which he was involved.

The critical apparatus which surrounds the text is longer than the poem itself – what Cibber in his *Letter* calls 'those loads of Prose Rubbish, wherewith you have smothered your *Dunciad*'.[56] Like Swift's *A Tale of a Tub*, it integrates in the footnotes and commentaries the voices of opponents and critics, the better

---

[51] I have developed this point in Tadié, 'Quarrelling', 542–57.
[52] See Weinbrot, *Menippean Satire Reconsidered*, 236.
[53] Pope, *The Dunciad*, 83, l. 164.
[54] Ibid., 93, ll. 251–2.
[55] Ibid., 133, l. 259.
[56] Cibber, *Letter from Mr. Cibber*, 9.

to ridicule them. The footnotes proliferate from the very first one, devoted to an exegesis of the title and a dialogue between different distinguished sources such as Theobald or Bentley, which takes over the page and the text. Such a technique stems from the paradox at the heart of satire itself. Indirection and opacity are necessary conditions of its composition and its existence (the dangers to the author were real, as Swift knew) but lead to a countervailing and equally necessary movement of clarification and commentary. The satirical text requires anonymity on the one hand, because of the system of surveillance and control which it attacks, and elucidation on the other, in order to be understood by its readers. Its intervention proceeds from the system under attack, takes place within that system, and in turn can become a target of that system.

The parody of the epic turns the contemporary world into a dystopian empire, ruled over by the goddess Dulness, while the politics of the age are satirically displayed as favouring this empire. King George appears in the very first lines of the poem ('Dunce the second'), while Walpole's presence can be detected in various parts. The text articulates a literary opposition (Cibber's poor talent, as viewed by Pope) and a political context (Cibber as poet laureate). It examines the state of the Republic of Letters (characterised by quarrels, skirmishes and fragmentation) and relates it to the political environment (the corruption of politics under Walpole). It constructs a world, the world of London, which is being taken over by the forces of darkness, where surveillance dominates. The goddess's empire appears in no uncertain words as one peopled with sycophants who are dutifully rewarded, and who embody the collapse in values, lambasted by Pope:

> And now the Queen, to glad her sons, proclaims
> By herald Hawkers, high heroic Games.
> They summon all her Race: An endless band
> Pours forth, and leaves unpeopled half the land.
> A motley mixture! in long wigs, in bags,
> In silks, in crapes, in Garters, and in rags,
> From drawing rooms, from colleges, from garrets,
> On horse, on foot, in hacks, and gilded chariots;
> All who true Dunces in her cause appear'd,
> And all who knew those Dunces to reward.[57]

At the beginning of book IV the reader witnesses the emergence of a bleak dystopian world. Here is the Queen:

> She mounts the Throne: her head a cloud conceal'd,
> In broad Effulgence all below reveal'd,

---

[57] Pope, *The Dunciad*, 297, ll. 17–26.

('Tis thus aspiring Dulness ever shines)
Soft on her lap her Laureat Son reclines;
Beneath her foot-stool, *Science* groans in Chains,
And *Wit* dreads Exile, Penalties and Pains.
There foam'd rebellious *Logic*, gagg'd and bound;
There, stript, fair *Rhet'ric* languish'd on the ground[58]

The despotic power of Dulness has subdued all the classical disciplines, science as much as rhetoric. Book IV parades its dunces, with Colley Cibber, 'the Antichrist of wit',[59] as the arch dunce, but it is Dulness who reigns supreme and whose restoration is the subject of book IV. By extolling Cibber, by asserting the triumph of Dulness and the demise of truth, philosophy, sciences, religion or morality, by the (absence of) vision of the final line of the poem, Pope shows that the forces of destruction have conquered the world and the principles of empty disputation have triumphed. The surveillance state reigns supreme.

VI. Conclusion

Satire thus enables Pope, as well as Swift, to think through a world which is being gradually invaded by the principles of surveillance, and furthermore to use the tools of surveillance – its secrecy, its encoded language and closeted allusions – against itself. The utopian constructions of Bacon or, to some extent, of Defoe are fragmented into worlds without values, in which the social and political predicament of individuals resonates within the wars of the Republic of Letters. Through these inchoate forms of surveillance, satire exposes the embeddedness of the language and practice of surveillance in thinking about the world, and in particular about its (utopian) future.

Bacon thought that technological advancement was indeed a prerequisite for all advancement of knowledge, suggesting, a few hundred years before our own technological age, that the nature of innovation and knowledge production positions surveillance as a modality of technical and social progress.[60] Defoe implied not only that the construction of the modern subject and of the liberal polity had to face issues of control and dominance but that the whole project was itself dependent on colonialism and slavery. In Swift's satire the contradictions faced by utopian projects, specifically around questions of surveillance, sight and oversight, were exposed as insurmountable. Pope's great poem finally sees the defeat of arts and science under the armies of Dulness,

---

[58] Ibid., 342, ll. 17–24.
[59] Ibid., 297, l. 16.
[60] Cohen, 'Studying Law Studying Surveillance'.

and the surveillance state they ushered in, as the dystopian future of Britain. But where Bacon and Defoe looked forward to the developments of science and the progress of society, Swift and Pope show through satire the doomed prospects of such hopes. Gulliver's willing journey to the borders of animality or the progress of Dulness finally restored to her throne emphasise the risk we incur in surrendering ourselves to the forces of conformity and control without resistance. For both Swift and Pope, perhaps for all satirists, this resistance lay first and foremost in words, in satirical practice – as veiled as surveillance but employed for diametrically opposed ends. Martinus Scriblerus, in his opening remarks on *The Dunciad*, claims that 'our Author, in his very laughter, is not indulging his own Ill nature, but only punishing that of others'.[61] Pope's satirical move mischievously reveals to the public the full vacuity of his opponents. But instead of simply winning the argument or the fight, it is through the reader's laughter thus provoked that he achieves his goal.

VII. Bibliography

Bacon, Francis. *New Atlantis*. 1627. In *The Works of Francis Bacon*, edited by James Spedding, Robert L. Ellis, and Douglas D. Heath, vol. 3, 119–66. London: Longman, 1859.

Bender, John. *Imagining the Penitentiary: Fiction and the Architecture of Mind in Eighteenth-Century England*. Chicago: University of Chicago Press, 1987.

Carey, Daniel. 'Reading Contrapuntally. *Robinson Crusoe*, Slavery, and Postcolonial Theory.' In *The Postcolonial Enlightenment: Eighteenth-Century Colonialism and Postcolonial Theory*, edited by Daniel Carey and Lynn Festa, 105–36. Oxford: Oxford University Press, 2013.

Cibber, Colley. *A Letter from Mr. Cibber*. London, 1742.

Cohen, Julie E. 'Studying Law Studying Surveillance.' *Surveillance & Society* 13, no. 1 (2015): 91–101.

Defoe, Daniel. *Robinson Crusoe*. Edited and introduction by Thomas Keymer and co-annotated by James Kelly. Oxford: Oxford University Press, 2008.

Harcourt, Bernard E. *Exposed: Desire and Disobedience in the Digital Age*. Cambridge, MA: Harvard University Press, 2015.

Henry, John. *Knowledge is Power: How Magic, the Government and an Apocalyptic Vision Helped Francis Bacon to Create Modern Science*. Cambridge: Icon, 2002.

Marin, Louis. *Utopiques: jeux d'espaces*. Paris: Éditions de Minuit, 1973.

Pearl, Jason H. *Utopian Geographies and the Early English Novel*. Charlottesville: University of Virginia Press, 2014.

Pope, Alexander. *The Dunciad*. Ed. James Sutherland. 3rd ed. Revised. London: Methuen, 1963.

[61] Pope, *The Dunciad*, 19.

Pritchard, Jonathan. 'Social Topography in *The Dunciad, Variorum*.' *Huntington Library Quarterly* 75, no. 4 (2012): 527–60.

Rogers, Pat. 'Gulliver's Glasses.' In *The Art of Jonathan Swift*, edited by Clive T. Probyn, 179–88. New York: Barnes and Noble, 1978.

Rosen, David, and Aaron Santesso. *The Watchman in Pieces: Surveillance, Literature, and Liberal Personhood*. New Haven, CT: Yale University Press, 2013.

Swift, Jonathan. *The Correspondence of Jonathan Swift, D.D.* Edited by David Woolley. Frankfurt am Main: Peter Lang, 1999–2014.

———. *Gulliver's Travels*. Edited by David Womersley. Cambridge: Cambridge University Press, 2012.

———. *A Tale of a Tub and Other Works*. Edited by Marcus Walsh. Cambridge: Cambridge University Press, 2010.

Tadié, Alexis. *Francis Bacon. Le continent du savoir*. Paris: Classiques Garnier, 2014.

———. 'Quarrelling.' In *The Oxford Handbook of Eighteenth-Century Satire*, edited by Paddy Bullard, 542–57. Oxford: Oxford University Press, 2019.

Weinbrot, Harold. *Menippean Satire Reconsidered: From Antiquity to the Eighteenth Century*. Baltimore, MD: Johns Hopkins University Press, 2005.

Williams, Aubrey. *Pope's* Dunciad: *A Study of its Meaning*. London: Methuen, 1955.

Zuboff, Shoshana. *The Age of Surveillance Capitalism: The Fight for the Future at the New Frontier of Power*. London: Profile Books, 2019.

4

Digital Technology during Times of Crisis: Risks to Society and Fundamental Rights

Yves Poullet

I. Introduction

In the introduction to his 2012 work entitled *Crisis(es) and Law*, Jacques Larrieu defines crisis as a 'disorder' causing 'the disintegration of the norms that usually regulate society'.[1] This disorder can in turn give rise to a 'law of circumstance' which is to be considered dangerous but which can also be a source of progress as it invites specialists to conceive of a 'new legal system that draws lessons from the crisis'.

Digital technology is an important part of the response to crises, and its use in the service of the struggle against them plays a major role in the disruption of the functioning of our legal system, in an undoubtedly more insidious than conscious manner. Of course, the upheaval that digital technology causes in the legal system is not specific to times of crisis. What is unmistakably specific to such times, however, is how this tool is used during periods of unrest, and how its legitimisation makes the law forget its own foundations. If digital technology is sometimes the object of specific legislation, it is above all because it constitutes the very condition of the effectiveness of the regulatory measures taken by our governments, an effectiveness that runs the risk of negating certain freedoms.

Should the use of such effective tools therefore be abandoned? The answer is 'no', but it is undoubtedly necessary to limit their implementation with a legal framework adapted to these exceptional times. The goal of this reflection, therefore, is to guide the development of such a framework, in the same way as Gligorijević attempts to do in Chapter 5 of this collection.

---

[1] Larrieu, 'Avant-propos', 9–12. In the same vein can be added the reflections of the authors of a thematic edition of the magazine *Droit et Société* devoted to the COVID crisis (Abitboul et al., 'Ce que 2020 a fait au droit'), who conclude that if 'the crisis denies the law', it nonetheless does not deny 'reflection that is specific to it'.

The present reflection covers two areas of application. The first concerns the lessons learned during the struggle against the pandemic.[2] The measures implemented today against COVID-19, or those envisaged for use against future pandemics, all have a restrictive impact on freedoms that goes beyond their simple limitation and sometimes represents a challenge to their very essence. Digital technology is omnipresent in these measures: the use of artificial intelligence in the search for new tools (vaccines and others) and in the analysis of the causes of the pandemic, its spread, its prevention and its impacts;[3] the creation of databases, whether it be of infected persons, the vaccinated, or of caregivers; the monitoring of people, for example through the use of systems put in place in our mobile phones with the goal of detecting the presence of contaminated people in one's entourage; the use of drones to monitor compliance with travel restrictions, and so on.[4] The biopolitical foundations of such policies are investigated by Sabot in Chapter 2 of this collection.

The second area of application focuses on the use of digital technology in the fight against crime in one area in particular: the use by police or intelligence services of data kept by communication service providers.[5] Digital evidence is now a major tool used in solving a growing number of crimes. Examples of this can be found in Grabosky and Urbas's chapter on application to online child exploitation,[6] as well as in the French Code of Criminal Procedure, which has been revised several times, and allows for

the installation of a technical device whose purpose is, without the consent of the interested parties, to access computer data in any place, to record, store and to transfer it, whether it is stored in a computer system, displayed on a

[2] In this regard, see the following studies: Poullet, 'Pandémie, numérique et droits de l'homme', 246–63; Parsa and Poullet, 'Les droits fondamentaux à l'épreuve du confinement et du déconfinement', 137–203; Poullet, 'COVID et libertés'.

[3] In this regard, see the OECD's response to Coronavirus on 23 April 2020, 'Using artificial intelligence to help combat COVID-19', available at https://www.oecd.org/coronavirus/policy-responses/using-artificial-intelligence-to-help-combat-covid-19-ae4c5c21/.

[4] To take just one example from Belgium: on 12 January 2021, a simple decision of the Minister of the Interior modified the previous ministerial decision of 28 October 2020, which organises emergency measures to limit the spread of the COVID-19 coronavirus. The modification intended to give the National Office of Social Security the power to use datamining and AI across various administrative databases, for the purpose of profiling, monitoring and surveillance of the Belgian population.

[5] Today, only traditional service providers are targeted, but we know that tomorrow, the European Union, in the context of the revision of the ePrivacy Directive (2002/58/EC, 12 July 2002), intends to extend data retention obligations to any communication and information platform, and therefore to new services on the Internet, such as Voice over Internet Protocol (VoIP), instant messaging, messages exchanged through social networks such as Twitter and Facebook, and e-mail, instead of traditional communication services.

[6] See Grabosky and Urbas, Chapter 7 of this collection.

screen for the user of an automated data processing system, or entered by typing out characters or received and transmitted by remote devices.[7]

Finally, the use of machine learning systems (artificial intelligence) also represents an opportunity for law enforcement.[8] Returning to our primary interest in this matter, the legal possibility is acknowledged, under Article 15 of the ePrivacy Directive,[9] for Member States to oblige communication providers to retain communication data (but not its content) and to allow police and judicial authorities as well as intelligence services to access such data. A recent decision of the Court of Justice of the European Union (CJEU) concerns the conditions of this access.[10] According to the Court, only a strictly defined state of emergency can justify the obligation of communication providers to preserve data beyond the simple limitations which, in normal circumstances, are provided by Article 52 of the Charter of Fundamental Rights of the European Union (EU Charter).

Whether it concerns the pandemic, tracking down criminal offenders or terrorist operatives, or the struggle against global warming or natural disasters, the use of the resources of digital technology and the development of ever more powerful applications of such resources is clearly a strong temptation for our leaders. The Commission on Information Technology and Liberties[11] refers to

---

[7] The French Code of Criminal Procedure, through the Act of 14 March 2011 on the orientation and programming for the performance of internal security, already included this possibility of access to digital evidence (L. 2014-1353, 13 November 2014, JORF, 14 November). The law of 13 November, whose tendency was to strengthen the provisions relating to the fight against terrorism singularly expanded this recourse and a law of 3 June 2016 (L. 2016-731, 3 June 2016, JO 4 June) further extended these possibilities of real-time and remote access to all flagrante or preliminary investigations for cases of crime and organised delinquency upon authorisation of the judge of liberties and detention and upon request of the Public Prosecutor. A 2019 decree (2019-1602 published in the JO of 31 December 2019) specifies the contours of this capturing of digital evidence.

[8] In the face of increasingly numerous data collected in an increasingly ubiquitous manner, the processing capacities of computers make it possible to facilitate both the tasks of prevention and the detection of offences and their authors. For example: detecting racist messages on the Internet; using emotional analysis systems to analyse the reactions of suspects or, by means of facial recognition, identifying a criminal or a person suspected of terrorism in a crowd; using the cross-referencing of multiple socio-economic data, including consumption, mobility and expenditure, to track down a criminal or to predict how dangerous a person may be; calculating how dangerous a convicted person may be in the future (see *State v Loomis* (2016) WI 68, 371 Wis. 2d 235, 881 N.W.2d 749).

[9] 2002/58/EC, 12 July 2002.

[10] *Privacy International and others* (C-623/17, C-511/18, C-512/18 and C-520/18) (CJEU, 6 October 2020).

[11] CITL Ruling, 'Ruling No. 2020-046, 24 April 2020 on a proposed mobile application called "Stop-Covid"', available at https://www.cnil.fr/fr/publication-de-lavis-de-la-cnil-sur-le-projet-dapplication-mobile-stopcovid.

this as 'technological solutionism',[12] defined as the convenient recourse to the tool of technology as a response to the challenges posed by emergency situations, with the belief that it will solve the problem.

Furthermore, it is not surprising that these two areas are being brought together. Could it not be argued that the same technologies of surveillance and control are at work in both cases,[13] and that the privilege granted to the use of such technologies could be explained by a similar logic? That is to say, in light of the state of emergency and the seriousness of the situation, such technologies provide an unparalleled efficiency in the service of the given priority, whether it be regarding individual liberties and the right to health on the one hand, or the right to public security on the other. Indeed, the trade-off is often set in terms of liberty versus security, but it need not be so, as Gligorijević explains in Chapter 5 of this collection.

The 'Pandemic' law, recently adopted by the Belgian Parliament, establishes the procedure that must be put in place in order to declare such a state of emergency. In addition, Article 15 of the Council of Europe's Convention on Human Rights (ECHR) provides a strict overarching framework for this state of emergency.

The potential of digital technology fully justifies the anxiety of judges, data protection authorities and civil liberties associations in the face of what tomorrow may be a commonplace tool in the hands of governments or, even worse, of certain companies acting in the service of private interests or at the very least in a vaguely defined notion of the 'public good'. This is the main theme throughout the following reflection, as well as elsewhere in the volume. Indeed, to reflect the tandem between surveillance and 'public good', Brunon-Ernst, in Chapter 6 of this collection, describes the concept of bien(sur)veillance coined by Cynthia Fleury.

This discussion therefore begins with the examination of the CJEU 2020 judgment in *Privacy International and others* on access to communications data by law enforcement authorities. The second point of discussion studies Article 15 of the ECHR, the application of which was recommended to the Member States during their fight against the pandemic, and then compares

---

[12] At the 2008 South by Southwest festival, Facebook founder Mark Zuckerberg said, 'As the world faces many major issues, what we are trying to build as a company is an infrastructure on which to unravel some of them.' Along the same lines, Eric Schmidt, executive chairman of Google, announced at a 2012 conference, 'If we get it right, I think we can fix all the world's problems.' Laugee, 'Solutionisme'.

[13] On this point, refer to the examples given by Calay, 'L'empire des logiciels', 18; Tesquet, *État d'urgence technologique*, 48–52.

the Belgian law voted on 15 July with the requirements of this article. The third point broadens the discussion, relying on the importance of implementing an even more radical limitation of the use of digital technology outside of this state of emergency. The conclusions drawn here call on our legislators to act in order to ensure, in the name of the rule of law, a collective and democratic control of the development of digital technology in the service of freedom, without neglecting the common good.

II. The CJEU's 2020 Judgment on the Widespread Retention of Communications Data

The data retention obligation imposed on Internet service providers and content hosts to retain the traffic, location and civil identity data of all their users in a widespread and undifferentiated manner, for a period of one year, is based on the permissive provisions of Article 15(1) of the ePrivacy Directive. Beyond this precise legal reference, should this not also be considered as an interference justified by the right to security guaranteed in Article 6 of the EU Charter and by the requirements of national security, for which the responsibility lies solely with the Member States by virtue of Article 4 of the Treaty on the European Union (Maastricht Treaty)? The petitioning associations and companies contested the absence of measures governing the implementation of this obligation and, consequently, the right of the police and intelligence services to collect and process the data thus stored by the providers.

Concerning the dispute, the CJEU ruled as follows:

> in situations where a Member State is facing a serious threat to national security that proves to be genuine and present or foreseeable, that Member State may derogate from the obligation to ensure the confidentiality of data relating to electronic communications by requiring, by way of legislative measures, the general and indiscriminate retention of that data for a period that is limited in time to what is strictly necessary, but which may be extended if the threat persists.[14]

The Court added that the injunction must be proportionate, implemented for a time period limited to what is strictly necessary, and is to be subject to effective monitoring controls, either by a court or by an independent administrative body. The latter are to be tasked with verifying the implementation

---

[14] *Privacy International and others* (C-623/17, C-511/18, C-512/18 and C-520/18) (CJEU, 6 October 2020).

of the conditions and guarantees provided by the Court. If these are met, the automated analysis of data must be permitted, particularly that relating to the traffic and location of all users of electronic communications.

This judgment has been interpreted differently by the French Conseil d'État (Council of State) and the Belgian Constitutional Court. In France, the Council of State leaves the interpretation of the emergency situation – which the CJEU cites as a reasonable justification for the widespread retention of communication data – to the discretion of the national executive powers, considering that in light of recent events there exists a threat of terrorism:

> France is faced with a threat to its national security, assessed with regard to all the fundamental interests of the Nation listed in Article L. 811-3 of the Interior Security Code, which, by its intensity, is considered serious and real . . . Moreover, France is particularly exposed to the risk of espionage and foreign interference, notably because of its military capabilities and commitments as well as its technological and economic potential.[15]

The Belgian Constitutional Court adheres to the strict interpretation of the Court.[16] It notes, following European jurisprudence, that the widespread retention measure poses a far greater threat to privacy and freedom of expression than any other measure of limited access to data concerning particular citizens. It emphasises that data retention should be used only in response to serious threats to national security such as terrorism and not to public safety objectives such as serious crime.[17] The Belgian Court therefore considered that,

> In order to satisfy the requirement of proportionality, the legislation must lay down clear and precise rules governing the scope and application of the

---

[15] Conseil d'État [Council of State; the highest court in the administrative legal system], *French Data network et al.*, 21 April 2021, n 393099, 394922, 397844, 397851, 424717, 424718. As a justification of the generalised obligation for data retention, the Council of State added that 'France is also facing serious threats to public peace, linked to an increase in the activity of radical and extremist groups. These threats are of such a nature as to justify the obligation of the generalised and undifferentiated retention of connection data' and, in an even more critical manner towards the European judge, 'the obligation for the judge to set aside the provisions of national law imposing a generalised and undifferentiated retention of connection data for purposes other than safeguarding national security would deprive of effective guarantees the objectives of constitutional value of preventing breaches of public order, in particular breaches of the security of persons and property, and of tracking down the authors of criminal offences'.

[16] Judgment 57/2021, *OBFG et al.*, 21 April 2021, n 6590, 6597, 6599 and 6601.

[17] As held by the CJEU in *Privacy International and others* (C-623/17, C-511/18, C-512/18 and C-520/18) (CJEU, 6 October 2020), 136.

measure in question and imposing minimum safeguards, so that the persons whose personal data is affected have sufficient guarantees that data will be effectively protected against the risk of abuse. That legislation must be legally binding under domestic law and, in particular, must indicate in what circumstances and under which conditions a measure providing for the processing of such data may be adopted, thereby ensuring that the interference is limited to what is strictly necessary.[18]

On this basis, the Court considered that a decision ordering electronic communications service providers to carry out such data retention must be subject to effective review either by a court or by an independent administrative body, such as the CJEU has required.[19]

When assessing the risks to our freedoms that are involved, what is undoubtedly striking in both the European and Belgian decisions is the emphasis on accounting for the potential of the use of digital technology in the implementation of regulatory provisions. Thanks to powerful AI systems, these new risks revolve in particular around the profiling of individuals, the automated detection of sensitive data, and geolocation, as well as the illicit use of communication data. It is in this light that the annulment of the national provisions authorising the widespread conservation of communication data and the prohibition in principle of any instrument of mass surveillance are justified.[20]

Recent developments in digital technology have unmistakably permitted a far greater effectiveness within criminal law than the traditional tools of police and judicial investigation, and even of intelligence services, and as such, the infringements on our individual and collective liberties must have appropriate limits placed upon them. Therefore, as the Belgian Constitutional Court notes,

> The judgment of the Court of Justice of 6 October 2020 imposes a change of perspective with respect to the choice that the legislator has made: the obligation to retain data relating to electronic communications must be the exception, not the rule. Regulations providing for such an obligation must also be subject to clear and precise rules concerning the scope and application of the measure in question as well as imposing minimum requirements. This

---

[18] Judgment 57/2021, *OBFG et al.*, 21 April 2021, 132.

[19] Ibid., 139.

[20] In the same vein, with regard to the questioning of the 'Privacy Shields' agreements entered into by the European Commission in the context of trans-border data flows to the United States for not meeting the requirements of the GDPR, see the *Schrems II* decision (*Facebook Ireland v Schrems* (C-311/18, 16 July 2020)).

regulation must ensure that interference is limited to what is strictly necessary and that it 'must always meet objective criteria that establish a connection between the data to be retained and the objective pursued'.[21]

Therefore, it would clearly be useful to elaborate on how this state of emergency is defined and enacted, based on the lessons drawn from Article 15 of the ECHR. The latter provides a rudimentary framework for these systems of emergency measures and was recently invoked in the context of the pandemic.

III. From the Fight against the Pandemic to Article 15 of the European Convention on Human Rights

1. The Struggle against the Pandemic and Restrictions on Our Freedoms

There can be no doubt that what is misrepresented as the 'war' on COVID-19[22] can be used to justify certain decisions in the context of a technological 'emergency' that is itself justified by the 'health emergency' the world currently faces. Today, it is time to measure the extent of the damage inflicted upon our freedoms. The right to education, to assemble in public, to worship, to free expression and free enterprise, to mobility and to privacy are all either limited or suspended or, in any event, sacrificed so as to safeguard public health at all costs. Garapon writes, 'the measures adopted in the emergency resemble an immense medical prescription extended to the entire population, more than to the law',[23] whose only guide is statistics such as those concerning the lack of hospital beds, those of the deaths that nobody likes to count, as well as those concerning vaccinations that some governments have made compulsory for at least some professions.

At the same time, what are even more worrying are the societal risks that this torrent of emergency measures conceals, such as the gradual disappearance of the rule of law and of democratic rights. The European Parliament Resolution of 13 November 2020 on the pandemic and the rule of law echoes this concern:

> these measures have an impact on democracy, the rule of law and fundamental rights as they affect the exercise of individual rights and freedoms, such as freedom of movement, freedom of assembly and of association, freedom

---

[21] Judgment 57/2021, *OBFG et al.*, 21 April 2021, 132, 133.

[22] In particular, see President Macron's statements on 16 March 2020, where he announced to the French public that containment measures were necessary to curb the spread of COVID-19, declaring in a serious tone that 'We are at war', available at https://www.lemonde.fr/politique/article/2020/03/17/nous-sommes-en-guerre-face-au-coronavirus-emmanuel-macron-sonne-la-mobilisation generale_6033338_823448.html.

[23] Garapon, 'Un moment d'exception'.

of expression and information, freedom of religion, the right to family life, the right of asylum, the principle of equality and non-discrimination, the right to privacy and data protection, the right to education and the right to work.[24]

In support of the regulatory measures taken, we note the multiplication of data processing and databases created throughout the COVID-19 pandemic, which have been used to trace the disease and therefore the individuals carrying or likely to carry the virus. It is on these measures that the debates inciting the strongest resistance have been focused, especially those led by the data protection authorities, the guarantors of our data protection.[25] The European Parliament Resolution summarises the importance of digital technology in the fight against COVID-19 and the related risks:

> measures to combat the pandemic that restrict the right to privacy and data protection should always be necessary, proportionate and temporary in nature, with a solid legal basis; new technologies have played an important part in the fight against the pandemic, but at the same time bring significant new challenges and have raised concerns; the governments of some Member States have resorted to extraordinary surveillance of their citizens through the use of drones,[26] police surveillance cars with cameras, tracking by means of location data from telecommunications providers, police and military

---

[24] European Parliament resolution of 13 November 2020 on the impact of COVID-19 measures on democracy, the rule of law and fundamental rights (2020/2790(RSP)), 13 November 2020, P9 TA(2020)0307. The resolution builds on the Commission's 30 September 2020 Communication 'Rule of Law Report 2020 – The State of the Rule of Law in the European Union' (COM(2020)0580) and the accompanying twenty-seven chapters organised by country on the rule of law in the Member States (SWD(2020)0300-0326), which address the impact of COVID-19-related measures taken by Member States on democracy, the rule of law and fundamental rights.

[25] The reader will find a complete and impressive list of opinions, statements, etc. of Data Protection Authorities and other national and international data protection bodies at https://globalprivacyassembly.org/covid19/. See also the very extensive site of the LSTS research team of the VUB (Brussels): 'Data Protection Law and the COVID 19 Outbreak', available at https://lsts.research.vub.be/en/data-protection-law-and-the-covid-19-outbreak.

[26] On the use of drones for pandemic control purposes, it should be noted that, in a summary order issued on 18 May 2020, the Council of State ordered 'the State to cease, without delay, carrying out surveillance measures by drone in Paris, out of respect for the health security rules applicable to the decontamination period'. It ruled that these drones were used outside the framework provided by the 'Informatique et Libertés' Act and were a 'serious and manifestly illegal infringement of the right to privacy'. French Council of State, Juge des référés, 18/05/2020, 440442, available at https://www.legifrance.gouv.fr/ceta/id/CETATEXT000041897158/.

patrols, monitoring of mandatory quarantines via house calls by the police or mandatory reporting via an app; some Member States have introduced contact tracing apps, even though there is no consensus about their effectiveness and the most privacy-friendly, decentralised system is not always used; in some Member States the reopening of public spaces has been accompanied by the collection of data through mandatory temperature checks and questionnaires and the obligation to share contact details, sometimes without due regard for the obligations that stem from the General Data Protection Regulation.[27]

Are all these measures simple limitations of our freedom or are they more radical suspensions of it? Do they even perhaps constitute an attack on its very essence, which Article 52 of the EU Charter prohibits? Article 52 does in fact sanction the possibility of limitations to the fundamental rights set out in the EU Charter, but it also imposes guidelines on these limitations:

> Any limitation on the exercise of the rights and freedoms recognised by this Charter must be provided for by law and respect the essence of those rights and freedoms. Subject to the principle of proportionality, limitations may be made only if they are necessary and genuinely meet objectives of general interest recognised by the Union or the need to protect the rights and freedoms of others.[28]

Where then can the basis for the suspension of fundamental rights and freedoms be found, at a time when digital technology is granting the regulatory provisions, sometimes even simply of the local municipal police, a much more significant impact on our freedoms? Is freedom of assembly, including that of trade unions, still possible when drones monitor gatherings and have a dissuasive effect on the population? Vaccination, even if it is presented as a moral 'obligation', is imposed on citizens who know they are being 'tracked' by a widely accessible database, even when going to a pharmacy to obtain medicine not related to COVID-19, or when seeking to sit down at a restaurant or participate in a so-called mass event.[29]

The limitation of fundamental rights should therefore not be confused with the derogation or suspension of these rights. Derogations 'suspend' fundamental freedoms for a given time period, in given exceptional circumstances,

---

[27] 2020/2790(RSP), 13 November 2020, P9 TA(2020)0307.
[28] Article 52 of the EU Charter.
[29] It is beyond the scope of this chapter to discuss the questions raised by compulsory vaccination. On this point, see the recent reflections of Bioy, 'Vers la vaccination obligatoire contre la Covid?'

such as a state of health emergency, terrorist attacks or a state of war.[30] Article 15 of the ECHR states that they can only be justified in exceptional circumstances. It follows then that states are no longer obliged to meet the conditions of justification imposed for restrictions on fundamental rights when they find themselves in the specific circumstances and conditions of derogation laid out in Article 15.[31] In view of the extent of the restrictions imposed by the laws, ordinances and even decrees of all kinds issued by the public authority, the latter should have referred to Article 15 of the ECHR in order to justify them. Article 52 of the EU Charter does not prohibit this recourse,[32] but imposes it in the case where derogations or suspensions of freedoms are envisaged. Article 15 of the ECHR establishes a system of sanctions which, while authorising significant restrictions on freedoms in the name of well-specified higher public interests, are nonetheless delineated in order to maintain the rule of law, which is precisely what is endangered in such circumstances.[33] For this reason, both French and Belgian constitutional writers have justifiably regretted that the governments of these two countries did not implement this article when they took measures to combat the pandemic.[34]

[30] Colella, 'Chapter 1: L'acception des notions de restriction, limitation et dérogation', 126.

[31] De Schutter, *International Human Rights Law*, 585n. See also the strong statement of the Secretary General of the Council of Europe, Pejčinović Burić, on 7 April 2020 at the moment of publication of the 'toolkit' for all European governments on respect for human rights, democracy and the rule of law during the COVID-19 crisis, available at https://rm.coe.int/sg-inf-2020-11-respecting-democracy-rule-of-law-and-human-rights-in-th/16809e1f40.

[32] As an authoritative interpreter of the EU Charter, the FRA (European Agency for Fundamental Rights) notes: 'The Charter does not affect the possibilities of Member States to avail themselves of Article 15 of the ECHR, allowing derogations from ECHR rights in the event of war or of other public dangers threatening the life of the nation, when they take action in the areas of national defence in the event of war and of the maintenance of law and order, in accordance with their responsibilities recognised in Article 4(1) of the Treaty on European Union and in Articles 72 and 347 of the Treaty on the Functioning of the European Union.'

[33] On the totalitarian shift facilitated by so-called states of emergency, see the work of Basilien-Gainche, *État de droit et états d'exception*, 125: 'The rule of law refers to the law and the norm, to normality and the ordinary: it is a political goal of the State, a horizon of perfection nourished by the separation of powers and the guarantee of rights. As for states of emergency, they evoke disorder and the extraordinary, the concentration of powers and the restriction of rights.'

[34] Thus, in France, Sudre's post on the *Club des juristes* website 'La mise en quarantaine de la Convention européenne des droits de l'Homme', 20 April 2020 as well as that of Costa, 'Le recours à l'article 15 de la Convention européenne des droits de l'homme'; in Belgium, Ost, 'Nécessité fait loi?', 26–7; Verdussen, 'Droits humains et crise sanitaire'.

2. *The Legal Regime of Article 15 of the ECHR*

In contrast to France and Belgium, no fewer than ten signatory countries of the ECHR wished to enact Article 15 in the context of the pandemic.[35] Article 15 authorises derogations of rights and freedoms in a state of emergency, subject to prior notification of the Secretary General of the Council of Europe:

> In time of war or other public emergency threatening the life of the nation any High Contracting Party may take measures derogating from its obligations under this Convention to the extent strictly required by the exigencies of the situation, provided that such measures are not inconsistent with its other obligations under international law.[36]

This provision of the ECHR introduces the theory of the state of necessity to justify the exceptions,[37] while imposing strict conditions on Member States in order to control the exercise of such exceptions. While it can clearly be invoked in relation to situations of public order disturbance such as war or terrorist threats, can Article 15 be applied to situations such as a pandemic? According to the jurisprudence of the ECHR,[38] the interpretation of the words 'other public emergency threatening the life of the nation' allows this to be extended to cases of pandemic and has been implicitly approved by the Council of Europe by the very fact of its publication in 2020 of the 'toolkit' for the use of Article 15, on the subject of the pandemic.

---

[35] It is interesting to note that while both France and Belgium have not (yet) made use of this exception during the pandemic, other countries have started the procedures since mid-March 2020. See Venice Commission, 'Interim Report on the measures taken in the EU member States as a result of the Covid-19 crisis and their impact on democracy, the Rule of Law and Fundamental Rights', 8–9 October 2020 (CDL-AD(2020)018-e), para. 35, available at https://www.venice.coe.int/webforms/documents/?pdf=CDL-AD(2020)018-e. See also Council of Europe (Press Unit), 'Fact Sheet: Derogation in Time of Emergency', 2, available at https://www.echr.coe.int/documents/fs_derogation_eng.pdf; and, for detailed information on the context in which these derogations were formulated, the web page of the Council of Europe Treaty Office.

[36] Regarding this Article invoked by some member countries of the Council of Europe on occasions other than the pandemic and often for reasons of combating terrorism, see, in particular, Renucci, *Droit européen des droits de l'homme*, 33–5.

[37] It should also be noted that Article 17 of the ECHR sets out in a more general way the principle of prohibition of abuse, in particular by public authorities.

[38] In this regard, we cite the *Lawless v Ireland* judgment (1/7/61), in which the court held that the terms of Article 15 refer to 'a situation of crisis or exceptional and imminent danger which affects the entire population and constitutes a threat to the organised life of the community making up the State', and the *Ireland v UK* judgment of 18 January 1978 (Series A No. 25, para. 207), which leaves States a wide margin of manoeuvre in interpreting the concepts of Article 15.

Among the conditions set for the system of derogations from the ECHR, three material conditions can be distinguished:[39] first, the occurrence of serious circumstances, of public dangers threatening the life of the nation; second, the absolute necessity of being able to derogate from individual liberties; and third, the respect of other obligations arising from international law. In addition to these substantive conditions, a formal condition must be added, namely notification to the Secretary General of the Council of Europe of both the measures taken and the reasons for them, in accordance with the third paragraph of Article 15. States must also inform the Secretary General of the Council of Europe of the date on which '*the provisions of the Convention are again fully implemented*'. Finally, the Secretary General, at the moment of the publication of the 'toolkit' on the use of Article 15 during the Coronavirus pandemic on 7 April 2020, recalled that, according to the jurisprudence of the Council of Europe, derogations must be proportionate and framed, if possible, by legislative measures:

> At the same time, any derogation must have a clear basis in domestic law in order to protect against arbitrariness and must be strictly necessary to fighting against the public emergency. States must bear in mind that any measures taken should seek to protect the democratic order from the threats to it, and every effort should be made to safeguard the values of a democratic society, such as pluralism, tolerance and broadmindedness. While derogations have been accepted by the Court to justify some exceptions to the Convention standards, they can never justify any action that goes against the paramount Convention requirements of lawfulness and proportionality.[40]

Thus, the state of necessity does not take precedence over the legality and proportionality of the proposed restrictive measures.[41]

---

[39] 'Guide on Article 15 of the European Convention on Human Rights: Derogation in Time of Emergency', updated 30 April 2021, available at https://www.echr.coe.int/documents/Guide_Art_15_ENG.pdf.

[40] 'Toolkit' for all European governments on respect for human rights, democracy and the rule of law during the COVID-19 crisis, available at https://rm.coe.int/sg-inf-2020-11-respecting-democracy-rule-of-law-and-human-rights-in-th/16809e1f40.

[41] With regard to this Article, see the comments of the Council of Europe advisory body European Commission for Democracy through Law (Venice Commission) in its report 'Interim Report on the measures taken in the EU member States as a result of the Covid-19 crisis and their impact on democracy, the Rule of Law and Fundamental Rights', 8–9 October 2020 (CDL-AD(2020)018-e), available at https://www.venice.coe.int/webforms/documents/?pdf=CDL-AD(2020)018-e.

There are therefore three arguments in favour of following the procedure and the conditions of Article 15 of the ECHR:

1. Openness: Article 15 requires transparency and legitimacy of both the measures and the reasons.
2. Verification by peer review and the Council of Europe itself: the communication to the Council of Europe of the measures taken or envisaged allows a *benchmarking* of the decisions in relation to those of other states and is done so under the vigilant eye of the organs of the Council of Europe, which, on this comparative basis, can question the states on the proportionality of the measures.
3. Need for democratic parliamentary deliberation, insofar as the Council of Europe will be bound by a text that has received the assent of the legislature after a comprehensive legislative process has been carried out.[42]

Other advantages can also be added, including the obligation to set a duration for the emergency measures that does not exceed the length of the health emergency, any extension to which must be justified and duly investigated by the Council of Europe; and the requirement to demonstrate that the measures taken are necessary, adequate and strictly proportionate. Finally, the distinction between limitation and restriction or suspension of freedoms invites reflection on the notion of the 'essence' of freedoms and rights introduced by Article 52 of the EU Charter. This notion implies that we have consideration of not only the content of the prescriptions but also the measures of effectiveness of such prescriptions, particularly those consisting in the use of digital technology. In any case, it is an invitation to distinguish, as did the French bill that has now been abandoned,[43] between the measures taken to

[42] 'A declaration of a state of emergency may be issued by parliament or by the executive. Ideally, it should be declared by parliament or by the executive subject followed by immediate approval by parliament. In urgent cases, immediate entry into force could be allowed – however the declaration should be immediately submitted to parliament, which can confirm or repeal it.' Venice Commission, 'Interim Report on the measures taken in the EU member States as a result of the Covid-19 crisis and their impact on democracy, the Rule of Law and Fundamental Rights', 8–9 October 2020 (CDL-AD(2020)018-e), para. 34, available at https://www.venice.coe.int/webforms/documents/?pdf=CDL-AD(2020)018-e. The Venice Commission is a body created by the Council of Europe on the situation of the rule of law in different countries.
[43] It is known that the project was finally withdrawn by the French government following criticism from the Council of State and the senators, insofar as the planned measures did not allow for sufficient control by the Parliament. See https://www.publicsenat.fr/article/parlementaire/urgences-sanitaires-le-gouvernement-retire-un-projet-de-loi-controverse-186392.

curb the pandemic – those justified by the crisis situation 'in case of serious health threats and situations'[44] – from those required by the state of health emergency, that is to say, 'in case of a health disaster endangering, by its nature and gravity, the health of the population'.[45] It is solely in this second case that the state of emergency which justifies restrictions to freedoms and not simple limitations should be applied in accordance with the prescriptions of Article 15 of the ECHR. It is certain, therefore, that in the name of the state of emergency, the government adopted measures that went beyond the simple limitation of freedoms and in reality were a true suspension of such freedoms, which it could only justify by recourse to Article 15 of the ECHR.

These 'essential' restrictions and the consequent suspension of rights and freedoms must be subject to an analysis of proportionality and to an even more careful analysis of their motivations beyond mere simple limitations, insofar as they must be of an exceptional nature for a situation that is universally judged to endanger the safety of the nation.[46] Here, we are faced

---

[44] French Council of State, 'Opinion on a draft law instituting a permanent health emergency management system', 21 December 2020: 'The state of health crisis will be declared by simple decree "in case of threat or serious health situation". It will be extended, every two months. During this system, the Prime Minister and the Minister of Health will be able to take or authorise the prefects to take measures of an essentially sanitary nature (individual decisions to place or maintain patients in quarantine or isolation, measures to make health products available to patients, necessary measures for the organisation and operation of the health care system, temporary price control measures and requisitions). This system of measures could intervene in particular in the event of a global, national or local epidemic, a nuclear or industrial accident, an earthquake, an attack [. . .].'

[45] Ibid.: 'The state of health emergency will be declared, as it is the case today, for one month "in case of a health disaster endangering, by its nature and gravity, the health of the population". In addition to the measures provided for in the state of health crisis, the Prime Minister may also take measures other than health measures (administrative police measures) as he did for the COVID-19 epidemic: regulation of the movement of people and the opening of establishments available to the public, prohibition of leaving the home, limitation of gatherings in public places, and any other measure restricting the freedom of enterprise. The Prime Minister may also make access to certain places and the exercise of certain activities conditional on screening or preventive or curative treatment (as is currently the case, for example, for compulsory tests before traveling by plane).'

[46] In this respect, see the clear statement of the French Council of State: 'The necessary, proportionate and appropriate character of such a measure cannot be considered as excluded in the perspective, which is that of the bill, of having perennial legal means of response to health disasters whose gravity cannot be anticipated. The measure can make it possible, by itself, to reconcile, in the event of particularly serious epidemics, the effective exercise of certain freedoms with the objective of protecting public health, instead of more generalised or more restrictive measures of the freedoms in question, in particular the freedom of movement and the freedom of enterprise.' Ibid.

with the restrictive interpretation of the state of emergency developed by the CJEU in relation to the obligation of the widespread retention of communication data, for which the application of Article 15 ECHR should have also been envisaged. In the case of the data retention obligation, the right to security is used to justify restrictions on our freedoms and, in the name of efficiency, democratic processes are brought into question; in the second case, it is the right to health that justifies this same movement.

3. The So-Called Belgian 'Pandemic' Law

Is Belgium's response in the form of the so-called 'Pandemic' law adequate?[47] There is no doubt that the text voted on is problematic. To be sure, the law transforms the state of emergency in fact into a state of emergency in law, insofar as it is Parliament that declares said state of emergency.[48] Fortunately, the legal text confers great importance on what forms the starting point of the emergency measures even though the law, regrettably, does not contain any reference to the procedure of Article 15 ECHR. The state of emergency is declared by the King following a judgment issued by the Council of Ministers after consultation with experts and on the advice of the Minister of Public Health. This judgment, which comes into effect as soon as it is published, is subject to parliamentary discussion at short notice and must be confirmed by a law also adopted at short notice. The same procedure must be followed, and the same conditions apply, in the case of an extension.

The law is partial and is only targeted at the health emergency.[49] Beyond the provisions relating to the pandemic, however, should a general system of measures for the state of emergency not have been implemented, as the CJEU recommended when it opened the debate on the widespread retention of communication data? Secondly, the text seems to us to miss the main point, which is of maintaining the rule of law in the context of a state of emergency. Regarding this last point in particular, it insufficiently takes into account the 'technological' element, a consideration of which is essential to the maintenance of such a rule of law. These two points are developed below.

In the context of a state of emergency, it is surprising that the clearly central question of freedoms has not led to the questioning of what constitutes the very condition and guarantee of the latter, namely respect for the rule

---

[47] Law on administrative police measures during an epidemic emergency, 14 August 2021, (Mb., 20 August 2021).

[48] We cannot go into the details of all the arguments submitted in our report to the Parliament March 2021, at the request of its president. Some extracts are published in Poullet, 'La société et les droits fondamentaux aux risques du numérique en temps de crise', 185–95.

[49] A notion which is too broadly defined by the 'Pandemic' law (see article 3 2°).

of law. The European Parliament Resolution of 13 November 2020 on the impact of COVID-19 measures on democracy, the rule of law and fundamental rights, which has already been discussed here, highlights this danger.[50]

This European Parliament affirmation of the necessary respect for the rule of law leads in particular to its demand that the legislature and the judiciary be able to play their role in support of freedom:[51]

> whereas government-led emergency measures that respect the rule of law, fundamental rights and democratic accountability are needed to combat the pandemic and should be the cornerstone of all efforts to control the spread of COVID-19; whereas emergency powers require additional scrutiny to ensure that they are not used as a pretext for changing the balance of powers more permanently; whereas measures taken by governments should be necessary, proportional and temporary; whereas emergency powers carry a risk of abuse of power by the executive and of remaining in the national legal framework once the emergency is over, and consequently appropriate parliamentary and judicial oversight, both internal and external, and counterbalances have to be ensured to limit this risk.[52]

---

[50] The Resolution provides: 'whereas the functioning of democracies and the checks and balances to which they are subject are impacted when a health emergency situation causes shifts in the distribution of powers such as allowing the executive to acquire new powers to limit individual rights and to exercise competences usually reserved for the legislature and local authorities [. . .]. Such is the situation when the courts can no longer meet or are reluctant to rule in cases of emergency, and when the bodies responsible for controlling legality or constitutionality cannot rule insofar as the norms adopted by the executive are beyond their control. This is the case at a time when associations can no longer express themselves in the street and when even the media have difficulty welcoming the detractors of anti-COVID-19 measures, in the name of a broad conception of misinformation, far from the principle of the freedom of expression affirmed by the jurisprudence of the Council of Europe since the *Handyside* case: freedom of expression is applicable not only to 'information' or 'ideas' that are favourably received or regarded as inoffensive or as a matter of indifference, but also to those that offend, shock or disturb the State or any sector of the population. Such are the demands of that pluralism, tolerance and broadmindedness without which there is no 'democratic society'".' Quotations in the judgment are from *Handyside v The United Kingdom*, no. 5493/72, Judgment Strasbourg, 7 December 1976, 49.

[51] On the difficulty of the legislature to play its role in the crisis caused by COVID-19, see The Robert Schuman Foundation, 'The impact of the health crisis on the functioning of parliaments in Europe', available at https://www.robert-schuman.eu/en/doc/ouvrages/FRS_Parliament.pdf.

[52] In the same sense, see the article in *Le Soir* of 23 March 2021, which denounces the 'heist of the century on the private life of Belgians'. The article aims at 'blowing the whistle' by declaring that there is 'an unprecedented amount of incompetence, [. . .] of a system of state management that is beyond parliamentary control, beyond the reach of the Council of State or the citizen's right of appeal, and beyond the reach of a supervisory authority that is increasingly devoid of its substance'.

On this basis, the European Parliament makes a number of recommendations, in particular:

- to ensure that if legislative powers are transferred to the executive, any legal act emanating from the executive is subject to subsequent approval by parliament and ceases to have effect if not approved within a specified period, and to address the excessive use of fast-track and emergency legislation
- to examine how to more effectively safeguard the central role of parliaments in crisis and emergency situations, especially their role in monitoring and overseeing the situation at the national level.

In order for Parliament to play its role in overseeing the executive, Belgian law should have specified the procedure that Parliament should follow so as to assess the proportionality and necessity of measures proposed by the government, otherwise the legislature runs the risk of being nothing more than an endorsement chamber.

Our second point concerns the absence of any provision relating to the use of digital technology in the fight against COVID-19. Initially, the text included an article calling to mind the requirements laid out in the data protection legislation. For reasons of unclear wording and fear of a provision that would appear to circumvent the mandatory European provisions and their translation into Belgian law, the Data Protection Authority (DPA), together with others, had argued for this article to be withdrawn.[53]

We find this regrettable. First, as has already been mentioned, the administrative police measures, the use of which are regulated by the 'Pandemic' law, often involve as a condition of their efficacy the processing of personal data. It is therefore important to keep in mind the rules surrounding the creation of such databases. Second, while each administrative or police measure involves an apparently distinct implementation of data processing, it would have been useful if, on this occasion, Parliament would be entitled to request access to a global and unfragmented view of the processing thus created and the links between them. Third, it was a good opportunity to recall the principles of legality, minimisation and transparency in regards to the individual citizen,[54] principles that are at the heart of data protection legislation and that guarantee the respect of the rule of law. Fourth, certain obligations should have been imposed such as 'Privacy by design' or 'Privacy by default', for instance the obligation to carry out a 'Privacy Impact

---

[53] This is the notice 24/2021 of 2 March 2021 on the draft law on administrative police measures during a pandemic emergency.

[54] Transparency undoubtedly requires that all the elements provided for in Article 6.4 of the GDPR are to be included in the text for the creation of data processing to combat COVID-19.

Assessment' and to establish the modalities of its drafting (i.e. who participates in this assessment? Who evaluates the report? Is the report published? etc.).

Other points include the questions of medical confidentiality and, more broadly, of access to databases containing medical information which could have been the subject of a provision making reference to the prohibition in principle of access to persons not covered by medical confidentiality and which provided the procedure that, if necessary, should be followed to allow such access to persons not covered by confidentiality; as well as the question of the limited duration of the data processing created in the framework of the fight against COVID-19. Finally, the principle affirmed by the European Data Protection Board (EDPB) could have also been highlighted:

> The EDPB generally considers that data and technology used to help fight COVID-19 should be used to empower, rather than to control, stigmatise, or repress individuals. Furthermore, while data and technology can be important tools, they have intrinsic limitations and can merely leverage the effectiveness of other public health measures. The general principles of effectiveness, necessity, and proportionality must guide any measure adopted by Member States or EU institutions that involve processing of personal data to fight COVID-19.[55]

As such, the need to put technology at the service of citizens certainly is the message sent by data protection authorities.

Beyond data protection issues, should we not address the question of freedom of expression and the fight against the misinformation that the business models of our communication platforms only intensify through their algorithms which exploit machine learning technologies and the profiling of Internet users? Should we not also reflect on the social justice issues raised by the digital revolution? We know that illiteracy excludes certain portions of the population from any use of applications or information that require access to or even the handling of technology,[56] and that vaccination databases are also a tool for the exclusion from certain places of a subset of the population which, for good or bad reasons, refuses vaccination, the merits of which are not up to the authorities to discuss.

---

[55] 'Guidelines 04/2020 on the use of location data and contact tracing tools in the context of the COVID-19 outbreak', adopted 21 April 2020, 3, available at https://edpb.europa. eu/sites/default/files/files/file1/edpb_guidelines_20200420_contact_tracing_covid_with_annex_en.pdf.

[56] In France, it is considered that almost a fifth of the population does not have access to or does not know how to use a smartphone. In addition, this portion of the population is largely made up of the elderly as well as the economically vulnerable, those most at risk. There is also the need to take into consideration foreign populations who are often ill-informed due to the language barrier.

The 'Pandemic' law does not validate the existence, however necessary, of the societal debates raised by the sometimes too rapid adoption of technological tools. This adoption should have been subject to a mandatory evaluation prior to the design of such information systems. Above all, the need for a comprehensive evaluation of such systems, often hastily built, during and at the end of periods of crisis, should be legally affirmed.[57]

IV. Digital Technology, the State of Emergency and the Rules of Lawlessness

Let us begin by recalling the importance of the principles of minimisation and proportionality: the state of emergency in itself never justifies the creation of any kind of processing procedure. As mentioned in the legal notice issued by the Chambre de connaissance (Knowledge Centre) of the DPA,[58] the following conditions must be met:[59] first, that the data processing effectively allows the accomplishment of the objective pursued. It is therefore necessary to demonstrate, on the basis of factual and objective elements, the effectiveness of the processing of personal data in achieving the stated aims. Second, that this processing of personal data is the least intrusive measure with regard to the right to privacy. This means that if it is possible to achieve the intended purpose by means of a measure that is judged less intrusive in reference to the right to privacy or the right to protection of personal data, the data processing originally envisaged cannot be carried out.[60] This requires detailing and being able to demonstrate, with factual and objective evidence, why other less intrusive measures are not sufficient to achieve the desired objective.[61]

---

[57] Calay, 'L'empire des logiciels', 39, speaks of a 'data coup d'état' during the pandemic.

[58] DPA Notice no. 124/2021 of 12 July 2021, already quoted above, no. 41 and 42, 13–14.

[59] This is what Van Drooghenbroek calls the triple test. See *La proportionnalité dans le droit de la Convention européenne des droits de l'homme*, 31–8. The requirement of this triple test is recalled in many of the DPA's opinions on anti-COVID-19 measures. See in particular DPA opinion no. 34/2020, 28 April 2020; Request for an opinion concerning a preliminary draft of Royal Judgment no. XXX implementing article 5, § 1, 1°, of the law of 27 March 2020 empowering the King to take measures against the spread of the coronavirus COVID-19 (II), in the context of the use of digital contact tracing applications as a preventive measure against the spread of the coronavirus COVID-19 among the population (CO-A-2020-041).

[60] It is in this sense that the preference given to the anonymisation of location data in the context of automatic tracing is conceivable.

[61] The EDPB's 'Guidelines 04/2020 on the use of location data and contact tracing tools in the context of the COVID-19 outbreak', adopted 21 April 2020, no. 14 onwards, available at https://edpb.europa.eu/sites/default/files/files/file1/edpb_guidelines_20200420_contact_tracing_covid_with_annex_en.pdf. The application of these requirements has fuelled the discussion in many of our countries about the choice between the DP-3T

If the necessity of data processing is established, it must still be demonstrated that the processing is proportionate (in the strict sense) to the objective this one pursues, that is, it must be shown that there is a fair balance between the various interests involved and the rights and freedoms of the persons concerned.

The benefits of the data processing in question must therefore outweigh the disadvantages for the individuals concerned. Once again, evidence must be provided that this analysis was performed prior to the implementation of the processing. An enshrinement in law of these guidelines for interpreting the principles of proportionality and minimisation would have been useful in guiding those who design the various data processing operations to be implemented, which in turn must be subject to a procedure that respects the principle of legality.

The analysis conducted by some authors of 'Datacracy'[62] or 'algorithmic governmentality'[63] notes the disappearance of a public space for discussion and the increase in power of both private and public actors who collect and manage this data and invest it with meaning through the power of digital technology, and above all through ever greater recourse to artificial intelligence. This artificial intelligence, based on algorithms that work in a more or less opaque way, purportedly represents reality and deduces its future behaviour, putting its power in the hands of its users, who are first of all the companies that implement it, then secondly government departments, and finally private citizens, if necessary.

This conclusion is consistent with Banita's appraisal, in Chapter 10 of this collection, of predictive policing through algorithms in the present volume. What other choice is there but to blindly follow this truth that emerges from computers, even if it means legitimising it through laws that organise its production through the creation of databases and instruments for collecting the necessary information, all the while entrusting obscure organisations

protocol (Decentralised Privacy Preserving Proximity Tracing), chosen by many European countries (Belgium, Germany, Italy, Portugal, etc.), and the competing Pan-European Privacy-Preserving Proximity Tracing (PEPP-PT) protocol, chosen by France for its TOUSANTICOVID application. Both use Bluetooth Low Energy technology to track our meetings with other users and record them on the system installed on our mobiles. The protocols differ in their reporting mechanism: PEPP-PT requires clients to upload contact logs to a central reporting server; with DP-3T, on the other hand, the central reporting server never has access to the contact logs and is not responsible for processing and informing the contact clients, and therefore it appears to offer a better guarantee of protection of our data and makes it part of the system design itself.

62 Guyader et al., 'La Datacratie'; Cardon, 'Le pouvoir des algorithmes'; Blandin, 'La gouvernance du monde numérique', 50–6.

63 Supiot, *La gouvernance par les nombres*; Rouvroy, '"Adopt AI, Think Later"'; Rouvroy and Berns, 'Le nouveau pouvoir statistique', 88–103; Rouvroy and Berns, 'Gouvernementalité algorithmique et perspectives d'émancipation', 163–96.

with the task of expressing it? It should be noted that this artificial intelligence relies on a 'reductionism' of human beings, viewed in all their diverse aspects.[64] The urgency of the fight against terrorism as well as the urgency of protecting the health of citizens justifies all the more the use of the solutions offered by digital technologies and their truth. It is a matter of relying on the virtues of multiple hastily constructed processes to give citizens the comforting illusion of the presence of Big Brother. Thus, as Supiot notes, a 'government by numbers' is emerging,[65] that is to say, a government which relies solely on statistics claiming to give a better account of reality than that made through contact and dialogue with people.[66] Sabot, in Chapter 2 of this collection, makes a similar contention.

As the DPA's Knowledge Centre rightly notes about the cooperation agreement relating to the health passport, 'COVID Safe',

> A reasonable boundary must therefore be drawn between what is a matter of individual freedom and responsibility and what may be a matter of social control, taking care to impose restrictions on fundamental rights and freedoms only when strictly necessary and proportionate to the public interest objective pursued. In this evaluation, the Authority insists on the need to be particularly attentive to the real risk of creating a 'phenomenon of dependency', which could lead us in the future to accept that access to certain places (including everyday places) be subject to the disclosure of proof that the person concerned is not a carrier of infectious diseases nor any other pathologies. The Authority draws attention to the importance of ensuring that the solution put in place authorising access to certain places or events does not result in a shift towards a surveillance society.[67]

Furthermore, we note, following Rappin, that cybernetics is the 'privileged instrument' used by government to curb crises: 'One cannot help but be struck by the proximity between the cybernetic project, implemented by a government of, and by, emergency, and the "shock doctrine".'[68] The author is referring here to a concept coined by Naomi Klein: 'This is how the shock doctrine works: Like a terrorised prisoner who gives up the names of his comrades and renounces his faith, societies in a state of shock abandon rights that, under other circumstances, they would have jealously defended.'[69]

---

[64] On this point, see my reflections in Poullet, *Éthique et droits de l'homme*, no. 40 onwards; Rouvroy's interview in Bherer, 'En 2018, résistez aux algorithmes avec la philosophe Antoinette Rouvroy'.
[65] Supiot, *La gouvernance par les nombres*.
[66] In this respect, see the conclusions of Ost, 'Nécessité fait loi?', 32.
[67] DPA Notice no. 124/2021 of 12 July 2021, 14.
[68] Rappin, 'Algorithme, management et crise', 109–10.
[69] Klein, *Shock Doctrine*.

Thus, the state of emergency is discreetly and sustainably put in place through the use of technological tools during times of crisis. If the usefulness, even if it is questionable, of these tools may be justified in times of crisis, it is nevertheless to be feared that they will be maintained in the name of the services rendered, of the interests of those who manage or contribute to them, of the investments made in them, and of the habitual familiarity towards them developed by citizens who have become docile. If the state of emergency readily explains the recourse to digital technology, in turn digital technology takes over the state of emergency and turns it into a 'permanent emergency', with the unconscious complicity of the populace. Beyond the crisis of the pandemic, what digital technology does to the law is to reinforce a state of lawlessness through its consecration of the state of emergency.

V. Conclusion

In this respect, and so to be clear, it is useful to reiterate the assertion of Morozov, an ardent critic of technological solutionism, that 'technology is not the enemy; our enemy is the romantic and revolutionary problem solver who resides within'.[70] To be more precise, it is the overconfidence, undoubtedly backed by the interests of some digital actors, relayed by our governments and progressively instilled in the population that leads to such a situation. This observation therefore requires prudence, transparency and democratic control of our tools, as well as putting them to use in the service of society and of the rule of law, even in times of crisis.

That the crisis in all its forms, and not only the health crisis, requires a state of emergency, and in this context in particular, the implementation of technological tools and information systems able to fight it, we are in complete agreement. However, it is also important to add that this state of emergency warrants guidelines that are to be found within the framework of the ECHR and, we believe, in a Belgian law that frames the actions and procedures which must be followed in these contexts of crisis. These measures are essential in order that the guidelines capable of guaranteeing the maintenance of our freedoms, social justice and our rule of law are imposed *in tempore non suspecto*. Within the framework of this law, which reconciles a state of emergency with the rule of law,[71] it is even more important to consider provisions relating to information systems, for there is a strong temptation, in the name

---

[70] Morozov, *To Save Everything, Click Here*, 358.

[71] On the difficulty of reconciling the rule of law and the state of emergency, see the thesis by Basilien-Gainche, *État de droit et états d'exception*, 263ff., in which the author examines the eleven conditions for the respect of the rule of law by the rulers in case of recourse to the state of emergency.

of urgency and effectiveness of the measures taken, to build a society of excessive profiling and surveillance through technological solutions.

VI. Bibliography

Abitboul, Serge, Alberto Alemanno, Emmanuelle Barbara, Jean Cattan, Christine Coslin, Mireille Delmas-Marty, Jean-Gabriel Flandrois, Laura Kövesi, Hans W. Micklitz, Hubert de Vauplane, and Jean Ziegler. 'Ce que 2020 a fait au droit.' *Le Grand Continent*, 4 January 2021. https://legrandcontinent.eu/fr/2021/01/04/ce-que-2020-a-fait-au-droit/.

Basilien-Gainche, Marie-Laure. *État de droit et états d'exception: une conception de l'État*. Paris: Presses universitaires de France (Collection Fondements de la politique), 2013.

Bherer, Marc-Olivier. 'En 2018, résistez aux algorithmes avec la philosophe Antoinette Rouvroy.' Interview. *Le Monde*, 29 December 2017. https://www.lemonde.fr/idees/article/2017/12/29/en-2018-resistez-aux-algorithmes-avec-la-philosophe-antoinette-rouvroy_5235555_3232.html.

Bioy, Xavier. 'Vers la vaccination obligatoire contre la Covid? Que dit le droit de la santé? Que répondent les droits fondamentaux?' *Le Club des juristes*, 8 July 2021. https://blog.leclubdesjuristes.com/vers-la-vaccination-obligatoire-contre-la-covid/.

Blandin, Annie, 'La gouvernance du monde numérique: que fait l'Europe?' *Comprendre la souveraineté numérique, Cahiers français* 415 (May–June 2020): 50–6.

Calay, Vincent. 'L'empire des logiciels, menace pour les démocraties?' *Cahier de prospective de l'IWEPS* 5 (July 2021). https://www.iweps.be/wp-content/uploads/2021/07/CAPRO05-150721-1.pdf.

Cardon, Dominique. 'Le pouvoir des algorithmes.' *Pouvoirs* 164, no. 1 (2018): 63–73.

Colella, Stéphanie. 'Chapter 1: L'acception des notions de restriction, limitation et derogation.' In *La restriction des droits fondamentaux dans l'Union européenne*. Brussels: Bruylant, 2018.

Costa, Jean Louis. 'Le recours à l'article 15 de la Convention européenne des droits de l'homme.' *Le Club des juristes*, 27 April 2020. https://blog.leclubdesjuristes.com/recours-article-15-cedh/.

De Schutter, Olivier. *International Human Rights Law: Cases, Materials, Commentary*. 2nd ed. Cambridge: Cambridge University Press, 2014.

Garapon, Antoine. 'Un moment d'exception.' *Esprit* 464 (May 2020): 87–92.

Guyader Alain et al. 'La Datacratie.' *Pouvoirs* 168, no. 1 (2018): 7–18.

Klein, Naomi. *The Shock Doctrine: The Rise of Disaster Capitalism*. Toronto: Vintage Canada, 2007.

Larrieu, Jacques. 'Avant-propos.' In *Crise(s) et droit*, 9–12. Toulouse: Presses de l'Université Toulouse 1 Capitole (Collection Institut fédératif de recherche 'Mutation des normes juridiques'), 2012.

Laugee, François. 'Solutionisme.' *Revue européenne des médias et du numérique* 33 (2014), reprinted on the journal's website, 30 July 2021. https://la-rem.eu/2015/04/solutionnisme/.

Morozov, Evgeny. *To Save Everything, Click Here: The Folly of Technological Solutionism.* New York: Public Affairs, 2013.

Ost, François. 'Nécessité fait loi? La santé n'a pas de prix? Ce que le Covid fait au droit.' In *La pandémie de Covid-19 face au droit*, edited by Saba Parsa and Marc Uyttendaele, 17–43. Limal: Anthemis, 2020.

Parsa, Saba, and Yves Poullet. 'Les droits fondamentaux à l'épreuve du confinement et du déconfinement.' In *La pandémie de Covid-19 face au droit*, edited by Saba Parsa and Marc Uyttendaele, 137–213. Limal: Anthemis, 2020.

Poullet, Yves. 'COVID et libertés: quelques considérations.' In *L'utilisation du numérique dans la lutte contre la COVID – enjeux techniques, éthiques et juridiques*, edited by Yves Poullet and David Doat, 75–125. Paris: L'Harmattan, 2022.

———. *Éthique et droits de l'homme dans notre société du numérique.* Brussels: Belgian Royal Academy (Collection Mémoires de l'académie), 2020.

———. 'La société et les droits fondamentaux aux risques du numérique en temps de crise – plaidoyer pour un régime légal strict de l'état d'exception.' In *Droit et pandémie*, edited by Françoise Tulkens and Saba Parsa, 165–205. Limal: Anthemis, 2022.

———. 'Pandémie, numérique et droits de l'homme – un étrange cocktail!' *Journal de droit européen* 270, no. 6 (2020): 246–63.

Rappin, Baptiste. 'Algorithme, management et crise: le tryptique du gouvernement de l'exception permanente.' *Quaderni* (2018): 103–14.

Renucci, Jean-François. *Droit européen des droits de l'homme.* 6th ed. Paris: LGDJ, 2015.

Rouvroy, Antoinette, '"Adopt AI, Think Later": The Coué Method to the Rescue of Artificial Intelligence.' https://www.academia.edu/42067794/_Adopt_AI_think_later_The_Cou%C3%A9_method_to_the_rescue_of_artificial_intelligence.

Rouvroy, Antoinette, and Thomas Berns. 'Gouvernementalité algorithmique et perspectives d'émancipation. Le disparate comme condition d'individuation par la relation?' *Réseaux* 177 (2013): 163–96.

———. 'Le nouveau pouvoir statistique ou quand le contrôle s'exerce sur un réel normé, docile et sans événement car constitué de corps "numériques" [. . .].' *Multitudes* 40 (2019): 88–103.

Sudre, Frédéric. 'La mise en quarantaine de la Convention européenne des droits de l'Homme.' Post. *Le Club des juristes*, 20 April 2020. https://blog.leclubdesjuristes.com/la-mise-en-quarantaine-de-la-convention-europeenne-des-droits-de-lhomme/.

Supiot, Alain. *La gouvernance par les nombres. Cours au Collège de France (2012–2014)*, Paris: Fayard, 2015.

Tesquet, Olivier. *État d'urgence technologique. Comment l'économie de la surveillance profite de la pandémie.* Paris: Premier Parallèle, 2021.

Van Drooghenbroek, Sébastien. *La proportionnalité dans le droit de la Convention européenne des droits de l'homme – prendre l'idée simple au sérieux.* Brussels: Bruylant, 2001.

Verdussen, Marc. 'Droits humains et crise sanitaire – l'état mis au défi.' *La libre Belgique*, 19 July 2020.

5

Privacy as Liberty and Security: Implications for the Legitimacy of Governmental Surveillance

Jelena Gligorijević

I. Introduction

Privacy is implicated whenever surveillance policies and practices are implemented. In liberal democracies, the onus rests upon those using surveillance, especially governments, to justify incursions on individual privacy. A prominent argument for justifying governmental surveillance is collective security. Security concerns about criminality have seen police use surveillance, including phone-tapping. National security concerns have seen larger-scale surveillance, including metadata collection. Medical security is a growing concern raised to support surveillance, including cellular monitoring of individuals' movements.

Security, however, is not a moral panacea for justifying the privacy-intrusive nature and consequences of surveillance. This is because security, alongside liberty, is embedded in the concept of privacy, and is a reason why privacy is valued. Positioning a broad conception of security against privacy is, therefore, an inaccurate opposition, and arguing privacy must give way whenever large-scale security concerns are raised presents a false conflict.

Other chapters in this collection assume the central value of individual privacy to the humanities tradition[1] – and rightly so. These contributors use the tools of sociology, literature and history. They provide us with a literary and social context for this value. This chapter looks more closely at the concept of privacy itself, and, specifically, the form it takes in law. It explores the complex normative underpinnings of privacy, which complexity may give rise to a greater readiness to circumvent privacy when broad utilitarian concerns are raised in apparent opposition to it. The multifaceted nature of privacy,

---

[1] Sabot, Chapter 2; Tadié, Chapter 3; Brunon-Ernst, Chapter 6.

however, does not make it a fluid or weak moral concern: the two fundamental principles of liberty and security both permeate the various normative justifications for protecting privacy. This problematises arguments that surveillance is a justified incursion on privacy, based upon a general appeal to collective security. Particularised, evidence-based arguments are required to address the principles of individual security and liberty, protected within privacy itself, and to discharge the onus of justifying each instance of surveillance.

II. Dealing with Privacy: Surveillance as Security

Although there is no universal, settled definition of privacy, concretely delineating its scope,[2] broadly understood, privacy acknowledges an individual's interest not to be subjected to unwanted observation or access by others in certain, normatively defined, circumstances;[3] or the concern that an individual's family, home, intimate and 'non-public' life not be interfered with by others, including the state, the press or other individuals.[4] There are different ways of delineating the privacy interest, and protecting that interest in law.[5] Nevertheless, few would dispute that surveillance interferes with privacy. In liberal democracies, governmental surveillance must be justified to account for this interference.[6] This is because, in liberal democracies, the existence and exercise of governmental power is morally justified as being for the benefit of individuals subject to it, and not for the benefit of the governing authority

---

[2] Solove, 'Conceptualising Privacy'; Solove, 'Taxonomy of Privacy'.

[3] Gavison, 'Privacy and the Limits of the Law'; Moreham, 'Protection of Privacy'; Allen, *Uneasy Access*.

[4] Warren and Brandeis, 'Right to Privacy'; Hughes, 'Behavioural Understanding of Privacy'; Moreham, 'Unpacking'.

[5] In the UK and New Zealand, tort law protects a 'reasonable expectation of privacy': *Murray v Big Pictures Ltd* [2008] 3 WLR 1360; *Hosking v Runting* [2005] 1 NZLR 1. The US has constitutional protection of privacy interests (Fourth Amendment), which has begotten protections against state surveillance and governmental interference with individuals' decision-making capacity (*Katz v US* 389 US 347(1967); *Roe v Wade* 410 US 113(1973)). Tort law also protects privacy interests in the US (American Law Institute, *Second Restatement of the Law, Torts* (1977), § 652B–§ 652E). Canada has qualified privacy protection in the Canadian Charter of Rights and Freedoms 1982 (Canadian Charter), and varying protection in states' legislation and common law (e.g. *Jones v Tsige* [2012] ONCA 3; *Jane Doe 464533 v D* [2016] ONSC 541). Article 8 of the ECHR codifies a right to a private and family life: see *Klass v Germany* (1978) 2 EHRR 214; *Liberty v United Kingdom* (App. No.58243/00). Many jurisdictions have regulatory regimes limiting governmental or commercial mass collection and usage of personal data: see Data Protection Act 2018 (UK); General Data Protection Regulation 2016/679 (EU); Privacy Act 1988 (Cth); Privacy Act 2020 (NZ).

[6] See also Poullet, Chapter 4; Cluzel-Métayer, Chapter 9, both in this collection.

itself.[7] The individual is presumed to have a moral, if not legal, entitlement to privacy. Surveillance, like other governmental interference, is presumed not to be the norm, and must actively be justified.

Some privacy interferences in liberal democracy are justified in general terms and on accepted principles of necessity for the direct and targeted protection of individuals' basic interests, including life and property. Criminalisation of serious harmful conduct against another individual, whether committed in private or public, is accepted because privacy should not obstruct the prevention of such wrongdoing. However, justification for other intrusive governmental actions or policies, including surveillance, is not so immediately and generally accepted. Direct and targeted protection of individuals' basic interests in life and property is not necessarily entailed in governmental surveillance, as it is in criminalising conduct that directly harms an individual's life or property. Surveillance may have sundry purposes, and protection of individuals' core interests is not necessarily one of them.

The reasons for surveillance must therefore be provided in the particular context where it is used, or whenever new surveillance laws are proposed.[8] There are different points at which justification for surveillance can be established in liberal democracies. For example, this justification can be made on the hustings, where a political party explains in its manifesto how and why, if elected to government, it would implement surveillance. The justification can also be made in parliamentary debates preceding enactment of surveillance laws. It can be made through governmental persuasion of individuals to subject themselves to surveillance,[9] and also within administrative procedures for granting surveillance warrants to officials in specific circumstances. That justification can likewise be made in ministerial statements justifying past or

[7] The relationship between individual and collective interests in liberal democracy is discussed below, particularly Sections III.1 and IV.

[8] For example, the UK Home Secretary's explanation of the Investigatory Powers Bill in 2016 (now the Investigatory Powers Act 2016) that 'privacy is hardwired into the Bill. It strictly limits the public authorities that can use investigatory powers, imposes high thresholds for the use of the most intrusive powers, and sets out in more detail than ever before the safeguards that apply to material obtained under these powers. The Bill starts with a presumption of privacy, and it asserts the privacy of a communication.' Hansard, HC Deb, 15 March 2016, cc 813–14, available at https://publications.parliament.uk/pa/cm201516/cmhansrd/cm160315/debtext/160315-0001.htm#16031546000001.

[9] For example, Australian government policy that individuals should download the 'COVIDSafe app' and thereby voluntarily subject themselves to increased surveillance in order to aid centralised tracking of the novel virus, 'to help [. . .] support and protect you, your friends and family'. 'COVIDSafe app', available at https://www.health.gov.au/resources/apps-and-tools/covidsafe-app.

present surveillance, as well as in adjudication, where the law sets justificatory thresholds for the use of surveillance against individuals. At any or all of these justificatory junctures, and whether or not justification is politico-moral or technical-legal, the governmental entity intending to use, or having used, surveillance must articulate why the privacy interference is justified.

This justificatory process can be complemented or complicated by media coverage of the current threat to the community, including through both traditional media and social media, which may present the threat in such a way as to support increased surveillance or to raise scepticism as to the need and consequences of that surveillance. They often do so by drawing on a common cultural imagination of surveillance. As Sabot so clearly illustrates in Chapter 2 of this volume, recourse to these mediatised forms of justification is increasingly a feature of public life.

Collective security, or security of the polity or group of individuals as a whole, is a common justification raised for surveillance.[10] The argument is that it is only through greater knowledge of individuals' activities and intentions that the state can discharge its duty to protect all individuals within its sphere of governance, against some identified large-scale threat, such as attacks by hostile actors, organised crime, or highly contagious diseases. Securitisation of a group (such as a nation-state) against such threats is presented as the end, with surveillance as (one of) the means, and the moral concern for individual privacy may appear automatically appeased, as a necessary and justified sacrifice in the pursuit of this collective end. Where a large-scale threat is identified, privacy is required to give way to security.

But such an argument neglects the centrality of security, no less than liberty, to the value of privacy itself. If we explore the reasons why privacy has moral significance and has in many liberal democracies attracted legal

---

[10] For example, the US Attorney-General's arguments for increasing governmental surveillance powers following the 9/11 attacks: 'We have used these tools to prevent terrorists from unleashing more death and destruction on our soil [. . .] to save innocent American lives [. . .] to provide the security that ensures liberty' (Speech of Attorney-General John Ashcroft about the Patriot Act, at Boise, Idaho, 25 August 2003, available at https://www.justice.gov/archive/ag/speeches/2003/082503patriotactremarks.htm); the Australian Signals Directorate Head's arguments that secret surveillance against Australians is 'the very capability that we use to keep Australia safe' (https://www.asd.gov.au/publication/speech-transparently-secret-asd); the Victorian Health Minister's justification for a six-month legislative extension of governmental emergency powers, including extreme surveillance measures, that failing to extend the state of emergency would mean 'we would literally fall off a cliff', and it was needed 'to safeguard Victorian lives' (Hansard, Vic LC, 1 September 2020, Ms Mikakos in First Reading of Bill, available at https://beta.parliament.vic.gov.au/parliamentary-debates/Hansard/HANSARD-974425065-7981/).

protection, we can recognise that privacy is itself founded upon deeper moral concerns for liberty and security. Given as much, interfering with privacy cannot be automatically or adequately justified by a broad appeal to collective security against a large-scale threat: suspending privacy entails suspending, rather than protecting, security, alongside liberty. Justifications for privacy-intrusive surveillance must satisfactorily address why, in the circumstances, each individual's overall security is better protected by suspending than by upholding individual privacy. That would require a particularised rather than a general argument.

III. Theorising Privacy: The Centrality of Liberty and Security

1. Liberty and Security

It is necessary to elucidate the meanings of 'liberty' and 'security' before these principles can be identified within the philosophical underpinnings of privacy. This entails understanding why liberty and security are important to the individual. The focus here is on the individual, because the individual is the most basic unit within a polity informed by liberal-democratic morality. Liberal democracy is founded upon a moral contract between each individual and the collective, which both creates and legitimises the interests of the collective itself.[11] Therefore, liberty and security are relational to the individual first and foremost. They are defined in terms of the interests of the individual. Any value of liberty or security to the collective (a nation-state or a society) originates in and is derivative of their value to the individual.

(a) Liberty

All of the three chief constructions of liberty – negative liberty, positive liberty and civic-republicanism – are important to ascertaining the meaning and significance of this principle. The state of being free facilitates, at least, an individual's ability and preparedness to make meaningful choices about his life.[12] This choice-making ability and preparedness is reflected in these main constructions of liberty and is a useful indicator of what it means to be free. Any value or norm whose function it is to maintain that choice-making capacity is informed by and protective of liberty.

The value of negative liberty to an individual lies in her ability to do something, including to make choices about her own life, having not been

---

[11] See either of the two main social contract theories: Hobbes, *Leviathan*; Locke, *Two Treatises of Government*.

[12] Berlin, *Four Essays on Liberty*, 52.

prevented from doing as much.[13] It is the absence of impediment. As a conceptual explication of liberty, it is a modal, non-normative rendition of liberty,[14] which requires ascertaining whether an individual is physically able to do something, in the sense of being unprevented by another from acting in that way,[15] rather than whether or not she is permitted to do something, having not been prohibited from doing it. Such a modal conception of liberty has been used to measure individuals' overall liberty in given settings, as an aggregate of their particular freedoms and unfreedoms, taking into account whether and how particular freedoms can be exercised conjunctively.[16] Negative liberty is concerned with, and valuable for, facilitating a most basic condition for choice-making capacity: an individual's ability to make choices in her own life – whether or not she does make choices, and whichever choices she might make.

Positive liberty requires more than freedom from interference. It conditions liberty on individuals acting in ways that enhance their lives: to be free is to have accomplished something of value or virtue.[17] The attainment of, and value in, liberty involves the individual himself actively participating in worthy endeavours. Liberty requires not only that an individual be able to make choices, but that he does make choices, and that he makes the right choices. Admittedly, this understanding of liberty exposes it to charges of paternalism or authoritarianism, in the form of coercion, commands or restraints.[18] Nevertheless, it is animated by the basic concern of ensuring an individual's ability and readiness to make choices about his own life.

The focus of civic-republican liberty is the absence of domination.[19] An individual's choice-making capacity hinges not only on her being unprevented from making a choice, but also that, in making her choice, she is not subject to another's dominant will. To guard against liberty-depriving situations of domination, individuals should participate as much as possible in their own system of governance, through exercising civic-communitarian virtue, or through political and legal structures targeted at participatory or

---

[13] Berlin, *Two Concepts of Liberty*; Berlin, *Four Essays on Liberty*; Cohen, *History, Labour, and Freedom*; Steiner, 'Individual Liberty'; Steiner, *Essay on Rights*; Cohen, *Self-Ownership*; Carter, *Measure of Freedom*; Kramer, *Quality of Freedom*.

[14] Kramer, *Quality of Freedom*, 15, 45.

[15] Ibid., 15.

[16] Ibid., 412, 428–41.

[17] Skinner, 'Republican Ideal of Political Liberty', 295–8; Kramer, *Quality of Freedom*, 91–3. See also Berlin, *Two Concepts of Liberty*.

[18] Berlin, *Two Concepts of Liberty*; Kramer, *Quality of Freedom*, 96–100.

[19] Skinner, 'Republican Ideal of Political Liberty'; Pettit, *Republicanism*; Skinner, *Liberty before Liberalism*; Pettit, *Theory of Freedom*.

representative government.[20] Such an approach is comparable to the description of a system of domination that is offered by panopticism,[21] since, although the individual may be physically free to do something, she is not prepared to do it due to her knowledge she is being observed and her awareness of potential consequences for acting in that way.[22] The dominance of another inhibits her preparedness to do something (including to make choices), even though it does not inhibit her physical ability. Civic-republicanism has been criticised as superfluous to negative liberty theory (with the latter better able to describe and exclude situations of dominance), and for not offering a means of accurately measuring overall liberty.[23] Whether or not it is so superfluous or imprecise, civic-republicanism is concerned that individuals be able and prepared to make choices about their lives – whatever the choices they might make.

Whether it is the bare minimum of liberty (a necessary but insufficient element) or the ultimate end of liberty (both necessary and sufficient), the concern that individuals have capacity to make choices in their own lives can be gleaned from each of the three main traditions of liberty. It is that concern for choice-making capacity that defines 'liberty' here.

(b) Security

Scholarship on security is often concerned with collective security vis-à-vis nation-states or the international order.[24] Much of the literature assumes security is valuable to individuals by virtue of their membership in a collective, rather than defining why and how security is valuable to the individual as such.

An etymological approach is useful to ascertaining the basic meaning of security as a value of significance to the individual. The ancient Greek word for 'security', *asphaleia*, is a negation of the verb *sphallo*, meaning to err, fall, fail or frustrate.[25] Security, then, is the state of being in which one is not tripped up or frustrated, and where one does not err, fall or fail. For the Greeks it was a mental state of serenity and confidence.[26] The Latin noun *securitas* ('security')

---

[20] Skinner, 'Republican Ideal of Political Liberty', 294–5; Kramer, *Quality of Freedom*, 105–11.
[21] Foucault, *Discipline and Punish*. See also Bentham, *Panopticon Postscript, Part II*.
[22] See Brunon-Ernst, Chapter 6 of this collection.
[23] Kramer, *Quality of Freedom*, 120–48.
[24] Dillon, *Biopolitics of Security*; Floyd, *Morality of Security*; Chandler, *Freedom versus Necessity*; Browning, *International Security*; Walton and Frazier, *Anthology*; Booth, *Theory of World Security*; Kaldor, *Global Security Cultures*; Chernoff, *Explanation and Progress*; Gilbert, *Terrorism, Security and Nationality*.
[25] Dillon, *Politics of Security*, 124; from Liddell and Scott, *Greek–English Lexicon*; Gros, *Security Principle*, 13–37.
[26] Gros, *Security Principle*, chap. 1.

comprises *sine* ('without') and *cura* ('troubling', 'carefulness' and 'anxiety').[27] Consistent with the Ciceronian use of *securitas* to denote tranquillity or peace of mind,[28] 'security' means a state (or sphere) of being in which individuals know they do not need to be wary of risks of harm or hindrance that may otherwise threaten them. Security can, therefore, be understood as the state (or sphere) of being in which individuals are or feel assured they will not be thwarted or injured, or harmed or hindered, by external forces that contour the boundaries of that state of being. That is what is meant by 'security' here.

Whereas liberty is recognised as preserving individuals' choice-making capacity, security can be construed, at an equally high level of abstraction, as individuals' capacity to control a defined sphere in their lives, to the exclusion of risks of external harm or hindrance. The greater the risk, or the more serious the harm or hindrance, the greater the degree of control required to achieve security. As such, depending upon the nature of risks and harms, individuals might choose to delegate the means of controlling and securing spheres of their lives to an entity more capable of achieving that; for example, delegations made to the state in wartime. However, the element of control and the value of security always fundamentally belong to and begin with the individual, and security in this basic sense is always presumed to be for the benefit of the individual first and foremost.[29] Any benefits derived from collective security are, therefore, measured and valued according to the security of the individuals who compose that group.

2. Liberty and Security Underpin Privacy

A complex value, privacy has many, diverse underpinnings, and there are multiple ways of explaining and justifying it.[30] There is, however, an important constancy beneath this complexity. Privacy comprises an allegiance to the deeper moral principles of liberty and security.

(a) Dignity and Personhood

Privacy has been theorised as safeguarding human dignity, and thereby protecting individual personhood.[31] Although 'dignity' has been criticised as

---

[27] Dillon, *Politics of Security*, 125; from Andrews, *Latin–English Lexicon*, 1380, 'securitas'.

[28] Andrews, *Latin–English Lexicon*, 1380, 'securitas'.

[29] Hobbes, *Leviathan*; Locke, *Two Treatises of Government*.

[30] Solove, 'Conceptualising Privacy', 1087; Busch, 'Privacy, Technology, and Regulation'; Scanlon, 'Thomson on Privacy', 315; Solove, 'Taxonomy of Privacy', 477.

[31] Fried, 'Privacy'; Reiman, 'Privacy, Intimacy and Personhood'; Bloustein, 'Privacy as an Aspect of Human Dignity'; Bloustein, 'Privacy is Dear at Any Price'; Gavison, 'Privacy and the Limits of the Law'.

being interpreted in different ways in different contexts,[32] a long-recognised explication of human dignity derives from Kant's categorical imperative that each individual be recognised as having inner worth so as to be an end in herself, and that, subsequently, no individual be used solely as a means to an end.[33] Insofar as privacy shields individuals from surveillance, it recognises that individuals are not merely entities which can and therefore should be observed, about whom information can and therefore should be freely obtainable. Private information should not be commodified and traded for profit,[34] given invasions of privacy 'injure [individuals] in their very humanity'.[35] Privacy recognises individuals as fundamentally entitled to manage their own life and identity, according to their own ends. This concern for dignity, as it underpins privacy, reflects a deeper moral allegiance to liberty and security, in the sense of protecting individuals' choice-making capacity and capacity to control a defined sphere in their lives: the private sphere.

In the same vein, a Dworkinian definition of dignity, under which everyone is responsible for identifying what counts as success or 'living well' in their own life,[36] construes privacy as 'respect for our personal identity'[37] and a crucial mechanism by which individuals identify how to maximise their success or 'good living'. Here, too, we can observe the deeper commitment of privacy to liberty and security. Dignity justifies privacy in shielding from surveillance those core and unavoidable aspects of every individual's life that we 'have been socialised into concealing', including grief, trauma and sex, exposure of which would create 'embarrassment and humiliation'.[38] For example, the inability to grieve privately, away from public attention, significantly affects relatives of victims of tragedies, impeding their ability to move on,[39] where moving on is intrinsic to identifying one's own purpose in life, and those things enabling one to 'live well', after the loss of a loved one. Privacy, through its connection with dignity, is concerned with protecting an individual's liberty, his choice-making capacity, in spite of the damage wrought by grief and trauma, as well as his security, his capacity to control that sphere of his life in which he experiences loss, grief and trauma. The denial of privacy in this context allows individuals, and their proximity to misfortune, to be treated thoroughly as a means to some external ends; and thus it also undermines individual liberty and security.

---

[32] Riley, 'Human Dignity'; Gajda, 'Trouble with Dignity'.
[33] Kant, *Groundwork of the Metaphysics of Morals*.
[34] Rössler, 'Should Personal Data Be a Tradable Good?'
[35] Fried, 'Privacy', 475.
[36] Dworkin, *Justice for Hedgehogs*.
[37] Lester, *Five Ideas to Fight For*, 145.
[38] Solove, 'Taxonomy of Privacy', 536.
[39] Moreham and Tinsley, 'Media Intrusion into Grief'.

(b) Autonomy

The autonomy justification for privacy is understood as an individual's ability to control her own life, including how much others know about her life.[40] The 'barriers' conception of privacy draws upon autonomy,[41] given the strongest barriers to intrusion result from individuals exerting control over their lives and defining who has access.

Given privacy is crucial to providing 'control over certain aspects in [one's] life',[42] it is lost or eroded when individuals lose control over their private information,[43] the manner in which that information is shared, or the extent to which the public can see into their lives: 'If the intimate details of my life are disclosed without my consent . . . something that is essentially *mine* to control has been taken from me.'[44]

This vision of and justification for privacy through the concern for autonomy, as ensuring a basic modicum of control over one's life, reflects clearly the deeper moral concern of privacy to protect individual security. Where an individual has that degree of control which the protection of her privacy ensures, she not only has a greater degree of autonomy in her life, but she also has a greater degree of security – she does not need to be wary of the risk of harm entailed in another's co-opting her personal information, including through surveillance.

Alongside control, autonomy also encompasses choice, and this is another way in which autonomy justifies privacy protection. This reveals that liberty, together with security, is embodied in the concern to protect privacy. An autonomous individual, like a free individual, has the capacity to choose how to live, what to think, and how much information about herself to share with others. Being able to reason, privately, about aspects of her life that are socially controversial or morally unsettled (for example, whether to consent to particular medical treatment, have an abortion, or seek assisted dying) allows an individual to make genuine choices on such matters, ensuring those choices are her own. Privacy is not necessarily dichotomous with publicity and does not necessarily entail secrecy or isolation. An autonomous individual, with privacy, might choose to vitiate that privacy.[45] The ability to choose

---

[40] Gross, 'Privacy and Autonomy'; Kupfer, 'Privacy, Autonomy, and Self-Concept'; Gavison, 'Information Control'.
[41] Hughes, 'Behavioural Understanding of Privacy'.
[42] Inness, *Privacy, Intimacy and Isolation*, 41.
[43] Taylor, 'Personal Autonomy and Caller ID'.
[44] Schauer, 'Free Speech', 223, original emphasis.
[45] Inness, *Privacy, Intimacy and Isolation*, 41–5.

is more important than the outcome, placing choice (as well as control) at the heart of privacy.[46] An individual subject to surveillance has diminished privacy because she has a diminished power of choice in how she lives her life. In such circumstances, the 'horror of uniformity, conformism, and mechanization of life is not groundless',[47] and it is a horror reflected in the absence of liberty.

(c) Psychological Sanctity

An individual's knowledge that her privacy is lost has the propensity to erode her psychological resilience and well-being. Here, the assertion that she who has nothing to hide has nothing to fear offers little solace.[48] The fear and psychological unrest following privacy intrusion arises not only from knowing others have gained knowledge about you, but from realising your life is open for others to access. The revelation of unfettered accessibility causes the grief, perplexity and lack of sanctity concomitant with privacy invasion. Such unfettered accessibility by others signifies a loss of control, and this is how psychological sanctity likewise reveals the deeper moral concern of privacy to protect individual security.

The negative psychological effects of loss of privacy have been documented in different contexts, including grief-journalism, where media coverage of tragedies has induced in victims' next-of-kin a fear even within their home and family lives, contributing to an emotional imbalance in dealing with their loss, and exacerbating their grieving experience.[49] Privacy intrusions within families also have psychological impacts: the exposure of children online by their parents has been linked to feelings of discomfort, vulnerability and powerlessness.[50] Psychological impacts of privacy intrusions have sometimes culminated in such fear and hopelessness as to lead to self-harm.[51]

The connection between such erosions of psychological sanctity and *insecurity* is obvious: in such states of being, the individual has no control over that sphere of her life defined as 'private', and because of that she is perpetually and incurably wary about risks of harms, in the form of further intrusions, or accessed aspects of her private life being used against her, or the use and revelation of her private life resulting in her being shamed or otherwise treated

---

[46] Scanlon, 'Thomson on Privacy'; Rachels, 'Why Privacy is Important'.
[47] Berlin, *Four Essays on Liberty*, 52.
[48] Feldman, *Civil Liberties and Human Rights*, 512.
[49] Moreham and Tinsley, 'Media Intrusion into Grief'.
[50] Children's Commissioner, *Life in 'Likes'*.
[51] For examples of cases of suicide following gross breaches of privacy, see Pilkington, 'Tyler Clementi'; Reynolds, 'Italy's Tiziana'.

badly. In protecting psychological sanctity, privacy protects individual security. The psychological ramifications of diminished privacy also affect individuals' choices about how they behave, where they go, how they interact with those closest to them, and with whom they associate themselves generally.[52] Once again we can see how privacy embodies an underlying conception of liberty as much as security.

Privacy can therefore be viewed as an antidote to the fear that the state or society is watching the individual when he does not want to be watched, passing judgment upon him, and, potentially, ostracising him.[53] The controlling device of panopticism[54] could be observed in both the McCarthyist United States and the totalitarian German Democratic Republic, for example, and the privacy-eroding surveillance tactics and effects of these regimes on human psychology have been well documented.[55]

(d) Personal Self-Reflection, Intellectual Development and Freedom of Expression

Privacy protection has also been justified on the basis that it safeguards individuals' ability to undertake self-reflection and intellectual development.[56] Not only does it enable introspection, critical thought and self-betterment, thus fostering personal and intellectual growth, it protects the individual from external pressures of conformism, and risk-averse thinking, which disable and discourage such personal development. Both security and liberty are reflected in this normative underpinning of privacy.

Away from others' 'unwanted gaze or interference',[57] when an individual has security and is confident others are not empowered to access how she thinks, she is free to test her convictions in ways that might not conform to a societal status quo. Empirical analysis of the effects of mass systemic surveillance has demonstrated that individuals who believe their patterns of behaviour might be watched by others subconsciously adjust their actions and thoughts to align themselves with status quo mores.[58] In that way, privacy-intrusive surveillance operates as a tool of auto-censorship, and it can be described as both the result of the insecurity entailed in such surveillance

---

[52] Lord Justice Leveson, 'Inquiry', Witness Statements of Gerald Patrick McCann; Sally and Bob Dowler; and Hugh Grant.
[53] Kafka and Kuhn, *Der Prozess*.
[54] Bentham, *Panopticon Postscript, Part II*; Foucault, *Discipline and Punish*.
[55] Miller, *The Crucible*; Becker, 'Der Verdächtige'; Funder, *Stasiland*.
[56] Richards, 'Intellectual Privacy'.
[57] Ibid., 389.
[58] Kaminski and Witnov, 'Conforming Effect'. See also Harcourt, *Exposed*.

and loss of privacy, and the manifestation of a lack of liberty consequent on such surveillance.

If privacy is justified for safeguarding secure and free personal and intellectual development, then privacy can be justified as enabling freedom of expression.[59] Privacy of thought gives individuals security, confidence and freedom to develop ideas and arguments, and also to express such ideas and arguments with equal security, confidence and freedom. A lack of privacy of thought transfers any resultantly conscious or subconscious auto-censorship to the sphere of expressive behaviour.[60] As such, the way in which privacy protects freedom of expression demonstrates that the deeper, fundamental concerns of privacy are the maintenance of security and liberty.

(e) Participation in Society

Privacy has also been said to support individuals as social beings, willing and able to cultivate relationships with others and to participate meaningfully in their society.[61] Indeed, privacy does not inherently undermine a community's social fabric, by producing silos of egotistical and socially careless individuals. As apparent in the preceding discussion, the cascading effects of adequate privacy protection, encompassing security and liberty, include more confident, outward-looking and socially active individuals. Safeguarding individual privacy stimulates socialisation and benefits the community by alleviating friction between the diverse values and interests held by individuals within that community.[62] It is precisely thanks to the security and liberty ensured by privacy that individuals can be more confident and ready to interact with others, form relationships, develop ideas for the betterment of their community, and share them.[63] On the contrary, victims' testimonies in the Leveson Inquiry, as well as observations of oppressive surveillance regimes, illustrate how diminished privacy drives individuals further into themselves, for fear of the scrutiny of their society or the apparatuses of power.

In giving individuals the security of their own psychological and physical space,[64] in which freely to make choices on how they develop and express their own values and beliefs, and in ensuring that personal space is guaranteed to

---

[59] Goold, 'How Much Surveillance is Too Much?', 42–3; Lever, 'Privacy, Democracy and Freedom of Expression'.

[60] Lever, 'Privacy, Democracy and Freedom of Expression', 168.

[61] Etzioni, *Limits of Privacy*; Feldman, 'Privacy-Related Rights', 18–23.

[62] Hughes, 'Social Value of Privacy', 230.

[63] Gavison, 'Privacy and the Limits of the Law', 455; Simitis, 'Reviewing Privacy', 732; Lever, *On Privacy*, 24–8.

[64] Zuboff has called this the 'right to sanctuary'. Zuboff, *Age of Surveillance Capitalism*.

all individuals in equal measure, privacy allows individuals to be content in living their lives according to their own mores, without having to compete with others. In this way, privacy can encourage mutual respect, even empathy, between individuals in their interactions, generating tolerance in a diverse society, and thereby maintaining pluralism in a liberal society.[65] On this reasoning, in spite of cultural differences, individuals with a guarantee of a private sphere will be willing and able more readily to develop meaningful relationships with others in their society. To that extent, privacy can ensure even the most pluralistic societies maintain cohesion. Increased participation in society, resulting from the security and liberty gained from privacy protection, is in turn valuable to the individual: it enlivens the cooperative and social role of human beings, and that is a vital element of human flourishing.[66] This reflexive socialisation value of privacy highlights the way in which protecting individual interests, including security and liberty, furthers collective interests, as derivative of individuals.

This is why, even when theorised through a societal lens,[67] privacy remains a uniquely individual interest. The societal benefits that accrue from protecting individual privacy provide further justifications for such protection, but the relevant interests in privacy remain those of the paradigmatic individual. Even though privacy's value to society is important and material to justifying why privacy is important, it is derivative of and secondary to the value of privacy to the individual. In this sense, privacy deserves protection when it enables individuals to perform social functions,[68] or protects them from certain social harms.[69] To the extent individuals with protected privacy can contribute more or better to their society in various ways, their privacy should be protected, and to the extent individual privacy is unattainable unless there is a universal minimal standard, privacy may be understood as a collective good,[70] derived from its value to the individual.

IV. Privacy as Liberty and Security: Problematising Surveillance

There is an enduring, deep and context-independent moral connection between the importance of privacy to the individual, and the prioritisation

---

[65] Bollinger, *Tolerant Society*; Raz, 'Free Expression'.

[66] Feldman, 'Privacy-Related Rights', 21.

[67] Regan, *Legislating Privacy*, 212–43; Feldman, 'Privacy-Related Rights'; Cockfield, 'Protecting the Social Value of Privacy'; Steeves, 'Reclaiming the Social Value of Privacy'; Nissenbaum, *Privacy in Context*; Hughes, 'Social Value of Privacy'; Regan, 'Privacy and the Common Good'.

[68] Feldman, 'Privacy-Related Rights', 15–16.

[69] Solove, *Understanding Privacy*, 91–2.

[70] Regan, *Legislating Privacy*; Nehf, 'Recognizing the Societal Value'; Nissenbaum, *Privacy in Context*, 87–8.

and preservation of individual liberty and individual security. Privacy is important because it preserves and protects liberty and security. The realisation that both liberty and security lie within the normative reasons for upholding privacy problematises the tendency to justify privacy-intrusive surveillance on the basis of a broad appeal to security. In order to justify surveillance, more is needed to address the fundamental concerns of liberty and security which buttress the value of privacy.

Whichever philosophical underpinning is invoked, whether it be dignity, autonomy, participation in society, or cultivation of relationships, for example, privacy is justified fundamentally because it is one way of protecting the choice-making capacity of individuals (individual liberty), and the capacity of individuals to control a defined sphere of their lives through an assurance of safety from potential external harm or hindrance (individual security). Not only does this constant and context-independent allegiance to individual liberty and security concretise privacy as an autochthonous value of significance to individuals even when placed in opposition to utilitarian reasons for interfering with privacy, it also problematises those utilitarian, collective reasons for interference which themselves invoke liberty or security. It is, in truth, not so straightforward comprehensively to justify interferences with individual privacy by invoking in broad terms the values of 'liberty' and 'security', as was the case in response to terrorist threats in, for example, the United States;[71] and as is the case currently in response to a novel virus: in addition to appeals to collective medical security, some governments appeared to be conditioning liberty on the adoption of privacy-intrusive surveillance tools to trace the spread of the virus.[72]

Any state wishing to employ surveillance on the basis of security (and liberty) must address the necessary incursion on the privacy of individuals who are purportedly being secured (or liberated). It is insufficient (though it may be necessary) to adduce generalised principles of just 'securitisation' to justify surveillance.[73] The normative strength and moral importance of

---

[71] Recall the US Attorney-General's arguments for increasing governmental surveillance: Speech of Attorney-General John Ashcroft about the Patriot Act, at Boise, Idaho, 25 August 2003, available at https://www.justice.gov/archive/ag/speeches/2003/082503patriotactrem arks.htm.

[72] For example, Australia's then Prime Minister stated on 29 April 2020 (about the 'COVID-Safe app'): 'I would liken it to the fact that if you want to go outside when the sun is shining, you have got to put sunscreen on [. . .] This is the same thing [. . .] If you want to return to a more liberated economy and society, it is important that we get increased numbers of downloads when it comes to the COVIDSafe app [. . .] This is the ticket to ensuring that we can have eased restrictions.' Hitch, 'Prime Minister Scott Morrison'.

[73] Floyd, *Morality of Security*.

privacy requires stronger, evidence-based and more targeted justifications. An appeal to collective security cannot in and of itself justify setting aside the deeper moral concerns for individual security (as well as liberty) embedded within the value of privacy. As discussed above, the interest of the greater unit (the collective) in some value cannot automatically set aside the interest of the smaller unit (the individual) in the same value, because it is the interests of the smaller that constitute and legitimate the interests of the greater.[74] Given the political morality of the social contract that creates and legitimises governmental power in liberal democracy, although the interests of the collective (or the state) can be fully expounded by reference to the interests of its individual members without being reducible to them,[75] the collective (or the state) exists and has interests contingent on its service to its individual members;[76] the interests of the collective and its individuals are, as a matter of moral principle, in alignment.

Therefore, it is inaccurate to place into opposition the concern for individual privacy and a broad concern for collective security. The calculus is not a generalised trade-off between the individual and the collective,[77] but rather it is an evidence-based assessment in the particular circumstances that pursuing a collective interest in, for example, collective security will serve individual interests in individual security better than pursuing or upholding individual security in the same circumstances. What is required is rather an evidence-based assessment in the particular circumstances that the threat is so great that the individual should, for the sake of the individual as such, delegate, for the time being, to the collective (the state), the power to safeguard their individual interests. Nothing less will suffice.

Given as much, neither is a broad appeal to utilitarian or collective ends sufficient to justify displacing individual privacy in general, and nor is a broad appeal to collective security and liberty sufficient to justify suspending individual privacy in specific circumstances of large-scale threat, whether it be the threat of warfare or a novel virus. Privacy is not a normatively fluid or weak value, and it requires more detailed, targeted and evidence-based politico-moral (and, as the case may be, legal) justifications for its interference, including when such justifications involve the securitisation of the collective against a large-scale threat.

---

[74] Recall, again, the basic understanding of liberal democracy as constitutive of a social contract, between individuals, as such, and the collective of individuals. Hobbes, *Leviathan*; Locke, *Two Treatises of Government*.

[75] Kramer, 'Rights Without Trimmings', 54.

[76] Kramer, 'Getting Rights Right'.

[77] For example, 'trade-off thesis'. Posner and Vermeule, *Terror in the Balance*.

In the European Court of Human Rights, which has presided over several challenges to state surveillance on the basis of the Article 8 right to a private and family life, Judge Pinto de Albuquerque criticised the reasoning of the Court for

> *assum[ing]* that the fight against terrorism *requires* a 'pool of information retrievable by the authorities applying highly efficient methods and processing masses of data, potentially about each person, should he be, one way or another, connected to suspected subjects or objects of planned terrorist attacks'.[78]

His Honour went on:

> [Such] optimistic language is indicative of an illusory conviction that global surveillance is the *deus ex machina* capable of combating the scourge of global terrorism. Even worse, such delusory language obliterates the fact that the vitrification of society brings with it the Orwellian nightmare of 1984. In practice, [using such language means] [. . .] condoning, to use the words of the European Parliament, 'the establishment of a fully-fledged preventive state, changing the established paradigm of criminal law in democratic societies whereby any interference with suspects' fundamental rights has to be authorised by a judge or prosecutor on the basis of a reasonable suspicion and must be regulated by law, promoting instead a mix of law-enforcement and intelligence activities with blurred and weakened legal safeguards, often not in line with democratic checks and balances and fundamental rights [. . .]'.[79]

His Honour's concerns relate to the specificity with which legal thresholds consistent with liberal democracy must be defined and applied to determine whether the liberal-democratic state may employ surveillance. Those concerns also reflect the politico-moral recognition that individual privacy (as one embodiment of individual security and liberty) is presumed to be the norm in a liberal democracy, so it is for the government wishing to interfere with privacy to justify that interference with sufficient specificity and in terms consistent with those values embodied in privacy. The liberal polity, including its executive government and its courts, must not lose sight of the moral principles which constitute and legitimise governmental power. This is the social contract, which recognises as paramount and foundational the interests of the individual. The moral understanding of privacy as liberty and security means any government in such a position must adduce specific evidence of how the particular type of surveillance will, in the circumstances of the particular threat, safeguard every

---

[78] *Szabo and Vissy v Hungary* (Application no. 37138/14) Fourth Section (12 January 2016) (*Szabo*), separate opinion of Judge Pinto de Albuquerque, [20], emphasis added; the judge was quoting from [78] of the Chamber's majority decision.

[79] *Szabo*, sep. op. Judge Pinto de Albuquerque, [20].

individual's security and liberty by interfering with individuals' privacy. This duty to justify surveillance on the basis of specific and evidence-based reasons – on the hustings, in political speeches, in parliamentary debates or in law reform proposals – must be discharged whenever a state wishes to interfere with the foundational norms of privacy.

One possible approach would be through the principle of proportionality. Such an analysis could demonstrate that, in the circumstances, surveillance safeguards each individual's security and liberty better than if each individual's privacy were left intact. Justification through proportionality would require the state to prove that surveillance, in the particular circumstances, is a rational response to the threat to security, a minimally necessary response to that threat, and, vitally, a means proportionate to achieving the objective (securitisation).[80] Indeed, in several liberal-democratic jurisdictions, proportionality is elemental to the legal justification of governmental interference with individual rights and liberties, or constitutional freedoms.[81]

V. Conclusion

Surveillance, and in particular governmental surveillance, interferes with privacy, and, in a liberal democracy, requires government to justify that interference. In view of the centrality of liberty and security to privacy, it is both inaccurate and insufficient to invoke broad claims to collective security (or overall liberty) as a way of opposing privacy interests and justifying surveillance. Privacy does not come into conflict with security or liberty; it embodies them, and therefore requires that surveillance be justified in terms consistent with those moral concerns to protect individual interests, and on reasons that are specific and evidence-based. The onus is on the state to show why the protection of individual liberty and security, as embodied in the value of privacy, is better achieved, in the circumstances, through the protection of collective liberty and security.[82] That onus cannot be discharged through appeals to existential threats without evidence connecting surveillance to

---

[80] Alexy, 'Constitutional Rights', 133.

[81] For example, English administrative law: *R v Headteacher and Governors of Denbigh High School, ex p Begum* [2007] 1 AC 100; ECHR, Article 8(2) (justified interference with private and family life): *Kennedy*; New Zealand Bill of Rights Act 1990, ss 4,5,6: *Hansen v The Queen* [2007] NZSC 7, [104]; Canadian Charter: *R v Oakes* [1986] 1 SCR 103; Australian constitutional law vis-à-vis interference with freedom of political communication: *Clubb v Edwards* [2019] HCA11.

[82] An example of when this onus can be discharged is in the context of mass vaccination in response to a novel virus, provided that in the particular circumstances there is sufficient and demonstrable medical evidence of the safety and efficacy of the vaccine in question, so that inoculation of individuals en masse is safer for all individuals than it is for individuals to remain exposed to the risks posed by that novel virus.

the furtherance of individual liberty and security. The weight of the onus is commensurate with the moral importance in liberal-democratic society of individual privacy as an embodiment of both liberty and security.

VI. Bibliography

Alexy, Robert. 'Constitutional Rights, Balancing, and Rationality.' *Ratio Juris* 16, no. 2 (2003): 131–40.

Allen, Anita L. *Uneasy Access*. Totowa, NJ: Rowman & Littlefield, 1988.

———. *Why Privacy Isn't Everything*. Lanham, MD: Rowman & Littlefield, 2003.

Andrews, E. A., ed. *Latin–English Lexicon*. 2nd ed. London: Sampson Low, Son & Marston, 1875.

Arendt, Hannah. *The Human Condition*. Chicago: University of Chicago Press, 1958.

Becker, Jurek. 'Der Verdächtige.' In *Nach der Ersten Zukunft*, 259. Frankfurt am Main: Suhrkamp, 1980.

Benn, S., and G. Gaus. 'The Liberal Conception of the Public and the Private.' In *Public and Private in Social Life*, edited by S. Benn and G. Gaus, 31–66. New York: St. Martin's Press, 1983.

———. 'The Public and the Private: Concepts and Action.' In *Public and Private in Social Life*, edited by S. Benn and G. Gaus, 3–27. New York: St. Martin's Press, 1983.

Bentham, Jeremy. 'Chapter IX: Ministers Collectively. Section 26. Architectural Arrangements.' In *Constitutional Code*, edited by F. Rosen, J. H. Burns, and L. J. Hume, vol. 1, 438–57. Oxford: Clarendon, 1983.

———. 'Postscript, Part 1. Containing further Particulars and Alterations relative to the Plan of Construction originally proposed; principally adapted to the purpose of a Panopticon Penitentiary-House.' In *The Works of Jeremy Bentham*, edited by John Bowring, vol. 4, 67–121. Elibron Classics, 2005.

———. 'Postscript, Part II. Principles and Plan of Management.' In *The Works of Jeremy Bentham*, edited by John Bowring, vol. 4, 121–72. Elibron Classics, 2005.

Berlin, Isaiah. *Four Essays on Liberty*. New York: Oxford University Press, 1969.

———. *Two Concepts of Liberty*. Oxford: Clarendon, 1958.

Bloustein, Edward J. 'Privacy as an Aspect of Human Dignity.' *New York University Law Review* 39 (1964): 962–1007.

———. 'Privacy is Dear at Any Price.' *Georgia Law Review* 12 (1977): 429–54.

Bollinger, Lee C. *The Tolerant Society*. New York: Oxford University Press, 1988.

Booth, Ken. *Theory of World Security*. Cambridge: Cambridge University Press, 2007.

Browning, Christopher S. *International Security*. Oxford: Oxford University Press, 2013.

Busch, Andreas. 'Privacy, Technology, and Regulation.' In *Social Dimensions of Privacy*, edited by Beata Rössler and Dorota Mokrosinska, 303–23. Cambridge: Cambridge University Press, 2015.

Carter, Ian. *A Measure of Freedom*. Oxford: Oxford University Press, 1999.

Chandler, David. *Freedom versus Necessity in International Relations: Human-Centred Approaches to Security and Development*. London: Zed Books, 2013.

Chernoff, Fred. *Explanation and Progress in Security Studies: Bridging Paradigm Divides in International Relations.* Stanford: Stanford University Press, 2014.

Children's Commissioner. *Life in 'Likes': Children's Commissioner Report into Social Media Use among 8–12 Year Olds.* London: Children's Commissioner for England, 2018.

Cockfield, Arthur J. 'Protecting the Social Value of Privacy in the Context of State Investigations Using New Technologies.' *University of British Columbia Law Review* 40, no. 1 (2007): 41–68.

Cohen, G. A. *History, Labour, and Freedom.* Oxford: Clarendon, 1988.

———. *Self-Ownership, Freedom, and Equality.* Cambridge: Cambridge University Press, 1995.

DeCew, Judith Wagner. 'The Feminist Critique of Privacy.' In *Social Dimensions of Privacy,* edited by Beata Rössler and Dorota Mokrosinska, 85–103. Cambridge: Cambridge University Press, 2015.

Dillon, Michael. *Biopolitics of Security: A Political Analytic of Finitude.* London: Routledge, 2015.

———. *Politics of Security: Towards a Political Philosophy of Continental Thought.* London: Routledge, 1996.

Dworkin, Ronald. *Justice for Hedgehogs.* Cambridge, MA: Belknap Press, 2011.

Etzioni, Amitai. *The Limits of Privacy.* New York: Basic Books, 1999.

Feldman, David. *Civil Liberties and Human Rights in England and Wales.* 2nd ed. Oxford: Oxford University Press, 2002.

———. 'Privacy-Related Rights.' In *Privacy and Loyalty,* edited by Peter Birks, 15–50. Oxford: Clarendon, 1997.

Floyd, Rita. *The Morality of Security: A Theory of Just Securitisation.* Cambridge: Cambridge University Press, 2019.

Foucault, Michel. *Discipline and Punish: The Birth of the Prison.* 1975. Translated by Alan Sheridan. 2nd ed. New York: Vintage Books, 1995.

Fried, Charles. 'Privacy.' *Yale Law Journal* 77 (1968): 475–93.

Funder, Anna. *Stasiland.* London: Granta Books, 2003.

Gajda, Amy. 'The Trouble with Dignity.' In *Comparative Defamation and Privacy Law,* edited by Andrew T. Kenyon, 246–64. Cambridge: Cambridge University Press, 2016.

Gavison, Ruth. 'Information Control.' In *Public and Private in Social Life,* edited by S. Benn and G. Gaus, 113–34. New York: St. Martin's Press, 1983.

———. 'Privacy and the Limits of the Law.' *Yale Law Journal* 89, no. 3 (1980): 421–71.

Gilbert, Paul. *Terrorism, Security and Nationality: An Introductory Study in Applied Political Philosophy.* Hoboken, NJ: Taylor and Francis, 2002.

Goold, Benjamin J. 'How Much Surveillance is Too Much?' In *Overvåkning i en rettsstat,* edited by D. W. Schartum, 38–48. Bergen: Fagbokforlaget, 2010.

Gros, Frédéric. *The Security Principle: From Serenity to Regulation.* 2012. Translated by David Broder. London: Verso, 2019.

Gross, Hyman. 'Privacy and Autonomy.' In *Privacy,* edited by J. Roland Pennock and John W. Chapman, 169–81. New York: Atherton, 1971.

Harcourt, Bernard E. *Exposed: Desire and Disobedience in the Digital Age*. Cambridge, MA: Harvard University Press, 2015.

Hitch, Georgia. 'Prime Minister Scott Morrison Flags Easing of Coronavirus Restrictions in Near Future.' *ABC News*, 29 April 2020. https://www.abc.net. au/news/2020-04-29/prime-minister-scott-morrison-coronavirus-restrictions-easing/12196562.

Hobbes, Thomas. *Leviathan (Reprinted from the 1651 Edition)*. Oxford: Clarendon, 1909.

Hughes, Kirsty. 'A Behavioural Understanding of Privacy and Its Implications for Privacy Law.' *Modern Law Review* 75, no. 5 (2012): 806–36.

———. 'The Social Value of Privacy.' In *Social Dimensions of Privacy*, edited by Beata Rössler and Dorota Mokrosinska, 225–43. Cambridge: Cambridge University Press, 2015.

Inness, Julie C. *Privacy, Intimacy and Isolation*. Oxford: Oxford University Press, 1992.

Kafka, Franz, and Heribert Kuhn. *Der Prozess*. Frankfurt am Main: Suhrkamp, 2000.

Kaldor, Mary. *Global Security Cultures*. Cambridge: Polity, 2018.

Kamenka, Eugene. 'Public/Private in Marxist Theory and Marxist Practice.' In *Public and Private in Social Life*, edited by S. Benn and G. Gaus, 267–79. New York: St. Martin's Press, 1983.

Kaminski, Margot E., and Shane Witnov. 'The Conforming Effect.' *University of Richmond Law Review* 49, no. 2 (2015): 465–518.

Kant, Immanuel. *Groundwork of the Metaphysics of Morals: A German–English Edition (German Text from Second Original Edition (1786))*. Edited by J. Timmerman. Translated by M. Gregor. Cambridge: Cambridge University Press, 2011.

Kramer, Matthew H. 'Getting Rights Right.' In *Rights, Wrongs and Responsibilities*, edited by M. Kramer, 28–95. London: Palgrave Macmillan, 2001.

———. *The Quality of Freedom*. Oxford: Oxford University Press, 2003.

———. 'Rights Without Trimmings.' In *A Debate Over Rights*, by M. Kramer, N. Simmonds, and H. Steiner, 7–111. Oxford: Clarendon, 1998.

Kupfer, Joseph. 'Privacy, Autonomy, and Self-Concept.' *American Philosophical Quarterly* 24, no. 1 (1987): 81–9.

Lester, Anthony. *Five Ideas to Fight For*. London: Oneworld, 2016.

Lever, Annabelle. *On Privacy*. London: Routledge, 2012.

———. 'Privacy, Democracy and Freedom of Expression.' In *Social Dimensions of Privacy*, edited by Beata Rössler and Dorota Mokrosinska, 162–80. Cambridge: Cambridge University Press, 2015.

Liddell, H. G., and R. Scott, eds. *A Greek–English Lexicon*. 9th ed. Oxford: Clarendon, 1940.

Locke, John. *Two Treatises of Government*. Cambridge: Cambridge University Press, 1988.

Lord Justice Leveson. 'An Inquiry into the Culture, Practices and Ethics of the Press, Report.' HC 780-I to HC 780-IV, 29 November 2012.

Miller, Arthur. *The Crucible: A Play in Four Acts. New York: Viking*, 1953.

Moreham, N. A. 'The Protection of Privacy in English Common Law.' *Law Quarterly Review* 121 (2005): 628–56.

———. 'Unpacking the Reasonable Expectation of Privacy Test.' *Law Quarterly Review* 134 (2018): 651–74.

Moreham, N. A., and Yvette Tinsley. 'Media Intrusion into Grief.' In *Comparative Defamation and Privacy Law*, edited by Andrew T. Kenyon, 115–35. Cambridge: Cambridge University Press, 2016.

Nehf, James P. 'Recognizing the Societal Value in Information Privacy.' *Washington Law Review* 78, no. 1 (2003): 1–91.

Newell, Bryce Clayton, Cheryl A. Metoyer, and Adam D. Moore. 'Privacy in the Family.' In *Social Dimensions of Privacy*, edited by Beata Rössler and Dorota Mokrosinska, 104–21. Cambridge: Cambridge University Press, 2015.

Nissenbaum, Helen. *Privacy in Context*. Stanford: Stanford University Press, 2010.

Pateman, Carole. 'Feminist Critiques of the Public/Private Dichotomy.' In *Public and Private in Social Life*, edited by S. Benn and G. Gaus, 281–303. New York: St. Martin's Press, 1983.

Pettit, Philip. *Republicanism: A Theory of Freedom and Government*. Oxford: Oxford University Press, 1997.

———. *A Theory of Freedom*. Cambridge: Polity, 2001.

Pilkington, Ed. 'Tyler Clementi, Student Outed as Gay on Internet, Jumps to His Death.' *The Guardian*. 30 September 2010. https://www.theguardian.com/world/2010/sep/30/tyler-clementi-gay-student-suicide.

Posner, Eric A., and Adrian Vermeule. *Terror in the Balance*. Oxford: Oxford University Press, 2007.

Rachels, James. 'Why Privacy is Important.' *Philosophy and Public Affairs* 4, no. 4 (1975): 323–33.

Raz, Joseph. 'Free Expression and Personal Identification.' *Oxford Journal of Legal Studies* 11 (1991): 303–24.

Regan, Priscilla M. *Legislating Privacy*. Chapel Hill: University of North Carolina Press, 1995.

———. 'Privacy and the Common Good.' In *Social Dimensions of Privacy*, edited by Beata Rössler and Dorota Mokrosinska, 50–70. Cambridge: Cambridge University Press, 2015.

Reiman, Jeffrey H. 'Privacy, Intimacy and Personhood.' *Philosophy and Public Affairs* 6, no. 1 (1976): 26–44.

Reynolds, James. 'Italy's Tiziana.' *BBC News*, 13 February 2017. http://www.bbc.co.uk/news/world-europe-38848528.

Richards, Neil M. 'Intellectual Privacy.' *Texas Law Review* 87 (2008): 387–445.

Riley, Stephen. 'Human Dignity: Comparative and Conceptual Debates.' *International Journal of Law in Context* 6, no. 2 (2010): 117–38.

Rössler, Beata. 'Gender and Privacy.' In *Privacies: Philosophical Evaluations*, edited by Beata Rössler, 52–72. Stanford: Stanford University Press, 2004.

———. 'Should Personal Data Be a Tradable Good?' In *Social Dimensions of Privacy*, edited by Beata Rössler and Dorota Mokrosinska, 141–61. Cambridge: Cambridge University Press, 2015.

———. *The Value of Privacy*. Translated by R. D. V. Glasgow. Cambridge: Polity, 2005.

Scanlon, Thomas M. 'Thomson on Privacy.' *Philosophy and Public Affairs* 4, no. 4 (1975): 315–22.

Schauer, Frederick. 'Free Speech and the Social Construction of Privacy.' *Social Research* 68, no. 1 (2001): 221–32.

Simitis, Spiros. 'Reviewing Privacy in an Information Society.' *University of Pennsylvania Law Review* 135, no. 3 (1987): 707–46.

Skinner, Quentin. *Liberty before Liberalism*. Cambridge: Cambridge University Press, 1998.

———. 'The Republican Ideal of Political Liberty.' In *Machiavelli and Republicanism*, edited by Gisela Bock, Quentin Skinner, and Maurizio Viroli, 293–309. Cambridge: Cambridge University Press, 1990.

Solove, Daniel J. 'Conceptualising Privacy.' *California Law Review* 90, no. 4 (2002): 1087–155.

———. 'A Taxonomy of Privacy.' *University of Pennsylvania Law Review* 154 (June 2005): 477–564.

———. *Understanding Privacy*. Cambridge, MA: Harvard University Press, 2008.

Steeves, Valerie. 'Reclaiming the Social Value of Privacy.' In *Lessons from the Identity Trail*, edited by Ian Kerr, Valerie Steeves, and Carole Lucock, 191–208. Oxford: Oxford University Press, 2009.

Steiner, Hillel. *An Essay on Rights*. Oxford: Blackwell, 1994.

———. 'Individual Liberty.' In *Liberty*, edited by David Miller, 123–40. Oxford: Oxford University Press, 1991.

Taylor, James Stacey. 'Personal Autonomy and Caller ID.' In *Information Ethics: Privacy, Property, and Power*, edited by Adam D. Moore, 265–75. Seattle: University of Washington Press, 2005.

Walton, David, and Michael Frazier, eds. *An Anthology of Contending Views on International Security*. New York: Nova Science, 2012.

Warren, Samuel D., and Louis D. Brandeis. 'The Right to Privacy.' *Harvard Law Review* 4, no. 5 (1890): 193–220.

Westin, Alan F. *Privacy and Freedom*. New York: Atheneum, 1967.

Zuboff, Shoshana. *The Age of Surveillance Capitalism: The Fight for the Future at the New Frontier of Power*. London: Profile Books, 2019.

Part 2

Spaces

6

Panopticon as a Surveillance Model

Anne Brunon-Ernst

I. Introduction: Timely Reassessment?

One of the aims of the present volume is to examine how the COVID-19 health crisis has concentrated and intensified the stakes and ambiguities of surveillance. In this investigation, both Sabot and Gligorijević feel the need to use the panoptic metaphor to further their arguments.[1] This scholarly resurgence is reflected in more general use in newspapers and media. The most telling of these is the newspaper article entitled 'Panopticon in Your Pocket' on the COVID tracing app.[2] With the exception of March 2004 and January 2017, the Internet search request 'Panopticon' has never trended so high.[3] In the stock of shared metaphors to characterise surveillance, the adjective 'Orwellian' is a strong contestant. However, Panopticon is a clear winner. But to what extent does this use reflect an appreciation or a misunderstanding of Foucault's work on the transformation of governmental power over the last two hundred years?

Many academics have tried to make sense of the unprecedented changes brought on by the COVID-19 pandemic. Judith Butler is one of them, writing:

> I see that there are writers and academics who are taking both utopian and dystopian positions. The utopians tend to celebrate the global time-out as an opportunity to remake the world and to realize the socialist ideals embodied in the communities of care that have recently emerged. I can understand that. *The dystopians tend to project into the future the intensification of state control and surveillance*, the loss of civil liberties and the unshackling of market forces, including the crude kinds of market rationality that intensify social and economic inequalities. I can understand that, too.[4]

---

[1] See Sabot, Chapter 2; Gligorijević, Chapter 5, both in this collection.
[2] Harcourt, *Exposed*; Bartos, 'Panopticon in Your Pocket'.
[3] Search request on 24 May 2020. Source: Google trends.
[4] Yancy, 'Judith Butler: Mourning is a Political Act', emphasis added.

The Panopticon as metaphor puts a dystopian spin on any investigation of the pandemic. This stand needs to be contrasted with Bentham's own reference to his panoptic project as utopian.[5] Using the term 'panoptic' as a characterisation of surveillance tips the perspective on the side of the dystopian and aims to bring to view all the unsatisfactory elements that members of society might not have seen or understood in their practices. The aim of this chapter is to show how the Panopticon alternates between dystopian (state and corporate surveillance) and utopian (transparency, publicity, accountability) models of surveillance. Indeed, as Tadié also explains in this volume, surveillance has both a utopian and dystopian legacy.[6]

As recently as a few years ago, many writers were hailing the death of the Panopticon. Indeed, at the turn of the millennium, David Lyon, and other sociologists, did not consider the Panopticon as a fit analytical tool to explore issues of surveillance, since it was a historically outdated conception based on discipline.[7] Closer to us, Bernard Harcourt considered that we had 'moved beyond biopower or securitarian logics' as they 'do not fully account for the new forms of power circulating today'. He wrote:

> Although the digital transparence at times feels panoptic, there is in truth little need for bars and cells and watchtowers – there is little need to place the subject in a direct line of sight. There is little need to extract information,

---

[5] In the *Panopticon Letters* of 1787, Bentham called his plan 'My own Utopia'. Bentham, *Panopticon*, 49, and Bentham, *Outline of a Work entitled Pauper Management Improved*, 437. The word 'utopia' was coined by Thomas More (1478–1535) in the eponymous *Utopia* (1516) as meaning 'no-place', that is, 'place which does not exist', or an 'imaginary place' (*ou-topos*), or then again 'happy place' (*eu-topos*). Dystopia, on the other hand, is built from the prefix *dys-* to which is added *utopia* to convey the meaning of a difficult or bad state.

[6] See Chapter 3 of this collection.

[7] Lyon, *Theorizing Surveillance*, 9. See also similar comments made in Poster, *Mode of Information*; Norris and Armstrong, *Maximum Surveillance Society*; Bauman, 'Social Issues'; Lyon, *Surveillance Society*. In Michel Foucault's words, Jeremy Bentham – the de signer of the Panopticon –'invented a technology of power designed to solve the problems of surveillance'. Foucault, *Discipline and Punish*, 148, qtd in Koskela, '"Cam Era"', 293. See also: 'The critique of the Panopticon, and of the technologies of control which the Panopticon symbolised so perfectly, has been passively projected by analysts of all convictions onto every possible setting and device of social regulation. Without much hesitation, we continue to take for granted that the wish to control is embedded in a project of shaping the self, and to accept uncritically that normative power is always exerted via the injection of values into the subject.' Lianos, 'Social Control after Foucault', 424. And also: 'not only is our society marked by small numbers watching large numbers, it is also marked by the phenomenon of very large numbers watching the activities of very few; and this reversal of the Panoptical polarity may have become so marked that it finally deconstructs the Panoptical metaphor altogether'. Lyon, *Electronic Eye*, 62.

because we are giving it freely and willingly, with so much love, desire and passion – and, at times, ambivalence and hesitation.[8]

The present research does not dismiss such assessments. Yet the Panopticon is and remains a 'figure of desire in welfare capitalism'.[9] The present chapter belongs to a long academic tradition of interpretation of the Panopticon, and is unlikely to be the last. Emmanuelle de Champs's interview in December 2019 for the French radio channel France Culture on the contemporary legacy of the Panopticon is one instance of this trend.[10] My task here, however, is to set out the fecundity of panoptic metaphors, from their eighteenth-century origins to twentieth-century models of disciplinary society, to a schema of generalised surveillance, and finally to a new genre of fiction. Across its long history, the panoptic metaphor has offered uniquely adaptive responses to the experience and practices of surveillance.

II. Panopticon in Bentham's Projects

The Panopticon was first devised by Samuel Bentham as a solution to extracting more work from the factory hands in the estate he was managing in Russia.[11] It was then adapted by his brother, Jeremy, as a circular prison with a central inspection tower from which all inmates could be monitored at all times. Because they never know when, how and by whom they are monitored (anybody can be an inspector and visitors are welcome), the panoptic system ensures that inmates comply with prison rules at very little cost. The panoptic system was thought by Bentham to be applicable to any closed structure requiring the performance of certain tasks by inmates – a prison, poor house, school, factory, ministerial office, and so on.[12]

1. Definition and Features

So, the Panopticon names a building design that allows the activities of inmates to be seen and monitored by a viewer to ensure their compliance with institutionally defined behaviour. Prevention of abuse is ensured by the reversal of the gaze and mutual control within the structure. This principle can then be backed by an array of non-architectural arrangements which further strengthen the compulsion to conform to the norms set by the institution. In different fields, it is now used as synonymous with excessive surveillance.

---

[8] Harcourt, *Exposed*, 17.
[9] Boyne, 'Post-Panopticism', 295.
[10] https://www.franceculture.fr/societe/le-panoptique-a-lorigine-de-la-societe-de-surveillance.
[11] Christie, *The Benthams in Russia*, 177. See also Bentham's comment in *Panopticon; or the Inspection-House*.
[12] Bentham, *Panopticon; or the Inspection-House*, 40.

It is important to grasp three distinctive features of the Panopticon, to avoid misunderstanding its operation. The first deals with its inmates, be they convicts, workers, the poor, insane, middle-class students, ministers, and even art students.[13] This means the Panopticon is not a system setting the governed against the governors.[14] The second has to do with compliance. Certainty of compliance, that is, rule observance, is key.[15] This means the Panopticon facilitates the reformation of inmates. And the third rests on the idea of a total system.[16] The Panopticon implies a whole array of technical, management, data collection innovations, relying only partly on the circular design of the building.

2. A New World View

So more than just a design innovation, the Panopticon presents a new world view, which it both builds upon and informs. First, it is a new penal system which posits that to act as a deterrent for crime, punishment needs to make sure that each and every infraction is systematically identified and punished, that the same punishment is applied to the same offence, and that the punishment is proportionate to the offence. These basic principles of penal rationality were first theorised by Beccaria.[17]

Second, the Panopticon introduces accountability for the parties involved (governed, governors and third parties) as a guarantee that the system will not operate tyrannically.[18] The Panopticon achieves this aim thanks to two mechanisms: through publicity and through architecturally built-in transparency, which make possible five levels of surveillance. It is not just the central gaze and its reversal that lie at the heart of the panoptic endeavour. In Janet Semple's typology, (1) inmates are overseen by staff; (2) the inspector oversees staff; (3) staff oversee the inspector; (4) inmates control each other; and (5) the building is open to the public. The gaze thus operates from the centre to the ring, and back, but also from points on the ring between them, thus allowing for any combination of sightlines and control.[19]

---

[13] See Samuel Bentham's project of an art school in Cottell and Mueller, 'From Pain to Pleasure'.
[14] Lyons, *Interest of the Governed*.
[15] Brunon-Ernst, 'La matrice panoptique'.
[16] Harcourt, *Exposed*.
[17] Beccaria, *On Crimes and Punishments*.
[18] See Leroy's work on the concept of reversed Panopticon: Leroy, 'Le panoptique inversé', 172.
[19] Semple, 'Bentham's Haunted House'.

III. Panopticism: From Prison to Society

1. Foucault's Panopticism

Foucault's engagement with the Panopticon started in the early 1970s when he was researching for his lecture series on psychiatric power.[20] However, it was only fully fleshed out in 1975 with the publication of *Discipline and Punish*.[21] His 1978 lecture series on biopolitics provided a reassessment of the place of panopticism in Bentham's work.[22]

Foucault's interpretation of the Panopticon evolved over time. The present chapter relies on his 1975 description of panopticism made in the wider discussion on disciplines. Foucault stresses first, the use of a spatial organisation that ensures the exact observation of human subjects; second, the reliance on an architecture that permits the isolation and confinement of the individuals who are watched, thus the omnipresence of the few who watch and the knowledge of constant surveillance; third, a perfect control over time that allows the maximum extraction of information and work from those who are under surveillance; fourth, a normalising form of judgment that 'compares, differentiates, hierarchizes, homogenizes, excludes'; and last, a generalised form of truth production, the examination, that constantly evaluates and judges those who are being watched, and which ultimately hides the gaze of the watcher, so that those watched begin to internalise the discipline themselves.[23]

2. Panopticon vs Panopticism

Foucault's panopticism is not Bentham's Panopticon.[24] The main reason is that Foucault did not take into account the ways in which Bentham's project evolved over time.[25] First, Bentham's brother, Samuel, invented the Panopticon in 1786 and applied it to factory work in the Russian estate he was overseeing. Bentham then resorted to the Panopticon design in 1787–91 to solve the problem of prison overcrowding and convict hulks on the River Thames, following

---

[20] Foucault, *Le pouvoir psychiatrique*; Foucault, *Psychiatric Power*.
[21] Foucault, *Surveiller et punir*; Foucault, *Discipline and Punish*.
[22] Foucault, *Birth of Biopolitics*.
[23] Foucault, *Discipline and Punish*, 6–7, 170–3, 183–92. See also Harcourt, *Exposed*, 85–7.
[24] Brunon-Ernst, *Beyond Foucault*.
[25] On the history of Bentham's Panopticon project, he himself entitles his project: *Outline of a Work entitled Pauper Management Improved*, 8; Bentham, *Chrestomathia*, ed. Smith, Burston, and Hume; Bentham, *Chrestomathia*, ed. and trans. Cléro. On the different Panopticon projects, see Brunon-Ernst, 'Les métamorphoses panoptiques'; Brunon-Ernst, *Beyond Foucault*.

American Independence and the loss of the transportation route to America.[26] Faced with food shortages in the winter of 1797–8, Bentham returned to the Panopticon to provide a model for wide-scale poor relief.[27] In 1816–17, Bentham sought to build a version of the Panopticon in his own garden as part of a project to provide schools for the children of the trading middle-classes.[28] Finally, at the end of his career, Bentham used the panoptic layout for government offices in the *Constitutional Code*.[29]

These were not just copycat projects. They were adapted to different users and aims. Foucault wrote that the Panopticon is a multi-use structure which can house 'a child learning to write, a worker at work, a prisoner correcting himself, a madman living in madness'.[30] He was correct, but he forgets about ministers of state.[31] Their inclusion changes our understanding of the accountability and deliberative features embedded in the design. Admittedly, Foucault acknowledged that the Panopticon was not meant to be a tyrannical machine. Indeed, he conceded, 'The seeing machine [. . .] has become a transparent building in which the exercise of power may be supervised by society as a whole.'[32] Such a more nuanced perspective influenced his later characterisation of biopolitics.[33] But his lack of early insight has made it difficult to think of the Panopticon beyond surveillance.

In describing the Panopticon, Foucault identified permanent visibility and isolation as key features.[34] However, Bentham quickly abandoned isolation, as

---

[26] For background on crime and punishment at the end of the eighteenth century, see Ignatieff, *Just Measure of Pain*; Davie, *Penitentiary Ten*. For Bentham's prison Panopticon project, see Bentham, *Panopticon; or the Inspection-House*; Bentham, 'Postscript, Part I'; Bentham, 'Postscript, Part II'. For major secondary sources on the pauper Panopticon, see Himmelfarb, 'Haunted House'; Semple, *Bentham's Prison*; Guidi, '"My Own Utopia"'.

[27] For Bentham's writings on the poor laws, see Bentham, *Essays on the Subject of the Poor Laws*; Bentham, *Pauper Systems Compared*; Bentham, *Outline of a Work entitled Pauper Management Improved*. For major secondary sources on the pauper Panopticon, see Zagday, *Bentham and the Poor Law*; Himmelfarb, *Idea of Poverty*; Bahmueller, *National Charity Company*; Quinn, 'Jeremy Bentham and the Relief of Indigence'; Quinn, 'Fallacy of Non-interference'; Brunon-Ernst, *Contrôle ou autonomie*; Brunon-Ernst, *Le panoptique des pauvres*; Brundage, *Making of the New Poor Law*.

[28] See Bentham, *Chrestomathia*.

[29] Bentham, 'Architectural Arrangements', 442.

[30] Foucault, 'Truth and Juridical Forms', 58. See also similar descriptions in Foucault, *Psychiatric Power*, 74–5. Both texts were written in 1973. The later chapter 3 in *Discipline and Punish* exhibits the same features two years later.

[31] Bentham, *Constitutional Code*.

[32] Foucault, *Discipline and Punish*, 207.

[33] Laval, 'La chaîne invisible'; Laval, 'Ce que Foucault a appris de Bentham'; Brunon-Ernst, *Utilitarian Biopolitics*.

[34] Foucault, *Psychiatric Power*, 103–4.

posing mental health risks to inmates, and even provided for limited privacy within the cells. Moreover, there are reasons to call into question the stress on isotopy in panopticism. Foucault believed that one key to the panoptic system lay in the way it ascribed a definite space to each individual in the system. This might be true in the prison and the poorhouse, but is erroneous in the school-room where the economy and efficacy of teaching relies on students moving across academic classes according to proficiency.[35] Lastly, 'everything that the individual does and says, is graded and recorded',[36] wrote Foucault. Again, while this may be true in most cases, Bentham allows for government secrecy as a protection of the privacy of individual applications in certain circumstances.

Key to Foucault's definition of panopticism is the idea that the norms imposed by the institution are being internalised by users, thanks to the con-stant monitoring gaze. But this too has been questioned.[37] Some academics have pointed out that the term 'internalisation' is anachronistic in the context of late eighteenth-century Britain. Indeed, they argue that the Panopticon tapped into the leverage of unremitting pressure of social observation on the individual to modify the nature of self and ultimately reform them according to the institution's aim.[38] The Panopticon relied on peer pressure rather than on the yet unknown psychological springs of internalisation.

Panopticism, therefore, needs to be understood as the reinterpreta-tion of the Panopticon to suit Foucault's own strategic narrative. However, Foucault was neither the first nor the last to use the panoptic motif to suit his own ends. By and large, in surveillance studies the Panopticon has been read exclusively through the lens of Foucault's interpretation, rendering it indistinguishable from panopticism.[39]

3. Panopticism in Surveillance Theories

There are three stances towards the relevance of panopticism to the study of sur-veillance: acceptance, rejection or qualified application. Several arguments may initially cause us to lean towards an outright rejection. First, the Panopticon, and indeed the related concept of discipline, is often rejected as no longer relevant in our digital age.[40] Second, the absence of resistance in panoptic surveillance –

---

[35] Ibid., 52–3.
[36] Ibid., 48–52.
[37] Foucault, *Discipline and Punish*, 201.
[38] Rosen and Santesso, *Watchman in Pieces*; Rosen and Santesso, 'Panopticon Reviewed'.
[39] Brunon-Ernst, 'La matrice panoptique'.
[40] Lianos, 'Social Control after Foucault', 413; Boyne, 'Post-Panopticism', 293; Poster, *Mode of Information*; Norris and Armstrong, *Maximum Surveillance Society*; Bauman, 'Social Issues'; Lyon, *Surveillance Society*.

the observation that the Panopticon is an unrealistic fantasy of absolute compliance[41] – is often identified as a shortcoming. Third, sociologists point to the rise in consumer society,[42] where enjoyment imperatives are paramount[43] and rank above any attempt at reforming the individual,[44] to show that the panoptic model is irrelevant. Crime prevention systems, for example, track objects rather than individuals.[45] Nevertheless, the resilience of the panoptic image in surveillance studies is evident in the multiplicity of its metaphoric uses: Super-Panopticon,[46] Post-Panopticon,[47] Electronic Panopticon,[48] Omnicon,[49] Ban-opticon,[50] Global Panopticon,[51] Panspectron,[52] Myoptic Panopticon,[53] Fractal Panopticon,[54] Industrial Panopticon,[55] Urban Panopticon,[56] Pedagopticon,[57] Polypticon,[58] Synopticon,[59] panoptic discourse,[60] social panopticism,[61] Cybernetic Panopticon,[62] Neo-Panopticon;[63] the list goes on. First, these metaphors point to one group which is controlled through isolation; second, the central monitoring gaze remains key to the panoptic analogy; third, surveillance is understood as exacting inescapable compliance; fourth, the Panopticon is all-pervasive; and fifth, it is presented as a mode of governing individuals.

4. Panopticism Revised in the Digital Age

For some, the emergence of the digital world has created a new paradigm. As Sabot exposes in Chapter 2 of this collection, exposure is the main mode

---

[41] Boyne, 'Post-Panopticism', 295; Mann, Nolan, and Wellman, 'Sousveillance', 333.
[42] Boyne, 'Post-Panopticism', 297.
[43] Bauman, 'On Post-modern Uses of Sex', 23; Vaz and Bruno, 'Types of Self-Surveillance', 281.
[44] Lianos, 'Social Control after Foucault', 423.
[45] Ibid., 426.
[46] Poster, *Mode of Information*.
[47] Boyne, 'Post-Panopticism.'
[48] Lyon, 'An Electronic Panopticon?'
[49] Groombridge, 'Crime Control or Crime Culture TV?'
[50] Bigo, 'Security'.
[51] Gill, 'Global Panopticon'.
[52] DeLanda, *War in the Age of Intelligent Machines*.
[53] Leman-Langlois, 'Myopic Panopticon'.
[54] De Angelis, 'Global Capital'.
[55] Butchart, 'Industrial Panopticon'.
[56] Koskela, '"Cam Era"'.
[57] Sweeny, 'Pedagopticon'.
[58] Allen, '"See You in the City!"'
[59] Mathiesen, 'Viewer Society'.
[60] Berdayes, 'Traditional Management Theory'.
[61] Wacquant, 'Penalisation of Poverty'.
[62] Bousquet, 'Space, Power and Globalization'.
[63] Mann, Nolan, and Wellman, 'Sousveillance'.

of identity formation. Harcourt traces the shift from the security concerns of biopolitical post-panoptic eras to a paradigm of enjoyment which characterises digital surveillance in the era of social networking. Technology makes it possible to target people individually at a low cost. Information is freely surrendered. Pleasure not reformation is the new catchphrase. Yet something of the Panopticon remains. Indeed, as Sabot argues, the language of exposure and that of surveillance cannot be entirely separated from each other; on the contrary, each is implicated in the other.

First, total awareness. Harcourt still thinks that some classic forms of the juridical exercise of power have survived into the digital age. If he thinks that the symmetries and asymmetries are different, he acknowledges that there is the same desire for 'total awareness' as in the Panopticon. Second, spatial metaphors endure in our efforts to understand the digital world. In the past, spatial metaphors were instrumental in describing discrete eras: the age of the spectacle was represented by the arena, that of disciplines by the Panopticon, and that of consumerism by the Mall of America. But even when he tries to characterise the digital world, Harcourt uses spatial images: the crystal palace and the steel cage.

IV. Fictional Panopticon

This chapter began with a quote by Judith Butler on the recent pandemic. In the same interview, she goes on to say:

> Our public institutions would do well to help us think through different media about persistence and loss, what connects and divides humans across communities, languages and regions, and what role the critical imagination has during times in which crisis and futurity are clearly the issues.[64]

Beyond the utopian or dystopian stands that one can take in relation to the pandemic Butler exhorts us to embrace 'critical imagination'. This last part therefore explores fictional Panopticons as a means of imagining, critically, what the future holds.[65]

1. Panoptic Fiction as Mode of Resistance

The investigation of surveillance issues arises in novels in contexts in which their authors make explicit or implicit reference to the Panopticon.[66] Panoptic

---

[64] Yancy, 'Judith Butler: Mourning is a Political Act'.

[65] Some elements of the present discussion have been developed in previous research with Wrobel. See Wrobel and Brunon-Ernst, 'Variations littéraires contemporaines'; Brunon-Ernst and Wrobel, 'Prisons in Panoptic Fiction'.

[66] For the relevance of the panoptic metaphor in literature or as a critical tool, see discussion in Bender, *Imagining the Penitentiary*; Miller, *The Novel and the Police*; Cohn, 'Optics and Power'.

fiction thus identifies a distinct genre.[67] Unsurprisingly, direct references to the Panopticon crop up mainly in works of fiction set in a prison environment. Panoptic fiction is a form of discourse which reflects reality,[68] foretells and anticipates reality,[69] and thus offers a particular response to the challenges the modern penitentiary poses by highlighting its abuse and inefficiency. Panoptic novels participate in the debate on the reform of the contemporary penitentiary, but literary criticism and fiction reinterpret the original Benthamite and Foucauldian panoptic projects for their own purposes. Thus, fiction does not provide a consistent critical discourse on the prison system.[70] Artists make strategic use of the Panopticon/panopticism features to enhance an artistic effect or to make a political point. The panoptic thus is presented as necessarily dystopic and aims to be critical of the failure of contemporary penitentiary systems and of a society that cannot deal with crime otherwise than through confinement and punishment. Panoptic fiction is not only about mapping modes of surveillance but also about showing how individuals navigate their place within a surveilled environment. This is where the concept of resistance becomes key to the genre.

Resistance is a concept that we have already encountered earlier on in this chapter. It was one of the reasons why the Panopticon was rejected as a fitting metaphor in surveillance studies. Indeed, there does not seem to be the possibility of resistance in Bentham's panoptic projects. This is precisely what makes it simultaneously utopian and dystopian. However, Foucault shows that resistance is coeval with the exercise of power.[71] And indeed, fiction fleshes out the various means of resistance available to the subject of the panoptic gaze, through images of prison riots,[72] drives of sex and desire,[73] writing and imagining one's future or identity,[74] and the satirical reversal of

---

[67] See for example Orwell, *Nineteen Eighty-Four*; Carter, *Nights at the Circus*; Willocks, *Green River Rising*; McGrath, 'Vigilance'; Fagan, *The Panopticon*; Eggers, *The Circle*.

[68] Nussbaum, *Poetic Justice*.

[69] See Bender, *Imagining the Penitentiary*, 1: 'Vehicles, not reflections of social change'; Rosen and Santesso, *Watchman in Pieces*, 10: 'novelists have often . . . been generators of [. . .] surveillance history'.

[70] Fludernik, 'Panopticisms'.

[71] This would be to misunderstand the strictly relational character of power relationships. Their existence depends on a multiplicity of points of resistance: these play the role of adversary, target, support, or handle in power relations. These points of resistance are present everywhere in the power network. Hence there is no single locus of great Refusal [. . .]. Instead there is a plurality of resistances.' Foucault, *The History of Sexuality*, 95–6.

[72] Willocks, *Green River Rising*.

[73] Carter, *Nights at the Circus*.

[74] Fagan, *The Panopticon*.

the Panopticon as a doughnut[75] or a zoo.[76] As Tadié suggests in Chapter 3 of this collection, satirical fiction is both a way of understanding the Panopticon and a way of resisting it.

The Circle by Dave Eggers is a novel on surveillance which exemplifies how art, and the novel in particular, participates in the project of giving imaginative specificity to the call for resistance. The following section analyses how surveillance – and resistance to it – are portrayed in James Ponsoldt's film adaptation of the book.

2. From Panopticon to The Circle

The Circle, starring Emma Watson and Tom Hanks, tells the story of a young graduate, Mae Holland (played by Watson), hired to work in a flashy tech company (owned by a tycoon played by Hanks) and chosen to be part of an experiment, called 'going fully transparent', which consists in having each moment in one's life live-streamed on social media.[77] Commentators on the novel and its adaptation focus on its genre: is it utopian or dystopian? Margaret Atwood in a review describes it as a 'satirical utopia',[78] a label rejected by Lyon, who points out the mainly dystopian features of the narrative and concludes that 'the world Mae is so enamored with – and in the end won over by – appears utopian but is in fact dystopian'.[79] The interest of the utopian/ dystopian discussion for the present chapter is how it links up with panoptic features in *The Circle*. As Tadié shows in Chapter 3, the tradition of satirical utopias is precisely to show how close the line between utopia and dystopia is, and specifically the dual effect of surveillance in this respect.

While there is no direct mention of the Panopticon, indirect references are rife in the logo of the company, its name and the architecture of its head-quarters. Lyon points to the Bentham-like features in the character of Baley.[80] Panoptic surveillance is also present in the story-line through the transparency of the glass building settings, the live feed of workers' private and work-related communications, fixed and mobile CCTV footage in public and private spaces, the round-shaped miniature camera, the storage of large amounts of data, and so on. In a similar vein, Atwood writes, 'What happens to us if we must be "on" all the time? Then we're in the twenty-four hour glare of the supervised prison. To live entirely in public is a form of solitary confinement.'[81]

---

[75] Carter, *Nights at the Circus*.
[76] Willocks, *Green River Rising*.
[77] Ponsoldt, *The Circle*.
[78] Atwood, 'When Privacy is Theft'.
[79] Lyon, *Culture of Surveillance*, 170–1.
[80] Ibid.
[81] Atwood, 'When Privacy is Theft'.

The Circle takes an intriguingly balanced approach. It identifies the benefits and cost-effectiveness of surveillance in relation to crime (unapprehended
convicts can be found in a matter of minutes), health (Mae's father has MS),
personal safety (Mae almost drowns and is saved by CCTV footage called
SeeChange) and reformation (Mae comes clean about having broken the law
by trespassing and borrowing a kayak at night); but also the drawbacks of
giving access to so much personal data to a company. Ultimately, the narrative overcomes the risk of misuse of personal data by a full and effective
application of the core principle of transparency. Bentham would certainly
have subscribed to such a step, though Foucault, as noted above, has far less
to say about it. Full transparency is applied not only to workers and politicians, but also to the CEOs and founders of the tech giant. In so doing, *The
Circle* furnishes a sympathetic narrative in which true adherence to panoptic
principles of mutual and reversible transparency prevents the abuse of power.

From the perspective of the present research, which investigates resistance to surveillance, the ending of *The Circle* is both unexpected and baffling. Just where we might have expected a call for better privacy protection,
such as that advanced in Chapter 5 of this volume by Gligorijević, the film
moves in a different direction. Fleshed out by Eric Stoddart, the concept
of 'surveillance *for* others'[82] highlights the positive outcomes arising from
certain types of surveillance. This concept is a forerunner of French phi-
losopher Cynthia Fleury's 'bien(sur)veillance', the latest type of surveillance
to be born at the time of COVID-19,[83] which theorises the use of surveillance technologies in the field of health as a benevolent and efficient tool to
fight the pandemic. The benevolent aim of electronic surveillance echoes a
certain nineteenth-century paternalism, artfully circumventing any fears of
hi-tech invasions of privacy by 'the dubious promise that these technologies are [. . .] the indispensable keys to keeping ourselves and our loved
ones safe',[84] as Gligorijević points out in Chapter 5. The conclusion to *The
Circle* echoes this trend. It channels resistance away from calls to overhaul
the system to gear it towards its beneficial use. Would this mean trading
privacy for security?

We do not yet know how surveillance will change in the age of COVID-19,
from telehealth to remote working and learning to humanless contactless technologies, all of it generating and exploiting an unprecedented stream of data.[85] We
can be sure, however, of a rise in Panopticon-inspired works of fiction critically

[82] Stoddart, *Theological Perspectives*.
[83] Fleury, 'Journal d'une confinée'.
[84] Klein, 'How Big Tech Plans to Profit from the Pandemic'.
[85] Klein writes about 'pandemic shock doctrine' or the 'Screen New Deal' in ibid.

mirroring our rapidly changing reality. In that respect, *The Circle* might be construed as a model of a panoptic narrative in the digital age.

V. Conclusion: Out-Dated Model?

Harcourt explains that ready-made, off-the-shelf, dystopian Panopticon analogies are inadequate to reflect on the new challenges of our digital post-COVID age. Notwithstanding this damning assessment, the panoptic paradigm is clearly not dead. Major publications hail the death of panopticism, but in so doing reassert the importance of the panoptic paradigm.[86] In the field of surveillance and critical studies, law and fiction, there is still room for panopticism as a methodological and substantive tool. Above all, it is through fiction that the Panopticon reveals its value as a mode of resistance. Indeed, the panoptic metaphor fulfils a very important function: it taps into the collective psyche and activates primal fears that individuals can have of surveillance and loss of liberties and self. As Lyon explains, 'imaginaries provide the sense of what living with surveillance entails'.[87] Very few works of fiction offer an even-handed view of panoptic surveillance; yet *The Circle* achieves a delicate balance, highlighting in the process new avenues of resistance to make surveillance a force for good.

VI. Bibliography

Allen, Matthew. '"See You in the City!" Perth's Citiplace and the Space of Surveillance.' In *Metropolis Now: Planning and the Urban in Contemporary Australia*, edited by Katherine Gibson and Sophie Watson, 137–47. Sydney: Pluto, 1994.

Atwood, Margaret. 'When Privacy is Theft: Dave Egger's "The Circle".' *The New York Review of Books*, 21 November 2013.

Bahmueller, Charles. *The National Charity Company: Jeremy Bentham's Silent Revolution.* Berkeley: University of California Press, 1981.

Bartos, Michael. 'Panopticon in Your Pocket.' *Inside Story*, 27 April 2020.

Bauman, Zygmunt. 'On Post-modern Uses of Sex.' In *Love and Eroticism*, edited by Mike Featherstone, 19–23. London: Sage, 1999.

———. 'Social Issues of Law and Order.' *British Journal of Criminology* 40 (2000): 205–21.

Beccaria, Cesare. *On Crimes and Punishments, and Other Writings.* 1764. Edited by Richard Bellamy. Cambridge: Cambridge University Press, 1995.

Bender, John. *Imagining the Penitentiary: Fiction and the Architecture of Mind in Eighteenth-Century England.* Chicago: University of Chicago Press, 1987.

---

[86] See Gary Marx's comment on the back cover of Lyon, *Theorizing Surveillance*: 'This volume paradoxically serves both to undermine and strengthen the idea of panopticism as a theoretical construct.'

[87] Lyon, *Culture of Surveillance*, 33.

Bentham, Jeremy. *Chrestomathia*. Edited by M. J. Smith, W. H. Burston, and L. J. Hume. Oxford: Clarendon, 1983.

———. *Chrestomathia*. 1816–17. Edited by Jean-Pierre Cléro. Paris: Cahiers de l'Unebévue, 2004.

———. *Constitutional Code*. Edited by F. Rosen, J. H. Burns, and L. J. Hume. Oxford: Clarendon, 1983.

———. *Essays on the Subject of the Poor Laws*. 1797. In *The Collected Works of Jeremy Bentham: Writings on the Poor Laws*, edited by Michael Quinn, vol. 1, 1–140. Oxford: Oxford University Press, 2001.

———. *Outline of a Work entitled Pauper Management Improved*. 1797. In *The Works of Jeremy Bentham*, edited by John Bowring, vol. 8, 369–439. Bristol: Thoemmes Press, 1995.

———. *Panopticon; or the Inspection-House: Containing the Idea of a New Principle of Construction Applicable to Any Sort of Establishment, in Which Persons of Any Description Are to Be Kept under Inspection*. 1790. In *The Works of Jeremy Bentham*, edited by John Bowring, vol. 4, 37–172. Elibron Classics, 2005.

———. *Pauper Systems Compared, or A Comparative View of the Several Systems Establishable as well as Established in Relation to the Poor*. 1797. In *The Collected Works of Jeremy Bentham: Writings on the Poor Laws*, edited by Michael Quinn, vol. 1, 141–216. Oxford: Oxford University Press, 2001.

———. *The Works of Jeremy Bentham*. Edited by John Bowring. Edinburgh: W. Tait, 1843.

Berdayes, Vicente. 'Traditional Management Theory as Panoptic Discourse: Language and the Constitution of Somatic Flows.' *Culture and Organization* 8 (2002): 35–49.

Bigo, Didier. 'Security, Exception, Ban and Surveillance.' In *Theorizing Surveillance: The Panopticon and Beyond*, edited by David Lyon, 46–68. Cullompton: Willan Publishing, 2006.

Bousquet, G. 'Space, Power and Globalization: The Internet Symptom.' *Societies* 4 (1998): 105–13.

Boyne, Roy. 'Post-Panopticism.' *Economy and Society* 29, no. 2 (2000): 285–307.

Brundage, Anthony. *The Making of the New Poor Law: The Politics of Inquiry, Enactment, and Implementation, 1832–1839*. New Brunswick, NJ: Rutgers University Press, 1978.

Brunon-Ernst, Anne, ed. *Beyond Foucault: New Perspectives on Bentham's Panopticon*. Aldershot: Ashgate, 2012.

———. *Contrôle ou autonomie: Les propositions de Jeremy Bentham sur l'assistance aux pauvres en Angleterre, 1795–1798*. Lille: ANRT, 2004.

———. 'La matrice panoptique dans les formes contemporaines de la surveillance.' In *Deux siècles d'utilitarisme*, edited by Malik Bozzo-Rey and Émilie Dardenne, 145–56. Rennes: Presses universitaires de Rennes, 2011.

———. *Le panoptique des pauvres: Jeremy Bentham et la réforme de l'assistance en Angleterre*. Paris: Presses de la Sorbonne Nouvelle, 2007.

———. 'Les métamorphoses panoptiques: de Foucault à Bentham.' *Cahiers critiques de philosophie* 4 (2007): 60–71.

————. *Utilitarian Biopolitics: Bentham and Foucault on Modern Power*. London: Chatto and Pickering, 2012.

Brunon-Ernst, Anne, and Claire Wrobel. 'Dystopic Prisons in Panoptic Fiction.' CLAH Research Seminars, Australian National University, 24 July 2019.

Butchart, Alexander. 'The Industrial Panopticon: Mining and the Medical Construction of Migrant African Labour in South Africa, 1900–1950.' *Social Science and Medicine* 42, no. 2 (1996): 185–97.

Carter, Angela. *Nights at the Circus*. London: Chatto & Windus, 1984.

Christie, Ian. *The Benthams in Russia, 1780–1791*. Oxford: Berg, 1993.

Cohn, Dorrit. 'Optics and Power in the Novel.' *New Literary History* 26, no. 1 (1995): 3–20.

Cottell, Fran, and Marianne Mueller. 'From Pain to Pleasure: Panopticon Dreams and Panopticon Petal.' In *Bentham and the Arts*, edited by Anthony Julius, Malcolm Quinn, and Philip Schofield, 244–69. London: UCL Press, 2020.

Davie, Neil. *The Penitentiary Ten: The Transformation of the English Prison, 1770–1850*. Oxford: Bardwell Press, 2017.

De Angelis, M. 'Global Capital, Abstract Labour, and the Fractal Panopticon.' *The Commoner 2001*, no. 2 (2004): 1–19.

DeLanda, Manuel. *War in the Age of Intelligent Machines*. New York: Zone, 1991.

Eggers, Dave. *The Circle*. London: Hamish Hamilton, 2013.

Fagan, Jeni. *The Panopticon*. London: Windmill Books, 2013.

Fleury, Cynthia. 'Journal d'une confinée, par Cynthia Fleury: "Nous entrons dans une ère de bien(sur)veillance".' *Télérama*, 9 April 2020.

Fludernik, Monika. 'Panopticisms: From Fantasy to Metaphor to Reality.' *Textual Practice* 31, no. 1 (2017): 1–26.

Foucault, Michel. *The Birth of Biopolitics: Lectures at the Collège de France 1978–1979*. Edited by Michel Senellart. Translated by Graham Burchell. New York: Palgrave Macmillan, 2008.

————. *Discipline and Punish: The Birth of the Prison*. 1975. Translated by Alan Sheridan. London: Allen Lane, 1977.

————. *Essential Works of Michel Foucault, 1954–1984. Vol. 3: Power*. Edited by James D. Faubion. Translated by Robert Hurley and others. New York: New Press, 2000.

————. *The History of Sexuality*. 1976. Translated by Robert Hurley. London: Penguin Books, 1998.

————. *Le pouvoir psychiatrique: cours au Collège de France, 1973–1974*. Edited by Michel Senellart. Paris: Gallimard, 2003.

————. *Psychiatric Power: Lectures at the Collège de France, 1973–74*. Edited by Jacques Lagrange. Translated by Graham Burchell. New York: Palgrave Macmillan, 2006.

————. *Surveiller et punir: naissance de la prison*. 1975. Paris: Gallimard, 2000.

————. 'Truth and Juridical Forms.' In *Essential Works of Michel Foucault, 1954–1984. Vol. 3: Power*, 1974, edited by James D. Faubion, translated by Robert Hurley and others, 1–89. London: Penguin Books, 2001.

Gill, Stephen. 'The Global Panopticon: The Neo-liberal State, Economic Life, and Democratic Surveillance.' *Alternatives* 20, no. 1 (1995): 1–49.

Groombridge, Nic. 'Crime Control or Crime Culture TV?' *Surveillance & Society* 1, no. 1 (2003): 30–45.

Guidi, Marco. '"My Own Utopia". The Economics of Bentham's Panopticon.' *European Journal of Economic Thought* 11, no. 3 (2004): 405–31.

Harcourt, Bernard E. *Exposed: Desire and Disobedience in the Digital Age.* Cambridge, MA: Harvard University Press, 2015.

Himmelfarb, Gertrude. 'The Haunted House of Jeremy Bentham.' In *Victorian Minds*, 32–81. New York: Knopf, 1968.

———. *The Idea of Poverty: England in the Early Industrial Age.* London: Faber, 1985.

Ignatieff, Michael. *A Just Measure of Pain: The Penitentiary in the Industrial Revolution.* London: Macmillan, 1978.

Klein, Naomi. 'How Big Tech Plans to Profit from the Pandemic.' *The Guardian*, 13 May 2020. https://www.theguardian.com/news/2020/may/13/naomi-klein-how-big-tech-plans-to-profit-from-coronavirus-pandemic.

Koskela, Hille. '"Cam Era" – the Contemporary Urban Panopticon.' *Surveillance & Society* 1, no. 3 (2003): 292–313.

Laval, Christian. 'Ce que Foucault a appris de Bentham.' *Revue d'études benthamiennes* 8 (2011). http://etudes-benthamiennes.revues.org/259.

———. 'La chaîne invisible.' *Revue d'études benthamiennes* 1 (2006). http://etudes-benthamiennes.revues.org/63.

Leman-Langlois, Stéphane. 'The Myopic Panopticon: The Social Consequences of Policing through the Lens.' *Policing and Society* 13, no. 1 (2003): 43–58.

Leroy, Marie-Laure. 'Le panoptique inversé: théorie du contrôle dans la pensée de Jeremy Bentham.' In *La production des institutions*, edited by Christian Lazzeri, 155–77. Besançon: Presses universitaires Franc-Comtoises, 2002.

Lianos, Michalis. 'Social Control after Foucault.' *Surveillance & Society* 1, no. 3 (2003): 412–30.

Lyon, David. *The Culture of Surveillance: Watching as a Way of Life.* Cambridge: Polity, 2018.

———. *The Electronic Eye: The Rise of Surveillance Society.* New ed. Cambridge: Polity, 1994.

———. 'An Electronic Panopticon? A Sociological Critique of Surveillance Theory.' *The Sociological Review* 41, no. 4 (1993): 653–78.

———. *Surveillance Society: Monitoring Everyday Life.* Buckingham: Open University Press, 2001.

———, ed. *Theorizing Surveillance: The Panopticon and Beyond.* Cullompton: Willan Publishing, 2006.

Lyons, David. *In the Interest of the Governed.* Oxford: Oxford University Press, 1973.

McGrath, Patrick. 'Vigilance.' *Conjunctions* 14 (1989): 198–209.

Mann, Steve, Jason Nolan, and Barry Wellman. 'Sousveillance: Inventing and Using Wearable Computing Devices for Data Collection in Surveillance Environment.' *Surveillance & Society* 1, no. 3 (2003): 331–55.

Mathiesen, Thomas. 'The Viewer Society: Michel Foucault's "Panopticon" Revisited.' *Theoretical Criminology* 1, no. 2 (1997): 215–34.

Miller, D. A. *The Novel and the Police*. Berkeley: University of California Press, 1989.

Monahan, Torin. 'Surveillance as Cultural Practice.' *The Sociological Quarterly* 52 (2011): 495–508.

Norris, Clive, and Gary Armstrong. *The Maximum Surveillance Society: The Rise of CCTV.* Oxford: Berg, 1999.

Nussbaum, Martha Craven. *Poetic Justice: The Literary Imagination and Public Life.* Boston, MA: Beacon Press, 1995.

Orwell, George. *Nineteen Eighty-Four*. London: Penguin Classics, 2021.

Ponsoldt, James, director. *The Circle*. STX Entertainment, 2017. 1 h., 50 min.

Poster, Mark. *The Mode of Information: Poststructuralism and Social Context.* Chicago: University of Chicago Press, 1990.

Quinn, Michael. 'The Fallacy of Non-interference: The Poor Panopticon and Equality of Opportunity.' *The Journal of Bentham Studies* 1 (1997). http://www.ucl.ac.uk/Bentham-Project/journal.

———. 'Jeremy Bentham and the Relief of Indigence: An Exercise in Applied Philosophy.' *Utilitas* 6 (1994): 81–96.

Rosen, David, and Aaron Santesso. 'The Panopticon Reviewed: Sentimentalism and Eighteenth-Century Interiority.' *ELH* 77, no. 4 (2010): 1041–59.

———. *The Watchman in Pieces: Surveillance, Literature, and Liberal Personhood.* New Haven, CT: Yale University Press, 2013.

Semple, Janet. 'Bentham's Haunted House.' *The Bentham Newsletter* 11 (1987): 35–44.

———. *Bentham's Prison: A Study of the Panopticon Penitentiary.* New York: Clarendon, 1993.

Stoddart, Eric. *Theological Perspectives on a Surveillance Society: Watching and Being Watched.* London: Routledge, 2011.

Sweeny, Robert W. 'The Pedagopticon: Other Eyes in the 21st Century Classroom.' *Journal of Social Theory in Art Education* 28/29 (2009): 30–41.

Vaz, Paulo, and Fernanda Bruno. 'Types of Self-Surveillance: From Abnormality to Individuals "at Risk".' *Surveillance & Society* 1, no. 3 (2003): 272–91.

Wacquant, Loïc. 'The Penalisation of Poverty and the Rise of Neo-liberalism.' *European Journal on Criminal Policy and Research* 9 (2001): 401–12.

Willocks, Tim. *Green River Rising*. New York: Avon, 1995.

Wrobel, Claire, and Anne Brunon-Ernst. 'Variations littéraires contemporaines autour du panoptique de Jeremy Bentham: une histoire fantasmée de l'administration pénitentiaire.' Colloque du CERSA 'Des scribes et des écrivains: une histoire littéraire de l'administration', Université Paris-Panthéon-Assas, 6–7 June 2019.

Yancy, George. 'Judith Butler: Mourning is a Political Act Amid the Pandemic and Its Disparities.' Interview. *Truthout*, 30 April 2020. https://truthout.org/articles/judith-butler-mourning-is-a-political-act-amid-the-pandemic-and-its-disparities/.

Zagday, M. I. *Bentham and the Poor Law*. London: G. W. Keeton and G. Schwarzenbeger, 1948.

7

Online Undercover Investigations and the Role of Private Third Parties

Peter Grabosky and Gregor Urbas

I. Introduction

Over the past quarter century, a great deal of crime has migrated from physical space to cyberspace. What was formerly achieved with a can of spray paint can now be engineered with SQL injections and file transfer protocols.[1] Extortion demands, once made face to face, by letter or through a telephone call, can now be made online. Extortion payments, previously delivered in a paper bag or briefcase, can now be accomplished by electronic funds transfer.[2] Sexually explicit images of children, once circulated by hand or purchased in disreputable bookstores, are now reproduced and disseminated instantaneously, in real time. Adults no longer need to lurk near schoolyards to arrange illicit assignations, preferring less obtrusive encounters in chatrooms frequented by young people.[3]

Predictably, a great proportion of criminal investigation has also migrated to cyberspace. Cyber forensics, once an esoteric specialty, is becoming increasingly central to crime control. Law enforcement agencies are scrambling to keep abreast of their criminal adversaries. Accompanying the activities of state agencies are those of private citizens. Just as police in recent years have invited a degree of citizen 'co-production' in conventional crime control through initiatives such as Neighbourhood Watch and Crimestoppers, contemporary law enforcement agencies have established online reporting protocols and hotlines. The FBI's *Internet Crime Complaints Center (IC3)* and the Australian *ReportCyber* are two examples.[4]

---

[1] Balduzzi et al., *Deep Dive.*

[2] Grabosky, Smith, and Dempsey, *Electronic Theft.*

[3] Davidson and Gottschalk, *Internet Child Abuse.*

[4] Federal Bureau of Investigation, *Internet Crime Complaint Center*; Australian Cyber Security Centre, *ReportCyber*; Chang, Zhong, and Grabosky, 'Citizen Co-production'; Cheong and Gong, 'Cyber Vigilantism'.

Throughout history, state police have used covert or undercover methods to complement more visible, transparent investigative techniques. The reasons are pragmatic: certain types of activity, such as serious organised crime and complex criminal conspiracies, are less amenable to interdiction by means of overt, conventional police practices.

Undercover policing has been described as a 'necessary evil' because of its potential for misuse. By their very nature, covert methods are open to abuse and to the avoidance of accountability. One need look no further than totalitarian states of the twentieth century for grim illustrations. But even in democratic states that present themselves as paragons of governmental accountability and champions of human rights, abuses can and do occur.[5]

Covert policing is by no means the monopoly of state policing and security services. Nor, as the editors of this volume note, is it a uniquely modern phenomenon. Private individuals, members of non-governmental organisations and commercial entities have all engaged in investigation for a variety of motives, including a sense of civic responsibility, moral indignation or commercial gain. In Chapter 3 of this volume, Alexis Tadié reminds us that concerns about the 'surveillance state' go back centuries. Jonathan Wild, a private investigator in early eighteenth-century London, made a comfortable living recovering stolen property for a fee. He was regarded as so successful that he was consulted by the Privy Council regarding methods of crime control. On the side, he operated a gang of thieves who ensured an ongoing demand for his services.[6]

The cultural basis of surveillance noted in the Introduction to this volume was strongly evident throughout the history of the United States. It could be seen in the vigilante tradition during the westward expansion throughout much of the nineteenth century, and in the practice of lynching in southern states from the end of the Civil War until well into the twentieth century.[7] Concerned citizens in early twentieth-century New York engaged private investigators to infiltrate brothels, gambling dens and radical political organisations. Disapproving of such practices as racial mixing, entirely legal in New York at the time, they reported these objectionable pastimes to the police.[8]

And just as agencies of the state may transgress the law and avoid accountability, so too can non-state actors.

This chapter explores the use of covert online investigative methods by state agencies, and by individuals and institutions in civil society. Our focus is primarily on active investigations of online child exploitation. The universe of

---

[5] Marx, *Undercover*; Fijnaut and Marx, *Undercover: Police Surveillance*.
[6] Howson, *Thief-Taker General*.
[7] Brown, *Strain of Violence*; Marx and Archer, 'Citizen Involvement'; Garland, 'Penal Excess'.
[8] Fronc, *New York Undercover*; Hochschild, 'All-American Vigilantes'.

	Public	**Private**
Passive	Police 'patrolling' chatrooms	Private actors 'patrolling' chatrooms Citizen 'hotlines' for reporting anomalies
Active	Police stings Undercover impersonation Police hacking	Citizen vigilantes Citizen hackers Citizen impersonators

Figure 7.1 Typology of online undercover investigation.

online undercover investigations may be mapped according to Figure 7.1. On the vertical axis, investigations may be *passive or active*. Passive investigations are limited to the collection of information available in locations accessible to the public. *Active* investigations involve deceptive techniques such as impersonation of a child, or the facilitation of child exploitation online. The horizontal axis differentiates between *state* investigations conducted by public officials, and *private* activities undertaken by non-state actors.

We deal in this chapter with activities represented as taking place in the lower half of Figure 7.1. In particular, we are concerned with two types of investigative activity: (1) an investigator's active deceptive impersonation of a child, or of a facilitator of child exploitation, online; and (2) techniques of accessing and compromising information systems used for the purpose of child exploitation. While these investigative methods may have a legitimate place in contemporary crime control, they are not without disadvantages. We look first at their potential for abuse by state agencies, and the remedies available to the targets of illegal or otherwise questionable state practices. We then turn to non-state investigators, and note that the targets of private investigation have even less protection.

It should be noted, of course, that many investigations involve cooperation between public and private actors. For example, police may draw on expertise or information held by individuals or corporations in the commercial world, such as the Microsoft Digital Crimes Unit.[9] Other examples of public–private interaction in law enforcement are plentiful.[10] But given

---

[9] Microsoft Digital Crimes Unit, 'Digital Crimes Unit'.
[10] Ayling, Grabosky, and Shearing, *Lengthening the Arm of the Law.*

the potential for abuse by public and private actors when operating independently, we will make some observations about how their collaboration, orchestrated or spontaneous, should be managed with great caution.

We conclude by articulating some standards by which the propriety of state and non-state covert online investigative activity, separate or collaborative, may be evaluated. Bearing in mind the focus of this volume, and noting in particular the argument mounted by Gligorijević for the centrality of privacy in liberal democratic society, one might ask just how much surveillance – public, private or hybrid – can be justified?[11]

II. Investigative Practices by State Agents

Covert investigation may use various technologies. These can include telecommunications interception, the installation of listening devices, compromising and accessing information systems, imaging, infiltration of a target organisation, active deceptive impersonation, passive observation, and, in recent years, Big Data analytics.[12]

Whatever the tools employed, investigation may serve a number of objectives. These include the acquisition of intelligence, the disruption of a criminal enterprise, and – our primary focus here – the collection of evidence for use in a criminal prosecution. The use of technologies may necessitate a search warrant, the specificity of which will vary across jurisdictions. In the United States, whose constitutional foundations were influenced profoundly by the draconian system of crime control established during the reign of King George III, search warrants must specify in considerable detail the nature of evidence to be sought, and the anticipated location of the evidence in question. Similar requirements exist in Australia.[13]

In the United States, the abuse of power by government agents did not end with the War of Independence. Decades of overzealous policing led to considerable restraints on state power, to the extent that evidence collected by illegal means, from coerced confessions to the fruits of warrantless searches, is generally inadmissible in criminal proceedings. Here we explore two basic

---

[11] See Gligorijević, Chapter 5 of this collection.
[12] Marx, *Windows into the Soul*; Završnik, *Big Data*; Harcourt, *Exposed*.
[13] For example, under s.3E(5) of the Crimes Act 1914 (Cth), a search warrant issued by an officer must state: (a) the offence to which the warrant relates; (b) a description of the premises to which the warrant relates or the name or description of the person to whom it relates; (c) the kinds of evidential material that are to be searched for under the warrant; (d) the name of the constable who, unless he or she inserts the name of another constable in the warrant, is to be responsible for executing the warrant; (e) the time at which the warrant expires; and (f) whether the warrant may be executed at any time or only during particular hours.

principles relating to evidence obtained as a result of questionable practices by law enforcement: entrapment and outrageous government conduct.

1. Entrapment

In *Sorrells v United States*, the United States Supreme Court defined entrapment as the 'conception and planning of an offense by an officer, and his procurement of its commission by one who would not have perpetrated it except for the trickery, persuasion, or fraud of the officer'.[14] When the defence of entrapment is raised, the government, in order to negate or rebut it, must show that the accused was predisposed to commit the crime. Entrapment, in other words, relates to the state of mind of the defendant. Sorrells, found by the court to have been 'an industrious, law-abiding citizen', had sold a bottle of whisky following 'repeated and persistent solicitation'[15] by an undercover prohibition agent representing himself as a fellow veteran of World War I. In essence, the issue of entrapment is a question of fact, to be presented to the jury.

A more recent entrapment case involved Mr Jacobson, who had purchased a publication containing pictures of underage males at a time when such publications were entirely legal. Some weeks later, following the enactment of the Child Protection Act 1984, the material became proscribed by law. As part of an aggressive campaign to enforce the new legislation, United States government agencies obtained the mailing lists of the bookseller from whom Jacobson had bought the magazine. Over the course of twenty-six months, the United States Postal Service and United States Customs Service sent Jacobson repeated overtures from bogus civil liberties and opinion research organisations, urging him to purchase the illicit materials. He finally did so and was convicted. Jacobson appealed to the United States Supreme Court, which found in his favour. The court held that 'the prosecution must prove beyond reasonable doubt that the defendant was disposed to commit the criminal act prior to first being approached by Government agents'.[16]

2. Outrageous Government Conduct

Outrageous government conduct, by contrast, focuses on the *conduct of the police*. In *Rochin v California* the United States Supreme Court held that it could 'nullify any state law if its application shocks the conscience'.[17] Rochin had swallowed two suspicious capsules in the presence of police officers

---

[14] *Sorrells v United States*, 287 U.S. 435 (1932) at 454.
[15] Ibid. at 441.
[16] *Jacobson v United States*, 503 U.S. 540 (1992) at 549.
[17] *Rochin v California*, 342 U.S. 165 (1952) at 175.

following their warrantless entry into his residence. He was then forcibly taken to a hospital and immobilised while a tube was pushed into his mouth and an emetic solution injected into his stomach. The regurgitated capsules were found to have contained morphine. Unlike entrapment, which rests on a finding of fact by the jury, the determination of whether the conduct of law enforcement is sufficiently outrageous to constitute a denial of due process is determined by the court. In *United States v Russell*, the Supreme Court addressed policing practices 'so outrageous that due process principles would absolutely bar the government from invoking judicial process to obtain a conviction'.[18]

3. 'Hybrid Improprieties' in Other Common Law Jurisdictions

In contrast to United States jurisprudence, other common law countries offer no defence of entrapment or outrageous conduct *per se*.[19] This involves a balancing exercise, requiring

> the weighting against each other of two competing requirements of public policy, thereby seeking to resolve the apparent conflict between the desirable goal of bringing to conviction the wrongdoer and the undesirable effect of curial approval, or even encouragement, being given to the unlawful conduct of those whose task it is to enforce the law.[20]

The Australian case of *Ridgeway* is illustrative. Ridgeway was a convicted drug offender, who, upon his release from prison, contacted a fellow ex-prisoner, Lee, who had been deported to Malaysia. The objective was to import a quantity of heroin into Australia. Unbeknownst to Ridgeway, his accomplice had become a registered informer for the Royal Malaysian Police Force. A joint operation between Malaysian and Australian police services resulted in the arrival in Australia of Lee, his supervisor (an undercover Malaysian police officer) and the heroin. The operation culminated in Ridgeway's arrest when he took possession of the drugs. Ridgeway was convicted, and he appealed.

The High Court of Australia held that there was no substantive defence of entrapment under Australian law. A trial judge may exclude evidence illegally or otherwise improperly obtained, when concerns for the integrity of the judicial process outweigh the public interest in convicting the guilty. At the

---

[18] *United States v Russell*, 411 U.S. 423 (1973) at 431.
[19] Hofmeyr, 'Problem of Private Entrapment'.
[20] *Bunning v Cross* (1978) 141 CLR 54, per Stephen and Aickin JJ at 74–5 discussing the Australian and English authorities.

time, Australian laws prohibiting the importation of drugs provided for no exceptions. Therefore, both Australian and Malaysian police had themselves engaged in criminal activities. The High Court noted that penalties for heroin importation were extremely severe. Ridgeway's conviction was quashed and a permanent stay on any further prosecution on the importation offences was ordered.[21]

Following the *Ridgeway* decision, the Commonwealth Parliament of Australia speedily enacted legislation authorising 'controlled operations' by police, which has since been expanded to include covert investigations of serious crimes other than drug offences.[22] In particular, the list of 'serious Commonwealth offences' for the investigation of which a controlled operations authorisation may be sought includes those involving 'misuse of a computer or electronic communications' and 'dealings in child abuse material'. At around the same time, the law of evidence was largely codified in Commonwealth statute, with the common law public policy discretion reformulated in terms of an exclusionary rule, so that illegally or improperly obtained evidence is 'not to be admitted unless the desirability of admitting the evidence outweighs the undesirability of admitting evidence that has been obtained in the way in which the evidence was obtained'.[23]

The common law has either evolved or been statutorily modified in a similar manner in other common law countries. In the United Kingdom, for example, the Police and Criminal Evidence Act 1984 (PACE) provides for the discretionary exclusion of evidence

[21] *Ridgeway v The Queen* (1995) 184 CLR 19, with a majority of 6:1 in favour of allowing the appeal. In a dissenting judgment, McHugh J would have dismissed the appeal on the basis that the police conduct did not induce the commission of the crime: 'The appellant's possession of the heroin was the result of his own initiatives, formed without any inducement from the police officers.'

[22] Part IAB of the Crimes Act 1914 (Cth), and note also Part IAC dealing with assumed identities. Similar authorisations can be found in all Australian jurisdictions. Both kinds of authorisation may be used in the investigation of online child exploitation, though there is no legal requirement that necessitates their use.

[23] Section 138 of the Evidence Act 1995 (Cth); with a list of factors that the court must take into account including: (a) the probative value of the evidence; (b) the importance of the evidence in the proceeding; (c) the nature of the relevant offence, cause of action or defence and the nature of the subject-matter of the proceeding; (d) the gravity of the impropriety or contravention; (e) whether the impropriety or contravention was deliberate or reckless; (f) whether the impropriety or contravention was contrary to or inconsistent with a right of a person recognised by the International Covenant on Civil and Political Rights; (g) whether any other proceeding (whether or not in a court) has been or is likely to be taken in relation to the impropriety or contravention; and (h) the difficulty (if any) of obtaining the evidence without impropriety or contravention of an Australian law.

if it appears to the court that, having regard to all the circumstances, including the circumstances in which the evidence was obtained, the admission of the evidence would have such an adverse effect on the fairness of the proceedings that the court ought not to admit it.[24]

4. Online Entrapment

Digital technology lends itself to entrapment, as illustrated by the following case from the United States. Mark Poehlman, a married father of two children, disclosed to his wife that he had an irresistible desire to wear women's clothing. This confession met with her considerable displeasure, leading to their divorce. In addition, Poehlman was dismissed from the United States Air Force, where he had served honourably for seventeen years.

In search of a new partner, he joined an online chat group devoted to alternative lifestyles. There, he made online contact with a person called Sharon. With complete candour, and seeking to establish a sustainable romantic partnership, he freely revealed his fashion preferences. Sharon seemed potentially receptive but focused persistently on her three daughters. After a lengthy exchange of emails, it became clear that she was seeking a partner who would provide participatory sex education to her children. Desperate to find a companion, Poehlman agreed, and travelled to California to meet them. Sharon welcomed Poehlman to California, presented him with pornographic magazines and photographs of her children, and invited him to meet them in an adjoining room. There he was greeted not by 'Sharon's' daughters, but by her colleagues: federal and state law enforcement agents.

Based on his conduct upon arrival in California, Poehlman was charged and convicted under state law of attempted lewd acts with a minor. As a result, he served one year in prison. Two years after his release, he was charged and convicted under United States federal law for a crime relating to his behaviour leading up to the same incident, namely crossing state lines for the purpose of engaging in sex acts with a minor. For this, he was sentenced to 121 months in federal prison. Poehlman appealed his conviction, claiming that the idea of crossing state lines for illegal purposes was implanted only after extensive email correspondence with the FBI (in other words, Sharon), and there was no evidence of predisposition. His appeal was upheld.[25]

5. Outrageous Government Conduct in Cyberspace

The case of outrageous government conduct is a difficult one to make, in cyberspace no less than in the physical world. A recent case from the State of

---

[24] Stone, 'Exclusion of Evidence', 4. See also Bronitt, 'Sang is Dead', for a comparative perspective.
[25] *Poehlman v United States*, 217 F.3d 692 (2000).

Washington involved a female detective posing as a young girl in an online chatroom ostensibly catering for adults. She engaged with the defendant, Solomon, who claimed that he had relied on the web banner statement that individuals in the chatroom were over eighteen years old. During the conversation, the detective made the statement that, 'Oh, by the way, I'm 14, almost 15.' Solomon replied, 'I'm not willing to get into trouble [. . .] maybe hit me up in 3 years if your [sic] still around [. . .] I take everything back not interested at all this is a setup by cops or a website good luck to you.'

The detective persisted, but despite Solomon's attempts to discontinue the relationship on seven occasions, the chats continued. The detective sent scores of messages, some shockingly explicit, to Solomon about wanting to meet him for sex. The suspect found them irresistible.[26] The trial judge called the language used by the detective in the messages 'repugnant' and dismissed all charges. The State appealed, but the appeal was unsuccessful, the Court of Appeals holding that the trial court was entirely justified in exercising its discretion to dismiss the charges against Solomon.

Elsewhere, seductive communication alone is not enough to support a claim of outrageous government conduct. In one Ohio case, it was asserted by the defence that an undercover investigator had sent the suspect a photograph that was 'so overly enticing that use of it by [the investigator] was outrageous'. The appeals court held that 'the photograph may have been sufficient in the Defendant's mind to warrant driving [. . .] five hours from Tennessee, but is not so overwhelming to launch a thousand ships. The Helen of Troy Defense is not applicable here.'[27]

An Ohio court has also held that a motion to dismiss based on outrageous government conduct required two factors: (1) that the offence in question was created by the state; and (2) the investigation involved an element of coercion.[28] This could also be found to include repeated and persistent overtures, combined with evidence of significant reluctance on the part of the target, as reported in *Jacobson* and *Solomon*.[29]

In 2015, the FBI arrested the administrator of The Playpen, a child pornography Internet bulletin board on the 'dark web'.[30] Unbeknownst to thousands of Playpen users, the FBI immediately took over administration of the site, and operated it for two weeks. The transition was seamless,

[26] The language used was too graphic for reproduction in this chapter. See *State v Solomon*, Court of Appeals of the State of Washington No. 76298-2-I. 29 May 2018, available at http://www.courts.wa.gov/opinions/pdf/762982.pdf.

[27] *State v Cunningham*, 156 Ohio App.3d 714, 2004-Ohio-1935 at 720.

[28] *State v Bolden*, 2004-Ohio-2315.

[29] More, Lee, and Hunt, 'Entrapped in the Web?'

[30] Chen, 'Graymail Problem'; Mayer, 'Government Hacking'.

and the bulletin board thrived under government stewardship. The FBI quickly obtained a warrant to install what it called a Network Investigative Technique (NIT) on the Playpen servers. The NIT consisted of malware allowing the FBI access to the computers of Playpen users, regardless of their location in physical space. Hundreds of arrests followed, including Kim's. Although many suspects in the Playpen investigation challenged the validity of the warrant on the grounds of jurisdiction and insufficient specificity, Kim took issue with the FBI's management of the website when it became apparent that at least 22,000 pictures, videos and links to child pornography were downloaded during the period of FBI administration. Kim's counsel moved to dismiss the indictment, on the grounds that each of the downloads was a criminal offence, and that thousands of such actions thereby constituted outrageous government conduct.

In *United States v Kim*,[31] the court held that any harm to third parties was offset by benefits flowing from the investigation. As the government asserted in a previous case, the FBI maintained that its agents regularly assessed the continued benefits of the investigation and shut the website down as soon as it concluded that the costs of the operation outweighed the benefits. In addition, it claimed to have continuously monitored postings to the website and took immediate action where it determined that a child was in imminent danger. Forty-nine children subjected to abuse were reportedly identified or rescued as a result.[32] The court held that Kim's rights had not been infringed; any harm that may have befallen third parties was irrelevant to his case.

In Australia, courts have discretion to exclude evidence obtained by illegal or improper means.[33] Despite some intriguing defence arguments, the power has not been used to exclude evidence of child grooming activities detected by undercover officers posing as children. Indeed, in an illustrative Australian Capital Territory Supreme Court case, the (then) Chief Justice quoted the Gospel of St Matthew in support of his Honour's view that community attitudes towards such offences and offenders 'would support the use of covert operations to detect them in a manner that does not place an actual young person at risk'.[34]

---

[31] *United States v Kim*, 16-CR-191 (PKC) (E.D.N.Y. Jan. 27, 2017).

[32] The court in *Kim* noted the government's submission to the court in a case arising from the same investigation, *United States v Anzalone* 2016 WL 6476939 at 4.

[33] Evidence Act 1995 (Cth), s.138.

[34] *R v Stubbs* [2009] ACTSC 63 (26 May 2009), per Higgins CJ at [69]–[70]. See also *R v Priest* [2011] ACTSC 18 (11 February 2011), which arrived at a similar conclusion in relation to a joint Australian–United States covert operation that targeted a defendant who was engaged in grooming underage boys. In neither of these cases were controlled operations authorisations used, as police acted on the basis that no illegality was involved in these sting operations. See Urbas, 'Protecting Children'.

Jurisdictions whose domestic laws impose restraints on investigative practices may benefit from circumstances in which legally questionable methods have been tacitly 'outsourced' to willing foreign agencies. When a friendly foreign police service acquires evidence through illegal means, should this evidence be admissible in those jurisdictions whose laws forbid such practices on the part of their own investigators?[35] Queensland Police Task Force Argos, whose investigative practices are relatively unconstrained, is reported to be a potential partner sought after by foreign law enforcement agencies.[36]

III. Investigative Practices by Private Actors

1. Vigilante Hacking

Police have traditionally drawn on third parties such as individuals, community groups and businesses to provide information and assistance in specific cases or, more broadly, to assist in crime prevention and surveillance. This information can be provided by third parties unilaterally, as the result of an explicit request, or pursuant to an open invitation. The information in question may be collected by legal or illegal means. Its disclosure may be voluntary or required by law.[37] Our concern here is with unilateral private covert investigations by individuals or hacker groups.

Law enforcement and security agencies are not alone in their occasional inclination to engage in overzealous conduct. As noted elsewhere in this collection, surveillance practices in the digital age are transforming every aspect of social life. An exclusive focus on the power of the state will fail to appreciate both the extent and the perils of excessive surveillance. In 2011, the hacker group Anonymous undertook a unilateral campaign of harassment against online purveyors of child pornography, briefly disrupting the service of forty sites, and publishing the names of 1,500 alleged users of 'Lolita City'.[38] Feminist groups have targeted online misogynists.[39] In Thailand, fascist vigilante groups use Facebook to engage with political dissidents, then report them to the police.[40] 'Cyber troops' in the Philippines, encouraged

---

[35] Kerr and Murphy, 'Government Hacking'; Warren, Mann, and Molnar, 'Lawful Illegality'.
[36] By contrast, Taskforce Argos must have used controlled operations authorisations to compromise child exploitation websites and fora, to administer them for months at a time, and for evidence obtained in the process to be presented in court. See Bleakley, 'Watching the Watchers'.
[37] Ayling, Grabosky, and Shearing, *Lengthening the Arm of the Law*; Greenwald, *No Place to Hide*; Chang, Zhong, and Grabosky, 'Citizen Co-production'.
[38] BBC News, 'Hackers Take Down'.
[39] Jane, 'Online Misogyny'.
[40] Schaffar, 'New Social Media'.

by the state, orchestrate campaigns of bullying and harassment against critics of the government.[41]

Individuals too have engaged in criminal conduct explicitly to assist law enforcement. In July 2000, police in Montgomery, Alabama, received an email from an anonymous individual, 'Unknownuser', who claimed to be in Turkey. The message was accompanied by material depicting an adult person abusing a girl aged five or six years. Unknownuser wrote, 'I know his name, Internet account, home address, and I can see when he is online. What should I do? PS he is a Doctor or Paramedic.'

Unknownuser had accessed a chatroom frequented by devotees of child pornography. There he inserted a Trojan horse virus allowing him access to the computers of chatroom visitors, including one Dr Steiger. The matter was referred to the FBI, whose agents obtained a warrant and conducted a search of the suspect's residence. The search produced an abundance of incriminating evidence. Steiger was convicted and received a seventeen-and-a-half-year prison sentence. He appealed on the grounds that the evidence was obtained pursuant to an illegal search by Unknownuser, who had become an agent of the state. The United States Court of Appeals held that Unknownuser had acted at all times as a private individual and that the government was a passive recipient of unsolicited information. Steiger's appeal was dismissed. The FBI agent who had been in contact with Unknownuser thanked him and said, 'If you want to bring other information forward, I am available.'[42]

After a hiatus of several months, Unknownuser again contacted the Montgomery Police and identified another suspected child pornography offender, one William Jarrett. The Montgomery officer obtained the evidence collected by Unknownuser and forwarded it to the FBI. A prosecution ensued. At the trial, the defence argued that an agency relationship existed between the government and the hacker, and that evidence derived from Unknownuser should be suppressed. The court denied the motion, and Jarrett entered a conditional plea of guilty to one count of manufacturing child pornography. Prior to sentencing, the government disclosed an earlier email exchange between Unknownuser and the FBI. It revealed that following Jarrett's arrest, the FBI agent on the case had thanked Unknownuser for his assistance. The agent added:

> I cannot ask you to search out cases such as the ones you have sent us [. . .] but if you should happen across such pictures as the ones you have sent us and wish us to look into the matter, please feel free to send them to us [. . .] We also have no desire to charge you with hacking.[43]

[41] Sombatpoonsiri, *Manipulating Civic Space.*
[42] *United States v Steiger* 318 F.3d 1039 (2003).
[43] *United States v Jarrett*, 338F.3d 339 at 343.

This disclosure prompted the defence to file a new motion to suppress the evidence on the grounds that an agency relationship existed between the government and Unknownuser. The motion succeeded and the evidence was suppressed. The government then appealed, successfully, with the court holding that prior affirmative encouragement by the state is required for a search to be deemed a government search. Communications after the arrest of the suspect had no bearing on the admissibility of evidence obtained earlier in the investigation. The court further held that the government was under no obligation to affirmatively discourage Unknownuser from hacking.

Far from the activities of the Turkish cyber-vigilante, a self-styled 'private computer cop' from Canada devised a Trojan horse virus that allowed him access to between 2,000 and 3,000 computers being used to visit websites of interest to paedophiles. In May 2000, a California Judge visited such a website for reasons unrelated to his profession, and inadvertently downloaded the Trojan. The Canadian 'cop' collected incriminating evidence, which he then forwarded to a citizens' group active against child pornography. The group in turn brought it to the attention of United States authorities, and a prosecution followed. In the federal court, defence counsel argued that the vigilante thought of himself as an agent for law enforcement, and that he was motivated to act for law enforcement purposes. This, said the defence, made him an agent of the state, and thereby implicated the Fourth Amendment bar to the admissibility of evidence gathered as a result of searches subsequent to and derived from the vigilante's criminal act. The United States Court of Appeals held that these considerations were insufficient. It reaffirmed that some degree of government knowledge of, and acquiescence in, the search before the fact is essential for the private party to be deemed a state agent.[44]

2. Entrapment by Private Actors

The issue of private entrapment has been easily resolved, at least as far as United States law is concerned. In one case, an adult male attempted to contact a young female on her MySpace page. Upon learning of this, the child's mother set up her own MySpace page under an assumed name, pretending to be a fifteen-year-old girl. The male made contact with her as well, and after a series of chats he asked her for sex. She reported this to the FBI, who took over the investigation. Appealing his conviction, the offender claimed that the person he thought was a minor was not a law enforcement officer, but was rather a private person who had entrapped him. The appeals court seized upon this opportunity to reaffirm that there is no defence of private entrapment, so there is no exclusionary

---

[44] *United States v Kline*, 112 Fed Appx. 562 (2004).

rule applicable to evidence obtained in such a manner by private persons. The court held that, if any remedy existed, it lay in prosecuting the vigilante.[45] In the United Kingdom, a defendant entrapped by a private party also remains culpable, although a stay of prosecution is potentially available in cases where the actions of the private party constitute 'sufficiently gross' misconduct.[46]

At least in theory, the remedy of prosecuting the vigilante is also available in cases of other third party illegality, such as hacking. Online vigilantes may be at risk of committing numerous other crimes in the course of their efforts to assist the state. By providing illegal content to a target in an effort to establish trust or create an opportunity to commit crime, a vigilante investigator may be committing an offence. By pretending to be a minor, a vigilante may be engaging in criminal impersonation, if the relevant law is sufficiently broad.[47] By inviting an adult suspect to engage in illegal activity, the vigilante may be implicated in a criminal conspiracy or be seen to be inciting, or aiding and abetting, a criminal act.[48] However, it would seem that, absent egregious behaviour or evidence of ulterior motives on their part, vigilantes can usually operate with impunity. Both Unknownuser and the Canadian self-styled cyber cop were located outside the United States. To activate the machinery of mutual assistance and extradition may be cumbersome and time consuming. Law enforcement agents in most jurisdictions may be disinclined to turn against the very individual who has done them a service, even when a crime has been committed in the process. A few notable exceptions are discussed below.

Using an online avatar posing as a young Filipina girl called 'Sweetie' in chatrooms known to be frequented by adults seeking webcam sex encounters with children, Dutch researchers for the Swiss child protection organisation Terre des Hommes in 2013 detected thousands of apparent child predators and were able to provide identifying information to police in numerous cases, leading to prosecutions in Australia and elsewhere. A more sophisticated

---

[45] *United States v Morris* 549 F.3d 548 (2008). See also Yaffe, "'The Government Beguiled Me'".

[46] *R v TL* Court of Appeal (Criminal Division) [2018] EWCA Crim 1821 at 32. See Starke, 'Non-State Entrapment'.

[47] Under New York law, criminal impersonation is committed when an individual '[i]mpersonates another and does an act in such assumed character with intent to obtain a benefit or to injure or defraud another'. NY Penal Law § 190.25.

[48] Police are generally protected against liability for aiding and abetting the commission of criminal offences as part of their undercover work, by virtue of the fact that they lack the requisite accessorial criminal intent that the offence be completed; rather, they are usually engaged in the effort to prevent offences such as child abuse from occurring. However, where there is any doubt, mechanisms such as controlled operations and assumed identities authorities can be used, which serve both to protect investigators from liability and ensure the legality of the exercise and the admissibility of evidence thereby obtained.

version, 'Sweetie 2.0' involving artificial intelligence chatbot functionality, shows that such investigations can in principle be automated and scaled up to new levels. However, the legality of police being able to use such techniques depends very much on each country's legislation and judicial limits on covert online investigations, with some drawing the line at entrapment.[49]

3. Downside Risks of Online Vigilante Activity

Fifty years ago, Marx and Archer noted that citizen involvement in law enforcement processes posed a greater risk of miscarriage, and serious conse- quences of abuse, than did public policing alone.[50] These warnings are no less apposite today. Notwithstanding the benefits of citizen contributions to the control of online child exploitation, private investigation can entail signifi- cant social costs. These may be borne by the targets of investigation, as well as by innocent third parties. In addition, vigilante investigations may impair the criminal process and erode the rule of law more generally.[51] We focus first on the adverse unintended consequences of covert investigations to targets and to third parties.

In Adelaide, Australia, a vigilante who had reported two alleged child sex offenders to police was himself arrested and charged with aggravated assault against one of his targets while attempting a 'citizen's arrest'. In addition, the vigilante was charged with two counts of using a carriage service to menace, harass or cause offence, and one count of publishing the identity of a person charged with a sexual offence, an offence under South Australian law.[52]

In the UK, two men were allegedly blackmailed by a paedophile hunter and later physically beaten by groups of people when their identities were disclosed. Both the vigilante and the two men were charged.[53] Elsewhere in the UK, members of a group called Letzgo Hunting identified a target, who was beaten and otherwise threatened when his image was posted online. He was compelled to quit his job and relocate elsewhere in Britain. Police reviewed the materials collected by the vigilante group and found no evidence of any sexual offences.[54]

Being caught in a sting can result in much more than humiliation or a beating. Another target of Letzgo Hunting was tempted by an online imper- sonation of a fourteen-year-old female, only to be confronted at their agreed meeting place by the impersonator, an adult male. The target committed

---

[49] Terre des Hommes, *Sweetie 2.0*; Schermer et al., *Legal Aspects of Sweetie*.
[50] Marx and Archer, 'Citizen Involvement'.
[51] Kosseff, 'Hazards of Cyber-Vigilantism'.
[52] Dowdell, 'Self-Proclaimed Paedophile Hunter Arrested'. A 'carriage service' is *not* a mode of transportation but rather refers to a telecommunications facility.
[53] Sabin, 'Vigilante Paedophile Hunter Arrested'.
[54] Booth, 'Vigilante Paedophile Hunters Ruining Lives'.

suicide.[55] 'Perverted Justice', an anti-paedophile group in the United States, collaborated with local police and a major television network to orchestrate a sting targeting a public prosecutor in Texas. The operation was to be broadcast as part of the television series *To Catch a Predator*. For dramatic effect, the sting culminated in a raid on the suspect's home by a police SWAT team. As police entered his home, the suspect took his own life. His surviving sister sued the television network for damages, and the case was settled out of court for an undisclosed amount.[56]

Gratuitous harm to an alleged offender may arise from private motives such as revenge, vindictiveness or greed in addition to moral indignation and perceived civic responsibility. One case, ostensibly involving the intended public shaming of four suspected offenders, elicited accusations of ulterior motives on the part of the vigilante. Explicit 'selfie' images and texts posted by the four to a person thought to be a young female were published on a website. A lawyer for the four implied that the website was a profitmaking venture, reliant on advertising revenue and donations for income. He is quoted as having said, 'This website is a total scam. They're not solving crimes. They don't report people to the authorities. They're just making money.'[57] The lawyer succeeded in having the website taken down, only to have it reappear shortly thereafter in another location. The four threatened to sue for criminal impersonation and for theft of intellectual property, claiming that their moral rights in their images and texts had been violated.

A variety of other cases reported in the United Kingdom and Australia illustrate the risks to both vigilante and suspected offender that may arise from private enforcement.[58] Moreover, harm to third parties is not uncommon in the annals of police undercover investigation.[59] The targets of a vigilante investigation may have family members or other close associates, entirely innocent of wrongdoing, who themselves may be stigmatised or harassed as a result of disclosures.

4. Interference with Police Operations

Police value citizen assistance, but only to a point. 'Wannabe cyber cops' can get underfoot. They can tamper with evidence, intentionally or accidentally.[60]

[55] BBC News, 'Letzgo Hunting'.
[56] *Conradt v NBC Universal, Inc.*, 07 Civ. 6623, United States District Court (S.D. New York); Stelter, 'NBC Settles'.
[57] Gregorian, 'Four Men Ensnared'.
[58] Crabtree, '"Vigilante" Ryan Naumenko'; Campbell, 'Suspended Sentence'; Gorrey, 'Canberra Teen'; Rowe, 'Adam Brookes'; Portelli, 'Paedophile-Hunter'.
[59] Joh and Joo, 'Sting Victims'.
[60] e Silva, 'Vigilantism and Cooperative Criminal Justice'.

They can create crime and, as we have seen, use their purported 'good works' to mask criminal activity of their own. Non-intrusive investigative methods may also go astray, and even genuine civic-minded individuals can impede police investigations. Nhan et al. report that citizens seeking to contribute to identifying perpetrators of the Boston Marathon bombings in 2013 misidentified several individuals as potential suspects. Police were deluged with communications from citizens, compounding the burdens they were facing, under time pressures in an urgent situation with the perpetrators still at large.[61]

To their credit, police in a number of jurisdictions have been known to issue public statements advising well-meaning citizens (and those not so well-meaning) to act within the law. Primary concerns are the risk of jeopardising investigations, by inadvertently alerting the target, or impeding the collection of evidence. There is also the risk that the integrity of that evidence which has been collected may have been corrupted.

Regarding the Adelaide case discussed above, a senior South Australian detective was quoted as warning, '[i]t is not appropriate for individuals to take matters into their own hands because no matter how well intentioned they may be, this can significantly obstruct and hinder what police are empowered to do.' Noting the potential for violence in such matters, he added, '[t]here is a very real risk to both parties when someone chooses to take the law into their own hands.'[62]

A forty-seven-year-old Welshman, who fifteen years earlier had been convicted for possession of indecent images of children, was convicted in 2015 after posing as a young girl and eliciting indecent images from unwitting men. By embedding computer viruses in his communications, he was able to obtain the men's personal details and additional incriminating material. Over a period of two and half years, he made approximately £40,000 by blackmailing his targets. He was convicted of thirty-one offences and sentenced to nine years' imprisonment. In response to this sentence, a South Wales Police Detective remarked, 'I hope this will send a clear message that we take blackmail and computer hacking offences very seriously – in whatever context they are conducted.'[63]

5. Aggravation of Systemic Pathologies

Unregulated private searches may have an adverse impact on the criminal process and on society more generally. When police passively condone, or

---

[61] Nhan, Huey, and Broll, 'Digilantism'.
[62] Dowdell, 'Self-Proclaimed Paedophile Hunter Arrested'.
[63] Readhead, '"Paedophile Hunter" Jailed'.

even actively approve of, vigilante illegality, it may be perceived as encouraging it. When evidence illegally obtained by private actors is admitted in court, this may be seen as the court's implicit imprimatur. The court's independence or authority may be tarnished by explicit indifference to inappropriate police conduct, or by seeming to tolerate questionable private conduct.

The normative unity of the criminal process is such that questionable behaviour by one institution – police, prosecution or the judiciary (unless that institution is held unambiguously to account) – reflects adversely on all three. If the provision for acquittal or for exclusion of evidence on grounds of outrageous conduct or entrapment is intended to protect the integrity of the judicial process, prosecution based on similarly dubious activity by a 'private party investigator' likewise risks undermining the legal system. In theory, the independence of each of these institutions should serve as a check on the potential transgressions of the others. In practice, this is not always the case.

IV. Safeguards and Remedies

What steps might be taken to reduce the risks of abuse intrinsic to undercover investigations? First, they should not be employed gratuitously. Rare indeed is the law enforcement agency that can boast of more resources than it needs. If online child exploitation is as rampant as it is said to be, more strategic application of limited resources is in order. Second, the targeting of investigations should be focused. Rather than lurking in websites ostensibly established for legitimate purposes, such as adult dating and alternative lifestyles, detectives should aim for sites more explicitly devoted to criminal activity. Third, the procedures for engaging with targets should be closely circumscribed. Investigators should avoid persistent, unrelenting pursuit of a target who has expressed repeated reluctance to engage. It might be useful to compare the guidelines governing online investigations by the New Zealand Police with the investigative techniques employed in the *Solomon* case.[64]

These guidelines, of course, pertain to state officials, and not to private individuals. Given the complexity and sensitivity of criminal investigation, private individuals are at risk of harming targets and third parties well beyond what the law will tolerate. The above cases illustrate an unfortunate paradox: protections from overzealous investigation by agents of the state, themselves far from perfect, are not matched by safeguards against abuses by private citizens.

There may be no simple solutions to this conundrum. The provision of official guidelines to non-state actors may render them agents of the state,

---

[64] New Zealand Police, *Principles of Practice for Investigating On-line Grooming of Children under 16*. Reproduced in *R v Stubbs* [2009] ACTSC 63.

which could risk contamination of any prosecution that might flow from their efforts. In the meantime, it seems appropriate for law enforcement agencies firmly to apply the law when it is transgressed by vigilantes, and to continue publicly to discourage vigilante activities based on criminal conduct. The situation is even more complex when the illegal investigative activity, whether undertaken by a citizen or by a state agent, originates in a foreign jurisdiction. Of course, the state may still encourage the reporting of suspected criminal conduct occurring within public view, in cyberspace as on the street. But it should make it abundantly clear that any criminal activity engaged in by private citizens, no matter how well-meaning, will attract criminal sanctions.

V. Conclusion

Digital technology has transformed surveillance to the extent that it has become all but ubiquitous. Its enthusiastic embrace by security and policing agencies is evident throughout the world. In some states surveillance is undertaken responsibly, in others it is not. Undercover investigation appears to have become an indispensable method in response to cybercrime generally, and to online child exploitation in particular. In theory, abuses by government agents are subject to the accountability of the judicial process, at least in those jurisdictions that adhere to the rule of law and respect the rights of the accused. But the democratisation of digital technology has enabled ordinary citizens to assume the role of amateur 'cyber cops', for better or worse. The advent of social media has been a boon for Internet vigilantism. Not only has it created spaces to facilitate illicit overtures, but it has enabled the formation of vigilante communities. Today, any person with Internet access can create his or her own sex offender registry. One might question the extent to which law or policy should foster an ethos of bounty hunting that would not have been unfamiliar to Jonathan Wild. The state should certainly not create opportunities for extortion. A twenty-first-century democracy should not glorify, much less legitimise, the criminal activities of its citizens.

Rules of evidence and procedure quite rightly exist to protect the judicial process from contamination by the abuse of state power. Laws and guidelines exist to ensure the integrity of state investigative practices. But when the state passively condones private illegality in furtherance of public policy, it may subtly encourage high-tech lynching. If citizen involvement in online undercover investigation has a place in any jurisdiction, citizens should be held to a level of accountability no less than those required of agents of the state.

VI. Acknowledgements

An earlier version of this chapter was published in the *International Journal of Cyber Criminology*, January–June 2019. Vol. 13(1): 38–54. Reprinted with permission. It is based on prior presentations to the Tilburg Institute for Law, Technology, and Society (TILT), Netherlands, 2017; The National Judicial College of Australia, 2017; the British and Irish Law Education and Technology Association (BILETA) Conference, Braga, Portugal, 2017 (Urbas); and the School of Criminal Justice at Michigan State University, 2018 (Grabosky).

VII. Bibliography

Australian Cyber Security Centre, *ReportCyber*. https://www.cyber.gov.au/acsc/report.

Ayling, Julie, Peter Grabosky, and Clifford Shearing. *Lengthening the Arm of the Law: Enhancing Police Resources in the Twenty-First Century*. Cambridge: Cambridge University Press, 2009.

Balduzzi, Marco, Ryan Flores, Lion Gu, and Federico Maggi with Vincenzo Ciancaglini, Roel Reyes, and Akira Urano. *A Deep Dive into Defacement: How Geopolitical Events Trigger Web Attacks*. Irving, TX: Trend Micro, 2018. https://documents.trendmicro.com/assets/white_papers/wp-a-deep-dive-into-defacement.pdf.

BBC News. 'Hackers Take Down Child Pornography Sites.' *BBC News*, 24 October 2011. http://www.bbc.com/news/technology-15428203.

———. 'Letzgo Hunting Denies Blame for Man's Suicide.' *BBC News*, 18 September 2013. http://www.bbc.com/news/uk-england-leicestershire-24145142.

Bleakley, Paul. 'Watching the Watchers: Taskforce Argos and the Evidentiary Issues Involved with Infiltrating Dark Web Child Exploitation Networks.' *The Police Journal: Theory, Practice and Principles* 92, no. 3 (2019): 221–36.

Booth, Robert. 'Vigilante Paedophile Hunters Ruining Lives with Internet Stings.' *The Guardian*, 26 October 2013. https://www.theguardian.com/uk-news/2013/oct/25/vigilante-paedophile-hunters-online-police.

Bronitt, Simon. 'Sang is Dead, Loosely Speaking.' *Singapore Journal of Legal Studies* (2002): 374–87.

Brown, Janelle. 'Cyber Angels Antiporn Database Dies.' *Wired*, 14 March 1997. https://www.wired.com/1997/03/cyber-angels-antiporn-database-dies/.

Brown, Richard Maxwell. *Strain of Violence: Historical Studies of American Violence and Vigilantism*. New York: Oxford University Press, 1975.

Campbell, Claire. 'Suspended Sentence for Murray Bridge Man Who Tortured Elderly Man He Met on Grindr.' *ABC News*, 21 April 2021. https://www.abc.net.au/news/2021-04-20/man-who-tortured-elderly-man-after-meeting-on-grindr-sentenced/100080142.

Chang, Lennon, Lena Zhong, and Peter Grabosky. 'Citizen Co-production of Cyber Security: Self-Help, Vigilantes, and Cybercrime.' *Regulation and Governance* 12, no. 1 (2016): 101–14.

Chen, Christine. 'The Graymail Problem Anew in a World Going Dark: Balancing the Interests of the Government and Defendants in Prosecutions Using Network Investigative Techniques (NITs).' *Columbia Science and Technology Law Review* 19, no. 1 (2018): 185–215.

Cheong, Pauline, and Jie Gong. 'Cyber Vigilantism, Transmedia Collective Intelligence, and Civic Participation.' *Chinese Journal of Communication* 3, no. 4 (2010): 471–87.

Crabtree, Richard. '"Vigilante" Ryan Naumenko Avoids Jail after Exposing Mildura's "Creeps" Online.' *ABC Mildura-Swan Hill*, 24 May 2021. https://www.abc.net.au/news/2021-05-24/vigilante-ryan-naumenko-avoids-prison-in-mildura/100161746.

Davidson, Julia, and Petter Gottschalk, eds. *Internet Child Abuse: Current Research and Policy.* Abingdon: Routledge, 2011.

Dowdell, Andrew. 'Self-Proclaimed Paedophile Hunter Arrested, Charged with Assault and Revealing Identity of Person Charged with Sexual Offence.' *The Advertiser*, 22 December 2017. http://www.news.com.au/national/south-australia/selfproclaimed-paedophile-hunter-arrested-charged-with-assault-and-revealing-identity-of-person-charged-with-sexual-offence/news-story/cbc35c6a9c42a1f4b-cdbed074eb3964d.

e Silva, Karine K. 'Vigilantism and Cooperative Criminal Justice: Is There a Place for Cybersecurity Vigilantes in Cybercrime Fighting?' *International Review of Law, Computers and Technology* 32, no. 1 (2018): 21–36.

Federal Bureau of Investigation. *Internet Crime Complaint Center (IC3)* (2018). https://www.ic3.gov/default.aspx.

Fijnaut, Cyrille, and Gary T. Marx. *Undercover: Police Surveillance in Comparative Perspective.* Alphen aan de Rijn: Kluwer, 1995.

Fronc, Jennifer. *New York Undercover: Private Surveillance in the Progressive Era.* Chicago: University of Chicago Press, 2009.

Garland, David. 'Penal Excess and Surplus Meaning: Public Torture Lynchings in Twentieth-Century America.' *Law and Society Review* 39, no. 4 (2005): 793–833.

Gorrey, Megan. 'Canberra Teen Locked up for "Calculated Entrapment" of Men in Grindr Extortion.' *Canberra Times*, 12 May 2017. https://www.canberratimes.com.au/national/act/canberra-teen-locked-up-for-calculated-entrapment-of-men-in-grindr-extortion-20170512-gw3b4r.html.

Grabosky, Peter, Russell Smith, and Gillian Dempsey. *Electronic Theft: Unlawful Acquisition in Cyberspace.* Cambridge: Cambridge University Press, 2001.

Greenwald, Glenn. *No Place to Hide: Edward Snowden, the NSA, and the U.S. Surveillance State.* New York: Metropolitan Books, 2014.

Gregorian, Dareh. 'Four Men Ensnared by "To Catch a Predator" Type Website Sue to Get Personal Information Scrubbed from Web.' *New York Daily News*, 22 May 2015. http://www.nydailynews.com/new-york/4-men-sue-scrub-perv-info-web-article-1.2232881.

Harcourt, Bernard E. *Exposed: Desire and Disobedience in the Digital Age.* Cambridge, MA: Harvard University Press, 2015.

Hochschild, Adam. 'All-American Vigilantes.' *New York Review of Books*, 22 July 2021.

Hofmeyr, Kate. 'The Problem of Private Entrapment.' *Criminal Law Review* (2006): 319–36.

Howson, Gerald. *Thief-Taker General: Jonathan Wild and the Emergence of Crime and Corruption as a Way of Life in Eighteenth-Century England.* New Brunswick, NJ, and Oxford: Transaction Books, 1985.

Jane, Emma. 'Online Misogyny and Feminist Digilantism.' *Continuum* 30, no. 3 (2016): 284–97.

Joh, Elizabeth, and Thomas Joo. 'Sting Victims: Third Party Harms in Undercover Police Operations.' *Southern California Law Review* 88, no. 6 (2015): 1309–56.

Kerr, Orin S., and Sean D. Murphy. 'Government Hacking to Light the Dark Web: Risks to International Relations and International Law?' *Stanford Law Review* 70, no. 1 (2017): 58–69.

Kosseff, Jeff. 'The Hazards of Cyber-Vigilantism.' *Computer Law and Security Review* 32, no. 4 (2016): 642–9.

Marx, Gary T. *Undercover: Police Surveillance in America*. Berkeley: University of California Press, 1988.

———. *Windows into the Soul: Surveillance and Society in an Age of High Technology*. Chicago: University of Chicago Press, 2016.

Marx, Gary, and Dane Archer. 'Citizen Involvement in the Law Enforcement Process: The Case of Community Police Patrols.' *American Behavioral Scientist* 15, no. 1 (1971): 52–72.

Mayer, Jonathan. 'Government Hacking.' *Yale Law Journal* 127, no. 3 (2018): 570–660.

Microsoft Digital Crimes Unit. 'Digital Crimes Unit: Leading the Fight against Cyber-crime.' 3 May 2022. https://news.microsoft.com/on-the-issues/2022/05/03/how-microsofts-digital-crimes-unit-fights-cybercrime/.

Microsoft Trust Center. 'Cybercrime.' (2018). https://www.microsoft.com/en-us/trustcenter/security/cybercrime.

More, Robert, Tina Lee, and Robert Hunt. 'Entrapped in the Web? Applying the Entrapment Defense to Cases Involving Online Sting Operations.' *American Journal of Criminal Justice* 32 (2007): 87–98.

New Zealand Police. *Principles of Practice for Investigating On-line Grooming of Children Under 16*. Reproduced in *R v Stubbs* [2009] ACTSC 63.

Nhan, Johnny, Laura Huey, and Ryan Broll. 'Digilantism: An Analysis of Crowd-sourcing and the Boston Marathon Bombings.' *British Journal of Criminology* 57, no. 2 (2017): 341–61.

Portelli, Emily. 'Paedophile-Hunter Targeted Innocent Melbourne Businessman, Court Told.' *Herald Sun*, 14 April 2014. http://www.heraldsun.com.au/news/national/paedophilehunter-targeted-innocent-melbourne-businessman-court-told/news-story/ef00b800a742e95095fdf2ce09045512.

Readhead, Harry. '"Paedophile Hunter" Jailed for Hacking and Blackmail.' *Metro*, 8 December 2015. https://metro.co.uk/2015/12/08/paedophile-hunter-jailed-for-hacking-and-blackmail-5551111/?ito=cbshare.

Rowe, Joanne. 'Adam Brookes Lured Victim to His Home in Downham Gardens, Prest-wich, by Advertising on the Craigslist Website.' *Bury Times*, 10 December 2015. https://www.burytimes.co.uk/news/14136397.adam-brookes-lured-victim-to-his-home-in-downham-gardens-prestwich-by-advertising-on-the-craigslist-website/.

Sabin, Lamiat. 'Vigilante Paedophile Hunter Arrested over "Assault" and "Blackmail" of Two Men Accused of Attempting to Meet with Underage Girls.' *The Independent*, 20 April 2015. https://www.independent.co.uk/news/uk/crime/

vigilante-paedophile-hunter-arrested-over-assault-and-blackmail-of-two-men-accused-of-attempting-to-10188587.html.

Schaffar, Wolfram. 'New Social Media and Politics in Thailand: The Emergence of Fascist Vigilante Groups on Facebook.' *Austrian Journal of South-East Asian Studies* 9, no. 2 (2016): 215–34.

Schermer, Bart, Ilina Georgieva, Simone van der Hof, and Bert-Jaap Koops. *Legal Aspects of Sweetie 2.0.* Leiden: Center for Law and Digital Technologies, 2016.

Sombatpoonsiri, Janjira. *Manipulating Civic Space: Cyber Trolling in Thailand and the Philippines.* (GIGA Focus Asien, 3). Hamburg: GIGA German Institute of Global and Area Studies – Leibniz-Institut für Globale und Regionale Studien, Institut für Asien-Studien, 2018. https://nbn-resolving.org/urn:nbn:de:0168-ssoar-57960-4.

Stelter, Brian. 'NBC Settles with Family that Blamed a TV Investigation for a Man's Suicide.' *New York Times*, 26 June 2008. https://www.nytimes.com/2008/06/26/business/media/26nbc.html.

Starke, Findlay. 'Non-State Entrapment.' (2018). https://www.repository.cam.ac.uk/bitstream/handle/1810/287186/Non-State%20Entrapment%20-%20Repository%20Version.pdf?sequence=1.

Stone, Richard. 'Exclusion of Evidence under Section 78 of the Police and Criminal Evidence Act: Practice and Principles.' *Web Journal of Current Legal Issues* 3 (1995): 1–20. https://paginelegali.com/attachments/312.pdf.

Terre des Hommes. *Sweetie 2.0: Stop Webcam Childsex.* (2018). https://www.terredeshommes.nl/en/sweetie-20-stop-webcam-childsex.

Urbas, Gregor. 'Protecting Children from Online Predators: The Use of Covert Investigation Techniques by Law Enforcement.' *Journal of Contemporary Criminal Justice* 26, no. 4 (2010): 410–25. https://journals.sagepub.com/doi/abs/10.1177/1043986210377103.

Warren, Ian, Monique Mann, and Adam Molnar. 'Lawful Illegality: Authorizing Extraterritorial Police Surveillance.' *Surveillance & Society* 18, no. 3 (2020): 357–69.

Yaffe, Gideon. '"The Government Beguiled Me": The Entrapment Defense and the Problem of Private Entrapment.' *Journal of Ethics and Social Philosophy* 1, no. 1 (2005). http://jesp.org/index.php/jesp/issue/view/1.

Završnik, Aleš. *Big Data, Crime and Social Control.* London: Routledge, 2018.

8

Space and Surveillance in Jonathan Raban's Novel *Surveillance* (2006)

Aliette Ventéjoux

I. Introduction

It is no surprise that surveillance, today recognised as an unmistakable field of study,[1] is also a topic widely addressed in post-9/11 literature.[2] As Brunon-Ernst explains in Chapter 6 of this volume, the first wave of scholarship on surveillance and literature dates from shortly after the publication of Foucault's *Discipline and Punish* in 1975. Some of the best-known works are that of John Bender, *Imagining the Penitentiary*, published in 1987, and that of D. A. Miller, *The Novel and the Police*, published in 1988. Miller declares that his work 'centres not on the police, in the modern institutional shape they acquire in Western liberal culture during the nineteenth century, but on the ramification within the same culture of less visible, less visibly violent modes of "social control"'.[3] As Mark Vareschi underlines, '[t]aking the establishment of the modern police force in the nineteenth century as the historical backdrop, Miller argues for the novel's engagement in regimes of disciplinary power'.[4] As for Bender, he states that 'art, culture, and society are not separate or separable' and that '[n]ovels as [he] describe[s] them are primary historical and ideological documents; the vehicles, not the reflections, of social change.'[5] In his work, he takes a closer look at how prison and the penitentiary come to share concerns with the novel.

More recently, in *The Watchman in Pieces: Surveillance, Literature, and Liberal Selfhood*, Rosen and Santesso explore the idea that 'surveillance and

---

[1] See for instance Castagnino, 'Critique des *surveillances studies*', which discusses the evolutions and different aspects of this field.

[2] Surveillance has of course been a topic addressed by literature long before 9/11. For further discussion, see for instance Miller, *The Novel and the Police*; Breight, *Surveillance*.

[3] Miller, *The Novel and the Police*, viii.

[4] Vareschi, 'Surveillance Studies', 1–7.

[5] Bender, *Imagining the Penitentiary*, 1.

literature, as kindred practices, have light to shed on each other – on each other's theory, mode of operation, and ways of grappling, as it were, with the reality principle'.[6] In *Spaces of Surveillance: States and Selves*, Susan Flynn and Antonia Mackay take a closer look at how surveillance affects the space one inhabits and has an impact on one's identity. The authors state that '[t]he potential contained in surveillant technologies is [. . .] twofold: providing bodies with identities they may not want, but at the same time providing them with an identity that can be determined as real – I am watched, therefore I am.'[7] Taking an interest in photography, art and literature, the authors of this collection offer 'a unique insight into the ways in which bodies have both voluntarily and involuntarily been shaped and defined by changing technology'.[8] Changing experiences of space are coeval with the phenomenon of contemporary surveillance, and with the spatial overlap it entails; they are also discussed in this volume in Cluzel-Métayer's chapter on the way surveillance implemented in Smart Cities shapes urban spaces, as well as in Grabosky and Urbas's where online identities are explored in the fight against online child pornography.[9]

With the insight of these different critics, this chapter will focus on a 2006 novel whose title, *Surveillance*, could not be more explicit.[10] In this novel, the writer Jonathan Raban depicts a post-9/11 world where surveillance operates on different scales and spaces. The story takes place in Seattle, where Lucy Bengstrom, a freelance journalist, lives with her daughter, Alida. She is asked by *GQ* to write a piece about bestselling author August Vanags, whose memoir, *Boy 381*, recounts his childhood during World War II. However, she soon starts to wonder if he really wrote his own memoirs, because his recollection reminds her a great deal of *The Pianist*, by Władysław Szpilman. While trying to find out more about Vanags and his book, she also begins questioning his real identity. Suspicion and paranoia pervade the narrative, and there seems to be no escape from being watched and monitored, and hiding the truth. Tad Zachary, Lucy's best friend, thinks that he is being spied on, while using the Internet himself to spy on people. As an actor, he embodies the matter of one's fluctuating identity, a question that is reinforced by the fact that he plays the role of the surrogate father for Alida.

Raban's novel aims not only to make people aware of the fact that surveillance has pervaded everyone's lives but also that, as Georgiana Banita writes in *Plotting Justice,*

---

[6] Rosen and Santesso, *Watchman in Pieces*, 10.
[7] Flynn and Mackay, *Spaces of Surveillance*, 3.
[8] Ibid., 10.
[9] See Chapters 9 and 7 of this collection.
[10] Raban, *Surveillance*.

post-9/11 fiction [. . .] emplots surveillance as an ingenious frame for an overt critique of America's War on Terror. This politicized approach denounces permanent surveillance both as an instrument of state oppression and for its role in the design of modern communication and interpersonal relationships.[11]

Focusing on how surveillance affects different spaces in the novel, this chapter aims at taking a closer look not only at its critique of surveillance in the post-9/11 United States, but also at its treatment of questions of identity. As David Lyon reminds us, '[s]urveillance is not inherently sinister or malign. But the focused attention to persons and populations with a view to influencing, managing or controlling them – that we call "surveillance" – is never innocent either.'[12] Thus, it can have powerful consequences on people's lives and prompt new ways of shaping one's identity. In his novel, Raban finds various techniques to depict how different spaces, be they geographical or personal, are 're-mapped' and altered by surveillance. Exploring the different spaces that surveillance permeates, this chapter will focus not only on how surveillance rewrites identity, but also on how it is used to criticize the War on Terror.

II. Reshaping Seattle

Raban's novel is set in Seattle, and one important feature stands out concerning the city right from the beginning: its vulnerability both to earthquakes and to what Banita describes as the 'pending (albeit invisible) threat' that is the threat of terrorism.[13] The very first pages portray a devastated city, the air saturated by noise and commotion: 'He was cupping his hands to his ears, as if to spare himself the noise of sirens, car alarms, bullhorns, whistles, and tumbling masonry. [. . .] His mouth opened wide in a scream that was lost in the surrounding din.'[14] The multiple plosives and the repetition of the sound /z/ insist on the extent and violence of the cacophony that pervades the beginning of the novel. Moreover, the fact that the identity of the man is not given at first and that his scream is swallowed by the surrounding uproar stresses that that is not what is important here, that it is the catastrophe that matters and that the world is falling apart. The identity of the man dissolves in the environment although people are the ones that will be affected by the catastrophe. These first pages give the impression that people are fused into

---

[11] Banita, *Plotting Justice*, 267.
[12] Lyon, 'Surveillance after September 11'.
[13] Ibid., 268.
[14] Raban, *Surveillance*, 3.

the catastrophe and that they do not matter any more, whereas in fact they are its real victims.

The novel opens *in medias res*, and as Andrea Del Lungo reminds us, 'the incipit *in medias res* opens the space of uncertainty'.[15] Here, this uncertainty concerns the catastrophe itself, which is mentioned as early as the third word of the novel: 'After the explosion [. . .].'[16] But what kind of explosion was it? A terrorist attack, as the post-9/11 reader is prone to believe? Or just an accident? Whatever the cause, it is certain that the catastrophe is not just a threat any more, it is really happening.[17] Or is it?

Indeed, if the first pages depict the vivid picture of a world falling apart, it soon becomes clear that it is not an actual attack but a staged one in which Tad, as an actor, plays a part. All casualties are volunteers or homeless people, and a few actors filmed in close-up, like Tad. This end-of-the-world-like scene is just orchestrated for the show 'TOPOFF 27', put together by the Department of Homeland Security. The exercise is 'being monitored' in DC and is one of a great number, exploring different scenarios, treated as a 'dress rehearsals'.[18] For instance, 'TOPOFF 27' is

> the most realistic yet. A dirty bomb [. . .] had gone off in a container supposedly holding 'cotton apparel' from Indonesia [. . .]. A fireworks expert [. . .] created the terrific gunpowder explosion and the rockets laden with talc to simulate caesium. The tire fire had been set with gasoline, the broken glass supplied by volunteers standing on the roofs of neighbouring buildings. At least the pictures beamed to the other Washington would look great.[19]

The whole description highlights its theatrical quality, and a will to make it as realistic as possible. This results in a kind of accumulation of props and hyperboles: the bomb is not 'just a bomb', it is a 'dirty bomb'; the person in charge of the fireworks is an 'expert'; the explosion is 'terrific'; and in the end, the only thing that matters is that the pictures will 'look great'. People

---

[15] '[L]'incipit *in medias res* ouvre l'espace de l'incertitude [. . .].' Del Lungo, *L'incipit romanesque*, 14, my translation.

[16] Raban, *Surveillance*, 3.

[17] This opening reminds us of Don DeLillo's novel *Falling Man*, which also starts with the depiction of the catastrophe, of the 9/11 attacks in New York and the noise that saturates both the city and the pages: 'The roar was still in the air, the buckling rumble of the fall. This was the world now. Smoke and ash came rolling down streets and turning corners, busting around corners, seismic tides of smoke, with office paper flashing past, standard sheets with cutting edge, skimming, whipping past, otherworldly things in the morning pall.' DeLillo, *Falling Man*, 1.

[18] Raban, *Surveillance*, 7.

[19] Ibid., 6.

volunteer to throw glass; citizens take part willingly in the staging of the catastrophe. The attention is drawn not to the efficiency of the fake bomb, but to the sensationalism of the image that it will produce and the fact that it will be seen by many people.

However, part of the population seems to be more bored and annoyed than concerned by the staged catastrophe, as the words used by Lucy to refer to the event suggest: 'the bomb-scare shenanigans'.[20] The rehearsals are in fact ploys to keep the people in a state of constant fear in order to implement measures of surveillance such as a 'biometric National ID card':[21]

> The administration was in the business of manufacturing fear and methodi- cally spreading its infection from city to city. The lengths they went to – setting fires, showing make-believe corpses to the cameras – surely went far beyond what is needed to test the emergency services. How could you explain to a child that 'homeland security' meant keeping the homeland in a state of continuous insecurity?[22]

The accusation is clear: the aim of the administration is not improving preparedness but spreading fear. The choice of the term 'business' insists on the aloofness with which the administration treats matters of life and death. Moreover, as Paul Giles remarks, the expression 'homeland security' is paradoxical, and should be used with care:

> to turn a home into a 'homeland' is, by definition, to move from a zone in which domestic comforts and protection could be taken for granted to one in which they had to be guarded anxiously and self-consciously; in that sense, the very phrase 'homeland security' could be seen as a contradiction in terms, since it rhetorically evokes the very insecurity it is designed to assuage.[23]

So, the administration is playing with facts in order to spread a feeling of anxiety favourable to mass surveillance and its acceptance as something normal. Thus Lucy is reminded of the importance of getting the biometric National ID card 'soon':

> A soldier [. . .] demanded ID.
> She gave him her driver's license.
> 'National ID?'

[20] Raban, *Surveillance*, 8.
[21] Ibid., 14.
[22] Ibid.
[23] Giles, *Global Remapping*, 17.

'I d-d-d-d-don't have it yet.' No one she knew did.
'You know the deadline.'
'Yes.'
'Get it. Soon.'[24]

Although she has done nothing wrong, she finds herself stuttering in front of authority, whereas she is within her rights showing 'just' her driver's licence. The incongruity of this exchange is reinforced by the fact that she is not the only one without this new ID, as the aside 'No one she knew did' underlines. This exchange clearly demonstrates the pressure put on citizens to submit themselves to the will of the state. The last words of the soldier, two very short assertions, sound very final and brutal. Banita states that 'even more apparent are the resemblances between Raban's vision of a futuristic surveillance vortex and the forms of social control deployed in the War on Terror'.[25]

On the other hand, the real danger that looms over Seattle seems to be of little concern for the government: earthquakes are described as having a much stronger possibility of realisation than attacks, but they are barely addressed. They are mentioned, but in passing, and no surveillance system is linked to the idea of monitoring the earth and warning the population of a possible earthquake, for instance. 'I don't *not* believe in terrorism', says Lucy. 'It is just that there are more threatening things – greenhouse gases, earthquakes, whatever. Like Seattle gets millions of federal dollars for mock terror attacks but can't raise a federal cent for earthquake exercises, which is what it really needs.'[26]

She almost sounds like a kind of Cassandra, because what changes the face of the city in the end is indeed not an attack but an earthquake. One of the last scenes of the novel depicts Alida, Lucy's daughter, in the middle of the street, surrounded by noise, and thus echoing the opening scene:

she heard the car alarms, hundreds of them, coming from all across the city. [. . .] She heard the foundations of the building grinding, deep down, against rock [. . .]. From somewhere, she couldn't tell where, came the long, tumbling thunder of what must be a building coming down. [. . .] The chorus of car alarms was joined by a mad band of sirens and whistles, and, from somewhere close by, a thin and lonely cry, like a sheet being torn down the middle [. . .].[27]

[24] Raban, *Surveillance*, 62–3.
[25] Banita, *Plotting Justice*, 268.
[26] Raban, *Surveillance*, 51.
[27] Ibid., 254–7.

Once again, noise and destruction pervade the city, echoing the opening pages of the book. The description gives an impression of abundance, and noises saturate the air. The wheel has come full circle, chaos prevails but no one has predicted or tried to prevent this disaster. This time there are no walk-on actors throwing glass from a roof: the 'falling piece[s] of masonry' are all too real.[28]

This choice of ending suggests the limits of surveillance if used to no avail, or only to create an atmosphere of fear and to monitor people. Here, the failure to use surveillance properly in the novel leads to the literal destruction of the city after having staged it several times and prepared everyone for the potential destruction of its citizens in the end.

III. Spying on One Another

While surveillance fails to predict natural catastrophes, it nevertheless invades people's everyday life, taking different shapes. The biometric ID is by no means the only form that surveillance takes. For instance, each time Lucy takes the ferry to visit the author August Vanags, cars are stopped and searched. The first search that is described (page 65 and following) is that of a man driving a car with Canadian plates. If, at first, Lucy sides with the soldiers who arrest him, she soon changes her mind – in the following paragraph, in fact:

> Lucy was with the soldiers on this one. [. . .] Khaki-skinned, implausibly single, Canadian-plated, he looked like trouble incarnate, and shit-eating fraudulence was written all over that grin. [. . .] Then she jolted into reverse. This was stupid 'profiling'; no real bomber would so neatly fit the stereotype; and catching stereotypes was the ineffectual best that the army and police could do.[29]

Once again it is the army and the government that bear the brunt of her distrust, offering, by extension, a harsh criticism of the measures taken in the name of the War on Terror. The choice of the noun 'stereotype' is no coincidence, and reminds the reader of Nadine Naber's words:

> the federal government went after 'the CNN version of what a terrorist looks like. He was dark, Middle Eastern, and had a full beard. He was the typical terrorist looking guy – or at least the guy who CNN portrays as the terrorist. Timothy McVeigh is a terrorist, but he is not associated with terrorism because he does not look like the typical terrorist-looking guy.'[30]

---

[28] Ibid., 255.
[29] Ibid., 65.
[30] Naber, "'Look, Mohammed the Terrorist is Coming!'", 296.

By virtue of their origins or their appearance, some people suffer more from surveillance than others.

It is by no means simply the state that is playing the surveillance card. The new owner of Lucy's and Tad's apartments, Mr Lee, wants to install video surveillance in the building. The man is all about security: each time he appears in the novel, words like 'security', 'safe' and 'surveillance' materialize on the page.[31] He seems obsessed with surveillance and security, but it is soon revealed that he is less concerned about the well-being of his tenants than about that of his wallet. He is all about transformation and reshaping, if not the whole city, then at least the neighbourhood:

> 'What I see long term?' Mr Lee was speaking softly, facing her mom but almost talking to himself. 'I see you go out the door and you got the restaurant, nice restaurant, right there. You got the grocery store. You go the dry cleaners. And Starbucks. You got to have the Starbucks.'
> On *Adam Street*? [. . .]
> Alida was confused. Adam Street wouldn't be Adam Street, wouldn't be home. [. . .]
> 'Like I say, long term. Short term, you got to think security. [. . .]'[32]

Mr Lee's plans hint at more definitive changes: changes that transform a home into a mere house, turning a place where someone belongs into a place to take shelter. Mr Lee's version of safety, however, seems nearer to gentrification than to security. Starbucks implies a more middle-class neighbourhood and higher rents. If the neighbourhood changes, as Mr Lee hopes, the people currently living there (Tad and Lucy, for instance) might not be able to pay their rent any more, and will be forced to move. Ironically, then, Mr Lee's security is to be bought at the expense of that of his tenants.

However, even though the adults are not fooled by the landlord's words, Alida is filled with enthusiasm at the prospect of camera surveillance in the building. Her reaction is a perfect example of Castagnino's words: 'surveillance techniques are all the more efficient that they are considered as a factor of improvement of everyday life, and thus more easily accepted'.[33] This use of surveillance in an urban environment is further discussed by Cluzel-Métayer in Chapter 9 of this collection. Here Alida considers cameras not only as an improvement, but also as belonging to a new trend:

[31] Raban, *Surveillance*, 80, 83, 193, 194, 195, 218.

[32] Ibid., 82–3.

[33] '[L]es techniques de surveillances sont d'autant plus efficaces qu'elles sont considérées comme un facteur d'amélioration de la vie quotidienne, et ainsi plus facilement acceptées.' Castagnino, 'Critique des *surveillances studies*', 11, my translation.

'[. . .] What you need? Surveillance. Up here, bell ring – you got visitors. Who down there? You don't know. Oh, sure, you got intercom, but intercom ain't no security. Maybe friend says, "Is me," but maybe you got lowlife down there wait-ing to get in door with friend. Maybe friend don't see lowlife, maybe lowlife hold a gun to friend. How you know what going on down there? Easy, 'cause right here' – he shaped a rectangle with his hands at shoulder height beside the door – 'you got TV that show you the street, show everybody who there, fish-eye view!'

'Cool!' Alida said, the word escaping her involuntarily.

[. . .] That seemed a fair deal to Alida, who was still thinking of how cool it would be to see every visitor on a TV monitor, caught by the camera unawares.[34]

This exchange presents two contrasting visions of surveillance. On the one hand, we have Alida, rather naïve maybe, envisaging surveillance as a kind of reality TV show and finding it 'cool' to be able to observe people on a moni-tor. On the other hand, according to Mr Lee, surveillance equals security. In Chapter 5 of this volume, Gligorijević shows the complex ways in which surveillance is justified on grounds that security is portrayed as a necessary trade-off for privacy. Without the cameras in the lobby of the building, there is no way to be safe any more. The common space of the lobby becomes a hazardous place. One more time, just like with the 'TOPOFF' shows, a prospective danger effectively produced by those with power, be they the state or the landlord, is used to convince people that surveillance is for their own good. The same rationale is at work in the present COVID-19 health crisis, where surveillance in the form of COVID-tracing apps, for example, is imposed on grounds of protecting the health of populations, as Poullet shows in Chapter 4 of this volume. Here, Mr Lee's plans concerning his building are those of someone belonging to a panoptic society: 'For now, he meant to do little except watch. Watch and wait.'[35] He embodies the 'sovereign gaze' mentioned by Foucault.[36] Just like the structure of the Panopticon, analysed so carefully by Brunon-Ernst in Chapter 6 of this collection, the structure that Mr Lee imagines for his building is one that allows one person to observe everything around him.[37] 'The panoptic mechanism arranges spatial unities that make it possible to see constantly and to recognize immediately',[38] states Foucault, and that is precisely what Mr Lee hopes to achieve.

---

[34] Raban, *Surveillance*, 83–4.
[35] Ibid., 103.
[36] Foucault, *Discipline and Punish*, 317.
[37] On Bentham's Panopticon, see Brunon-Ernst, Chapter 6; Sabot, Chapter 2, both in this collection.
[38] Ibid., 200.

Mr Lee is an ambiguous figure. On the one hand, he seems the embodiment of surveillance: he wants to install video surveillance in the building that he has just bought; he terrorises one of his employees into spying on his colleagues and telling him their every move; and he even goes as far as prying through Lucy's apartment, drawers and underwear.[39] He goes from surveillance to voyeurism in the blink of an eye and abuses his position as a landlord. Lucy is no more than a means to an end for him: his gaze reifies her. He decides to marry her and makes a list of why he should, the first – and most important element – being that '[s]he had citizenship'.[40] The list goes on for a whole page, and Mr Lee notes everything that he has observed when inviting himself into her apartment. Nothing has escaped his gaze, not even the fact that she takes good care of her car. He uses his surveillance and sharp gaze to build a fantasy in which he becomes the epitome of the American dream.

But on the other hand, he is also being spied upon: Tad, suspicious of the landlord, googles him and finds that he might have usurped the real Mr Lee's identity:

> Tonight, though, he was doing a little data mining of his own, trawling through cyberspace for the new landlord. [. . .] The only name that fit was that of a social worker, Charles Ong Lee of Shoreline, who'd died in a one-car crash on Aurora Avenue in November 1999. [. . .] Could Mr Lee conceivably be guilty of identity theft?[41]

As Raban himself stated, 'we're all dataminers now',[42] and Tad is a perfect example. He speaks the almost exact same words: 'We're all spooks now',[43] asserting a new part of his identity. Trawling the Internet, he finds elements suggesting that their landlord has, in fact, taken the identity of a young man who died in a car crash some years before. After having found that information, he plays spy and pretends to be someone else working at the bank, while still surfing the Internet looking for information. As Susan

---

[39] Raban, *Surveillance*, 148–9.

[40] Ibid., 104.

[41] Ibid., 128–9.

[42] 'In the last few years, most of us – even instinctive technophobes like me – have become practiced in the dark art of surveillance. When I'm going to meet a stranger at dinner, I'll routinely feed her name to Google and LexisNexis to find out who she is and what she's been up to lately. If you know the person's street address, you can spy on her house with Google Earth, and inspect the state of her roof and how she keeps her garden. A slight tilt of camera angle, and you'd be able to see into her sock drawer and monitor the bottles in her liquor cabinet.' Raban. 'We Have Mutated'.

[43] Raban, *Surveillance*, 178.

Flynn and Antonia Mackay remind us, 'the Internet and, by extension, web imagery found on social media, has quickly become a form of individual surveillance'.[44] It is here used by Tad as a device to defend himself and Lucy against their greedy landlord, but also a way of shaping Tad's identity as existing through monitoring other people, while he strongly believes at the same time that he is a victim of constant surveillance.

IV. Cyberspace

Cyberspace is one of the spaces most affected by surveillance in the novel, and the most vulnerable one, because it is the only space where an attack really occurs. Tad's relationship with the Internet is twofold. He acts as a spy as far as his landlord is concerned, but he is also deeply convinced that the government is spying on him:

> Someone, somewhere, was watching as he tramped from site to site in cyberspace. The Patriot Act gave the federal government unlimited power to snoop on private citizens, and a daily visitor to Al-Jazeera must surely have aroused the interest of whoever was monitoring that site. Tapping out email, Tad had the sense that his messages were being scanned by an anonymous eavesdropper. Paranoia? Hardly. Internet service providers were required by law to render up complete records of their clients' every digital move if they were sent a 'national security letter' by the FBI.[45]

Tad is outraged at the idea of being spied on by the government. At the same time, however, he wears it as a badge of pride, despising the government and checking information on Al-Jazeera and in French newspapers. The famous phrase, 'Either you are with us or against us' is used again, and Tad is proud of being neither 'with' nor 'against' but rather someone capable of choosing his own source of information, even at the risk of being branded 'a traitor'.[46] Like it or not, Tad is driven into the camp of those 'against us' and embraces his identity. Thus Tad is at the same time both a vigilant eye and under the surveillance of the state's vigilant eye, a duality that shapes his identity. Flynn and Mackay's words seem to apply to him: 'Surveillance, therefore, features much more in the shaping of our identity than it may first appear to. [. . .] [O]ur sense of identity can be formed by the spaces of surveillance, the images of surveillance, and even the act of looking itself.'[47]

[44] Flynn and Mackay, *Spaces of Surveillance*, 5.
[45] Raban, *Surveillance*, 161–2.
[46] Ibid., 128.
[47] Flynn and Mackay, *Spaces of Surveillance*, 7.

Cyberspace is in fact the only space where a human threat materialises in the book, in the form of a young American teenager, albeit without any real consequences for the characters' everyday life. The episode serves only to remind them that the arsenal put in place to prevent attacks from happening is a mere pretence. Finn, a teenager in Alida's class, succeeds in spreading a Trojan horse named 'Freak' throughout Europe, America and Asia in one night, 'burgling people's address books and forwarding itself to unsuspecting millions. Sites like Amazon and eBay were temporarily down.'[48] Freak is described as

> 'a malicious act of cyber terrorism', which Lucy thought wildly overblown. Vandalism, certainly. Terrorism? Surely not. The cant word of the last few years was greying from repetition, decaying in a process of inevitable entropy – which, come to think of it, was another cant word from an earlier decade. Entropy itself had fallen victim to entropy.[49]

The (un)importance of this attack is highlighted a few pages later: 'The brouhaha over the Freak virus was over by lunchtime, when Lucy applied the patch and went onto the disinfected Internet.'[50] Here, the medical metaphor points out that this attack was no more than a virus and has been treated as such, that an antidote has been developed, and that life can go on as if nothing had happened. However, the fact that Finn was successful in launching his virus reminds the reader that the new technologies used for surveillance can also be exposed to assault, and that they might even open new doors for the attacks the government fears. They have become a kind of *pharmakon* which, as Derrida reminds us, is both a cure and a poison.[51]

This episode is a pretext for the state to extend its surveillance to everyone, even children. A man on TV gives advice to parents: 'A solemn fellow in a bow tie advised parents to ensure that their kid's computer was permanently located in a "family room," where they could constantly "monitor" the screen.'[52] The clothes of the man are meant to give him standing, importance, to make him look serious and professional, whereas his advice remains rather trite and futile. Moreover, the choice of the verb 'monitor' has a military connotation that links his recommendation more to surveillance and punishment

---

[48] Raban, *Surveillance*, 209.

[49] Ibid.

[50] Ibid., 213.

[51] Derrida, in 'La pharmacie de Platon', reminds us that the pharmakon is 'cette "médecine", ce philtre, à la fois remède et poison'. Derrida, 'La pharmacie de Platon', in *La dissémination*, 77–213.

[52] Raban, *Surveillance*, 215.

than to educating children about the dangers of the Internet. As such, from a young age children are supposed to be kept under surveillance and observed, rather than being taught how the world around them works and its dangers. Everyone becomes a potential suspect from early childhood, a proposition strongly rejected by Lucy, who still believes in privacy and a private space for her daughter, even in cyberspace.

Once again, Raban operates a kind of reversal: the real attack is mastered by an American teenager, not some unknown Other, and, despite all the surveillance deployed, it is not stopped in time. Raban stresses the paradoxical character inherent in surveillance and the impossibility of preventing each and every attack from happening. Moreover, while preparing to prevent or retaliate against attacks coming from outside the country, the United States tends to overlook the inside threat, the 'terrorist within' to use the words of Özden Sözalan.[53] Sözalan uses that term in order to qualify one of the characters of Don DeLillo's novel, Martin Ridnour, aka Ernst Hechinger, who might have been a member of the German group Kommune 1. According to Sözalan, 'DeLillo most succinctly introduces the "terrorist within" whose portrayal in the novel subverts, in more than one way, the binary opposition of "Us" and "Them".'[54] Through the figure of the terrorist within, post-9/11 literature reminds the reader that the threat is not just transnational.

V. Questioning Identity

The question of identity is raised on several levels, but the most uncertain identity is that of August Vanags. A historian and bestselling author, he now lives at Useless Bay, on a peninsula near Seattle, with his wife, Minna. His autobiography, entitled *Boy 381*, recalls his childhood during the Second World War. The book is a bestseller, but his editors have decided that it would be better if its author moved from the city to a quieter place, becoming 'a mystery man'.[55] This choice of hiding a man who has written his memoir, and thus recounted his whole life, is rather paradoxical. Lucy visits him there, first alone, then with her daughter, in order to interview him for *GQ*. Lucy and August are described as two very different characters that allow Raban to voice two contrasting opinions on surveillance, security, terrorism and American politics. Vanags is a supporter of the Vietnam War and the War on Terror, and the words 'we are at war' recur regularly in his speech.[56]

[53] Sözalan, *American Nightmare*, 25.
[54] Ibid.
[55] Raban, *Surveillance*, 34.
[56] Ibid., 48, for instance.

His opinions on such topics are unequivocal; he is the voice of American imperialism:

> '[E]very poor sap living under a dictatorship, when he dreams of being free he dreams of being an American. Most probably he doesn't know that. He doesn't say to himself "I want to be an American," but it's our freedom that he's dreaming of . . . We got to open that guy's eyes to what he's really feeling.'[57]

Although Vanags was a European immigrant, he has become American to the core, and has clear imperialist ideas. Raban places him on the side of global surveillance and securitisation.

However, if his ideas are well defined and voiced, his identity is less obvious. Working on her piece, Lucy discovers a review of Vanags's book written by a British woman, Marjie Tillman, calling him a fraud. According to this woman, the photograph on the book jacket was taken at her parents' farm in England, and not in a concentration camp. This accusation, and the fact that some passages in Vanags's memoir are similar to Władysław Szpilman's book, *The Pianist*, are enough for Lucy to start wondering if Vanags really experienced everything he describes in his memoir. Lucy becomes an agent of surveillance herself, as she looks him up on the Internet and contacts the woman who claims he is a fraud. The question of authorship is never answered, but nor is any judgement passed on Vanags's writing. As Banita asserts concerning post-9/11 literature, '[a]uthority itself is held up to scrutiny and indicted'.[58]

Having asked the question and voiced the possibility of a false memoir, Lucy ultimately cannot come to a definite conclusion. She chooses not to judge. As Banita remarks, her search, 'like many counterterrorist investigations lampooned in the book, ultimately remains fruitless'.[59] Once again the author suggests that the promise of certain and effective knowledge that surveillance holds out is destined to disappoint.

This resonates with Lucy's own words on her piece, when Vanags asks her if she has done it yet: 'It's odd – I find writing profiles harder and harder as I get older. It's that conclusive tone they tend to have, as if the journalist has gotten to the bottom of the subject's soul in a one-hour interview, and the piece is like the last word.' To which Vanags answers, 'Woe to those who conclude!'[60] In a larger sense, her assertion can be read as a metatextual comment, laying

---

[57] Ibid., 156.
[58] Banita, *Plotting Justice*, 254.
[59] Ibid., 270.
[60] Raban, *Surveillance*, 231–2.

emphasis on the difficulty for the author or the authorities to point the finger at the real threat in a post-9/11 world, or to put under surveillance those who are a definite threat.

Yet Lucy's discoveries – or lack thereof – about Vanags lead her to rethink her writing and her identity as a journalist. She decides that the time has come to write differently:

> She imagined it rather as she expected a post-modern New York might look – all the beams and pipes of its construction, its artifice, would be not only exposed but highlighted. They, as much as August Vanags, would be its subject. It would be full of tourist snapshots of Augie in the patio, on the beach, lecturing a dinner table, up in his study quoting Montaigne and E. B. White, or out kayaking with Alida, who had to be in the picture, too. [. . .] But they would be just that – snapshots, nothing more, disjointed one from another like the capricious jumble of images that every camera-toting traveler brings back from a trip, some more in focus than others. They wouldn't add up, wouldn't form a narrative, because the narrative of this piece would lie elsewhere. The *GQ* guy had spoken of a 'unicorn hunt.' She'd catch a multitude of glimpses of the elusive unicorn, but the piece would be about the comic intricacies of the chase, and its ultimate futility.[61]

The choice of snapshots alludes to both the strategic narrative adopted by the author, and the screens of tele-surveillance. Raban's narrative unfolds in the form of vignettes focusing on one or another character, giving rhythm to the text, and jumping from one story to the other, just like Lucy wishes to do with her piece. These vignettes also make one think of snapshots, as Lucy suggests, taken from people's lives without their consent, as if the novelist himself was spying on them.

Likewise, Raban's approach can be compared to the screens of video surveillance, on which scenes from the lives of different people appear at the same time. The person in charge can jump from one shot to the other, intruding on first one and then another without their knowledge. Surveillance takes many forms, and not even the writer is immune to its seductive charms.

VI. Conclusion

The work of Deleuze and Guattari offers useful insights on surveillance,[62] 'suggesting through some striking metaphors that the growth of surveillance systems is rhizomic; more like a creeping plant than a central tree trunk

---

[61] Ibid., 242.
[62] Deleuze and Guattari, *Mille plateaux*.

with spreading branches'.[63] Multiple examples in the novel make visible how several spaces are pervaded by surveillance, like branches reaching into every corner of public and private space.

The idea of vignettes that structures not only the novel but also Lucy's writing works as a strong reminder of the fragmented reality that surveillance puts forward. Throughout the novel, it is sometimes arduous to get a larger picture of what is actually going on. The Freak attack, perpetrated by a young American teenager who loves muffins, is the perfect example of this loss of perspective.

Moreover, as Timothy Druckrey reminds the reader, '[t]he sharply visualized panoptic space of contemporary culture is rapidly shifting towards a post-optic one in which observation is quickly giving way to information gathering systems, databases, and the monitoring of biological and chemical agents.'[64] Thus, Bentham's Panopticon and the fundamental character of vision are being replaced by less sizeable elements brought forward by new technologies or new biological discoveries. This is a point Bernard Harcourt makes in *Exposed*, and is discussed in Brunon-Ernst's chapter in this volume.[65]

Raban describes the 'TOPOFF' shows as theatre plays or films in order to make clear that the shift towards dystopia is slight. Ubiquitous surveillance might not be the answer to post-9/11 fears but rather another grounds for concern. The staged attacks maintain the population in a state of constant fear and alert, the feeling of security that the state claims to want to provide in fact undermined. Homeland security brings homeland insecurity; everyone becomes a potential threat; everyone can be put under surveillance for no reason. On a smaller scale, the landlord's desire to bring security to his tenants and to better their lives by installing new means of surveillance in the building is experienced instead as an infringement of their right to privacy, and a threat to their future in the very building.

Thus, surveillance is presented in the novel as an illusion: cyber attacks are not prevented, counter-terrorism investigations end without having really started, wrongly accused men are put in prison, and, in the end, the real catastrophe is not terrorism, for which everyone has been preparing, but an earthquake that no one seems to have anticipated. The reader is left to wonder if the strong link established by some characters, like Mr Lee, between surveillance and security might be an error, and if surveillance might be put to better use. Raban seems to agree with Lyon: '[s]urveillance

---

[63] Lyon, 'Surveillance after September 11'.
[64] Druckrey, 'Secreted Agents', 150–7, 151.
[65] See Chapter 6 of this collection.

can only anticipate [threats] up to a point, and in some very limited circumstances.'[66] On the contrary, Raban actually invites his readers to take a closer look at the vignettes and the narrative, rather than accumulating data that has become so enormous that it is not possible to make sense of it any more. Moreover, he insists on the personal and psychological fragmentation which the climate of surveillance produces, reminding the reader that surveillance happens at different scales, from the city to its buildings, from the inside of the characters' apartment to the web of the Internet. No place is left concealed, and as a result of constant surveillance, disorientation occurs.

VII. Bibliography

Banita, Georgiana. *Plotting Justice: Narrative Ethics and Literary Culture after 9/11.* Lincoln: University of Nebraska Press, 2012.

Bender, John. *Imagining the Penitentiary: Fiction and the Architecture of Mind in Eighteenth-Century England.* Chicago: University of Chicago Press, 1987.

Breight, Curtis C. *Surveillance, Militarism, and Drama in the Elizabethan Era.* New York: St. Martin's Press, 1996.

Castagnino, Florent. 'Critique des *surveillances studies.* Éléments pour une sociologie de la surveillance.' *Déviance et Société* 42, no. 1 (2018): 9–40.

Deleuze, Gilles, and Félix Guattari. *Mille plateaux.* Paris: Éditions de Minuit, 1980.

DeLillo, Don. *Falling Man.* New York: Scribner, 2007.

Del Lungo, Andrea. *L'incipit romanesque.* Paris: Éditions du Seuil, coll. 'Poétique', 2003.

Derrida, Jacques. *La dissémination.* Paris: Éditions du Seuil, 1972.

Druckrey, Timothy. 'Secreted Agents, Security Leaks, Immune Systems, Spore Wars . . .' In *Ctrl [Space]: Rhetorics of Surveillance from Bentham to Big Brother,* edited by Thomas Y. Levin, Ursula Frohne, and Peter Weibel, 150–7. Cambridge, MA: MIT Press, 2002.

Flynn, Susan, and Antonia Mackay, eds. *Spaces of Surveillance: States and Selves.* Cham: Palgrave Macmillan, 2017.

Foucault, Michel. *Discipline and Punish: The Birth of the Prison.* 1975. Translated by Alan Sheridan. 2nd ed. New York: Vintage Books, 1995.

———. *Surveiller et punir: naissance de la prison.* 1975. Paris: Gallimard, 2015.

Giles, Paul. *The Global Remapping of American Literature.* Princeton, NJ: Princeton University Press, 2011.

Lyon, David. 'Surveillance after September 11.' *Sociological Research Online* 6, no. 3 (2001). https://www.socresonline.org.uk/6/3/lyon.html.

Miller, D. A. *The Novel and the Police.* Berkeley: University of California Press, 1988.

Naber, Nadine. '"Look, Mohammed the Terrorist is Coming!": Cultural Racism, Nation-Based Racism, and the Intersectionality of Oppressions after 9/11.' In

---

[66] Lyon, 'Surveillance after September 11'.

Race and Arab Americans before and after 9/11: From Invisible Citizens to Visible Subjects. Edited by Amaney Jamal and Nadine Naber, 276–305. Syracuse, NY: Syracuse University Press, 2008.

Raban, Jonathan. *Surveillance: A Novel*. New York: Vintage, 2006.

———. 'We Have Mutated into a Surveillance Society – and Must Share the Blame.' *The Guardian*, 20 May 2006. https://www.theguardian.com/commentisfree/2006/may/20/comment.usa.

Rosen, David, and Aaron Santesso. *The Watchman in Pieces: Surveillance, Literature, and Liberal Personhood*. New Haven, CT: Yale University Press, 2013.

Sözalan, Özden. *The American Nightmare: Don DeLillo's Falling Man and Cormac McCarthy's The Road*. Bloomington: Authorhouse, 2011.

Vareschi, Mark. 'Surveillance Studies and Literature of the Long 18th Century.' *Literature Compass* (2017): 1–7.

9

Safe Cities: The French Experience

Lucie Cluzel-Métayer

I. Introduction

Predictive policing experiments have been developing in many countries in recent years. In the context of risks exacerbated by terrorist and health threats, the urban space explored in Jonathan Raban's novel *Surveillance* and discussed by Ventéjoux in Chapter 8 of this volume has become the privileged space for predictive policing experiments. In the United States, police forces in New York, Los Angeles, Atlanta and many other cities now rely on software, including the iconic PredPol discussed by Banita in Chapter 10 of this volume, in order better to deploy their forces and prevent public disorder through algorithmic 'predictions'. According to numerous press releases, this experiment has contributed to a significant decrease in the crime rate.[1] Although this positive outcome is questionable, some French cities, such as Nice, Marseilles, Dijon and Paris, have expressed a growing interest in them. Through the collection and analysis of a considerable amount of data – specifically, metadata – on the circumstances and modalities of past crimes and misdemeanours, police can better predict risks and combat them, especially by cross-referencing this data in real time with geolocalised data in public spaces. Such practices are highly seductive as they conjure up the utopia of a crime-free society. But the development of these techno-police experiments poses a risk for fundamental rights. It demonstrates in a familiar setting how our desire for everyday security in the towns and cities we live in can so readily be played off against the fundamental norms which, as Gligorijević argues in Chapter 5 in this volume, in fact sustain it. And it demonstrates how the very aspects that draw people to urban areas – their diversity, multiplicity, opportunity – can become the tools for a subtle and more all-encompassing surveillance.

---

[1] Some studies allege a drop by 20 per cent, or even 30 per cent in some cities, but no source seemed reliable enough to be cited. For a critical reading of these statistics, see Meijer and Wessels, 'Predictive Policing'; Raufer, 'Police prédictive'; Raufer, 'Cartographie criminelle'.

Some cities, by promoting a 'Smart City policy', are committed to this perspective of technology-based safety. The idea of a Smart City is believed to have emerged out of a discussion between President Clinton and John Chambers, then President of the CISCO systems company, in the second half of the 2000s. The European Parliament provides the following definition: 'A Smart City is a city seeking to address public issues via ICT-based solutions on the basis of a multi-stakeholder, municipally based partnership.'[2] Breaking with the traditional silo organisation of administrative services, the Smart City is based, first of all, on the transversality and interconnection between services and networks (energy, transport, urban lighting, waste management and car-parks, but also administrative procedures, education, and the like), which are part of the transformation of urban infrastructure. The Smart City is also characterised by the omnipresence of digital technology and data, large amounts of which are collected by sensors placed all over the city, and which can only be processed by increasingly sophisticated algorithms. The keyword for intelligent territories is cross-functionality, which entails rethinking the governance of territories by integrating not only elected officials and administrations, but also economic actors, associations and citizens.[3]

The advantages of Smart Cities are considerable and include the reduction of energy consumption, smoother journeys, better management of certain public services (waste, water and sanitation), better accessibility (particularly for people with reduced mobility), the strengthening of participatory democracy,[4] and increased risk-management capabilities. In this respect, it must be noted that, although the promises of intelligent cities are numerous and diverse, the benefit of increased security, in particular, often dominates.

In the present context of risks exacerbated by the threat of terrorism and health crises, Smart Cities are giving way to Safe Cities.[5] Cities are taking hold of digital technology in order to set up 'data surveillance', or 'dataveillance'.[6] Predictive police experiments are based on the use of various files that can now be cross-referenced with data which is collected by sensors located all over the cities, or which people carry with them. Experiments combining video surveillance, geolocation and biometrics are emerging in order to prevent threats, improve

[2] European Parliament, *Mapping Smart Cities*, 9.
[3] Townsend, *Smart Cities*; Auby, 'Les smart cities', 12–13; *Ville intelligente, ville démocratique?*
[4] Coming from Latin America, experiences of participatory budgets have recently been developing in France. Sintomer et al., *Les budgets participatifs dans le monde*; Cluzel-Métayer, 'Les budgets participatifs'.
[5] Ballesteros et al., 'Safe Cities'.
[6] Clarke defines dataveillance as 'the systematic monitoring of people or groups, by means of personal data systems, in order to regulate or govern their behaviour'. Clarke, 'Information Technology'.

the detection of potential breaches of the peace, and reduce the time required to mobilise available police forces. This system is referred to as 'intelligent video surveillance' and is based upon the analysis of images in order to detect signals of abnormality, sometimes coupled with facial recognition algorithms for identification purposes. Some systems aim to detect suspicious behaviour in real life, while others, such as PredPol in the United States, offer predictive analysis of the location of offences, enabling police forces to be deployed more effectively in the field. The use of these technologies will undoubtedly grow, given their purported security, health and financial benefits. This is already illustrated by the growing power of private operators and the increasing involvement of the population, which are working together towards a co-production of security, and have already led to a decline of the role of the state.

The issue is that the activity of private actors is not sufficiently supervised, and the protection of freedoms is not ensured, increasing the risk of a variety of violations of individual liberty.[7] As it is immersed in the realm of the invisible, the Smart City relies on the collection of data by sensors that multiply and are so small that their existence is forgotten. The mechanisms that are supposed to inform residents and obtain their consent to the collection and processing of their personal data cannot be an effective bulwark against the asymmetry and invisibility of this harvesting process, which gives rise to new forms of surveillance. This harm is amplified by two phenomena: first, the fact that 'data rarely remains compartmentalised in its original purpose',[8] leading to a loss of control, and, second, the fact that anonymisation is largely illusory due to the endless possibilities of cross-referencing.

Initially, population surveillance tools were firmly regulated by the law, under the control of constitutional judges, in order to prevent infringements of fundamental rights. However, the balance between the preservation of public order and the protection of fundamental rights is becoming increasingly difficult to strike. There are several reasons for this evolution: the context of terrorist threats, the current COVID-19 health crisis, and the transformation of our relationship with privacy in connection with digital technology. There is a lack of legal protection, first, because the regulations are still too fragmented, and, second, because the supervisory authorities (in France, the Commission Nationale Informatique et Libertés – CNIL; National Commission for Information Technology and Freedoms) are struggling to enforce them. But, as Sabot argues so convincingly in Chapter 2 of this volume, the question of surveillance is by no means limited to the power of the state. It is part and parcel of a social transformation to a 'society

---

[7] Kitchin, *Getting Smarter*.
[8] CNIL and LINC, *La plateforme d'une ville*, 38.

of exposition' in which digital transparency is increasingly understood as intimately connected to individual identity. In such a culture, surveillance becomes increasingly normalised, invisible and pervasive.

II. Cities under Surveillance

Cities are taking advantage of digital technologies in order to set up 'data surveillance' or 'data monitoring'.[9] This data can be of any kind: it can be 'public data'[10] that anyone can access, but very often it is personal, sometimes sensitive, data. These techniques, which are diverse and developed throughout France, involve more and more private operators, even average citizens, who are invited to collaborate actively in the preservation of public order.

1. Techno-police Experiments

While the idea of surveillance is 'inherent to the very institution of the State',[11] it has recently undergone profound change. Digital technologies are increasingly used in this context of new threats to public order and the reduction of government resources. Surveillance was initially file-based. Digitisation led to a multiplication of the number of files, and storage capacity was expanded. Fed with personal data and, increasingly, biometric data, some files were created to count or even identify individuals. Although the French have always typically been very hostile to a generalised filing system, they now seem to have accepted it. Created in 2016,[12] the 'Titres Électroniques Sécurisés' (TES; Secure Electronic Documents file), has enabled the Ministère de l'Intérieur (Home Office) to collect the personal and biometric data of all French ID cardholders.[13] This means that almost the entire French population can be registered. The adoption of this system, although not smooth, eventually succeeded, whereas in 1974 the SAFARI project had failed due to strong popular opposition.[14] The CNIL warned against the risks of misappropriation of a file that many administrative services can consult. These warnings did not prevent the creation of TES.

---

[9] Chevallier, 'La vie privée', 565.

[10] 'Les données publiques', Special Report in *Revue Française d'Administration Publique*.

[11] Chevallier, 'La vie privée', 565.

[12] Decree no. 2016-1460, 28 October 2016.

[13] Such as the identity, gender, eye colour, height, home address, data relating to parentage, digital image of the face and signature, email address and fingerprints of persons holding a French identity document.

[14] SAFARI stands for 'Système automatisé pour les fichiers administratifs et le répertoire des individus' (Automated System for Individuals' Administrative Files and Register), which was a project for the interconnection of the French administration's nominative files in 1974. Opposition prompted the government to create the National Commission for Information Technology and Freedoms (CNIL), founded 6 January 1978.

Police files are also on the rise, once again in order to monitor the population. The constant increase in the number of people subject to this registration system, and the possibilities of cross-referencing files, reveals a governmental will to implement generalised population surveillance, raising concerns for fundamental rights.[15] This form of surveillance runs alongside the increased intrusion into digital communication systems that was facilitated by the laws passed after the 2015 attacks in France. The 'Loi pour le renseignement' (Intelligence Act) of 24 July 2015, and the law of 30 November 2015 on 'Surveillance des communications électroniques internationales' (Surveillance of International Electronic Communications)[16] have allowed for the diversification of techniques of interception, and image and connection data capture. These laws have authorised the installation of 'black boxes', placed in the operators' premises in order to detect potential terrorist threats using cross-referencing of metadata. Indeed, article L851-3 of the 'Code de la sécurité intérieure' (Interior Security Code) authorises the general use of black boxes as a matter of principle, without the need for a 'menace réelle et actuelle' (real and current threat). The Court of Justice of the European Union has recently handed down an important ruling on this subject. It held that European law precludes legislative measures providing for generalised and undifferentiated retention of traffic and location data as a preventive measure.[17] Nevertheless, the French Parliament has approved the extension of what was supposed to be an experiment, in order to authorise the use of these black boxes by the intelligence services.[18]

In addition to these devices, increasingly sophisticated video surveillance networks are developing. In this respect, France, like many countries, seems to be catching up with the United Kingdom. The Criminal Justice and Public Order Act (1994) gives local authorities in England and Wales the power to install CCTV equipment without prior authorisation; the authorities themselves are responsible for drawing up codes of conduct.[19] This is linked, on

[15] See for example Decision 2017-670 QPC of 27 October 27 on the early erasure of personal data included in a criminal records file; or ECHR 22 June 2017 *Aycaguer v France*, application 8806/12, which ruled that the regime for storing DNA profiles in the FNAEG did not offer sufficient protection to the persons concerned because of its duration and the lack of possibility of erasure.

[16] 'Loi n° 2015-1556 du 30 novembre 2015 relative aux mesures de surveillance des communications électroniques internationales' (Statute 2015-1556 on the surveillance of international electronic communication, 30 November 2015). NOR: DEFX1521757L.

[17] C-511/18 La Quadrature du Net, C-512/18 French Data Network, C-520/18 'Ordre des barreaux francophones et germanophone' (Association of Bar Councils from French-speaking countries and German-speaking countries) and C-623/17 Privacy International.

[18] https://www.senat.fr/petite-loi-ameli/2020-2021/12.html.

[19] Heilmann and Mornet, 'L'impact de la vidéosurveillance'.

the one hand, to the extension of a network which can be defined as a 'fifth utility'[20] alongside gas, electricity, water and telecommunications, and, on the other hand, to the sophisticated tools that accompany this extension. Experiments combining video surveillance, geolocalisation and biometrics are beginning to emerge in order to prevent threats, improve the detection of events, and reduce the time required to mobilise police forces. 'Smart video surveillance' is based on image analysis which detects signals of abnormality, sometimes associated with facial recognition algorithms for identification purposes. Some systems, such as INDECT[21] or VOIE,[22] aim to detect suspicious behaviour in real life, while others, such as the emblematic and controversial PredPol in the United States,[23] offer a predictive analysis of the location of offences in order to optimise police intervention.

In early 2018, the city of Nice launched the 'Reporty project', which was based on a smartphone application that allowed citizens to report antisocial behaviour and offences by filming them and sending them via their smartphone to a 'Centre de supervision urbain' (Urban Supervision Centre). This project was invalidated by the CNIL, which considered that it was an extension of video surveillance based on citizen denunciation requiring a solid legal basis which was missing in this case.[24] However, this did not prevent the launch of another experiment based on a facial recognition system tested on 1,000 volunteers during the Nice carnival in February 2019.[25]

Also in 2018, the 'Observatoire Big Data de la tranquillité publique' (Big Data Observatory of Public Tranquillity) was inaugurated in Marseilles.[26] The project consists of an integration platform based on Big Data and machine learning methods. It is a tool intended to make it possible to aggregate multiple databases, such as that of the city's General Delegation for Security, which lists, among other things, police complaints and minor offences, or even, in the long term, data collected by their video surveillance network, hospital data or social networks.

---

[20] CNIL and LINC, *La plateforme d'une ville*, 4.

[21] http://www.indect-project.eu.

[22] 'Open and integrated video protection'. Project led by a consortium of eleven public and private players, coordinated by Thalès. See http://www.gouvernement.fr/sites.default/files/contenu/pièce-jointe/2016/09/fiche_demonstrateur_voie.pdf.

[23] https://www.predpol.com/; Benbouzid, 'From Situational Crime Prevention'; Benslimane, *Étude critique*.

[24] CNIL, Deliberation of 10 April 2018, Ref. IFP/AME/DI181074.

[25] The CNIL did not expressly authorise the experiment, but simply ensured that the free and informed consent of the volunteers was indeed collected beforehand. On this subject, see Rees, 'Reconnaissance faciale'.

[26] https://www.marseille.fr/prevention/s%C3%A9curit%C3%A9-et-pr%C3%A9vention/big-data-de-la-tranquillite-publique.

Since 2019, a neighbourhood in Saint-Étienne has been equipped with around twenty microphones designed to pick up 'weak signals of abnormality', including accidents or anti-social behaviour, ranging from simple screams or honks to detonations. Sound sensors trigger cameras which then focus on the origin of the suspicious noise and accelerate the arrival of the police or emergency services. This experiment may lead to the use of drones, which would prevent 'mobilising unnecessary resources'.[27] It may also lead to the creation of a reporting application, enabling citizens to report to the municipal police anti-social behaviour and other problems which they witness. For the time being, as these sound sensors are not programmed to pick up conversations of passers-by but only to detect acoustic signs, and as they do not record anything, the Saint-Étienne experiment does not raise the issue of personal data protection. This device is part of the legal framework of video protection, which has been considerably loosened since the regulations are now a type of *a posteriori* control (Article L. 251-1 et seq. of the Interior Security Code).[28]

2. Privatisation of Security

The digitalisation of law enforcement, which is growing along with urban data processing, contributes to the 'privatisation of security' which began in the 1990s in France,[29] a trend that is common in many English-speaking countries.[30] Two separate phenomena are apparent, namely, the increasing power of operators and the growing involvement of the population, both of which are intended to participate in the maintenance of public order.

While delegating policing activities to the private sector is prohibited in principle in France,[31] the rise of predictive policing largely undermines this general legal principle. Public contracts are entered into in order to enable well-known multinational corporations to develop these predictive policing

---

[27] La Quadrature du Net, 'Mouchards et drones à Saint-Etienne'.

[28] Bioy, 'Installation de micros à Saint-Etienne'.

[29] Cour des comptes [Audit Court], Annual report 2018, 'Les activités privées de sécurité', available at https://www.ccomptes.fr/fr/publications/le-rapport-public-annuel-2018.

[30] Mandel, *Armies Without States*, 169.

[31] Conseil d'État [Council of State; the highest court in the administrative legal system], 17 June 1932, Ville de Castelnaudary; Conseil Constitutionnel [Constitutional Council; the French court responsible for ensuring that all laws, institutional acts and international agreements are constitutional], Decision n° 2011-625 DC 10 March 2011, available at https://www.conseil-constitutionnel.fr/decision/2011/2011625DC.htm, based on Article 12 of the Declaration of Human and Civic Rights of 26 August 1789, which specifies that '[t]o guarantee the Rights of Man and of the Citizen a public force is necessary; this force is therefore established for the benefit of all, and not for the particular use of those to whom it is entrusted.'

systems. Thalès, Atos Bull, Bouygues Energies et Services, Citelum (an Electricity of France subsidiary), Suez and Engie Ineo remain the main players in this lucrative market.[32] In Marseilles, the Big Data Observatory of Public Tranquillity has been entrusted to Engie Ineo (a subsidiary of Engie specialising in Big Data), which is the leader in the video surveillance market, in partnership with IBM. The question is who, out of either local authorities or companies, ultimately controls the collected data. Because companies enforce their economic models,[33] which are based on the monetisation of individual data and advertising, there is a risk of 'privatization of the city'.[34]

On another level, the contract signed in 2016 and renewed in 2019 between the Head of the Home Office (DGSI) and American company Palantir was criticised in France for providing access to operational data which had been processed using its software.[35] The development of 'Smart City solutions' can generate the same fears if public local entities are not careful and relinquish their data to their partners. In Toronto, Google's Sidewalk Labs eco-neighbourhood project was abandoned in May 2020 precisely because of a data governance problem.[36] This resilient city development project, located on a vacant site in Quayside, was supposed to be a laboratory for the Smart City. While the project offered promising innovations (including heated streets, modular wooden buildings, and awnings that could be retracted depending on the weather), fears of invasion of privacy and the privatisation of public space ultimately led to its abandonment. The Digital Transparency in the Public Space program, which provided clear information on the use of residents' data, did not help to overcome those fears.[37]

Security measures proposed by the private sector also have the specificity of mobilising citizen vigilance. Using the many reporting applications available on

---

[32] Picaud, 'Peur sur la ville'.

[33] CNIL, Deliberation of 10 April 2018, 21.

[34] Belot, *De la smart city au territoire d'intelligence(s)*.

[35] See, in this regard, the hearing of Guillaume Poupard, Head of the Agence Nationale de la Sécurité des Systèmes d'Information (ANSSI; National Agency for the Security of Information Systems), before the Commission de la Défense nationale et des forces armées (National Defence and Armed Forces Committee) for the draft military programming law, 8 March 2018, available at https://www.assemblee-nationale.fr/dyn/15/comptes-rendus/cion_def/l15cion_def1718053_compte-rendu.

[36] Cecco, 'Google Affiliate Sidewalk Labs'.

[37] The program provided for a system of road signs to be displayed in the streets: yellow icons when the data can identify the person, blue when it is anonymous. The signs also specify the objectives of the collection: data used for safety, research or urban planning. They also specify who collects them, the city or private companies. Legros, 'À Toronto, la "ville Google"'.

smartphones or connected objects, citizens are called upon to participate actively in the surveillance of the city. For example, the 'Vigie citoyenne' application developed by the police headquarters in Paris and in Saint-Étienne enables users to report incidents. This contribution, or 'crowdsourcing',[38] is transforming the role of the police and therefore that of the state,[39] whose declining role in public surveillance is all the more problematic since the activity of private operators is not sufficiently supervised.

III. Regulation Applicability

In Chapter 5 in this volume, Gligorijević notes the centrality of privacy as a bulwark against excessive surveillance. In France, the Constitutional Council ruled that protection of privacy flows from Article 2 of the Declaration of 1789.[40] This right is also enshrined in Article 8 of the Convention for the Protection of Human Rights and Fundamental Freedoms, Article 7 of the Charter of Fundamental Rights of the European Union and, more specifically regarding personal data protection, in Article 6 of the General Data Protection Regulation,[41] which was introduced in France by the Protection of Personal Data Act of 20 June 2018. The Constitutional Council ruled that data protection law requires that 'the collection, recording, storage, consultation and communication of personal data must be justified by a reason of general interest and implemented in a manner that is adequate and proportionate to this objective'.[42] Nevertheless, current techno-policing experiments are putting this legal protection to the test, and the risks which these experiments pose to legal rights are unambiguously significant.

---

[38] Cluzel-Métayer, 'Les leviers numériques du *crowdsourcing*.'

[39] Jobard and de Maillard, *Sociologie de la police*, 241–8.

[40] Article 2 of the Declaration of Human and Civic Rights states, 'Le but de toute association politique est la conservation des droits naturels et imprescriptibles de l'homme. Ces droits sont la liberté, la propriété, la sûreté et la résistance à l'oppression' ('The aim of every political association is the preservation of the natural and imprescriptible rights of Man. These rights are Liberty, Property, Safety and Resistance to Oppression.')

[41] Regulation (EU) 2016/679 of the European Parliament and of the Council of 27 April 2016 on the protection of natural persons with regard to the processing of personal data and on the free movement of such data, and repealing Directive 95/46/EC (General Data Protection Regulation) and Directive (EU) 2016/680 of the European Parliament and of the Council of 27 April 2016 on the protection of natural persons with regard to the processing of personal data by competent authorities for the purposes of the prevention, investigation, detection or prosecution of criminal offences or the execution of criminal penalties, and on the free movement of such data, and repealing Council Framework Decision 2008/977/JHA.

[42] Constitutional Council, Decision 2012-652 DC, 22 March 2012.

1. Potential Freedom Violations

Smart surveillance systems have increased the risks of violations of legal rights and freedoms. These include invasion of privacy through the capturing, viewing and sometimes recording of images, where a person's identity could clearly be established, as well as sounds (even conversations) and biometric data (for example, body heat). They also include incursions on freedom of expression, opinion, conscience, movement and protest. This is exemplified by the Big Data Observatory of Public Tranquillity project in Marseilles, which provides, among other things, for the analysis of tweets and the monitoring of conversation threads in order to assess the risk of dangerous gatherings. Following the logic laid bare – and challenged – in Gligorijević's chapter in this volume, the gain in security entails a loss in privacy.[43]

How can the anonymity of individuals be ensured when the very aims of the Observatory are to aggregate and cross-reference a large amount of data, which allows for the identification of citizens? How can governments ensure that these tools will not be used to track members of a particular religious community, as was the case with a Muslim community in the United States,[44] and with the Uighur community in China?[45] The use of facial recognition algorithms to monitor ethnic minorities, as tested in China, would be illegal in France (Article 225-1 et seq. Criminal Code). The ultimate end for which this type of algorithm is developed is nothing less than direct discrimination. Even when discrimination is not meant to be built into the algorithm, its implementation may still have indirect discriminatory effects, thereby revealing hidden biases,[46] a phenomenon which reports have highlighted in connection with both ethnicity and gender discrimination.[47] As Banita's and Wrobel's chapters in this volume illustrate, ethnic and gender biases are particularly apt to be incorporated in, and reinforced by, surveillance.[48] As early as 2015, this issue became relevant when Google's facial recognition system identified African American people as gorillas. Today, although less explicit, bias is no less frequent. Amazon's algorithm for its premium delivery service avoids underprivileged

---

[43] See Gligorijević, Chapter 5 of this collection.

[44] New York City, for example, had set up a system in order to monitor the city's Muslim population. Pilkington, 'NYPD Settles Lawsuit'.

[45] See 'Comment la Chine organise la surveillance massive des Ouïgours'.

[46] Desmoulin-Canselier, 'Loyauté et vigilance', 2; Cluzel-Métayer, 'Décision publique algorithmique'.

[47] Angwin et al., 'Machine Bias'. See Hajian and Domingo-Ferrer, 'Direct and Indirect Discrimination Prevention Methods'.

[48] See Banita, Chapter 10; Wrobel, Chapter 13, both in this collection.

areas, and the algorithm used by its recruitment service favours male applicants.[49] The Compass algorithm, used in judicial procedures by some states of the United States to assess the risk of recidivism of prisoners, has also been denounced for its bias.[50] Using data which is apparently neutral (for example, current cases concerning the prisoner, his or her criminal record, housing, and employment situation and stability), this algorithm actually fosters racial discrimination, reproducing, and even amplifying, pre-existing bias. The result is that African American prisoners have a higher score in risk of recidivism than Caucasian prisoners.[51]

2. The Adaptability of the Legal Framework

The situation in France reveals an important paradox. While the right to privacy is protected by law, video surveillance is very poorly supervised. The setting up of a video surveillance system requires administrative authorisation,[52] which is issued by the prefect of the *département*.[53] Authorisation is quite easy to obtain and applies to several types of surveillance. Most importantly, these types of surveillance are defined in terms that are so general that cameras may be installed more or less anywhere. The different grounds used to justify the installation of cameras and thus the extension of video surveillance networks are: the protection of public buildings and their surroundings; traffic regulation; the recording of traffic violations; the prevention of attacks on people and property in places which are particularly exposed to risks of aggression, theft and drug trafficking; and, of course, the prevention of acts of terrorism.[54]

For example, the collection of abnormal sounds, which is enabled by the Saint-Étienne city system, may be seen as an extension of traditional video surveillance and therefore does not require the adoption of specific regulations or the intervention of the CNIL. The French Data Protection Act and the GDPR apply only if personal data is processed. They therefore do not apply where a sound signal is concerned. If the collection of data is associated

---

[49] CNIL, 'Comment permettre à l'Homme de garder la main?'
[50] Angwin et al., 'Machine Bias'.
[51] Ibid.
[52] Article L. 251-1 of the 'Code de la sécurité intérieure' (CSI; Interior Security Code).
[53] The main ninety-five administrative divisions of France are called *départements*. A *préfet* (prefect) is the representative of the State in the Department.
[54] A. L.251-2 CSI provides for other hypotheses, including: the safeguarding of installations useful for national defence; the prevention of natural or technological risks; the prevention of the abandonment of rubbish, waste, materials or other objects; and the safety of persons and property when places and establishments open to the public are particularly exposed to risks of aggression or theft.

with the storage of this data, as well as that of sound or images, this allows for a direct or indirect identification of individuals. The installation of thermal imaging cameras in some schools to measure the temperature of students, teachers and administrative staff in the context of the health crisis was thus considered by the administrative judges as falling within the scope of personal data protection law.[55] This was also the case for the implementation of facial recognition devices in high schools.[56]

However, even when data protection laws apply, they are rarely enforced. Techno-policing measures involve much more than simple video surveillance. They involve massive data collection. This data is then processed using sophisticated algorithms which direct the action of public authorities. Moreover, controlling these algorithms and data is complicated, particularly because of the lack of clear boundaries between the different possible uses. For example, data collected with a service-oriented purpose can easily 'slip' towards an objective of security.[57] Therefore, it is difficult to abide by the principles of the GDPR, such as the finality ('purpose limitation')[58] and proportionality ('data minimisation')[59] of data collection, in the context of the development of Safe Cities based on Big Data.

Finally, there is the problem of consent.[60] Consent must be informed, and therefore requires clear information to be given to the data subject. How could it be possible to inform and obtain the consent of passers-by when sensors are placed all over the city? Are the information panels placed in areas under video surveillance and messages concerning 'wifi tracking'[61] in shopping malls sufficient? The national and European legislative framework allows public authorities to set up these systems, but is not necessarily enforced to the letter. It is indeed up to the supervisory authorities to monitor their implementation, with the CNIL and administrative judges deciding upon the legality of this new digital tool.

---

[55] Council of State 26 June 2020, Ligue des droits de l'Homme, n° 441065.

[56] Administrative Court of Marseilles, 9th division, 3 February 2020, n° 1901249.

[57] Van Zoonen, 'Privacy Concerns'.

[58] GDPR Article 5 b.: 'Personal data shall be collected for specified, explicit and legitimate purposes and not further processed in a manner that is incompatible with those purposes [. . .].'

[59] GDPR Article 5 c.: 'Personal data shall be adequate, relevant and limited to what is necessary in relation to the purposes for which they are processed.'

[60] GDPR Article 6: 'Processing shall be lawful only if and to the extent that at least one of the following applies: (a) the data subject has given consent to the processing of his or her personal data for one or more specific purposes.'

[61] A technique aimed at geolocating individuals and tracking their movements based on the network identifiers attached to their mobile device when their wifi is switched on.

IV. The Emergence of Control by Public Authorities

1. The Rise of Soft Law

Since the GDPR came into force, the role of the CNIL has changed. It now focuses less on authorising data processing and more on advising and sanctioning those in charge of implementation. The GDPR and Directive 2016/280 abolished prior formalities and replaced them with new obligations for data controllers and their subcontractors. They must now implement 'appropriate technical and organisational measures' to ensure that they are at all times able to demonstrate that the processing they carry out complies with the GDPR or the Directive.[62]

Even though the GDPR defines in detail what data protection means, the practical operation and implementation of the DPPs, and Article 24, means that the enforcement of data protection laws is in effect placed in the hands of operators, and not those of the courts or the regulator. Data protection is defined concretely and continuously by the operators in charge of assessing the risks of infringement of fundamental rights and of implementing processing techniques that respect these rights. This is called *accountability*.[63] This paradigm shift considerably reduces the CNIL's control over the implementation of processing techniques. This means that Safe Cities solutions can be developed without the CNIL's approval. Processing operations relating to security, defence or criminal investigations and proceedings, as well as the processing of biometric or genetic data which is necessary for the authentication or control of the identity of individuals, carried out on behalf of the state, remain subject to an individual authorisation system (by ministerial order or decree) after the CNIL has approved them. However, this procedure no longer concerns the processing techniques which are implemented by and for local authorities. As a result, the CNIL has become more of an advisor and a guide that offers expertise and recommendations, thus participating in the construction of persuasive, non-binding soft law.

The problem is that the recommendations made by the CNIL are not always enforced. For example, when facial recognition techniques were experimented with in two high schools in Marseilles and Nice, the CNIL alerted public authorities that the device 'concerning students, most of whom are

---

[62] GDPR Article 24 and Directive (EU) 2016/680 of the European Parliament and of the Council of 27 April 2016 on the protection of natural persons with regard to the processing of personal data by competent authorities for the purposes of the prevention, investigation, detection or prosecution of criminal offences or the execution of criminal penalties, and on the free movement of such data, Article 19.

[63] Cluzel-Métayer and Debaets, 'Le droit de la protection des données personnelles'.

minors, with the sole aim of making access more fluid and secure [did not appear to be] necessary or proportionate to achieve these goals'.[64] The CNIL had even specified which requirements had to be respected in order to experiment with this technique, especially the collection of free and informed consent. This independent committee called for the elaboration of a solid legal framework in order to establish 'red lines beyond which no use, even experimental, can be admitted', and for a democratic debate on these questions.[65] While public local authorities do not seem very concerned about these warnings, several cases have been brought before the courts.

2. Judicial Control

Recent decisions by French administrative courts show that judges have taken the warnings of the CNIL into consideration. For example, the Administrative Court of Marseilles ruled that the installation of facial recognition cameras at the entrances to secondary schools did not comply with the GDPR and violated the principle of the right to consent:

> The administrative authority intended to legalise the processing of biometric data through the pupils' prior consent [. . .]. However, considering that consent is obtained with the pupil's signature, the administrative authority does not provide sufficient guarantees that it obtained consent from the pupils or their legal representatives for the collection of their personal data freely and in an informed manner, as there is a relationship of authority between the pupils and the school administration.[66]

This shows the strength of the principle of consent. The court added that the purposes of 'fighting identity theft and detecting unwanted movement' could be achieved by other, less intrusive means than facial recognition:

> La région PACA [Provence-Alpes-Côte d'Azur] n'établit ni ne fait valoir que les finalités poursuivies s'attachant à la fluidification et la sécurisation des contrôles à l'entrée des lycées concernés constituent un motif d'intérêt public ni même que ces finalités ne pourraient être atteintes de manière suffisamment efficace par des contrôles par badge, assortis, le cas échéant, de l'usage de la vidéosurveillance. Les requérantes sont donc fondées à soutenir que le traitement de données biométriques institué par la région PACA ne satisfait pas aux exigences prévues par le a) de l'article 9 du règlement général sur la protection

---

[64] CNIL, 'Expérimentation de la reconnaissance faciale'.
[65] CNIL, 'La reconnaissance faciale. Pour un débat à la hauteur des enjeux.
[66] Administrative Court of Marseilles, 3 February 2020, n° 1901249, discussed in Merabet, 'Chronique droit et intelligence artificielle', 1278.

des données telles qu'éclairées notamment par ses articles 4 et 7, ni davantage aux conditions énoncées par le g) du même règlement, et qu'il n'entre dans aucune des exceptions énumérées par le 2. de l'article 9 du règlement général sur la protection des données.[67]

The PACA [Provence-Alpes-Côte d'Azur] region has neither established nor asserted that the aims pursued in relation to the fluidification and securing of checks at the entrances to high schools constitute a reason of general public interest. Neither has it established or asserted that these purposes could not be achieved in a sufficiently effective manner by means of badge controls, accompanied, where appropriate, by the use of video surveillance. The claimants have therefore rightly argued that the processing of biometric data instituted by the PACA region does not meet the requirements listed in point a) of Article 9 of the General Data Protection Regulation as clarified in particular by Articles 4 and 7, that it also fails to satisfy the conditions set out in point g) of the same regulation, and that it does not fall within any of the exceptions specified in section 2. of article 9 of the General Data Protection Regulation.

Judges may also supervise the use of video surveillance systems to monitor compliance with health regulations. Concerning the use of thermal imaging cameras, the Council of State echoed the concerns of the CNIL and ruled that even if cameras do not store personal data, they shall be deemed to be systems allowing the collection and use of data. Since they lead to the collection of information authorising specific action, they have to abide by the GDPR. The Council of State considered that the function of these devices, implemented in some schools, corresponds to data processing and, more specifically, the processing of health data, which is protected by higher standards of processing. A formal decree stating the necessity of the procedure should have been obtained. Given there was no legal basis, the judge decided the use of the cameras constituted an unlawful violation of privacy. Indeed, the Council of State added that if a consent form had been sent to the families, 'the circumstance that the children's access to the school is subject to the acceptance of the use of temperature taking by thermal camera excludes in any case that the consent can be regarded as free'.[68] The judge thus reminded local authorities that the fight against the pandemic cannot justify everything.

In the same way, the Paris police have used drones with onboard cameras to ensure compliance with the lockdown measures at the end of the lockdown period, a practice which two associations for the protection of human rights – La Quadrature du Net and La Ligue des droits de l'Homme – have

[67] Ibid.
[68] Council of State 26 June 2020, Ligue des droits de l'Homme, n° 441065.

asked administrative courts to declare unlawful. The Council of State ruled in their favour.[69] It did not question the principle of the use of drones for surveillance purposes. It reasoned that the aim of the use of drones is 'to inform administrative police services so that police forces may be sent on site when necessary, in order to proceed to the break-up of crowds or the evacuation of sites forbidden to the public and to stop public disturbance and restore public order' (point 11). 'In the current circumstances, this objective is legitimate as it is necessary for public safety' (point 13). However, the Council of State decided that the state should immediately stop the use of drones for surveillance purposes. It ruled that drones equipped with powerful zoom lenses may collect data allowing the identification of individuals, even though it is not their primary objective (point 18). They can only be used if data protection rules are observed, which is guaranteed by official authorisation and approval by the CNIL (point 19).

Yet public authorities intend to bypass this decision. A draft bill has been discussed in Parliament to make drone surveillance possible.[70] It also plans to authorise the use of mobile cameras by police forces with transmission of images in real time to the command post and to equip all buses with cameras to film streets and, as a result, passers-by. These provisions reflect the public authorities' desire not only to supervise, but also to develop these digital systems with a view to monitoring the population as a whole. For the moment, the Constitutional Court has put a halt to drone surveillance.[71] But the government has just introduced a new, more precise, bill to circumvent the decision.[72]

V. Conclusion

The role of the courts, though reassuring, is nevertheless dependent on the heightened watchfulness of associations for the protection of fundamental freedoms. This raises the question, also discussed in Poullet's chapter in this

---

[69] Council of State ruling, 18 May 2020, n° 440442, 440445, Ass. La Quadrature du Net, Ligue des droits de l'homme.

[70] 'Proposition de loi relative à la Sécurité globale' (General Security Bill), 20 October 2020, National Assembly, which has become the 'Loi n° 2021-64625 du 25 mai 2021 pour la sécurité globale préservant les libertés' (Statute 2021-646 for general security and the preservation of freedoms, 25 May 2021).

[71] Constitutional Council. Decision n° 2021-817 DC, 20 May 2021, 'Loi pour une sécurité globale préservant les libertés' (Statute for General Security and the Preservation of Freedoms).

[72] 'Projet de loi, adopté par l'Assemblée nationale, relatif à la responsabilité pénale et à la sécurité intérieure, n° 849' (Bill passed by the National Assembly on penal responsibility and national security), introduced 23 September 2021.

volume, of whether judicial intervention is enough on its own.[73] The development of a comprehensive legislative framework would be a preferable approach. In some countries, the prospect of stricter and more efficient regulation of the use of algorithms by public authorities has arisen, with the Canadian Directive on Automated Decision Making of 1 April 2019, for instance. Future European Union AI regulation may bring better protection for citizens.[74] Ursula von der Leyen, President of the European Commission, stated:

> We will act to ensure that AI is fair and compliant with the high standards Europe has developed in all fields. Our commitment to safety, privacy, equal treatment in the workplace must be fully upheld in a world where algorithms influence decisions. We will focus our action on high-risk applications that can affect our physical or mental health, or that influence important decisions on employment or law enforcement. The aim is not more regulation, but practical safeguards, accountability and the possibility of human intervention in case of danger or disputes. We successfully shaped other industries – from cars to food – and we will now apply the same logic and standards in the new data-agile economy.[75]

The European Commission's White Paper of 19 February 2020 proposes a legal framework, based on essential requirements concerning the quality of the data used, its retention period, transparency, reliability, human control, and the right to an effective remedy against such AI applications.[76] As this project follows a risk-based approach, it will cover only 'high risk' AI applications such as health, social security, transport, energy, border control, judicial and law enforcement, but also protection of public order. It may therefore also cover Safe Cities devices. The question is whether this proposed European law is sufficiently demanding and does not come too late. Innovative practices are rapidly becoming routine and, as we have seen, it will be very difficult for judges to control them.

The search for security is leading to an increasing digital hold on the city. The flourishing digital security market naturally encourages this phenomenon.

---

[73] See Poullet, Chapter 4 of this collection.

[74] Proposal for a Regulation of the European Parliament and of the Council laying down harmonised rules on Artificial Intelligence (Artificial Intelligence Act) and amending certain union legislative acts COM/2021/206 final 21.04.2021.

[75] Ursula von der Leyen, Presentation of Commission's strategies for data and Artificial Intelligence, 19 February 2020, available at https://ec.europa.eu/commission/presscorner/detail/en/ac_20_260.

[76] Comm. UE (2020) 65, White paper, On Artificial Intelligence – A European approach to excellence and trust, 19 February 2020. Discussed in Marti, 'Concilier l'excellence et la confiance'.

Security is more than ever co-produced by public authorities and private actors – companies and citizens – who are called upon to participate in generalised surveillance, constituting a 'security continuum', infringing on freedom of movement, freedom of expression and of course privacy. As many of the chapters in this collection can attest – notably in the discussions by Sabot, and Grabosky and Urbas[77] – the line between police action and social attitudes, and between public and private interests, is vanishingly thin. The measures now being taken by Smart Cities further blurs these fundamental distinctions, weakening social cohesion by generating suspicion between individuals in a security ideal, instead of using digital technology to improve public service.

VI. Bibliography

Abiteboul, Serge, and Gilles Dowek. *Le temps des algorithmes*. Paris: le Pommier, 2017.

Angwin, Julia, Jeff Larson, Surya Mattu, and Lauren Kirchner. 'Machine Bias.' *ProPublica*, 23 May 2016. https://www.propublica.org/article/machine-bias-risk-assessments-in-criminal-sentencing.

Auby, Jean-Bernard. 'Les smart cities: un cadre nouveau pour les politiques sanitaires et les systèmes de santé.' In *Smart Cities et Santé*, edited by Antony Taillefait and Maximilien Lanna. Bayonne: Institut Universitaire de Varenne, 2019.

Ballesteros, Jaime, Mahmudur Rahman, Bogdan Carbunar, and Naphtali Rishe. 'Safe Cities. A Participatory Sensing Approach.' In *37th Annual IEEE Conference on Local Computer Networks*, edited by Tom Pfeifer, Anura Jayasumana, and Damla Turgut, 626–34. IEEE, 2012. DOI: 10.1109/LCN.2012.6423684.

Barnes, Susan B. 'A Privacy Paradox: Social Networking in the United States.' *First Monday* 11, no. 9 (April 2006). https://doi.org/10.5210/fm.v11i9.1394.

Belot, Luc. *De la smart city au territoire d'intelligence(s). Rapport au Premier Ministre sur l'avenir de la smart city*. 19 April 2017. https://www.gouvernement.fr/partage/9140-rapport-de-m-luc-belot-sur-les-smart-cities.

Benbouzid, Bilel. 'From Situational Crime Prevention to Predictive Policing: Sociology of an Ignored Controversy.' *Penal Field* 12 (2015). https://doi.org/10.4000/champpenal.9066.

Bensamoun, Alexandra, and Bertrand Brunessen, eds. *Le règlement général sur la protection des données*. Paris: Mare et Martin, 2020.

Benslimane, Ismaël. *Étude critique du système d'analyse prédictive: Predpol*. Grenoble: Grenoble University, 2015. http://www.innox.fr/uploads/9/1/8/9/9189649/benslimane.pdf.

Bioy, Xavier. 'Installation de micros à Saint-Etienne: une menace pour la vie privée?' *Le Club des juristes*, 15 March 2019. https://blog.leclubdesjuristes.com/installation-de-micros-a-st-etienne-une-menace-pour-la-vie-privee/.

---

[77] See Chapters 2 and 7 of this collection.

Bourcier, Danièle, Patricia Hassett, and Christophe Roquilly, eds. *Droit et intelligence artificielle*. Paris: Romillat, 2000.

Cecco, Leyland. 'Google Affiliate Sidewalk Labs Abruptly Abandons Toronto Smart City Project.' *The Guardian*, 7 May 2020. https://www.theguardian. com/technology/2020/may/07/google-sidewalk-labs-toronto-smart-city-abandoned.

Chevallier, Jacques. 'La vie privée à l'épreuve de la société numérique.' In *Penser le droit à partir de l'individu. Mélanges en l'honneur d'Élisabeth Zoller*, edited by Wanda Mastor, 563–76. Paris: Dalloz, 2018.

Clarke, Roger. 'Information Technology and Dataveillance.' Roger Clarke's Web-Site, 1987. http://www.rogerclarke.com/DV/CACM88.html.

Cluzel-Métayer, Lucie. 'Décision publique algorithmique et discriminations.' In *Nouveaux modes de détection et de prévention de la discrimination et accès au droit*, edited by Marie Mercat-Bruns, 109–19. Paris: Société de législation comparée, 2020.

———. 'Les budgets participatifs: une émancipation sous contrôle.' In *Finances publiques citoyennes*, edited by Jean-François Boudet and Xavier Cabannes, 171–81. Issy-les-Moulineaux: LGDJ (Collection Lextenso), 2017.

———. 'Les leviers numériques du *crowdsourcing* des services publics.' *JCPA* (December 2019): 24–7.

Cluzel-Métayer, Lucie, and Emilie Debaets. 'Le droit de la protection des données personnelles: la loi du 20 juin 2018.' *Revue française de droit administratif* 6 (2018): 1101–11.

CNIL. 'Comment permettre à l'Homme de garder la main? Les enjeux éthiques des algorithmes et de l'intelligence artificielle.' 15 December 2017. https://www.cnil. fr/fr/comment-permettre-lhomme-de-garder-la-main-rapport-sur-les-enjeux-ethiques-des-algorithmes-et-de.

———. 'Expérimentation de la reconnaissance faciale dans deux lycées: la CNIL précise sa position.' 29 October 2019. https://www.cnil.fr/fr/experimentation-de-la-reconnaissance-faciale-dans-deux-lycees-la-cnil-precise-sa-position.

———. 'La reconnaissance faciale: pour un débat à la hauteur des enjeux.' 15 November 2019. https://www.cnil.fr/fr/reconnaissance-faciale-pour-un-debat-la-hauteur-des-enjeux.

CNIL and LINC. *La plateforme d'une ville. Les données personnelles au cœur de la fabrique de la smart city*. Cahiers IP no. 5. Paris: CNIL, 2017.

'Comment la Chine organise la surveillance massive des Ouïgours.' *Le Monde*, 3 May 2019.

Desmoulin-Canselier, Sonia. 'Loyauté et vigilance: de nouveaux principes pour les algorithmes de recommandation?' *Dictionnaire permanent*. Bulletin no. 289 (February 2018).

Desmoulin-Canselier, Sonia, and Daniel Le Métayer. *Décider avec les algorithmes. Quelle place pour l'Homme, quelle place pour le droit?* Paris: Dalloz, 2020.

European Parliament. *Mapping Smart Cities in the EU*. Luxembourg: Publications Office, 2014.

Hajian, Sara, and Josep Domingo-Ferrer. 'Direct and Indirect Discrimination Prevention Methods.' In *Discrimination and Privacy in the Information Society: Data Mining and Profiling in Large Databases*, edited by Bart Custers, Toon Calders, Bart Schermer, and Tal Zarsky, 241–54. Berlin: Springer, 2013.

Heilmann, Eric, and Marie-Noëlle Mornet. 'L'impact de la vidéosurveillance sur les désordres urbains, le cas de la Grande-Bretagne.' *Les Cahiers de la Sécurité Intérieure* 46, no. 4 (2001): 197–211.

Jobard, Fabien, and Jacques de Maillard. *Sociologie de la police*. Paris: Armand Colin, 2015.

Kitchin, Rob. *Getting Smarter about Smart Cities: Improving Data Privacy and Data Security*. Dublin: Data Protection Unit, Department of the Taoiseach, 2016.

Latour, Xavier. 'La place du secteur privé dans la politique moderne de sécurité.' *AJDA* 12 (2010): 657–63.

Legros, C. 'À Toronto, la "ville Google" en quête d'une gouvernance de ses données numériques.' *Le Monde*, 14 June 2019.

Mandel, Robert. *Armies Without States: The Privatization of Security*. Boulder, CO: Lynne Rienner, 2002.

Marti, Gaëlle. 'Concilier l'excellence et la confiance en matière d'intelligence artificielle. Le Livre blanc de la Commission européenne cherche à réaliser la quadrature du cercle.' *Revue Pratique de la Prospective et de l'Innovation* (2020), file 5.

Martial-Braz, Nathalie, and Judith Rochfeld, eds. *Droit des données personnelles. Les spécificités du droit français au regard du RGPD*. Paris: Dalloz, 2019.

Meijer, Albert, and Martijn Wessels. 'Predictive Policing: Review of Benefits and Drawbacks.' *International Journal of Public Administration* 42, no. 1 (2019): 1031–9.

Merabet, Samir. 'Chronique droit et intelligence artificielle.' *La Semaine Juridique* (6 July 2020): 1278.

Picaud, Myrtille. 'Peur sur la ville: le marché des "safe cities".' *The Conversation*, 26 May 2020.

Pilkington, Ed. 'NYPD Settles Lawsuit after Illegally Spying on Muslims.' *The Guardian*, 5 April 2018. https://www.theguardian.com/world/2018/apr/05/nypd-muslim-surveillance-settlement.

La Quadrature du Net. 'Mouchards et drones à Saint-Etienne: le maire veut étouffer le débat.' La Quadrature du Net, 15 April 2019. https://www.laquadrature.net/2019/04/15/mouchards-et-drone-a-saint-etienne-le-maire-veut-etouffer-le-debat/.

Raufer, Xavier. 'Cartographie criminelle, surveiller et prédire.' *Le Monde des idées*, 5 January 2018.

———. 'Police prédictive: les belles histoires de l'Oncle Predpol.' *Sécurité globale* 3–4 (2015): 95–110.

Rees, Marc. 'Reconnaissance faciale: la ville de Nice n'a pas reçu "d'autorisation" de la CNIL.' NextInpact, 19 February 2019. https://www.nextinpact.com/article/29187/107628-reconnaissance-faciale-ville-nice-na-pas-recu-dautorisationde-cnil.

Sintomer, Yves, Carsten Herzberg, Giovanni Allegretti, with Anja Röcke. *Les budgets participatifs dans le monde – une étude transnationale*. Dialog Global, no. 25. Bonn: Engagement Global and Service pour les Communes du Monde, 2014.

Townsend, Anthony. *Smart Cities: Big Data, Civic Hackers, and the Quest for a New Utopia*. New York: W. W. Norton, 2013.

Van Zoonen, Liesbeth. 'Privacy Concerns in Smart Cities.' *Government Information Quarterly* 33, no. 3 (July 2016): 472–80.

Ville intelligente, ville démocratique? Proceedings of the annual meeting of the 'Cité des *Smart Cities*.' Boulogne-Billancourt: Berger-Levrault, 2015.

Part 3

Critique

10

Black Futures Matter: Racial Foresight from the Slave Ship to Predictive Policing

Georgiana Banita

> I arrive slowly in the world; sudden emergences are no longer my habit. I crawl along. The white gaze, the only valid one, is already dissecting me. I am *fixed*. Once their microtomes are sharpened, the Whites objectively cut sections of my reality. I have been betrayed. I sense, I see in this white gaze that it's the arrival not of a new man, but of a new type of man, a new species. A Negro, in fact!
>
> Frantz Fanon, *Black Skin, White Masks*

I. Post-Panopticism and the Visualisation of Race

Fanon's analysis speaks to the ineradicable synecdoche of seeing race. Upon entering the white field of vision, in Fanon's analysis, a Black man's opaque skin reflects every other Black man like himself – past, present and future.[1] He can no more be denuded of this epidermal mirror than he can shed his own skin. Fanon is fixated by a white gaze that he can sense and see; the white watcher does not have to be directly before one's eyes to do its work of dissecting. The conquering gaze could also inhabit a camera, or it may survey Black emergences indirectly by data gathering, statistics and prediction. What all these microtomes have in common is their inbuilt perception of blackness as a distinguishing category of experience that holds unspeakable dangers and must therefore be controlled and contained through permanent surveillance.

In his dread of being watched by a white observer – what we may call his racial scopophobia – Fanon articulates a deeply rooted pathology of American anti-Black racism.[2] As I suggest in what follows, throughout the history of

---

[1] Fanon, *Black Skin, White Masks*, 95.

[2] Fanon was deeply troubled by American racism, a fact that did not go unnoticed in the US. When he died in 1961 at Bethesda Naval Hospital, where he was being treated for leukaemia, he was under CIA watch. See Macey, *Frantz Fanon*, 486. On Fanon's reception in the US, see Gibson, *Rethinking Fanon*.

surveillance in the United States, suspicious blackness has provided an expedient template for determining who should look – or, as the case may be, point the camera – at whom. Consequently, any subversion of this template – the amateur video showing four LAPD officers brutally beating Rodney King, or sousveillance projects today – is automatically remarkable. So much so that it is easy to forget that no *a priori* surveillance system has ever demonstrated non-white subjects to be unrulier than the general population and thus in need of greater surveillance efforts; race was the reason why certain subjects were surveilled at all, in the firm expectation that they were inherently suspicious and thus susceptible to disorderly behaviour. Indeed, as Joy argues in Chapter 11 of this volume, this race-based suspicion underpins forms of surveillance that today perpetuate colonial power structures and the brutalisation of Indigenous peoples in Australia. In an enduringly colour-lined America, it is the optical construction of race that has summoned surveillance into everyday life, enabled the police to take root as an extension of the white gaze, and ultimately allowed non-optical police vigilance, such as pre-crime programs, to flourish.

As previous chapters have shown, although techniques and technologies have changed, the practice of surveillance, and our concerns about it, goes back centuries. But my purpose here is to insist that these practices are always and have always been racialised. Both by (white) states and by (white) citizens, from slavery and the colonial plantation onwards, the Black body has been targeted as the pre-eminent object of the sovereign gaze. The specific subject of this chapter is the untheorised chasm between an earlier era of passive surveillance – during which police patrols and federal law enforcement simply accumulated information that could be weaponised against suspicious citizens at a later date – and the newer, crystal-ball type of surveillance that feeds live data into pre-existing digital models able to instantly assess its value as predictive clues and actionable evidence against specific citizens (or non-citizens, for that matter). In Chapter 9 of this volume, Cluzel-Métayer has demonstrated the significance of predictive policing under the rubric of Safe Cities. She rightly notes that the application of predictive data points and algorithms is not equal. Some communities are far more vulnerable than others. Above all, as this chapter aims to show, in the United States in particular, the objects of these new technologies of study, prediction and enforcement are overwhelmingly Black lives. I shall argue that the shift from reactive to anticipative surveillance is closely linked to what I term 'racial foresight', a logic that ties race to future criminality and manifests itself most dramatically in police surveillance.[3] Law enforcement, then, is inseparable

---

[3] On the pre-vision of race, see also my forthcoming special issue, *Foreseeing Race: The Technology and Culture of Risk Prediction after the Datalogical Turn*, of the *Journal of American Studies*.

from the enforcement of white power over populations whose appearance and visual exposure limits them to a lesser citizenship. Though derived from American race relations, my argument can be applied beyond the borders of the United States. In this book, it is in fact echoed in Joy's chapter on the racialised surveillance of Indigenous peoples in Australia.

In this chapter, I suggest that, at root, surveillance itself is inseparable from racial foresight, starting with the proto-panoptic design of the slave ship, which immobilised the slaves and subjected them to round-the-clock observation by vigilant crew members. No form of surveillance, then, has ever been innocent – that is, a neutral, objective recording machine that trains its eyes indifferently on subjects that may or may not pose a threat. It was, rather, a sense of visible, racially inscribed danger that led surveillance to become a powerful instrument of sovereignty in the first place. This fact has been obscured by increasingly complex and covert observation systems that are neither themselves visible nor require having the target directly in sight. Wiretapping, intelligence and Big Data have blinded us to the visual origin of surveillance as the practice of literally keeping an eye on someone, usually a person who is discernibly different from the (white) norm. More recently, discussions of predictive surveillance too have left the role of visibility understated.

This has something to do with the fact that digital environments have nurtured new, arguably non-visual surveillance forms. Yet I write here in the conviction that a visual regime of racialised risk nonetheless continues to undergird surveillance practices, even in a post-panoptic world. It even sustains the methods of AI-based predictive policing, which are in essence also a practice of pre-vision or fore-sight.

As Brunon-Ernst notes in Chapter 6 of this collection, there is no question that the model of the Panopticon has been challenged by other forms of surveillance (Bentham's own 'constitutional Panopticon', or Thomas Mathiesen's synopticon, in which the many watch the few) that are either inversed or more dispersed, as more and more tech corporations promise individualised services in return for full transparency of their customers' online experience. That being said, Roy Boyne's conclusion that the panoptic paradigm has been rendered redundant by a 'post-panoptical' regime, in which surveillance is no longer spatial or architectural, is premature.[4] Though the infrastructures of observation have largely been digitised, the decision about which areas and which subjects to monitor still correlates with skin colour. While it cannot be denied that 'the emergent practice of pre-visualization'[5] – in which future danger is simulated on the basis of risk-predictive data, rather than observed in real time – has shifted the focus on non-visual data gathering, even such

[4] Boyne, 'Post-Panopticism'.
[5] Ibid., 299.

pre-visualising methods like those deployed by predictive policing programs ultimately project a visual threat on the retinas of patrolling officers.

The archive I have compiled for this diachronic argument begins with the human architecture of the slave ship, which I revisit in order to illustrate that 'overseeing' captive slaves during transportation is the Middle Passage equivalent of the modern panoptic racism that associates racial visibility (that is, both skin colour and its exposure to a dominating gaze) with criminal threat. I continue with the civil rights movement and the FBI's observation of its key advocates, especially Martin Luther King, Jr., to show that the hostile, often salacious spying on civil rights icons exposes the racial foresight at the very core of state-sanctioned surveillance. Third, I look into how broken windows policing in the 1990s laid the groundwork for the still popular policing doctrine that community disorder inevitably develops into large-scale social instability, which in turn facilitates crime and must therefore be met with a merciless, zero-tolerance approach. Fourth and finally, I explore how, in the shadow of the web, the over-policing practices of the 1990s have been increasingly obscured by a cloak of algorithmic invisibility. With pre-crime systems like PredPol and others, blatant racial profiling can now easily be disguised inside unintelligible technologies that continue to escape public scrutiny by feigning complexity and by painting themselves as unstoppable harbingers of the future.

II. The Slave Ship: Overseeing Race

As the historian Marcus Rediker has observed, the slave ship was 'a mobile, seagoing prison at a time when the modern prison had not yet been established on land'.[6] The Liverpool slave ship *Brookes*, for instance, was built in 1781, five years before Jeremy Bentham theorised the Panopticon. And yet the often-reproduced diagram of this ship shows an essential difference from Bentham's scheme (Figure 10.1). The Panopticon pivots on a gaze that radiates from the centre and fans out towards the margin in a lateral movement, the inmates and the security guard more or less at eye level. And with good reason: the object of observation is not so much the inmate as the entire space inside the cell. Since the inmate is able to move around, the guard's gaze must reach into the cell's perimeter.

On the slave ship, however, the human cargo is stowed away on platforms or shelves only two feet in height, even less than what prisoners would have been allotted on ships at the time. With the slaves crammed into every nook and cranny of the available space, there are no cells to speak of. The sailors

[6] Rediker, *Slave Ship*, 45.

PLAN SHEWING THE STOWAGE OF 130 ADDITIONAL SLAVES ROUND THE WINGS OR SIDES OF THE LOWER DECK BY MEANS OF PLATFORMS OR SHELVES (IN THE MANNER OF GALLERIES IN A CHURCH) THE SLAVES STOWED ON THE SHELVES AND BELOW THEM HAVE ONLY A HEIGHT OF 2 FEET 7 INCHES BETWEEN THE BEAMS AND FAR LESS UNDER THE BEAMS . See Fig I.

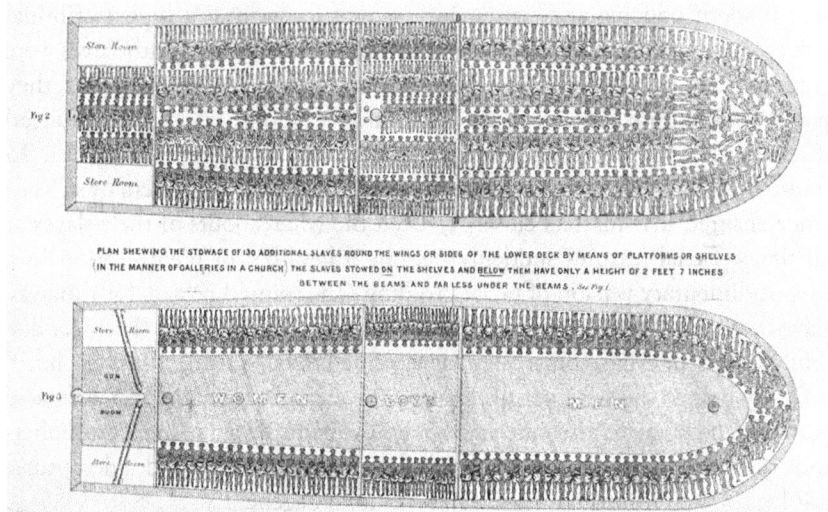

Figure 10.1 Stowage of the British slave ship *Brookes* under the Regulated Slave Trade Act of 1788. Library of Congress Rare Book and Special Collections Division, Washington, D.C. 20540 USA.

and other crew members working as guards would simply have looked down on the tightly packed rows of bodies. The diagram of the *Brookes* applies the same aerial vantage point. 'The neat and orderly ranks, graphically portrayed more like corpses than living beings, give little sense of place', writes the historian James Walvin;[7] what they do convey is a sense of visual domination. The panoptic design of the ship does not merely help discipline the slaves. The view from above, so poignantly highlighted by the abolitionist authors of the *Brookes* sketch, also seeks to massify and humiliate the captives.

The *Brookes* illustration in fact depicts the claustrophobically slotted slaves like tiny matchstick men whose only identifying feature is their blackness. The lack of any other personal markers dehumanises them by making their bodies appear interchangeable and therefore expendable. The drawing thus not only exposes the squalor of the ship, but also codifies the management of the slaves' bodies as a form of surveillance, of over-seeing. And in turn, oversight was prompted by foresight about the risk of losing too many of them – to suffocation or suicide – during the passage.

Disembarking the slave ship – only to step onto the plantation – hardly brought any freedom from disciplinary surveillance. In much the same way

[7] Walvin, *Black Ivory*, 46.

that modern policing and sentencing systems presuppose a higher criminal risk among Black Americans, in the nineteenth-century US South slaves were automatically considered a flight risk. Due to strict plantation routines, they posed little criminal threat apart from rare rebellions, yet they did indeed threaten to escape the criminal regime in which they were held captive. To forestall Black freedom and emancipation, an impermeable system of surveillance ensured that masters closely tracked the whereabouts of their slaves at all times. Facial features suddenly became a key tool of identification in a first, rudimentary version of racial profiling. The wanted posters for runaway slaves contained detailed physical descriptions of the fugitives. Features like 'blubber lips' or eyes so protrusive, they seemed to be 'starting out of his head' not only helped the slave patrols identify the escapees more quickly, but were paired with character assessments, too, many denoting some form of duplicitous disobedience. Such portraits did not just deter flight and aid capture, but legitimated it through caricatures of moral degeneracy.

The US police came into being as a network of social control during – and as a result of – slavery.[8] Indeed, the origins of the institution are impossible to imagine outside the deeply divided spaces of the plantation world. The idea of a slave patrol aligned perfectly with the values of antebellum America, particularly with the sense that Blacks could never hold fully-fledged human dignity and worth, validating slave owners' feeling that they themselves were intrinsically worthier of protection. This tainted genealogy impressed on police leaders and foot soldiers the notion that an entire section of the US population was to be denied the right to self-determination and agency. Evidence that the police remain committed to this mentality is hard to overlook, from the Jim Crow laws to the 'New Jim Code' – the term sociologist Ruha Benjamin has coined to describe algorithmic policing tools that target Blacks as relentlessly as earlier police forces fixated on the vagrant poor and the enslaved.[9] On the slave ship and on the plantation, the playbook by which slave owners kept an eye on their property is the original form of racial foresight that subsequently helped institutionalise surveillance as a tactic of racial control.

III. COINTELPRO and the Voyeurism of State Surveillance

As Simone Browne has observed, the surveillance of slaves both fulfilled a disciplinary function and, no less significantly, reduced the enslaved to the status of 'spectacle'.[10] In other words, the humiliation of being on permanent

---

[8] See for instance Hadden, *Slave Patrols*; Wagner, *Disturbing the Peace*; and sections of Vitale, *End of Policing*.

[9] Benjamin, *Race after Technology*; Benjamin, *Captivating Technology*; Jefferson, *Digitize and Punish*.

[10] Browne, *Dark Matters*, 42.

display objectified and sexualised the targets of surveillance. A very similar conflation of controlling and voyeuristic effects is evidenced by the FBI's relentless surveillance of Martin Luther King, Jr. at the height of his activism for civil rights. Through its Memphis field office, the FBI opened a security file on King in 1965. When King died in April 1968, his FBI file had already ballooned to about 190 pages.[11] King was counted among the subversive individuals that the FBI's COINTELPRO operation targeted covertly and illegally from 1956 to 1971. The list of Black artists and intellectuals surveilled, discredited and intimidated by the FBI in this period includes James Baldwin, Bob Marley, Malcolm X, Fred Hampton, Angela Yvonne Davis, Richard Wright, Ralph Ellison, Josephine Baker, Billie Holiday and Jimi Hendrix.

To burnish their reputation as effective enforcers of the law, the Federal Bureau of Narcotics kept Billie Holiday under close surveillance and persecuted her with multiple threats and arrests for her drug use in the 1950s.[12] But this federal agency, which lasted only until 1968, was gathering intelligence on the iconic singer primarily from the people in her inner circle. By the late 1960s, the government resorted to other means, including wiretapping and photography, to observe its targets. One photographer in particular is known to have supplied to the FBI numerous pictures of civil rights activists, including of his friend and frequent subject, Martin Luther King, Jr.

In 2010, the story broke that Memphis photographer Ernest C. Withers (1922–2007), a widely revered figure of the civil rights movement, had worked as an informant for the FBI in the 1960s. The revelation spurred a reconsideration of his images as perhaps less an act of historical documentation than one of covert surveillance. Withers's most famous photograph shows a group of sanitation workers on strike in Memphis, Tennessee, in March 1968. Each worker carries a sign proclaiming the obvious, yet in the segregated South still contested truth, 'I AM A MAN.' As an emblem of Black emancipation, the photo is memorable and moving. But in the context of Withers's work for the FBI, the image seems far more ominous. 'I never tried to monitor what they were doing (too closely)', Withers insisted, claiming that even though he was happy to record the public activism of the organisers, he refrained from exposing anything that went on during their secret meetings. 'I was always interested in their outside work but I tried not to know too much about the inside because I always had FBI agents looking over my shoulder and wanting to question me.'[13] The statement sounds

---

[11] Perrusquia, *Spy in Canaan*, 308. See also Lauterbach, *Bluff City*.

[12] As revealed in Andrew and Green, *Stars and Spies* and James Erskine's 2019 documentary *Billie*.

[13] Perrusquia, *Spy in Canaan*, 245.

disingenuous in light of his activities as an FBI informant, but it also testifies that Withers knew his connections and access were valuable – both to the movement and to the federal government.

After all, this was not just any ordinary photographer. Withers was present in King's hotel room the night the civil rights leader was shot, and he also photographed King's funeral. With his studio photographs of Black families, memorable snapshots of civil rights history, famous portraits of Black artists like Aretha Franklin and Tina Turner, or the pamphlet he published illustrating Emmett Till's death and the murder trial that followed, Withers provided an essential chronicle of Black life in the South.[14] Putting a face to the names and brutal slaying of Black Americans like Till and King was necessary as a call to arms in the battle for civil rights. So it seems especially perverse that the FBI should piggyback on the movement's own self-fashioning techniques to discredit and derail it from within.

The FBI had especially prurient interests when it came to King, keeping tabs on his illicit extramarital affairs and drinking habits by installing microphones in his hotel rooms. As an FBI-penned, anonymously posted letter to King reveals, the Bureau aimed to carry out its continued warrantless surveillance until King's purportedly 'filthy, fraudulent self' could be 'bared to the nation'.[15] Shortly after receiving the letter, instead of committing suicide as the letter encouraged him to, King travelled to Oslo to receive his Nobel Peace Prize. He was a world leader, public icon, and probably one of the most photographed people of his time; the tight mesh of surveillance woven around him inevitably reflected his global visibility and the increasingly iconographic publicity tools King himself used to advance the civil rights movement.

In an even more baffling twist, Withers had been a police officer in Memphis before starting his photography business on Beale Street. After serving as an Army photographer in World War II, he joined the police force as soon as it opened its ranks to Blacks.[16] And even though he quit after only three years, vestiges of a scrutinising surveillance gaze are still detectable in his photos. Yet he recasts the feelings of danger that emanate from civil rights activists – certainly in the eyes of police and white society – into a call for justice. In other words, he begins to watch the watchers, wielding his camera like a protest sign, staring down the white Southern establishment that marginalised and ignored the Black community for so long. The photo of William Edwin Jones pushing his baby daughter's stroller down the street, as three police officers look on from a squad car, is a case in point (Figure 10.2).

[14] In 2019 many of Withers's works were collected in a new book, *Revolution in Black and White*.
[15] Schwarz and Huq, *Unchecked and Unbalanced*, 22.
[16] Baldwin, *Freedom's March*, 18.

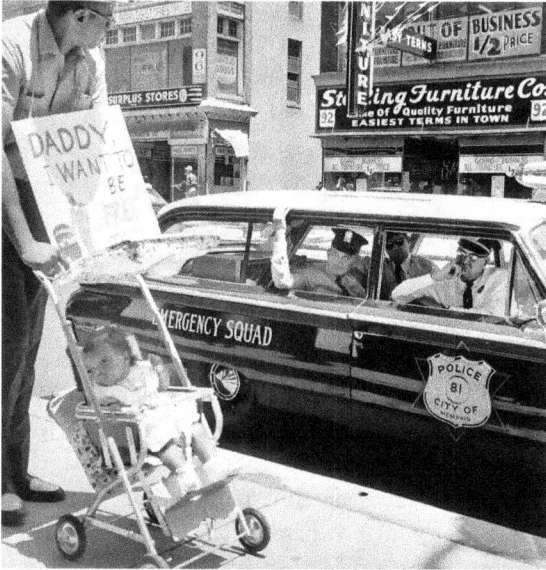

Figure 10.2 William Edwin Jones pushes daughter Renee Andrewnetta Jones
(8 months old, who grew up to become a doctor) during protest march on
Main St., Memphis, Tennessee, August 1961 (caption as written by Withers).
© Dr. Ernest C. Withers, Sr. courtesy of the Withers Family Trust.

The calculated *mise en scène* traces four intersecting gazes: the policemen's
half-bemused, half-intimidating looks, the father's defiant back-gazing, the
baby's precociously rebellious glance in the opposite direction, and Withers's
own probing scrutiny of the squad car. The effect captures the tension of
anti-Black policing, particularly the function of the street kerb as a barrier
between motorised, all-seeing police and visually exposed Black citizens.

IV. Eyes on the Street: Panopticops and Broken
Windows Policing in New York City

The street remained what Saidiya Hartman might call a 'scene of subjection'
well into the late twentieth century.[17] If in a previous era the FBI relied on
informants to obtain first-hand information about subversive individuals, in
the decades that followed, the kerbside surveillance depicted by Withers would
become a new norm in the state's strategy for crime containment. The shift
from intelligence gathering – by planting bugs and amassing photographic

[17] Hartman, *Scenes of Subjection*.

files on FBI targets – to face-to-face observation reaffirms the centrality of the police force to the visual regulation of Black freedom. J. Edgar Hoover spied on King through the photographic archive compiled by Withers; in the streets of America's urban centres in the 1990s, patrol cars were cruising slowly and demonstratively like mobile cameras. The overseers were on the move, doing their rounds in full view of the neighbourhood, with an eye to sowing fear and submission in their wake.

Cruise vehicles and foot patrols started out as key initiatives in a preventative form of neighbourhood policing. Initially focused on fostering positive relationships with community members and stakeholders, community policing soon devolved, however, into a stricter variant known as broken windows policing. First described in 1982 by George L. Kelling and James Q. Wilson in an influential article for the *Atlantic Monthly*, the broken windows theory pivots on the role of unchallenged neighbourhood disorder (such as vandalism, i.e. broken windows) in generating more serious crime.[18] In Kelling and Wilson's view, it is not enough to battle violent crime; the police must intervene much sooner to create a climate of safety by empowering (mostly) white foot-patrol officers to remove from the streets of Black neighbourhoods what the authors term 'disreputable or obstreperous or unpredictable people: panhandlers, drunks, addicts, rowdy teenagers, prostitutes, loiterers, the mentally disturbed'.[19] By maintaining a level of public order, and reducing the likelihood of 'distasteful, worrisome encounters' in these areas,[20] police patrols help residents feel reassured that they live in a safe neighbourhood. Crucially, Kelling and Wilson suggest that 'disorder and crime are usually inextricably linked, in a kind of developmental sequence';[21] in other words, by establishing public order at a lower level, more serious crime is less likely to take root. As they put it, 'one unrepaired broken window is a signal that no one cares'[22] – which in turn fosters the kind of social indifference and atomisation in which violent crime will flourish. So by cracking down on a wide range of so-called quality-of-life offences such as vandalism, turnstile jumping or jaywalking, the police can successfully tackle the larger crime problem plaguing US cities.

The cover of the *Atlantic Monthly* issue in which the Kelling and Wilson article appeared is both reductive and revealing (Figure 10.3). On the one hand, it downplays some of the article's distasteful racial undertones while, on the other, it lays bare the theory's true panoptic scope. The drawing by

[18] Kelling and Wilson, 'Police and Neighborhood Safety'. The argument presented in the article is extended and further illustrated in Kelling and Coles, *Fixing Broken Windows*.
[19] Kelling and Wilson, 'Police and Neighborhood Safety', 30.
[20] Ibid., 31.
[21] Ibid.
[22] Ibid.

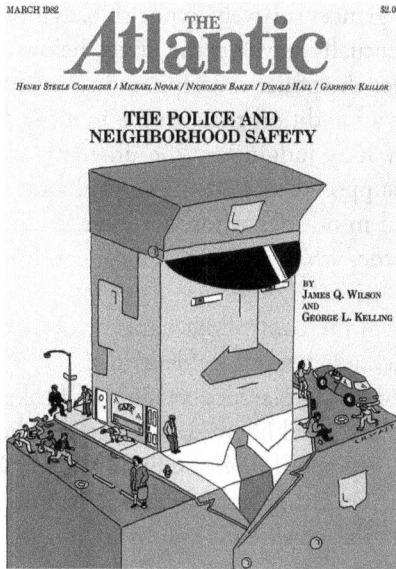

Figure 10.3 Cover of *Atlantic Monthly*, March 1982. © Seymour Chwast, 1982, printed with permission of the artist.

New York City graphic illustrator Seymour Chwast renders what Kelling and Wilson refer to as the 'inhospitable and frightening jungle' of a run-down neighbourhood in the pastel tones of the candy wrappers Chwast was designing at the time.[23] Though some of the people in the picture are Black – including teenagers outside a corner store, a loiterer slumped against a wall, and an inebriated citizen sleeping it off on the sidewalk – the image exudes playfulness and fun. It is the neighbourhood's panoptic architecture that fills the viewer with dread. The street wraps around the square face and shoulders of a police officer whose baby blue uniform, tie, cap and eyes convey a vigilant whiteness hovering over the carefree scene below. With the black brim of his cap partially obscuring his left eye, the panopticop melts into the urban landscape as he registers from his perch the comings and goings of the residents below – without having to move an inch.

It is not just racialised surveillance that mars the broken windows approach to policing, but also the idea that a neighbourhood which puts up with disorderly behaviour is 'vulnerable to criminal invasion', as Kelling and Wilson would have it.[24] In this view, disorder is another word for brutishness and blackness. The watchful figure on the magazine cover does not look

---

[23] Kelling and Wilson, 'Police and Neighborhood Safety', 31–2.
[24] Ibid., 32, 38.

down, but instead he glances furtively to one side, as if peering into the future 'jungle' that will eventually envelop the street below. Kelling and Wilson concede that the order the police are supposed to maintain is 'an inherently ambiguous term but a condition that people in a given community recognized when they saw it'.[25] Judging by the unseemly characters the broken windows police are supposed to rout – like panhandlers or vagrants, often poor populations and minorities whose progress is blocked by racial prejudice – to recognise order when you 'see' it means to live in a predominantly white area.

The extent to which the control mechanisms of increased police surveillance criminalise blackness became evident in the 1990s, when the NYPD adopted a bastardised, zero-tolerance version of broken-windows policing that blatantly ran afoul of civil liberties. With serious infraction rates plummeting at unprecedented speed, Police Commissioner William Bratton and Mayor Rudi Giuliani were duly celebrated for winning the war on crime. Bratton appeared on the cover of *Time* magazine in 1996, and in 1997 Giuliani won re-election with 57 per cent of the vote, a remarkable result for a Republican candidate in the staunchly Democrat New York. Bratton, who worked closely with Kelling during his tenure as chief of transit police, shared Kelling's view that if left unchecked, low-level, socially disruptive crime would negatively affect social stability.[26]

In essence, though, the NYPD's strategy weaponised an illiberal concept of public disorder to target the city's minorities. As the sociologist Alex Vitale aptly points out, '[t]he greater economic polarization of the late 1970s through the early 1990s contributed to the formation of an economic underclass that was drawn into prostitution, crime, and other forms of public disorder.'[27] To adapt Bill Clinton's famous adage from his 1992 presidential campaign, 'it's the economy, stupid' and not a propensity for crime that engenders social disorder. Yet Giuliani perceived urban crisis as a consequence of social permissiveness rather than economic decline. Under his leadership, instead of providing additional social services for the impoverished, the city set new enforcement priorities and new standards of orderly behaviour by cracking down on minor crimes.

It soon became apparent, however, that minority communities were bearing the brunt of Giuliani's aggressive policing. To soothe the fears of the white middle- and upper-class New Yorkers who voted in municipal elections, Giuliani castigated the allegedly antisocial 'subproletariat that mars the scenery and

[25] Ibid., 34.
[26] Kohler-Hausmann, *Misdemeanorland*, 25.
[27] Vitale, *City of Disorder*, 70.

menaces or annoys the consumers of urban space'.[28] What may have sounded like small interventions to restore order resulted in a climate of oppressive observation for the city's Black residents. Consistent with the broken windows pseudo-theory, the emphasis was not on making arrests that would result in successful prosecutions, but to expose majority Black neighbourhoods to permanent scrutiny and condescending harassment. The civil liberties of minorities were clearly swept aside as collateral damage in a brutal trade-off between fighting crime and safeguarding civil rights.

Giuliani's New York witnessed not only skyrocketing misdemeanour arrests, but also widespread police brutality. On 4 February 1999, the twenty-three-year-old Guinean immigrant Amadou Diallo was gunned down by four plainclothes NYPD officers outside his apartment on Wheeler Avenue in the Bronx. While on patrol in the neighbourhood, the officers pulled up to speak to Diallo, who caught their eye even though he was not engaged in any unsavoury activity. The police officers later claimed they mistook him for a serial rapist. As Keeling and Wilson callously contended, '[t]he unchecked panhandler is, in effect, the first broken window.'[29] For the police, the loitering Diallo was a broken window too, not a human being but a signal of disorder to come. And his infraction was nothing more than simply looking up and down the street. From the perspective of the police, he was surveying an area he had no business surveying. Diallo had transgressed the rules of zero-tolerance policing by daring to look, rather than hide away.

The shooting of Amadou Diallo illustrates the perils of racial foresight at its most extreme. After mistaking his wallet for a gun, the four police officers fired their semi-automatic weapons until they ran out of ammunition. A total of forty-one shots were fired at the immigrant, hitting Diallo nineteen times. The killing prompted national outrage, and Giuliani's approval ratings dipped to 40 per cent.[30] And yet the shooting of Diallo should have come as no surprise to anyone. A police force tasked with non-stop surveillance is bound to assume the worst about every Black man they encounter on the street. Surveillance itself – a searching gaze, a police car pulling up – becomes a sign of hostility. When the police look at you too closely, they are not on your side. And to be a target of police scrutiny is also a sure sign that society is probably not on your side either. The four police officers who shot Diallo were indicted on charges of second-degree murder and reckless endangerment, but were later acquitted of all charges.

---

[28] Wacquant, *Prisons of Poverty*, 16.
[29] Kelling and Wilson, 'Police and Neighborhood Safety', 34.
[30] Grunwald, 'Trial Puts Giuliani, NYPD on Defensive', A2.

V. Algorithms of Suspicion

When the LAPD created the first pre-crime algorithm, PredPol, in 2011, the invention was hailed as a game-changer in the perpetual war on crime. *Time* magazine cited the program as one of the fifty best inventions of the year 2011. In the history of law enforcement, however, predictive policing was by no means an innovation. NYPD Commissioner Bratton had famously 'pored over the evolution of criminal statistics daily with religious zeal' and pioneered a computerised statistical system (CompStat) to deploy police resources according to detailed, continuously updated data on petty daily infractions like drinking or littering.[31]

Bratton's crime statistics pale against the magnitude of modern pre-crime systems. And yet what links them most directly to the policing methods of previous eras is their racial fore-*sight*, that is, their optical racialisation of disorderly behaviour. Not just in the sense that predictive programs only process crime rate data available to the police; and since crimes committed by minorities are more often reported to the police and charges pressed, a racial bias is already baked into the police data cake. Programs like PredPol implicitly also draw a composite sketch of who the police ought to be on the lookout for in the street, typically African American males.[32] By targeting non-violent crimes like burglaries in majority Black areas, predictive policing is basically a continuation of broken windows policies by digital means.

Algorithms cannot see, of course, and race itself is not used as a metric to predict crime rates in a specific neighbourhood. But the police deployed to high-risk locations cannot – absent a mind-reading machine – do more than simply look around and settle on a suspect that ticks the usual (racial) boxes. Emboldened by algorithms that assign a higher crime risk to predominantly Black neighbourhoods or Black individuals (as in the Chicago Strategic Subject List), patrol police are more inclined to stop and frisk Black citizens. The purportedly 'post-panoptic' Big Data police generates an endemic, legalised and scientifically validated racial prejudice that can only be described as 'panoptic' in the classic sense of the term. The street replaces the prison and the patrol cars stand guard 'all along the watchtower' (Dylan/Hendrix) of their focal power structure. In much the same way that Bentham's Panopticon uses small lamps and mirrors to illuminate a prisoner's cell and conceal the watcher's presence, data sets function today as reflectors that light up every corner of a life in covert ways that shelter the watchers from scrutiny.

[31] Wacquant, *Prisons of Poverty*, 17.
[32] I have written a book on the importance of composite sketches and identikits for the cultural history of policing. See Banita, *Phantombilder*.

I am not the only one to grasp the design of Big Data surveillance as ultimately panoptic. To describe what he terms 'the management of unease' in the security sphere after 9/11, Didier Bigo coins the concept of the ban-opticon, an apparatus that operates globally along the borders of nation-states to separate those with rights of entry from suspicious subjects who must be monitored for possible detention and removal.[33] Bigo's construct reminds us that on a practical level, risk assessment is still highly racialised and premised on superficial factors, such as epidermal characteristics. Asylum seekers in particular are codified visually. Thus, it is partly due to intensified racial profiling at the borders that domestic policing, too, increasingly relies on visual markers to determine security risks.

We have contented ourselves for too long, I think, with critiques of precrime systems that only single out the unprecedented access of police forces to various databases, instead of digging deeper into the epidermal panopticism that secretly sustains – and is effectively camouflaged by – the tools of predictive policing. To redress this neglect, I now briefly turn to some artistic ways of bringing to the surface the true colours, so to speak, of predictive surveillance. While sociological critiques do make cogent points about the invasiveness and injustice of AI-based policing, it is artistic 'representations' of the subject that draw attention to the optical effects of police algorithms especially well.

The German documentary film *Pre-Crime* (2017) outlines the broader context in which predictive policing has arisen as a tool of law enforcement as well as a social and ethical threat.[34] The film addresses the invisible rhizome of Big Data, yet it also stresses the visible optics of suspicion that are inscribed in police algorithms. The directors, Matthias Heeder and Monika Hielscher, design an agile, constantly updating visual interface for the film that literally screens a person's criminal risk as calculated by an AI program in real time (Figure 10.4). By coupling footage of Black 'suspects' with the percentage points that indicate their individual threat levels, the filmmakers strikingly expose the optical calculus of pre-crime systems. While they may crunch only indirectly racialised data, their predictions do in fact correlate with the appearance of the citizens whom police patrols ultimately flag down. The film's visual effects provide a useful visualisation of computers that never really cease to 'see' race, even when they ostensibly operate race-blind.

The visual style of *Pre-Crime* made such an impression on me that I decided to smuggle it into the concept art for a radio play I conceptualised and produced in 2020 as a public-facing outreach campaign for a research

[33] Bigo, 'Globalized (In)Security'.
[34] Heeder and Hielscher, *Pre-Crime*.

Figure 10.4 Scene from *Pre-Crime*, directed by Matthias Heeder and Monika Hielscher. © Kloos & Co. Medien GmbH, 2017, printed with permission of the artist.

project on predictive policing. *Cassandra Rising* became a play rather than, say, a short film or a short story because I wanted to demonstrate how perplexing it can be – for police officers and the public alike – to be at the mercy of a black box algorithm.[35] Cassandra, the voice of the AI that emits warnings about criminal threats, sounds flat and uninvolved, as if she were reciting lottery numbers. The fortunes she tells, however, are pretty bleak. On the strength of her predictions, countless citizens are detained in quarantine spaces, a euphemism for jail cells to which both potential criminals and virus-carriers are summarily banished. Calling the shots from behind the scenes is a blind tyrant whose inability to see fuels his fantasy of a surveillance society. Cassandra, then, is her master's all-seeing eye (Figure 10.5). Even though her circuits run invisibly through the city's fortress-like walls, her piercing gaze settles on those who visibly stand out. In the play, her target is an underground movement whose recruits include visible minorities like Muslim migrants (the story is set in central Europe). The narrative is meant to be simple and accessible, but on a deeper level the blindness plot and the

---

[35] Written by Martin Heindel, the play is based on the results of my research project and inspired by various works of science fiction (literary, filmic and musical). *Cassandra Rising* was broadcast in Germany by Westdeutscher Rundfunk (WDR) and Südwest Rundfunk (SWR2). Grateful acknowledgement goes to the Volkswagen Foundation for funding both the research project and the radio play.

Figure 10.5 Concept art for *Cassandra Rising*. © Lenny Ward, 2020, printed with permission of the artist.

artwork I conceptualised and commissioned for the play leave no doubt that even the most inscrutable prediction systems rely on an optic perception of privilege – or what I called racial foresight – if only indirectly.

With her gorgon-like, circuit-sprouting head and metallic eyes, Cassandra is more than a supercomputer – that is, a merely mechanical collator of data – she is also an intelligent camera. The focus on her eyes in the poster art for the play suggests that both racial difference and racial foresight essentially depend on the separating effect of vision: one colour from another, one object from the one next to it. So, while in beaming down on the city Cassandra claims to see the future, she can only vaguely imagine it in an infrared spectrum that magnifies difference by perceiving colour as heat, Black as red, darkness as danger. The design is, of course, a playful homage to Stanley Kubrick's *2001: A Space Odyssey*, in which Hal, the iconic AI built into the Discovery 1 spacecraft, optically embodies an automated social environment. Above all, borrowing the gaze from Kubrick's famed design comments on the current practice of referring to high-risk urban areas as 'hot spots' – a roundabout way of redlining that makes sure only the most vulnerable, underserved communities feel the heat of over-policing.[36]

Underwriting pre-crime systems, then, is a fundamental suspicion that crime follows Black subjects around like an inseparable dark shadow, combined

---

[36] Safiya Noble uses the term 'technological redlining' to describe how automated processes marginalise social groups and perpetuate racial inequities. See Noble, *Algorithms of Oppression*, 1.

with the perceived duty to blunt this propensity. The outcome is a de facto segregation of Black and white futures – one dangerous, the other endangered. Moreover, predictive programs bestow on the automated watchers not only the hegemony of information, but also the privilege of plausible deniability. After all, neither the neighbourhood police nor the public can claim to understand exactly how these proprietary algorithms operate. This relegation of vigilance from the human to the digital realm breeds complacency among law enforcement stakeholders and demobilises systematic resistance in society at large, while bolstering an already prevailing sense of hopelessness among the watched.

VI. The Right to a Future Tense

What also distracts from the noxious effects of police surveillance in the age of Big Data is the sheer proliferation of surveillance in most realms of human experience. In her influential manifesto on surveillance capitalism, Shoshana Zuboff argues that mass surveillance, which enables accurate predictions of future behaviour, has become the engine of modern life in both business and pleasure. Her main interest lies in the economic uses and abuses of surveillance. Specifically, she locates surveillance capitalism in an economic architecture that funnels wealth, knowledge and power into the control of parasitic tech giants. And it does so, Zuboff explains, by extracting information and then moulding it into predictions of what people will desire and purchase next – often before consumers themselves become aware of what they want. Zuboff's key claim is that data-derived information, which she terms 'behavioral surplus', is processed into 'prediction products'.[37] What stands out about these products is their ability to harness automated data mining to automate – that is, calculate, shape and thereby control – human behaviour at scale.

Zuboff voices compelling misgivings about where our addiction to data will ultimately lead us, both individually and as a species. Surprisingly, she is far less concerned with the similar concentration of data in the digital circuits of the state, particularly of the police. To Zuboff, surveillance capitalism is 'as significant a threat to human nature in the twenty-first century as industrial capitalism was to the natural world in the nineteenth and twentieth'.[38] But she distinguishes too neatly in this analogy between industrial capital and governmentality, between private companies and executive power. In fact, an equally viable parallel can be drawn at the level of government control, namely between the stripping of individual freedoms by militarised police

[37] Zuboff, *Age of Surveillance Capitalism*, 8.
[38] Ibid., 'Definition', unpaginated.

patrols in the nineteenth and twentieth centuries and the usurpation of free will by prediction machines operated by desk police in the twenty-first.

What Zuboff's purely economic comparison leaves out is the unequal burden placed by surveillance on visible minorities and the poor. Surreptitious monitoring by tech giants inconveniences an Amazon customer much less than a pre-crime system upends the life of a citizen by using unreliable data – such as criminal records, postcode and affiliations – to stamp them as a future criminal. There is nothing convenient or free, which might be said of a dog blanket ad on the Amazon 'suggested items' feed of a dog owner, about being labelled a future criminal on the flimsiest of indicators. 'Evidence' would be too strong a word for such metrics as being friends with a victim of gang violence, suffering from a mental illness like depression, or being born to parents with a criminal record, all of which are frequently used in US courts to determine the risk of recidivism.

As soon as we move away from the behavioural control practised by Google and Meta towards policing systems, we notice another disparity, too. By purchasing smart home devices or using social media platforms, 'we now pay for our domination', as Zuboff has it.[39] Yet in the case of police surveillance, majority white populations fund, with their tax money, the pre-crime systems that dominate someone else – mostly minority, non-white groups – in order to guarantee the safety and certainty the public desires. So, if surveillance capitalism is self-enslaving, surveillance policing is enslaving, period. Crime prediction programs may be said to extract and process the behavioural information of non-white populations like so much digital chattel.

It was slaves who were uprooted and consumed as if they were nothing more than inanimate raw material. Zuboff, though, describes all of us, everyone whose data is tracked and saved by online platforms, as 'human natural resources'. In a surprisingly tone-deaf moment, she likens online surveillance to colonialism: 'We are the native peoples now whose tacit claims to self-determination have vanished from the maps of our own experience.'[40] It might seem appealing to cast the predominantly white victims of surveillance capitalism as a blamelessly disenfranchised group, whose 'needs for effective life vie against the inclination to resist' the 'bold incursions' of the surveillance systems that commodify their minds.[41] Such a partial reading of surveillance threatens, however, to inure us to the ways in which so many less privileged citizens lack the luxury to evade tracking and monitorisation, even if they wanted to. Their only desire is, quite simply, for life itself – be it effective or defective.

[39] Ibid., 10.
[40] Ibid., 100.
[41] Ibid., 11.

White-majority populations are the gleeful customers of companies like Meta and Google. They are also the beneficiaries of governmental social services like law enforcement. The detritus left behind by this transaction is Black life. But feeding on Black futures to engorge majority white prospects is neither effective nor sustainable. Working towards a safe future for the few and misery for the many is likely to result in insecurity for all. A new social contract is needed that disentangles race from digital danger, breaks the surveillance axis on which racial inequality manifests itself, and fashions ways to repurpose surveillance from a tool of control to one of care. After all, when Bentham conceived the Panopticon, he created more than a disciplinary architecture whose application was restricted to 'punishing the incorrigible, guarding the insane, reforming the vicious, confining the suspected', and other ways of corralling and controlling inspection-worthy persons.[42] Among the uses Bentham envisioned for his apparatus were also 'maintaining the helpless' and 'curing the sick'.[43]

Big Data policing accumulates information about, and from, Black citizens, but nor for them – not for their benefit or in ways that help them prosper. Rather than mine the depths of Black people's everyday lives in an extraction operation that benefits only the extractor, new protocols are needed to predict not Black risk, but Black vulnerability. Zuboff cleverly interprets surveillance capitalism 'as a challenge to the elemental *right to the future tense*, which accounts for the individual's ability to imagine, intend, promise, and construct a future'.[44] Even more elemental than the freedom to envision one's future is the right to live it, which is often withheld from the targets of predictive policing. Black immigrants like Amadou Diallo and the many African Americans swept up in the net of police suspicion ask not so much to 'imagine, intend, promise, and construct a future' as simply to preserve their right to live without harassment, outside a coffin or a jail cell.

'Racism', the feminist geographer Ruth Wilson Gilmore has noted, 'is the state-sanctioned and/or extralegal production and exploitation of group-differentiated vulnerability to premature death.'[45] An antiracist repurposing of surveillance would gather and process data as indices to the precariousness of non-white subjects, and deploy it to place these subjects in less vulnerable positions, for instance by marking them as more susceptible to health risks, such as infection with COVID-19 or a more serious form of the illness it causes. Instead, crime prediction systems condemn vulnerable populations to

---

[42] Bentham, *Works*, 40.
[43] Ibid.
[44] Zuboff, *Age of Surveillance Capitalism*, 20, original emphasis.
[45] Wilson Gilmore, *Golden Gulag*, 247.

social death in slow motion: longer prison sentences, life imprisonment after the third offence irrespective of its seriousness (in keeping with the three-strikes-law valid in twenty-eight US states), constant police harassment and greater risk of violence during so-called Terry Stops.[46]

In describing the effects of surveillance on Black subjects, Frantz Fanon listed a wide range of psychosomatic afflictions, from stress, fatigue and insomnia to light-headedness and a heightened predisposition to accidents.[47] To overcome the psychic numbing that continues to wither almost all public contest against racial foresight, we must first recognise the eye of the police not simply as a distant, frictionless, somehow impalpable screen that leaves no mark on the object of observation, but as what it truly is: a sharp instrument that carves deep scars into the flesh of real human beings.

The alternative would be a screening process of care, rather than a surveillance of risk. The target would not be the person, just as in a medical context one does not screen for cancer patients but for cancer. We are a long way away from instituting a crime-fighting system that targets crime itself rather than criminals. But surveillance is more malleable and polyvalent than has so far been recognised, going back to Bentham's panoptic architecture.[48] Instead of dismissing it as outdated, we might be better off – for the sake of the most vulnerable in our society – giving it a second chance: for Black lives, and their right to a safe future.

VII. Bibliography

Andrew, Christopher M., and Julius Green. *Stars and Spies: Intelligence Operations and the Entertainment Business*. London: Bodley Head, 2021.

Baldwin, Frederick C. *Freedom's March: Photographs of the Civil Rights Movement in Savannah*. Savannah, GA: Telfair Museum of Art, 2009.

Banita, Georgiana. *Phantombilder: Die Polizei und der verdächtige Fremde*. Hamburg: Edition Nautilus, 2022.

Benjamin, Ruha, ed. *Captivating Technology: Race, Carceral Technoscience, and Liberatory Imagination in Everyday Life*. Durham, NC: Duke University Press, 2019.

---

[46] A 'Terry Stop' is a brief detention and limited search of a person by law enforcement officers on reasonable suspicion of involvement in criminal activity, but short of probable cause to arrest. The name derives from the legal case *Terry v Ohio*, 392 U.S. 1 (1968), in which the Supreme Court established the legality of this measure.

[47] Browne, *Dark Matters*, 6.

[48] Most fitting here would be a kind of 'pauper-Panopticon', one of four distinct Panopticon versions identified by Brunon-Ernst in Bentham's writings. A modified pauper-Panopticon for the present day would be less a machine of control at the margins of society than an integrating and inclusive system, less a network or a dragnet than a safety net of pourveillance (a protective form of surveillance aimed at sheltering its target, not society from it). See Brunon-Ernst, 'Deconstructing Panopticism', 21.

———. *Race after Technology: Abolitionist Tools for the New Jim Code*. Cambridge, MA: Polity, 2020.

Bentham, Jeremy. *The Works of Jeremy Bentham*. Edited by John Bowring, vol. 4. Edinburgh: William Tait, 1843.

Bigo, Didier. 'Globalized (In)Security: The Field and the Ban-opticon.' In *Translation, Biopolitics, Colonial Difference*, edited by Naoki Sakai and Jon Solomon, 109–55. Hong Kong: Hong Kong University Press, 2006.

Boyne, Roy. 'Post-Panopticism.' *Economy and Society* 29, no. 2 (2000): 285–307.

Browne, Simone. *Dark Matters: On the Surveillance of Blackness*. Durham, NC: Duke University Press, 2015.

Brunon-Ernst, Anne. 'Deconstructing Panopticism into Plural Panopticons.' In *Beyond Foucault: New Perspectives on Bentham's Panopticon*, edited by Anne Brunon-Ernst, 17–41. London: Routledge, 2016.

Erskine, James, director. *Billie*. Altitude Film Entertainment, 2019. 1 h., 38 min.

Fanon, Frantz. *Black Skin, White Masks*. New York: Grove Press, 2007.

Gibson, Nigel C., ed. *Rethinking Fanon: The Continuing Dialogue*. Amherst, NY: Humanity Books, 1999.

Grunwald, Michael. 'Trial Puts Giuliani, NYPD on Defensive.' *Washington Post*, 30 March 1999.

Hadden, Sally E. *Slave Patrols: Law and Violence in Virginia and the Carolinas*. Cambridge, MA: Harvard University Press, 2003.

Hartman, Saidiya V. *Scenes of Subjection: Terror, Slavery, and Self-Making in Nineteenth-Century America*. New York: Oxford University Press, 2010.

Heeder, Matthias, and Monika Hielscher, directors. *Pre-Crime*. Kloos and Co. Medien, 2017. 1 h., 28 min.

Heindel, Martin. *Cassandra Rising*. Westdeutscher Rundfunk, 2020. 53 min.

Jefferson, Brian Jordan. *Digitize and Punish: Racial Criminalization in the Digital Age*. Minneapolis: University of Minnesota Press, 2020.

Kelling, George L., and Catherine Coles. *Fixing Broken Windows: Restoring Order and Reducing Crime in Our Communities*. New York: Free Press, 1996.

Kelling, George L., and James Q. Wilson. 'The Police and Neighborhood Safety.' *Atlantic Monthly* 249, no. 3 (March 1982): 29–38.

Kohler-Hausmann, Issa. *Misdemeanorland: Criminal Courts and Social Control in an Age of Broken Windows Policing*. Princeton, NJ: Princeton University Press, 2020.

Lauterbach, Preston. *Bluff City: The Secret Life of Photographer Ernest Withers*. New York: W. W. Norton, 2020.

Macey, David. *Frantz Fanon: A Biography*. New York: Verso, 2012.

Noble, Safiya Umoja. *Algorithms of Oppression: How Search Engines Reinforce Racism*. New York: New York University Press, 2018.

Perrusquia, Marc. *A Spy in Canaan: How the FBI Used a Famous Photographer to Infiltrate the Civil Rights Movement*. Brooklyn, NY: Melville House, 2018.

Rediker, Marcus. *The Slave Ship: A Human History*. New York: Viking, 2007.

Schwarz, Frederick A.O. Jr., and Aziz Z. Huq. *Unchecked and Unbalanced: Presidential Power in a Time of Terror*. New York and London: New Press, 2008.

Vitale, Alex. *City of Disorder: How the Quality of Life Campaign Transformed New York Politics*. New York: New York University Press, 2009.

———. *The End of Policing*. New York: Verso, 2018.

Wacquant, Loïc J. D. *Prisons of Poverty*. Minneapolis: University of Minnesota Press, 2009.

Wagner, Bryan. *Disturbing the Peace: Black Culture and the Police Power after Slavery*. Cambridge, MA: Harvard University Press, 2009.

Walvin, James. *Black Ivory: Slavery in the British Empire*. Hoboken, NJ: Wiley-Blackwell, 2001.

Wilson Gilmore, Ruth. *Golden Gulag: Prisons, Surplus, Crisis, and Opposition in Globalizing California*. Berkeley: University of California Press, 2007.

Withers, Ernest C. *Revolution in Black and White: Photographs of the Civil Rights Era*. Chicago: CityFiles Press, 2019.

Zuboff, Shoshana. *The Age of Surveillance Capitalism: The Fight for a Human Future at the New Frontier of Power*. London: Profile Books, 2019.

11

Fear of the Dark: The Racialised Surveillance of Indigenous Peoples in Australia

Rachel Joy

I. Introduction

The very nature of settler colonialism is to refuse to see our settler selves clearly and to fail to acknowledge how as settlers we act in the world. We stand before a mirror and see ourselves distorted and disfigured to fit a white nation-building agenda that proclaims we are part of a nation where fairness prevails.[1] In Australia the fair of face do rise, not so much through natural talent but because, as beneficiaries of colonisation, we are standing on the necks of others and especially of Indigenous others. It is with these facts very clearly etched in my mind that I commit words to print as a person of settler descent writing on surveillance and the colony. I do so in an attempt to interrogate the culture I was born into, a coloniser culture that perpetrates violence and brutality against those perceived as deficient due to their race and that privileges my white skin. In this sense I write from a place of autoethnography informed by critical race theory and Indigenous scholarship, with the intent to problematise surveillance as a tool of the occupation of the place now known as Australia. I also write from the unceded lands of the Wathawurrung people on the south coast of the continent and pay my respects to their Elders past and present.

This chapter is concerned with state surveillance of Aboriginal peoples as a tool of governance to maintain the occupation of Australia. It asks what surveillance contributes to the occupation, how it operates and how it shores up occupier sovereignty. It does not propose to write in detail about Aboriginal experiences of surveillance; Aboriginal people themselves are better placed to write on such matters. Rather, my object of analysis is not 'them' (Aboriginal peoples) but settler colonialism and surveillance as a form of power belonging to it.[2] This

---

[1] The national anthem of Australia is named 'Advance Australia Fair'.
[2] Povinelli, *Geontologies*, 22–3.

discussion begins from the premise that Australia is occupied territory and that settler sovereignty is exercised through what Aileen Moreton-Robinson describes as a race war to control the lives of Indigenous people.[3] For the most part, this race war no longer looks like armed conflict but rather is today ingrained in the structures and actions of governmental institutions. Racism becomes normalised in a culture built on racism,[4] to the point where it becomes so institutionalised and so socially acceptable that it is invisible to those unaffected by it. Debbie Bargallie reminds us that 'Australia is a racial state – since colonisation, race has been integral to the development of the nation-state through the power to exclude and include in racially ordered terms [. . .].'[5]

Everyday practices of surveillance have been fundamental to the conduct of this war, just as Banita has shown they were fundamental to the conduct of slavery and the institution of the plantation in the US, the monitoring of civil rights activists and the demoralisation of urban black youths.[6] They are an integral part of a racialised disciplinary society that needs to control black bodies. Australia has a history of disciplining black bodies by incarcerating Indigenous people and controlling their behaviour through law and by extension through the welfare and criminal justice systems. In the immediate aftermath of the British invasion, most Indigenous peoples were forced onto pastoral stations, reserves or missions where they could be surveilled, controlled and subjected to punitive actions by government-appointed administrators.[7] Such measures continue today and can been seen in the impacts of settler surveillance on contemporary Aboriginal communities in the form of 'The Intervention', carceral surveillance, and income management cards.

Because contemporary Australia cannot be understood in any meaningful way without an awareness of the political and ontological meaning of place, the chapter will examine the manner in which coloniser manipulation of space attempts to impact Indigenous bodies. As Achille Mbembe asserts, 'Colonial occupation itself was a matter of seizing, delimiting, and asserting control over a physical geographical area – of writing on the ground a new set of social and spatial relations.'[8] The British began their invasion using the bodies of convicts and later the bodies of sheep to fill the land and displace Indigenous peoples from their country. As Europeans laid claim to land as private property, they fenced it and began to assert control over it in

---

[3] Moreton-Robinson, 'Good Indigenous Citizen', 64.
[4] Delgado and Stefancic, *Critical Race Theory*, 8.
[5] Bargallie, *Racial Contract*, 49.
[6] Banita, Chapter 10 of this collection.
[7] Moreton-Robinson, 'I Still Call Australia Home', 4.
[8] Mbembe, 'Necropolitics', 26.

ways that excluded or regulated any Aboriginal people who belonged to that place. Settler colonialism differs from other forms of colonialism in that the settler stays, killing and displacing the original inhabitants and taking outright possession of the land.[9] In Australia the settler settled and, in that very process of occupation and settlement, began to change the environment. Europeans changed the land with their animals and plants,[10] their cities with their sprawling suburbs, and their mining of sacred Country.[11] The settler state changed the environment by curtailing Aboriginal land management practices, and traumatised people by removing them from Country and punishing the practice of language, and cultural and religious rites. Settlers established their racialised political environment with the lie of *terra nullius*[12] and subsequent legislative controls over black land, black bodies, black lives.[13] In this context settler sovereignty has the ability to 'define who matters and who does not, who is disposable and who is not'.[14] Settlers have surveilled Aboriginal people in a manner 'purposeful, routine, systematic and focused [. . .] for the sake of control, entitlement, management, influence, or protection'.[15] It is in this way that the spatial management of Aboriginal bodies through surveillance has always been and remains crucial to the production of the settler state.

II. The Lie of the Land

Despite the overwhelming body of evidence from both the academy and Indigenous Elders, the dominant 'genesis stories' of the modern Australian state continue to ignore the wars Aboriginal peoples fought for their Country.[16] Instead the state makes its claim to sovereignty through the authority of its sanitised narrative of settler history and identity, a narrative that is underpinned by the exercise of racial hierarchies. These fantasies

---

[9] Wolfe, 'Settler Colonialism', 388.
[10] Rose, *Wild Country*, 4.
[11] The word 'country' has different meanings to Indigenous and non-Indigenous people. In this text I will capitalise 'Country' as a proper noun when speaking of the Aboriginal or decolonised sense of the word and the small 'c' 'country' will be used to indicate settler constructions of land. Aboriginal epistemologies of 'Country' and their challenge to European concepts of land are detailed in Rutherford, 'Introduction', 4.
[12] See Dorsett and Mcveigh, 'Just So'; Rush, 'Surviving Common Law'; Rush, 'Altered Jurisdiction'; Muldoon, 'Thinking Responsibility'.
[13] See Yunupingu, *Our Land is Our Life*; Bartlett, *Native Title*; Hunter, 'Native Title'; Patton, 'Sovereignty'.
[14] Mbembe, 'Necropolitics', 27.
[15] Wood, *Report on the Surveillance Society*, 4.
[16] Reynolds, *Forgotten War*.

continue to gaslight Indigenous peoples about the truth of settler beginnings in this place because non-Indigenous Australians have not yet given a truthful account of how they come to be here and claim the land as they do.[17] In her essay 'I Still Call Australia Home', Goenpul woman and professor Aileen Moreton-Robinson establishes settler belonging in Australia in the dispossession of Aboriginal peoples contrary to international customary law.[18] More specifically, she differentiates between settler belonging and Indigenous people's relationship to land, stating:

> Indigenous people cannot forget the nature of migrancy, and we position all non-Indigenous people as migrants and diasporic. Our ontological relationship to land, the ways that country is constitutive of us, and therefore the inalienable nature of our relation to land, marks a radical, indeed incommensurable, difference between us and the non-Indigenous. This ontological relation to land constitutes a subject position that we do not share, that cannot be shared, with the postcolonial subject, whose sense of belonging in this place is tied to migrancy.[19]

The inability of most Australians to acknowledge our migrancy as who we really are and our dispossession of Aboriginal peoples as how we come to be here continues to be normalised. This in turn formalises the racial hierarchies extant in settler culture that condemn many Aboriginal people to lives of poverty and exclusion. It is these normalised racial hierarchies that provide the basis for the surveillance of Aboriginal communities normalised, to the point of quotidian ordinariness, in the workings of the occupier state – a state in which intensive surveillance exists concurrently with the refusal of settler society to uphold the human rights of Aboriginal people. The Colony,[20] as explicated by Chelsea Watego, turns both a blind eye to their suffering and an ever-watchful actuarial eye, as it formulates its racialised culture of death[21] in the most banal way.[22]

Successive Federal and State governments across the political divide have turned their backs on Indigenous peoples. From the failure to restore wages stolen from Aboriginal workers,[23] to the denial of compensation to the Stolen

---

[17] Butler, *Giving an Account*, 8.
[18] Moreton-Robinson, 'I Still Call Australia Home', 3.
[19] Ibid.
[20] Watego, *Another Day*.
[21] Mbembe, 'Necropolitics'.
[22] Arendt, *Eichmann in Jerusalem*.
[23] Curthoys and Moore, 'White People', 4–5; Gray, 'Elephant', 30; Jones, 'Working', 7.

Generations,[24] the refusal to act to stop Aboriginal deaths in custody[25] or to end 'The Intervention'[26] (Northern Territory Emergency Response; NTER), the list of state-sponsored political violence against Aboriginal peoples could go on *ad infinitum*. There has long been a social and political chasm between Indigenous people and non-Indigenous Australians fuelled by this refusal to acknowledge the nation's history of political violence towards the Indigenous population[27] or to condemn its current forms. The continued conflation of proud Australian nationalism with the silence over historical or/and contemporary wrongdoing sets a dangerous precedent for Australian identity.[28] If a politics that values difference is critical for successful dialogue,[29] then a politics that refuses to hear different viewpoints, such as those provided by the various Aboriginal voices of this country, is not able to engender ethical relations between the various peoples of this country. The construction of 'proud Australian identity' is exclusory and racialised: it disallows Indigenous voices unless, presumably, they subscribe to the whitewashing of history. Being proudly Australian and living with a consciousness of the violent history of the country are presented as mutually exclusive. Certainly, it may be difficult to reconcile these positions but, as I have argued elsewhere,[30] this is the inheritance settler Australians face.

III. Producing Settler Space

Politics creates the situations of our lived experience, but it does not function alone. It interacts with space, time and subjectivity, and in postcolonising[31] Australia it also interacts with colonialism to enshrine the relational politics that play out, on and through bodies.[32] In Australia, the settler logics that negatively affect black bodies to preserve the privileges of white bodies, and especially of capital, are produced by settler colonialism. Space is not merely a measurable entity but rather both a product of and a producer of relations between things.[33] In Australia space is deeply connected to place, and the

---

[24] Burns, 'Unfinished Business'.

[25] Dodson, '25 Years on'.

[26] Moreton-Robinson, 'Good Indigenous Citizen'.

[27] SBS, '7 Legacies'.

[28] Prime Minister John Howard, 'Opening Address to the Australian Reconciliation Convention-Melbourne', qtd in Behrendt, 'Morpeth Lecture', 42–3.

[29] See 'Uluru Statement from the Heart', in Pearson and Morris *Rightful Place*, 2.

[30] Joy, 'Very Becoming', 243.

[31] Moreton-Robinson, 'I Still Call Australia Home', 30.

[32] Philippopoulos-Mihalopoulos, *Spatial Justice*, 39.

[33] Paglen, 'Experimental Geography', 36.

meanings that it holds for people are informed conceptually by the competing narratives of law articulated by both the colonial state and the First Peoples of this country. Space as conceptualised by settler logics is absolute, stable and calculable, and through these spatial practices the coloniser creates a 'compartmentalized world'.[34] It is this understanding of space that has been so critical to the particular manifestation of settler colonialism and so problematic for relations between Indigenous peoples and settlers. According to Deleuze, space does not simply manifest as a singular point; rather, it folds and unfolds to encompass many experiences.[35] In this way both the material and immaterial may be held in their continually becoming forms, in the same space, and competing logics may also exist in the spacing of the fold, folded into each other in their difference. Thus, in the *spacing*[36] that is contemporary Australia, there may exist folded into each other the corroboree ground and the local park, birthing trees and a highway, a sacred site and a juvenile detention centre. This spacing is not one of continuity but rather one of rupture, dissonance or Derridean difference,[37] and yet it is contained within the fold.

Space is productive of relations between bodies, society and law.[38] As we have seen in previous chapters, particularly in Part 2 of this collection, surveillance operates in the first instance by the definition, ordering and disciplining of space. Before surveillance takes material or digital forms, it defines and orders space, including who is entitled to be in it and under what conditions. The space produced by the political reality of settler colonialism produces the manifold living conditions enjoyed or endured by the various citizens of Australia. Bodies inhabit space within the fold, folded with other bodies and co-forming the Deleuzian manifold. The housing, health, education, welfare services and policing data of remote Aboriginal communities and the Aboriginal town camps that exist outside many Australian country towns resemble those of people living in the poorest underdeveloped nations. In the same country, in the same space, there exists a very different place where the same services are provided in such a way as to produce vastly different social welfare outcomes. Thus, within the fold of Australian public health infrastructure, non-Indigenous peoples turn on a tap in their homes and receive potable drinking water while many Indigenous peoples turn a tap and receive dirty water that leads to a range of preventable health conditions.[39] The space of

[34] Fanon, *Wretched of the Earth*, 3.
[35] Deleuze, *The Fold*.
[36] Harvey, 'Spacetime', 12.
[37] Derrida, *Margins*.
[38] Hubbard et al., *Thinking Geographically*.
[39] Calma, *Social Justice Report*.

racialised public health inequities produces both of these realities. This occurs because of lack of access to mainstream services and lower levels of access to health services, including primary health care, and the substandard provision of health infrastructure in many Indigenous communities. The inequality in health outcomes experienced by Aboriginal and Torres Strait Islander peoples is 'both avoidable and systemic'.[40] The bodies produced in town camps by the political choices of coloniser culture are more likely to suffer acute illness like heart disease[41] and kidney failure,[42] more likely to suffer the health-related consequences of poor public health infrastructure,[43] and more likely to suffer diseases associated with dysfunctional social settings such as foetal alcohol syndrome,[44] acquired brain injury,[45] and domestic violence.[46] They are less likely to finish high school or go to university, less likely to be in employment and more likely to be dependent on welfare payments to meet family needs,[47] and they are likely to die approximately eleven years earlier than non-Indigenous Australians.[48] Within the space of the criminal justice system the data is similarly dire. What produces such profound systemic injustices in structural racism as it is constituted by settler colonialism?

IV. Racialised Surveillance

Surveillance may be a largely discreet yet accepted part of life for most people living in late capitalist Western democracies such as Australia. Yet as other authors in this collection have clearly shown, not all citizens are surveilled in the same way. Surveillance is racialised. It is a technology of whiteness which draws boundaries that 'Blacks cannot cross and whites cannot see'.[49]

Put another way, the surveillance carried out by the settler state has very different purposes and outcomes for Aboriginal people and non-Aboriginal people. In her book *Dark Matters*, Simone Browne explicates how methodologies of contemporary surveillance subjugate people of colour by weaponising the white gaze. For Browne, racialising surveillance means a kind of control

---

[40] Royal Australasian College of Physicians, *Inequity and Health*, 3.
[41] Thomson and Brooks, 'Cardiovascular Disease', 186.
[42] Australian Institute of Health and Welfare, *Chronic Kidney Disease*, 22.
[43] Australian Institute of Health and Welfare and Australian Bureau of Statistics, *Health and Welfare*, xxii.
[44] Fitzpatrick et al., 'Prevalence of Fetal Alcohol Syndrome'.
[45] Katzenellenbogen et al., 'Burden of Stroke'.
[46] Wilkinson, 'Ourselves and Others'.
[47] Australian Bureau of Statistics, *Population Characteristics*, 66.
[48] Australian Institute of Health and Welfare, *Trends*, 3.
[49] Fiske, 'Surveilling the City', 69.

where 'surveillance practices, policies and performances concern the production of norms pertaining to race and exercise a "power to define what is in or out of place"'.[50] Settler colonial narratives that associate Aboriginal people with danger help to maintain the unspoken hierarchies of racialised power and fuel perceptions that surveillance of Aboriginal people is warranted.[51]

Racialised surveillance is a critical element in the normative and constitutive acts of violence pertaining to the settler state, tabulating, malforming and constricting Indigenous life. Surveillance perpetrated by social welfare, criminal justice and other governmental systems provides the data that allows policy to be written and enacted to the detriment of Aboriginal communities. Acts of surveillance are thus at the heart of the settler colonial project. Surveillance of the Indigenous population manifests in iterations of government financial management programmes, such as the 'BasicsCard', an income management tool which controls and surveils[52] the spending of those (largely Indigenous peoples) who are forced to use it, despite reporting no problems with financial management or drug and alcohol addiction.[53] It is present in the gaze of police officers racially profiling the population[54] as they cruise neighbourhoods from the comfort of their climate-controlled vehicles. It reveals itself as government welfare conditionality,[55] the sentencing impacts of prior convictions or outstanding warrants, to name but a few iterations.[56] Its racist outcomes are visible in every negative statistic emanating from the criminal justice system, from the hyper-incarceration of Indigenous youth[57] to the disproportionate number of prisoners with mental illness or cognitive impairment who also happen to be Indigenous.[58] It is extant in the disturbing number of Aboriginal women in custody[59] and the numbers who do not report domestic violence against them for fear their children will be stolen – again.[60] All these numbers are people, Indigenous people whose existence problematises settler sovereignty.

Racism is ordinary, not aberrational.[61] The military invasion of Aboriginal communities in the Northern Territory in June 2007 might seem exceptional,

---

[50] Browne, *Dark Matters*, 16.
[51] Fredericks and Bradfield, '"I'm Not Afraid of the Dark"'.
[52] Dalley, 'The "White Card" is Grey', 53.
[53] Marston et al., *Hidden Costs*, 9.
[54] Law Reform Commission of Western Australia, *Aboriginal Customary Laws*, 192.
[55] Wacquant, *Punishing the Poor*, 288.
[56] Cunneen, *Conflict, Politics and Crime*, 34–6.
[57] Cunneen, White, and Richards, *Juvenile Justice*, 140.
[58] Baldry et al., *Predictable and Preventable Path*, 1.
[59] Cunneen and Tauri, *Indigenous Criminology*, 89.
[60] Ibid., 101–2.
[61] Delgado and Stefancic, *Critical Race Theory*, 8.

but it was entirely consistent with the systemic racism of the settler colonial project. 'The Intervention' afforded the Commonwealth powers to intervene, surveil and monitor the lives of Indigenous people in the Northern Territory at a level 'unmatched by any other policy declaration in Aboriginal affairs in the last forty years'.[62] It restricted the rights of Indigenous people living in seventy-three communities and town camps across the Northern Territory. Police were given powers to enter houses and seize property without a warrant, and citizens' rights to access social security, alcohol and computers, and to manage their land were curtailed. Although 'The Intervention' was an extreme example of state violence, it is important to understand it as consistent with colonialism, not aberrant. When does the exception become the rule? When it is the law of sovereign exception. Giorgio Agamben's concept of the law of sovereign exception is particularly useful in understanding 'The Intervention' as a political tool and can be applied to the settler state vis-à-vis Aboriginal peoples more broadly. The law of sovereign exception is put into practice by an all-powerful sovereign when they determine that a particular group is exempt from all legal protections and that a state of emergency exists whereby the usual rules of engagement have been suspended. In contemporary Australia we see this manifest in the government's Northern Territory 'Intervention'. This military incursion into Indigenous communities was executed through the suspension of the Racial Discrimination Act 1975. Aboriginal communities subject to it have been divested of political status and reduced to living what Agamben describes as 'bare life' without rights, and subject to a constant and remorseless scrutiny.[63]

The compartmentalisation and delimiting of life and bare life guarantees that 'the life of the settler, is nurtured through forms of biopower that builds hospitals, sanitation, education and employment: while the unworthy life of the native is the target of necropower – doomed to servitude and violence and considered disposable'.[64] Conservative politicians have repeatedly described the outstations and homelands where Aboriginal people live on their traditional lands in a largely self-governing capacity as 'lifestyle choices',[65] blaming Indigenous communities themselves for government failures to provide access to basic services such as sewerage, schools and medical clinics.[66] In Western Australia in 2015, the state government surveilled and calculated the assets of the remote Aboriginal communities within its territory. It then attempted to

---

[62] Hinkson, 'Introduction', 1.
[63] Agamben, *Homo Sacer*.
[64] Blagg and Anthony, '"Stone Walls Do Not a Prison Make"', 265.
[65] Davidson, 'Explainer'.
[66] Hansard, Legislative Council of Western Australia, 15 June 2017.

force the closure of over 150 remote Aboriginal outstations on the grounds that they were too costly to support. Yet other small towns inhabited by largely non-Aboriginal people were never endangered.

In removing services, stymying Indigenous-controlled enterprises and increasing policing of remote Aboriginal communities, federal and state governments have attempted to remove from them the conditions of life. Indeed, they have tried to condemn them to 'bare life' and turn thriving communities into 'camps' as theorised by Agamben. The camp in this context should be understood as a form of spatial management that disciplines populations and enforces compulsory visibility. In 'The Camp as Nomos of the Modern', Agamben links colonialism to the creation of 'the camp' as a political tool. He points to the 'campos de concentraciones' created by the Spanish in Cuba in 1896 to suppress the popular insurrection of the colony, and the 'concentration camps' into which the English herded the Boers towards the start of the century as being the first 'camps' to appear.[67] The important element in both examples is that 'a state of emergency linked to a colonial war is extended to an entire civil population'.[68] Since the invasion of the Australian continent by the British, their occupation has been met with resistance by the already extant population. This resistance took many forms including armed resistance, and the British understood themselves to be engaged in wars with various groups.[69] In a pattern typical of British colonialism elsewhere, the British in Australia began their invasion with violent attacks followed by the enclosure of land and the exclusion and containment of entire populations of Indigenous peoples in variously named missions, reserves and boarding schools that were all iterations of 'the camp' or what Mbembe describes as 'topographies of cruelty'.[70] Indeed, one might argue that the entire continent is a giant colonial 'camp' where Aboriginal people live in conditions of 'bare life'. Right across civil society from the over-surveillance of black kids on push bikes to the CCTV of maximum security prisons, the distinction between life inside/outside the 'camp' has disappeared. The 'logic of the camp' now applies to all the zones Aboriginal people are confined to such that they exhibit the conditions of 'bare life'[71] and space begins to function as one immense, heavily surveilled carceral continent.

If life on the inside is not especially different from life on the outside, then prison can be understood as one camp among many, as part of what Wacquant

---

[67] Agamben, *Homo Sacer*, 137.
[68] Ibid.
[69] Reynolds, *Forgotten War*.
[70] Mbembe, 'Necropolitics', 40.
[71] Diken and Laustsen, 'Zones of Indistinction'.

describes as a 'carceral continuum' where state- and church-run services impose carceral controls, and prisons offer social services.[72] Surveillance underpins this carceral continuum, its hidden presence regulating welfare data and parole, child services and solitary confinement. Sentencing Aboriginal people to longer carceral sentences accords with the settler colonial logic of assimilation and elimination, by which Aboriginal peoples were supposed to disappear. By imprisoning them in jails and watch houses in enormous numbers, we do, for a time, make them disappear – from our streets – only to reappear at a later date within the carceral continuum. Meanwhile, what are known as 'paperless arrests' allow the Northern Territory police to surveil the streets of Darwin and use their discretion to detain anyone they deem a public nuisance for a period of a few hours. Because these are not formal arrests no paperwork is required (hence the name), but the object of concern has been removed.

Certain places, especially those sites of detention produced by the interactions between architecture, knowledge, power and colonialism, hold particular trauma for Indigenous communities. These might be termed 'architectures of terror' and they consist of police watch houses, lock-ups, divisional vans, prisons and remand centres. Most of these places are monitored by CCTV and all of them are part of the carceral continuum. These architectures of terror are consistent with the merging of military and civilian architectures in the frontier.[73] They are expressed through a colonial lens and utilised in accordance with the law of exception as theorised by Giorgio Agamben[74] and, before him, Hannah Arendt in her work on totalitarianism.[75] When surveillance technology shows us Indigenous people being murdered or left to die within various architectures of terror, the practices and perpetrators responsible for such a dystopian gaze recede into the shadows. One might be conscious of the negative outcomes of surveillance on those who are surveilled, but those who produce and rely on such tools of governance are strangely absent. Its victims are highly, indeed obscenely, visible; its perpetrators are nowhere to be seen.

Watching the CCTV footage of a cellblock with a shadowy figure prone on the floor has become banal. So many dead: we count the numbers, write it down, wring our hands. While the purpose of CCTV and other surveillance measures in carceral settings might appear to be to provide security, it affords little to no protection for criminalised Aboriginal people. Perhaps the reason for this is that the eye at the other end of the CCTV is white and surveillance is a tool of

[72] Wacquant, 'Deadly Symbiosis', 97.
[73] Weizman, *Geometry of Occupation*, 2.
[74] Agamben, *Homo Sacer*.
[75] Arendt, *Origins*.

control that instrumentalises the white gaze,[76] a gaze that sees black bodies as objects of fear, disdain or dismissal. This is also the reason why Aboriginal people confined to cells with CCTV can fall, hit their heads and stop moving, all under the eye of the white gaze, and officers of the settler state do nothing. In July 2017 the Australian Broadcasting Corporation televised CCTV footage from a youth detention centre in Darwin of guards committing brutal acts of violence on Indigenous children without fear and in clear sight of CCTV cameras and senior officers. A Royal Commission into the detention and protection of children in the Northern Territory resulted. It found, among other things that 'Indigenous boys and girls were arbitrarily placed in segregation cells for 23 hours per day, treated like "dogs", denied food, water and basic hygiene and stripped naked by guards; they were reduced to bare life.'[77] They were imprisoned in a 'camp' and subject to the random violence afforded *homo sacer*. Surveillance did not prevent it; on the contrary, it saw it and did nothing.

V. A Protection Racket

The settler state looms as an early colonial era 'Protector' controlling and threatening the very survival of the family through a range of surveillance types not limited to but including surveillance by police, welfare administration, cashless debt cards, parole, and bail restrictions. Under 'The Intervention', government and allied agencies would be deployed using the rhetoric of protecting 'vulnerable children' as a means to justify the extended surveillance of Aboriginal families.[78] 'The Intervention' established administrative surveillance controls that would shift control over the provision of all services out of Indigenous hands and into the domain of government service providers or allied agencies. Once again the settler state deployed the language of 'protection' and the trope of the 'neglectful Aboriginal mother'[79] to establish control and undermine any efforts towards self-sufficiency and sovereignty. Aboriginal families and especially Aboriginal women are treated as *homo sacer* in a variety of contexts including situations of child welfare concerns and family violence.[80] When accusations of child abuse are levelled at white families, they are resolved by engaging with the family where abuse is alleged, and not by involving their entire community and certainly not by punishing that community with police-enforced curfews and other militaristic measures.

---

[76] Browne, *Dark Matters*, 16.
[77] Blagg and Anthony, '"Stone Walls Do Not a Prison Make"', 267.
[78] Mal Brough, in Commonwealth of Australia, *Parliamentary Debates*, 8.
[79] Haebich, *Broken Circles*, 233.
[80] Nancarrow et al., *Accurately Identifying*.

Indigenous peoples live with socio-economic disadvantage on all the major indicators.[81] It suits the colonial project to keep Aboriginal people in poverty. Research indicates that poverty is a major stressor contributing to poor mental and physical health.[82] However, when Aboriginal peoples are in control of their own enterprises, the results are overwhelmingly positive.[83] For example, adult Aboriginal mortality rates from all causes have been up to 40 per cent lower in Aboriginal homelands with Aboriginal-run health services than among Aboriginal peoples in the Northern Territory generally.[84]

But the success of Aboriginal-run communities and their enterprises threatens the protection racket and makes them a target for the race war of the settler state. Income control through the imposition of cashless debit cards is another iteration of racialised surveillance which, under the rubric of protection, infantilises and impoverishes Aboriginal people. Welfare quarantining, in the form of income management, was first introduced in 2007 as part of the NTER. The stated aim of income management, according to the Auditor General, is to 'assist income support recipients to manage their fortnightly payments – such as Newstart/Youth Allowance, parenting or carer payments, and the Disability Support Pension – for essentials like food, rent and bills'.[85] It has since been trialled in several other Indigenous communities where it was also imposed without consultation.[86] The effect of cashless debit cards is to control, limit choices and surveil spending. Their funds can only be spent on government-defined priority needs at government-approved retailers or service providers. In parliamentary debates about the income management card, Indigenous welfare recipients were portrayed by Minister for Indigenous Affairs Mal Brough as deficient for receiving 'passive welfare'.[87] This infantilises Aboriginal people, assuming they cannot wisely manage their own money, the implied judgement being based in white notions of spending priorities. Income management measures were also claimed to be necessary 'to ensure that priority needs are met and to encourage better social and parenting behaviours'.[88] Once again, a narrative of deficit and 'poor parenting' is employed to justify settler state surveillance of Aboriginal lives and the denial of Aboriginal peoples' sovereignty over their own lives and communities.

---

[81] Calma, *Social Justice Report*, 4.
[82] Shaw, Dorling, and Smith, 'Poverty'.
[83] Dwyer, Silburn, and Wilson, *National Strategies*, 91–106, Appendix.
[84] Rowley et al., 'Morbidity and Mortality'.
[85] Australian National Audit Office, *Implementation and Performance*, 7.
[86] Vincent, Submission 23, 16; Mal Brough, in Commonwealth of Australia, *Parliamentary Debates*, 6, 7, 11.
[87] Mal Brough, in Commonwealth of Australia, *Parliamentary Debates*, 11.
[88] Ibid., 3.

Right back to mission days there was always some *whitefella* watching. Pastor, protector, policeman: watching, always watching. Counting. Marking down in neat rows how many Aboriginal ears were nailed to the homestead as trophies,[89] making space for how many head of cattle, how many 'full bloods' to keep an eye on,[90] how many women for the station kitchen.[91] Protectors even kept a record of all the wages stolen from Aboriginal people deemed incapable of managing their money,[92] the same logic that today informs the cashless debit card. In the white settler colonial fantasy there is no place for blackness, so merely appearing is a disobedient act and one that challenges the white nation. Being Indigenous and present in place on your Country is to disobey the racialised spatial management of settler colonialism. Indigenous self-actualisation reveals the lie of *terra nullius*, of assimilation, and of deficit politics. It is this fear of sovereign blackness that fuels the violence of settler colonialism, and it is up to settlers to resolve their fear of the dark. Racialised surveillance acts like a roo shooter's spotlight in the darkness, hunting down Indigenous people and treating them like prey.[93] Surveillance is weaponised through systems of settler governance to light up and expose the 'bare life' of Aboriginal people within the carceral colony that is occupied Australia.

VI. Bibliography

Agamben, Giorgio. *Homo Sacer: Sovereign Power and Bare Life*. Translated by D. Heller-Roazen. Stanford: Stanford University Press, 1998.

Arendt, Hannah. *Eichmann in Jerusalem: A Report on the Banality of Evil*. New York: Penguin Books, 1994.

———. *The Origins of Totalitarianism*. London: Penguin, 2017.

Australian Bureau of Statistics. *Population Characteristics, Aboriginal and Torres Strait Islander Peoples 2001*. ABS cat. no. 4713.0. Canberra: Commonwealth of Australia, 2002.

Australian Institute of Health and Welfare. *Chronic Kidney Disease in Aboriginal and Torres Strait Islander People 2011*. Cat. no. PHE 151. Canberra: AIHW, 2011.

Australian Institute of Health and Welfare. *Trends in Indigenous Mortality and Life Expectancy 2001–2015*. Cat. no. IHW 174. Canberra: Commonwealth of Australia, 2017. https://www.aihw.gov.au/getmedia/bbe476f3-a630-4a73-b79f-712aba55d643/aihw-ihw.

---

[89] Evans and Thorpe, 'Indigenocide', 32.

[90] Haebich, *Broken Circles*, 135–6.

[91] Haskins, 'From the Centre to the City'.

[92] Kinnane, Harrison, and Reinecke, 'Finger Money'.

[93] Kangaroo hunters typically use powerful car-mounted spotlights to sight their nocturnal prey. Video evidence of Aboriginal deaths in custody also note police officers dragging the unconscious bodies of Aboriginal people 'like dead kangaroos'. See Whittaker, '"Dragged Like a Dead Kangaroo"'.

Australian Institute of Health and Welfare and Australian Bureau of Statistics. *The Health and Welfare of Australia's Aboriginal and Torres Strait Islander Peoples 2005.* ABS cat. no. 4704.0. Canberra: Commonwealth of Australia, 2005. www.aihw. gov.au/publications/ihw/hwaatsip05/hwaatsip05.pdf.

Australian National Audit Office. *The Implementation and Performance of the Cashless Debit Card Trial.* Auditor-General Report No. 1 2018–19. Barton: ANAO, 2018.

Baldry, Eileen, Ruth McCausland, Leanne Dowse, and Elizabeth McEntyre. *A Predictable and Preventable Path: Aboriginal People with Mental and Cognitive Disabilities in the Criminal Justice System.* Sydney: University of New South Wales, 2015.

Bargallie, Debbie. *Unmasking the Racial Contract: Indigenous Voices on Racism in the Australian Public Service.* Canberra: Aboriginal Studies Press, 2020.

Bartlett, Richard H. *Native Title in Australia.* 2nd ed. Chatswood: LexisNexis Butterworths, 2004.

Behrendt, Larissa. 'Morpeth Lecture: Mind, Body and Spirit: Pathways Forward for Reconciliation.' *Newcastle Law Review* 5, no. 1 (2001): 42–3.

Bird Rose, Deborah. *Reports From a Wild Country: Ethics for Decolonisation.* Sydney: University of New South Wales Press, 2004.

Blagg, Harry, and Thalia Anthony. '"Stone Walls Do Not a Prison Make": Bare Life and the Carceral Archipelago in Colonial and Postcolonial Societies.' In *Human Rights and Incarceration,* edited by Elizabeth Stanley, 257–83. Cham: Springer, 2017.

Browne, Simone. *Dark Matters: On the Surveillance of Blackness.* Durham, NC: Duke University Press, 2015.

Burns, Marcelle. 'The Unfinished Business of the Apology: Senate Rejects Stolen Generations Compensation Bill 2008 (Cth).' *Indigenous Law Bulletin* 7[s. l.], no. 7 (2008): 10–14.

Butler, Judith. *Giving an Account of Oneself.* New York: Fordham University Press, 2005.

Calma, Tom. *Social Justice Report 2005: The Indigenous Health Challenge.* Sydney: Australian Human Rights Commission, 2005.

Commonwealth of Australia. *Parliamentary Debates: House of Representatives.* 7 August 2007. (Mal Brough, Minister for Families, Community Services and Indigenous Affairs and Minister Assisting the Prime Minister for Indigenous Affairs).

Cunneen, Chris. *Conflict, Politics and Crime: Aboriginal Communities and the Police.* New York: Routledge, 2001.

Cunneen, Chris, and Juan Tauri. *Indigenous Criminology.* Bristol: Policy Press, 2016.

Cunneen, Chris, Rob White, and Kelly Richards. *Juvenile Justice: Youth and Crime in Australia.* Oxford: Oxford University Press, 2013.

Curthoys, Ann, and Clive Moore. 'Working for the White People: An Historio-graphic Essay on Aboriginal and Torres Strait Islander Labour.' *Labour History* 69 (1995): 1–29.

Dalley, Cameo. 'The "White Card" is Grey: An Anthropological Perspective of the Cashless Debit Card in an East Kimberley Town.' *Australian Journal of Social Issues* 55 (2020): 51–60.

Davidson, Helen. 'Explainer: The Facts behind the Outrage over Tony Abbott's Indigenous "Lifestyle Choice" Remarks.' *The Guardian*, 12 March 2015. https://www.theguardian.com/australia-news/2015/mar/12/behind-the-outrage-over-tony-abbotts-indigenous-lifestyle-choice-remarks.

Delgado, Richard, and Jean Stefancic. *Critical Race Theory: An Introduction*. New York: New York University Press, 2017.

Deleuze, Gilles. *The Fold: Leibniz and the Baroque*. Minneapolis: University of Minnesota Press, 1993.

Derrida, Jacques. *Margins of Philosophy*. Translated by Alan Bass. Brighton: Harvester Press, 1982.

Diken, Bülent, and Carsten Bagge Laustsen. 'Zones of Indistinction: Security, Terror, and Bare Life.' *Space and Culture* 5, no. 2 (2002): 290–307.

Dodson, Patrick. '25 Years on from Royal Commission into Aboriginal Deaths in Custody Recommendations.' *Indigenous Law Bulletin* 8, no. 23 (2016): 24–9.

Dorsett, Shaunnagh, and Shaun Mcveigh. 'Just So: The Law which Governs Australia is Australian Law.' *Law and Critique* 13 (2002): 289–309.

Dwyer, Judith, Kate Silburn, and Gai Wilson. *National Strategies for Improving Indigenous Health and Health Care, Aboriginal and Torres Strait Islander Primary Health Care Review: Consultant Report No. 1*. Canberra: Commonwealth of Australia, 2004.

Evans, Raymond, and Bill Thorpe. 'Indigenocide and the Massacre of Aboriginal History.' *Overland* 163 (2001): 21–39.

Fanon, Frantz. *The Wretched of the Earth*. New York: Grove Press, 2005.

Fforde, Cressida, Lawrence Bamblett, Ray Lovett, Scott Gorringe, and Bill Fogarty. 'Discourse, Deficit and Identity: Aboriginality, the Race Paradigm and the Language of Representation in Contemporary Australia.' *Media International Australia* 149, no. 1 (2013): 162–73.

Fiske, John. 'Surveilling the City: Whiteness, the Black Man and Democratic Totalitarianism.' *Theory, Culture and Society* 15, no. 2 (1998): 67–88.

Fitzpatrick, James P., Jane Latimer, Maureen Carter, June Oscar, Manuela L. Ferreira, Heather Carmichael Olson, Barbara R. Lucas, Robyn Doney, Claire Salter, Julianne Try, Genevieve Hawkes, Emily Fitzpatrick, Marmingee Hand, Rochelle E. Watkins, Alexandra L. C. Martiniuk, Carol Bower, John Boulton, and Elizabeth J. Elliott. 'Prevalence of Fetal Alcohol Syndrome in a Population-Based Sample of Children Living in Remote Australia: The Lililwan Project.' *Journal of Paediatric Child Health* 51, no. 4 (2015): 450–7.

Fredericks, Bronwyn, and Abraham Bradfield. '"I'm Not Afraid of the Dark": White Colonial Fears, Anxieties, and Racism in Australia and Beyond.' *M/C Journal* 24, no. 2 (2021).

Gray, Stephen. 'The Elephant in the Drawing Room: Slavery and the "Stolen Wages" Debate.' *Australian Indigenous Law Review* 11, no. 1 (2007): 30–53.

Haebich, Anna. *Broken Circles: Fragmenting Indigenous Families 1800–2000*. Fremantle: Fremantle Arts Centre Press, 2000.

Hansard. Legislative Council of Western Australia Prevention of Forced Closure of Remote Aboriginal Communities Bill 2017. Introduction and First Reading Bill introduced, on motion by Hon Robin Chapple, Thursday, 15 June 2017.

Harvey, David. 'Spacetime and the World (2005).' In *The People, Place and Space Reader*, edited by Jen Jack Gieseking, William Mangold, Cindi Katz, Setha Low, and Susan Saegert, 12–16. New York: Routledge, 2014.

Haskins, Victoria. 'From the Centre to the City: Modernity, Mobility and Mixed-Descent Aboriginal Domestic Workers from Central Australia.' *Women's History Review* 18, no. 1 (2009): 155–75.

Hinkson, Melinda. 'Introduction: In the Name of the Child.' In *Coercive Reconciliation: Stabilise, Normalise, Exit Aboriginal Australia*, edited by Jon Altman and Melinda Hinkson, 1–12. Melbourne: Arena Publication, 2007.

Howard, John, MP. 'Opening Address to the Australian Reconciliation Convention-Melbourne.' Department of the Prime Minister and Cabinet. https://pmtranscripts.pmc.gov.au/sites/default/files/original/00010361.

Hubbard, Phil, Rob Kitchin, Brendan Bartley, and Duncan Fuller. *Thinking Geographically: Space, Theory and Contemporary Human Geography*. London: Continuum, 2002.

Hunter, Ian. 'Native Title: Acts of State and the Rule of Law.' *The Australian Quarterly* 65, no. 4 (1993): 97–109.

Jones, Jilpia. 'Working for the White People.' *Culture, Law and Colonialism* 6 (2004): 1–8.

Joy, Rachel. 'Very Becoming: Transforming Our Settler Selves in Occupied Australia.' In *Testimony and Trauma: Engaging Common Ground*, edited by Christina Santos, Adriana Spahr, and Tracy Crowe Morey, 235–54. Leiden: Brill, 2019.

Katzenellenbogen, Judith M., Theo Vos, Peter Somerford, Stephen Begg, James B. Semmens, and James P. Codde. 'Burden of Stroke in Indigenous Western Australians: A Study Using Data Linkage.' *Stroke* 42, no. 6 (2011): 1515–21.

Kinnane, Steve, Judy Harrison, and Isabelle Reinecke. 'Finger Money: The Black and White of Stolen Wages.' *Griffith Review* 47 (2015): 49–70.

Law Reform Commission of Western Australia. *Aboriginal Customary Laws, Final Report*. Perth: LRCWA, 2006.

Marston, Greg, Philip Mendes, Shelley Bielefeld, Michelle Peterie, Zoe Staines, and Steven Roche. *Hidden Costs: An Independent Study into Income Management in Australia*. Brisbane: University of Queensland, 2020.

Mbembe, Achille. 'Necropolitics.' *Public Culture* 15, no. 1 (2003): 11–40.

Medhora, Shalailah, Calla Wahlquist, Daniel Hurst, and Helen Davidson. 'Noel Pearson Blasts Abbott's "Lifestyle Choice" Comments as "Shameless".' *The Guardian*, 11 March 2015. https://www.theguardian.com/australia-news/2015/mar/11/noel-pearson-blasts-abbotts-lifestyle-choice-comments-as-shameless.

Moreton-Robinson, Aileen. 'Imagining the Good Indigenous Citizen: Race War and the Pathology of Patriarchal White Sovereignty.' *Cultural Studies Review* 15, no. 2 (2009): 61–79.

———. 'I Still Call Australia Home: Indigenous Belonging and Place in a Postcolonizing Society.' In *The White Possessive: Property, Power, and Indigenous Sovereignty*, 3–18. Minneapolis: University of Minnesota Press, 2015.

Muldoon, Paul. 'Thinking Responsibility Differently: Reconciliation and the Tragedy of Colonisation.' *Journal of Intercultural Studies* 26, no. 3 (2005): 237–54.

Nancarrow, Heather, Kate Thomas, Valerie Ringland, and Tanya Modini. *Accurately Identifying the 'Person Most in Need of Protection' in Domestic and Family Violence Law*. Sydney: Australia's National Research Organisation for Women's Safety, 2020.

Paglen, Trevor. 'Experimental Geography: From Cultural Production to the Production of Space.' In *Critical Landscapes: Art, Space, Politics*, edited by Emily Eliza Scott and Kirsten Swenson, 34–42. Oakland: University of California Press, 2015.

Patton, Paul. 'Sovereignty, Law, and Difference in Australia: After the Mabo Case.' *Alternatives* 21 (1996): 149–70.

Pearson, Noel, and Shireen Morris. *A Rightful Place: A Road Map to Recognition*. Collingwood: Black, 2017.

Philippopoulos-Mihalopoulos, Andreas. *Spatial Justice: Body, Lawscape, Atmosphere*. New York: Routledge, 2015.

Povinelli, Elizabeth A. *Geontologies: A Requiem to Late Liberalism*. Durham, NC: Duke University Press, 2016.

Reynolds, Henry. *Forgotten War*. Sydney: NewSouth Publishing, 2013.

Rowley, Kevin G., Kerin O'Dea, Ian Anderson, Robyn McDermott, Karmananda Saraswati, Ricky Tilmouth, Iris Roberts, Joseph Fitz, Zaimin Wang, Alicia Jenkins, James D. Best, Zhiqiang Wang, and Alex Brown. 'Lower than Expected Morbidity and Mortality for an Australian Aboriginal Population: 10-year Follow-Up in a Decentralised Community.' *Medical Journal of Australia* 188, no. 5 (2008): 83–287.

Royal Australasian College of Physicians. *Inequity and Health – A Call to Action – Addressing Health and Socioeconomic Inequality in Australia – Policy Statement 2005*. Canberra: RACP, 2005.

Rush, Peter. 'An Altered Jurisdiction: Corporeal Traces of Law.' *Griffith Law Review* 6 (1997): 144–68.

———. 'Surviving Common Law: Silence and the Violence Internal to the Legal Sign.' *Cardozo Law Review* 27, no. 2 (2005): 753–66.

Rutherford, Jennifer. 'Introduction: Kairos for a Wounded Country.' In *The Poetics of Australian Spaces*, edited by Jennifer Rutherford and Barbara Holloway, 1–10. Crawley, WA: UWA Publishing, 2010.

SBS. '7 Legacies of John Howard's Government.' The Point, SBS television website. Aired 3 March 2016. https://www.sbs.com.au/nitv/the-point-with-stan-grant/article/2016/03/03/7-legacies-john-howardsgovernment.

Shaw, Mary, Danny Dorling, and George Davey Smith. 'Poverty, Social Exclusion, and Minorities.' In *Social Determinants of Health: The Solid Facts*, 2nd ed., edited by Michael Marmot and Richard Wilkinson, 211–39. Oxford: Oxford University Press, 2006.

Thomson, Neil, and Janette Brooks. 'Cardiovascular Disease.' In *The Health of Indigenous Australians*, edited by Neil Thomson, 186–206. Melbourne: Oxford University Press, 2003.

Vincent, Eve. Social Security (Administration) Amendment (Income Management and Cashless Welfare) Bill 2019, Submission 23.

Wacquant, Loïc. 'Deadly Symbiosis: When Ghetto and Prison Meet and Mesh.' *Punishment and Society* 3, no. 1 (2001): 95–133.

————. *Punishing the Poor: The Neoliberal Government of Social Insecurity.* Durham, NC: Duke University Press, 2009.

Watego, Chelsea. *Another Day in the Colony.* St Lucia: University of Queensland Press, 2021.

Weizman, Eyal. *The Geometry of Occupation.* Centre of Contemporary Culture of Barcelona 2004. Conference lecture at the cycle 'Borders'. CCCB, 1 March 2004.

Whittaker, Alison. '"Dragged Like a Dead Kangaroo": Why Language Matters for Deaths in Custody.' *The Guardian*, 8 September 2018. https://www.theguardian.com/commentisfree/2018/sep/07/dragged-like-a-dead-kangaroo-why-language-matters-for-deaths-in-custody.

Wilkinson, Richard G. 'Ourselves and Others – for Better or Worse: Social Vulnerability and Inequality.' In *Social Determinants of Health: The Solid Facts*, 2nd ed., edited by Michael Marmot and Richard Wilkinson, 341–58. Oxford: Oxford University Press, 2006.

Wolfe, Patrick. 'Settler Colonialism and the Elimination of the Native.' *Journal of Genocide Research* 8, no. 4 (2006): 387–409.

Wood, David Murakami, ed. *A Report on the Surveillance Society*. Wilmslow: Office of the Information Commissioner, 2006.

Yunupingu, Galarrwuy, ed. *Our Land is Our Life: Land Rights – Past, Present, Future.* St Lucia: University of Queensland Press, 1997.

12

Policing and Surveillance of the Margins: The Challenges of Homelessness in California

Yvonne-Marie Rogez

I. Introduction

In California, an estimated 108,000 people sleep outdoors, while 40,000 sleep in shelters every night, which is more than in any other state in the United States.[1] Furthermore, in 2019, the U.S. Department of Housing and Urban Development noted in its Annual Homeless Assessment Report that in one year, the rate of increase in the state (an additional 21,306 people, or 16.4 per cent) was 'more than the total national increase of every other state combined'.[2] California represents 12 per cent of the country's population but accounts for about 24 per cent of the total homeless population in the United States. It is home to a very high number of court cases challenging what is referred to as the criminalisation of homelessness, which both justifies and fosters surveillance practices. The homeless crisis, which is the state's most visible and persistent problem,[3] also crystallises all the challenges of contemporary surveillance: categorisation, visibility and invisibility, crime and criminalisation, surveillance under the guise of charity or 'care' work, privacy issues, policing, and the use of surveillance devices and technologies by local authorities. As surveillance regulates boundaries and relations,[4] it involves all strata of society and a wide range of social actors from neighbourhoods and local charities and police forces all the way up to the President of the United States.

---

[1] The figures are provided for 2020. See https://endhomelessness.org/homelessness-in-america/homelessness-statistics/state-of-homelessness-2020/. Counts for 2021 are not available and thus the numbers do not reflect any of the changes potentially brought about by the crisis (see Section V of this chapter). See https://www.usich.gov/homelessness-statistics/ca/.

[2] https://archives.hud.gov/news/2020/pr20-003.cfm.

[3] Hoeven, 'California Homeless Crisis'.

[4] Monahan and Wood, *Surveillance Studies*, xx.

David Lyon includes behaviours practised by the homeless, petty criminals and passers-by alike in his definition of surveillance. He notes that 'police officers watching someone loitering in a parking lot would be an example' of watching 'over those whose activities are in some way dubious or suspect'.[5] Public policies aimed at dealing with the presence of the homeless in city centres definitely require specific action which aims to both manage and protect. Surveillance lies at the heart of governmental and police action, as evidenced by several chapters in this collection.[6] This chapter examines examples of surveillance used in action by the government and the police, as 'dubious' and 'suspect' behaviours are qualified as crimes, while suggesting what the elements of the surveillance practices that apply to the homeless might be.[7]

Homelessness is the target of an impressively large array of surveillance techniques, even though they rarely are acknowledged as such,[8] that extend beyond the 'focused, systematic and routine attention to personal detail for the purposes of influence, management, protection or direction',[9] to incorporate a wide range of practices of social control, administration and policing. The distinctive character and variety of these strategies is hardly surprising. Deprived of a fixed home, settled income and the trappings of uninterrupted digital connection, the homeless stand outside the mechanisms of information-gathering and monitoring applied to other sections of society.[10] Surveillance practices vary from acts of control (excessive power, abuse, violation of privacy, etc.), to softer forms of control such as government-sanctioned encampments, and to protection (gathering of personal information for healthcare and safety purposes). Indeed, policies dealing with homelessness touch on the two opposite poles of the surveillance continuum, for instance in the case of homeless sweeps, as acts of control, and the work of charities, as protection.[11]

[5] Lyon, *Surveillance Studies*, 14.

[6] See for example Grabosky and Urbas, Chapter 7; Banita, Chapter 10; and Joy, Chapter 11, all in this collection.

[7] 'Before one can establish whether a particular set of sociotechnical relations constitutes surveillance various observable elements might need to be present. Little, if any, work so far has attempted to identify and confirm what the elements of surveillance might be across different empirical contexts.' Ball and Haggerty, 'Doing Surveillance Studies', 129.

[8] 'As we sometimes mask our own research intentions, research which names surveillance as surveillance may be seen as a direct challenge to the legitimacy of wide sets of organisational practices which they would also prefer to keep normalised or even secret.' Ibid., 134.

[9] Ibid.

[10] This chapter will not look at surveillance tools such as censuses (although they have consequences on policing when they are due, as local authorities aim to clean up the streets in order to keep the numbers down) or data collection used by charities.

[11] See the definition of 'surveillance' provided in the Introduction to this collection.

The policies which apply to the homeless cover all the usual goals of surveillance – security, economic control and growth, social harmony, and welfare – and they may be examined through the work of police and local authorities.[12] This chapter aims to examine what David Lyon terms the 'culture of surveillance',[13] as it applies to the homeless in California, as well as the varied roles of its practitioners and constituents. In order to participate in the culture of surveillance as Lyon defines it, one needs to have access to social media, digital devices (that the homeless often own, but then access to electricity becomes crucial) and consumer goods (that the homeless are not likely to own). The originality of this chapter lies in considering the specificity of the homeless, not mainstream consumers. The chapter demonstrates how this underclass of people, although they are by definition excluded from such a culture, experience surveillance otherwise and are asked to participate in their own surveillance differently. When it comes to the homeless, surveillance needs to be located alongside indifference, active policies of invisibilisation and outbursts of attempts at social control. This chapter looks at the surveillance tools used by local authorities, local ordinances targeting the homeless, and policies developed in the context of the COVID-19 pandemic. These diverse elements highlight the multidirectional and complex nature of surveillance in the specific and challenging context of homelessness. This chapter scrutinises the different types of surveillance to which the homeless are subjected, evaluating the legitimacy of their aims, their respect for individuals, and their adherence to their primary objective.[14]

This chapter thus first considers the homeless as a category of the population and looks at the challenges they pose to conventional practices of surveillance. It then assesses how the different players in the homelessness debate navigate these challenges, from the conflicting aims of visibility and invisibility sought to be imposed on the homeless by different levels of government. The fourth section focuses on the effective criminalisation of homelessness in California. Finally, an in-depth study of the surveillance of the homeless in the current COVID-19 health crisis in California suggests both new challenges and solutions, while providing new perspectives on the surveillance of marginalised social groups.

II. Categorisation and Control

David Barnard-Wills defines surveillance as linked to social sorting and discrimination. It is 'about power and therefore fundamentally political'.[15]

---

[12] Castagnino, 'Critique des *surveillances studies*'.
[13] Lyon, *Culture of Surveillance*, 7.
[14] Castagnino, 'Critique des *surveillances studies*', 33.
[15] Barnard-Wills, *Surveillance and Identity*, 2.

It is both easy and extremely difficult to precisely identify the homeless as a homogeneous group. The homeless are unhoused. On the one hand, here then is a community that is extremely difficult to trace and track for any length of time. On the other hand, as Foucault would be the first to point out, public policy requires detailed mechanisms of disaggregation, prioritisation and categorisation. Are those living in shelters, cars or RVs, or couch-surfing the same population as those living in tents? As Bart van Leeuwen notes, 'the population of the homeless is so diverse, and routes to homelessness so different, that they seem to defy any categorisation at all'.[16] He goes on, 'a major reason why the problem of homelessness is distinctive and unfit for a general theory of social rights is this sheer diversity of individuals with their particular problems, needs and chaotic living conditions'.[17] For many scholars, this tension is linked to issues of categorisation that are as detrimental as they are essential, as 'sympathy can turn into contempt as the part comes to stand for the whole and aggregation obscures the discriminations necessary for effective policy'.[18]

Indeed at the heart of the problem of definition lie the contradictory motives that shape efforts to regulate and control the increasing homeless population: on the one hand, a recognition of their special needs; on the other, the anxiety to control 'anarchy, bedlam, madness'.[19] In 'Helping and Hating the Homeless. The Struggle at the Margins of America', Peter Marin notes, '[d]rinking, doping, loitering, panhandling, defecating, urinating, molesting, stealing – the litany went on and on, was repeated over and over, accompanied by fantasies of disaster: the barbarian hordes at the gates, civilization ended.'[20] It is therefore an individual's behaviour and place 'on the pavement', more than their 'unhoused' situation, that marks them as 'homeless' for surveillance purposes. Up to 90 per cent of homeless people in California are addicted to drugs or alcohol, a number that has increased since the beginning of the opioid crisis,[21] further exacerbating the feeling of insecurity of citizens in some neighbourhoods. While shelters often aim to rehabilitate the homeless, policing, as well as judicial decisions and urban laws, have increasingly aimed to control the homeless population, to stamp out undesirable behaviour and simply to make it less visible.

---

[16] van Leeuwen, 'Edge of the Urban Landscape', 597.
[17] Ibid.
[18] Katz, *Undeserving Poor*, 233.
[19] Lopez, 'Dysfunction of L.A. Homeless Policy'.
[20] Marin, 'Helping and Hating the Homeless'.
[21] Wells, 'Downplaying the Reality of Addiction'.

Focusing on the consequences of homelessness, while it may help create a more socially useful category, is a double-edged sword, mirroring the paradoxes that bedevil solutions to the problem. For policy and thus surveillance purposes, the homeless are those who occupy the public space in ways that are not viewed as socially acceptable by the communities in which they reside. They are seen as vectors of insecurity and crime. This approach generates two complementary types of policies. One consists in displacing the homeless to make them less visible, either in shelters or by the dismantling of homeless camps and seizing of property (see Section III). This is itself paradoxical, arising out of the two opposite ends of the surveillance spectrum: drastic control on the one hand and care and protection on the other. The other, relying partly on tools and practices of surveillance, consists in criminalising homeless people's occupation of the public space (Section IV).

III. The Goals of Control and Surveillance: From Visibility to Invisibility

Homelessness reveals surveillance issues that are complex and paradoxical. While institutions where surveillance is exercised generally render those inside more visible,[22] shelters and rehabilitation centres ultimately aim to make them invisible – to make the problem go away. Visibility refers to the growing presence of the homeless in the public space and invisibilisation to the goal of law enforcement. However, their visibility is also considered by homeless advocates as a necessity as it reminds the population of the reality of this issue on a daily basis. The homeless may also be described as invisible in the sense that they do not participate in the life of mainstream society (even though some have jobs and pay taxes) and are 'non-citizens'.[23] Becoming visible would then also conversely mean access to a place within society. Invisibilisation which is not the result of housing is therefore systematically considered by advocates as avoiding and displacing the issue, rather than solving it. Some city ordinances aim to push the homeless over city and state lines.[24] Others are founded on the belief that, by displacing the belongings of homeless individuals, these individuals will have no choice but to move. These 'anti-homeless' ordinances arise out of pressure on politicians from local residents and, more particularly, business owners.[25] They are part of the

---

[22] Foucault, *Discipline and Punish.*
[23] Van Leeuwen, 'Edge of the Urban Landscape', 589.
[24] Baudrillard, *America.*
[25] National Coalition for the Homeless and National Law Center on Homelessness & Poverty, with the National Homeless Civil Rights Organizing Project, *Illegal to be Homeless.*

political arsenal of neoliberal and conservative groups who strongly support the harshest types of surveillance and policing.

The increasing presence of the homeless in public space threatens the evolution of urbanisation, real estate and gentrification.[26] Marin writes:

> [As] property rose in value, the nooks and crannies in which the homeless had been able to hide became more visible. Doorways, alleys, abandoned buildings, vacant lots – these 'holes' in the cityscape, these gaps in public consciousness, became real estate. The homeless, who had been there all the time, were overtaken by economic progress, and they became intruders.[27]

Marin is describing a form of privatisation of public space, in which the presence of the homeless is seen as a threat to private property and private security. Homeless people set up 'camps', on the basis that for them too there is safety in numbers. But this only exacerbates social anxieties about crime and disease. Authorities then decide that the camps must go.

But moving on the homeless only brings the illusion of disappearance. It is not linked to rehabilitation, deterrence or social reintegration. The tension between the continuing visibility of the homeless and the desire to make them invisible defines responses to homelessness. Michael Katz notes that:

> This attempt to render the poor invisible has introduced a schizophrenic character into homelessness policy. The progressive thrust of federal policy is countered by more inconsistent policies at the local level – on the one hand supporting programs to assist the homeless, while on the other, trying to keep them away from public spaces.[28]

On the one hand, then, homelessness advocates do not in fact wish the homeless to disappear from city centres, pavements and roadsides, as they would then also disappear from our consciousness.[29] On the other hand, opposition to the 'right to sleep on sidewalks' comes not just from neoliberal politicians or real estate agents but from advocates themselves, who see such a right as a sign of failure and surrender.[30] Banning sleeping on sidewalks may force governments to find more efficient and long-term solutions.[31] These paradoxes mount

---

[26] Katz, *Undeserving Poor*, 231.
[27] Marin, 'Helping and Hating the Homeless'.
[28] Katz, *Undeserving Poor*, 231.
[29] Rogez, 'Shopping Carts', 181.
[30] Lopez, 'Dysfunction of L.A. Homeless Policy'.
[31] Wright notes that if beggars were out of sight as a result of anti-homeless legislation, they would be easily forgotten by the very people who might come to their assistance. Wright, 'Not in Anyone's Backyard', 175.

up, resulting in a blurring of intentions and a form of discouragement for all sides of the political spectrum. If surveillance and control practices aim to render the homeless invisible, the failures of this process lead to their increasing visibility, which in turn becomes either the only way they might be taken care of, or a reason for more drastic control. Invisibilisation with no solution but displacement will only lead to more visibility, while visibility, while it may lead to better care, might in the long run bring more perennial invisibility.

IV. The Police and the Courts: Digital Technologies and Privacy Issues

In February 2022, a new type of programme targeting homelessness was proposed by Governor Gavin Newsom of California. It aims to create a mental health branch in counties' civil courts called 'care courts'. No doubt the phrase seems like an oxymoron, combining as it does both conservative policies of control and tracking and liberal values of protection. Even though the programme was elaborated with the homeless crisis in mind, it is not limited to homeless people and could apply to anyone. People with severe mental illnesses would be forced to accept treatment, and counties would be mandated to provide services.[32] If they refuse treatment, such people could be placed into conservatorships. This programme is both a response to the increasing visibility of the homeless on the streets as a result of the pandemic and a political move as part of the campaign leading up to the mid-term elections in November 2022. Homeless rights activists have criticised it as yet another form of surreptitious criminalisation. Coercive treatment is not efficient, Sam Levin argues,[33] noting that Newsom's scheme 'would take us back to the bad old days of confinement, coercive treatment and other deprivations of rights targeting people with disabilities'.[34]

The tendency for Democratic governments and authorities to lean towards draconian measures is also exemplified in San Francisco Mayor London Breed's decision in December 2021 to declare a state of emergency in the Tenderloin district, following high levels of homelessness and a rise in overdose deaths and related crime. The plan includes increased police presence and surveillance, as well as faster access to shelter, counselling and medical care.[35] Breed also called for more access to surveillance technology for the police. Critics have expressed their surprise as such legislation exists but has been under- or misused, noting that the real purpose of the announcement of the plan might be to 'circumvent

[32] Levin, 'California Proposal'.
[33] Ibid., mentioning Kisely, Campbell, and Preston, 'Compulsory Community and Involuntary Outpatient Treatment', and Rugkåsa, Dawson, and Burns, 'CTOs'.
[34] Eve Garrow, qtd in Levin, 'California Proposal'.
[35] Breed, 'Safer San Francisco'.

San Francisco's nationally lauded privacy law'.[36] They also note that the new plan would undermine the Acquisition of Surveillance Technology Ordinance 2019,[37] which placed limits on police surveillance, banning the use of facial recognition technology, with limited exceptions, and requiring public posting and approval of current surveillance technologies in the possession of or used by city departments.[38] To date, only two of the fifty technologies currently listed have been formally approved.

The expansion of police surveillance and access to surveillance technology in this new plan have raised considerable concerns.[39] Mano Raju, a public defender, has denounced the measures as targeting those who are already 'underserved and overpoliced'.[40] This encroachment on privacy is not new for the homeless. Long before the rise in modern surveillance technologies, many policies in practice denied the homeless any right to privacy, criminalised what would otherwise be described as common behaviour, and limited their access to public space.[41]

The privacy of the homeless is a right which is difficult to protect, as they necessarily live in public space. As Bart von Leeuwen argues,

> Although the homeless are trapped in public, at the same time they are not considered to be part of the public. Besides their outcast status, the homeless are effectively noncitizens in the sense in which they are unable to meaningfully participate in any civic or social function. In that sense, the homeless person is not only without a private sphere but effectively also without a public sphere.[42]

Policies aimed at controlling the presence and visibility of the homeless often negate any right to privacy. During homeless sweeps, for example, their belongings are seized and moved. Such practices, accompanied by the upsurge of recent policies which place a heavy emphasis on surveillance and control, suggest an evolution in policy-making. At least in part, this has been in response to a worsening crisis brought on by the unprecedented challenge

---

[36] Balakrishnan, 'Mayor's Drive to Override Surveillance Law'.
[37] Chapter 19B: Acquisition of Surveillance Technology Ordinance.
[38] San Francisco Police Department, '19B Surveillance Policies'.
[39] Canon, 'San Francisco Mayor'.
[40] Mano Raju, quoted in ibid.
[41] This raises the issue of the concept of privacy as applied to the homeless. The specificity of the homeless status – or lack thereof – means that the very concept of privacy needs to be redefined as it applies to homeless people. Indeed, how can one have a 'private sphere' when one does not have a home? Is there a perception that by living on the street, and therefore in public view, one forgoes privacy? Also, it seems that in addition to privacy, freedom of movement and freedom 'not to move' are being infringed upon.
[42] van Leeuwen, 'Edge of the Urban Landscape', 589.

of the COVID-19 pandemic, even though this evolution was short-lived and some of the plans that were implemented are being suspended as the virus seems less threatening.

V. COVID-19: Attempts at Controlling the Outbreak of the Disease

As early as 2009, surveillance specialist and now Assistant District Attorney Jamie Michael Charles wrote that 'many of the new ordinances result in the forced migration of the homeless, and are proliferating with virus-like speed as cities attempt to divert those displaced by other towns from their communities'.[43] Earlier still, the opioid epidemic which started in 1999 increased both the number of newly homeless people and mortality rates. Epidemics and infections are a common point of comparison. During epidemics, taking care of the homeless is no longer a matter of choice and charity but of survival, answering the urgent need for risk management. The homeless have often been metaphorically described as zombies, for example by Baudrillard.[44] Such images are all the more potent as people become afraid that those at large in the streets are 'infected' and spread disease. According to LAPD Detective Shannon Geaney, who runs a team of eight specialised officers in Hollywood, homelessness is the greatest threat to public safety, streets and people's lives in general.[45] This attitude to the homeless is not new.

In such circumstances, US local authorities use an efficient but ambivalent tool of surveillance and management: government-sanctioned or 'safe' campsites. A grid system allocates spaces for tents, providing the homeless with isolation both from each other and from the rest of society, access to sanitation facilities, and a sense of safety (Figure 12.1[46]). These encampments allegedly stopped the spread of a hepatitis A epidemic in San Diego in 2017.

So too in spring 2020, COVID-19 gave new impetus to the fear of the homeless as vectors of uncontrollable contamination and a danger to the population as a whole. Indeed, in fear of the spread of the pandemic, the homeless voluntarily consented to their own surveillance and quarantine. During the COVID-19 pandemic, photographs of rectangles and geometric shapes, such as San Francisco's civic centre, occupied by homeless people's tents, were published in newspapers and online, and quickly went viral. They have come to symbolise the US's response to the issue of homelessness during the pandemic.

---

[43] Charles, 'America's Lost Cause', 315. See also on pre-trial electronic surveillance Charles, 'Commonwealth v Norman'.

[44] Baudrillard, *America*.

[45] Lopez, 'Dysfunction of L.A. Homeless Policy'.

[46] The picture shows the San Francisco Civic Center in front of City Hall. The statue is the Pioneer Monument.

Figure 12.1 'Vertical aerial shot of homeless camps on Fulton St in San Francisco during pandemic' by Wirestock.

Another intermediate solution used by city governments consists in 'sanctioning' already existing camps, such as the Echo Park Lake camp in Los Angeles, where barriers surrounded more than a hundred tents. The camp was dismantled in March 2021, against the advice of the CDC.

Sanctioned camps show government responses to an uncontrollable crisis and therefore play a real political role. It may fail as public health but still succeed as propaganda. How, one might ask, can a city impose a lockdown on those who are locked out? The profusion of zipped-up tents, lines, barriers, limits and boundaries provide viewers and citizens with a reassuring feeling of control, whether they witness it from their windows during lockdowns or through the media. Meanwhile, perhaps for the first time, the city is able to keep a constant eye on the homeless population – an impossibility under normal circumstances (see Section II). Encampments bring an illusion of order to chaos. Replacing the disorder of pavement tents and sleeping bags with the regularity of a grid makes homeless people look like chess pieces and heightens their dehumanisation for disease control purposes. The encampment successfully brings control and immobility to a population whose disorder and instability is precisely at the heart of the moral panic they incite. Indeed, here we might recall Michel Foucault's writing on 'biopolitics'.[47] The government is interested not in the rights of individuals but in the preservation of life

---

[47] Foucault, *Birth of Biopolitics*.

and the management of populations through a process of exclusion (from the rest of society into camps) and inclusion (from a diffused margin to a concentrated centre). Those contained, no less than the wider population, are protected from infection, medical services are managed and organised, welfare is traded off at the expense of freedom. Whether the camp is a shelter or a prison is largely beside the point. As Foucault writes, the management of the plague was (and still is) the paradigm of modern governance:

> The plague is met by order; its function is to sort out every possible confusion: that of the disease, which is transmitted when bodies are mixed together; that of the evil, which is increased when fear and death overcome prohibitions. It lays down for each individual his place, his body, his disease and his death, his well-being, by means of an omnipresent and omniscient power that subdivides itself in a regular, uninterrupted way even to the ultimate determination of the individual, of what characterizes him, of what belongs to him, of what happens to him.[48]

The striking shape of a San Francisco sanctioned camp in Figure 12.1 allocates spread-out spaces for tents and is reminiscent of the grid-like types of surveillance used in times of plague, as Foucault describes them. Foucault's 'quadrillage' describes the policies implemented during plague outbreaks. First, 'quadrillage' refers to the repartition of individuals for surveillance purposes. Each individual is allocated a specific space. The aim of this repartition is to prevent the disappearance of individuals, their roaming around, and avoid dangerous gatherings. It is a technique against desertion, vagrancy and clusters.[49] Then, when applied during epidemics, 'quadrillage' refers to the utopia of the perfectly governed city, using a profound organisation of surveillance and control.[50] Foucault notes that '[t]he moment of the plague is one of an exhaustive sectioning (*quadrillage*) of the population by political power, the capillary ramifications of which constantly reach the grain of individuals themselves, their time, habitat, localization, and bodies.'[51] The COVID-19 pandemic provided California with such an opportunity.

In California in 2020, the homeless who lived in these camps were not passive subjects. They took part in this act of surveillance, renouncing some of their freedom in exchange for a combination of safety and control. Surveillance may result in a pact between the governing body and the

---

[48] Foucault, 'Panopticism', 3.
[49] Foucault, *Discipline and Punish*, 145.
[50] Ibid., 200.
[51] Foucault, *Abnormal*, 47.

governed, not unlike the social contract.[52] With these camps, the homeless were – in a significant departure from previous policies – enjoined to take part to an extent in the culture of surveillance as defined by David Lyon, comprised of 'the participation and engagement of surveilled and surveilling subjects'.[53] Previous writers have argued that '[s]afe camping sites are a public policy pariah. Homeless service providers, advocates for the homeless and local politicians often balk at the idea. Sanctioned camps can be difficult to manage and can seem like a city is just giving up.'[54] One may question the authorities' true intentions, which could well be interpreted as aimed rather at protecting the general population from the homeless, than the homeless from the disease. All the same, under the exigencies of the pandemic emergency, the turn to highly visible encampments represents a remarkable about-face in public policy.

The 'quadrillage' of the homeless population could have led to an unprecedented opportunity to both control them and offer them the services they need. However, the camps would have had to include the totality of the homeless population. The number of these camps remained very low, notwithstanding their visibility. Their enormous cost is also a problem, as encampments cost more per tent than a typical one-bedroom apartment in Los Angeles.[55] Like other social policies concerning the homeless, what appears to be a solution may also be considered a trap for good intentions. Short-term relief does not offer any long-term benefit. And yet the COVID-19 epidemic placed a new focus on the existence of homeless populations in communities. To some people, 'the coronavirus pandemic is exposing deep rifts in American society, underscoring the flaws in how our society has dealt with massive social problems, especially homelessness'.[56] The epidemic also brought to life the dreams of advocates for the homeless: 'purchasing motels, waiving environmental and regulatory hurdles for emergency shelters, expanded federal funding'.[57]

---

[52] Another form of pact is described by Sabot, Chapter 2 of this collection. He mentions Harcourt's work on the 'expository society' we live in, where citizens enter the hall of mirrors willingly, as the pleasure of being watched justifies the surveillance that they place themselves under.

[53] Lyon, *Culture of Surveillance*, 16. Lyon defines the culture of surveillance as a culture of consumers who watch films and have social media accounts and smart homes. The culture of surveillance as it applies to the homeless requires taking into consideration their place on the margins of mainstream society, where access to this culture is either absent, or sporadic and partial. Their participation in the experiment of the necessary lockdown was therefore also different, and the freedom that they renounced was replaced by a sense of safety and access to facilities.

[54] Tinoco, 'Government-Run Homeless Camps'.

[55] Scott, 'High Cost of Los Angeles Homeless Camp'.

[56] Tinoco, 'Government-Run Homeless Camps'.

[57] Levin, 'California is Scrambling'.

The combination of the consequences of the economic crisis caused by COVID-19 and the already existing but still increasing opioid crisis might, however, trigger an unprecedented period of homelessness.[58] In the meantime, it is identifiable in the death count. Nearly 1,500 people died between March 2020 and July 2021 on the streets of Los Angeles. The vast majority were homeless; the most common cause of death was accidental overdose.[59] This does not include those who died in hospitals or parked vehicles. Another consequence of the pandemic can be seen in the failure of many Californian counties to properly count the numbers of homeless people now living on the streets. An important tool used in the surveillance of the homeless, point-in-time counts,[60] relies on data provided by service providers and volunteers but these counts have been postponed due to the pandemic.[61]

VI. Conclusion

Sabot's comments on contemporary surveillance *dispositifs* in Chapter 2 of this collection perfectly describe governmental responses to homelessness during the pandemic. They arise 'from contradictory desires and [. . .] ambiguous divisions', here between visibility and invisibility.[62] Indeed, different versions of this paradox, which in particular affects the victims of discrimination, can be seen in the chapters on race, by Joy, and gender, by Wrobel.[63] These oppositions are not new and will not disappear. However, the policies that were implemented during the pandemic are not likely to survive it, and the policies that are now implemented might even be more drastic than before due to the unprecedented strength of the crisis, as described in Section IV. Policies in relation to homelessness come from opposite ends of the surveillance spectrum: they either criminalise the homeless and their behaviour, or are only intended to provide provisional, temporary and underfunded care, for instance through the work of charities. Neither approach is working. Society needs to move on from what Marin decried: 'We are moved either to "redeem" the homeless or to punish them.'[64]

If efforts are not also made to better integrate the homeless into society using mental health care, treatment for addiction and social care, merely providing them with housing will not be sufficient. Likewise, merely focus-

---

[58] Holpuch, "'I Am Beside Myself'".
[59] Levin, '1,500 Unhoused LA Residents Died'.
[60] https://www.hud.gov/program_offices/comm_planning/coc/pit-count.
[61] Hoeven, 'California Homeless Crisis'.
[62] Sabot, Chapter 2 of this collection.
[63] Joy, Chapter 11; Wrobel, Chapter 13, both in this collection.
[64] Marin, 'Helping and Hating the Homeless'.

ing on their visibility is a dead end. In terms of surveillance practices and taking into account all the paradoxes raised in this chapter, we need a policy mix that is drawn from right across the spectrum and far more willing to acknowledge the vast diversity of situations and circumstances which lead to homelessness. We might then be able to offer a combination of control and care responsive neither to optics nor populations but framed in terms of each individual's specific needs and problems. The US seems to be caught in a trap. The financial cost of policies has always been higher than their social benefits, and the financial benefits (for business owners) come at a very high social cost. The COVID-19 pandemic acted as double-edged sword, provoking unprecedented solutions while potentially sowing the seeds for a new devastating crisis. All the same, it allowed for a real-life illustration of the potential efficacy of Foucault's system of 'quadrillage'. It provided city governments with a new type of surveillance policy that evolved from a system of exile towards the logic of encampments. Reading Foucault, Gilles Deleuze shows that strict grid patterns, used for the plague, are 'a grid of daily life, from the most miniscule moments of quotidian life, the control of everyday life, the control of everydayness. This is much more important than exile, it is a function other than exile.'[65] With government-sanctioned camps, the government no longer cuts the homeless from society.[66] Instead, it moves towards a grid system within the larger grid system of the city,[67] aiming to manage, control and integrate the population of both. The pandemic offered the possibility for the homeless to re-enter society, in camps, shelters or motels, and therefore, using Deleuze and Guattari's image of smooth and striated spaces,[68] allowed for them to leave the smooth space of the pavement and enter the striated space of the sedentary, where they may be watched, *surveilled*, and perhaps even cared for, like the rest of the population. Affirming Brunon-Ernst's argument in Chapter 6 of this volume as to his continuing salience in the contemporary world, Foucault writes, with uncanny foresight, 'the exile of the leper and the arrest of the plague do not bring with them the same political dream. The first is that of a pure community, the second that of a disciplined society.'[69]

---

[65] Deleuze, 'Foucault / Lecture 07'.

[66] Deleuze notes that exile was for lepers, while the plague allowed for the control of everyday life. According to Foucault, the plagued village is what established the grid of cities. Ibid.

[67] This 'grid within the grid' system also applied during lockdowns due to the pandemic, where the camp appeared as a lockdown space for the unhoused while the rest of the population was in lockdown in their own houses.

[68] Deleuze and Guattari, *Thousand Plateaus*.

[69] Foucault, 'Panopticism', 4.

VII. Bibliography

Allard K. Lowenstein International Human Rights Clinic. *"Forced into Breaking the Law": The Criminalization of Homelessness in Connecticut*. Allard K. Lowenstein International Human Rights Clinic, Yale Law School, November 2016. https://law.yale.edu/sites/default/files/area/center/schell/criminalization_of_homelessness_report_for_web_executive_summary.pdf.

Anderson, Colin L. 'Median Bans, Anti-homeless Laws and the Urban Growth Machine.' *DePaul Journal for Social Justice* 8, no. 2 (2015): 405–54.

Balakrishnan, Eleni. 'Experts Say Mayor's Drive to Override Surveillance Law Misstates Law's Restrictions.' *Mission Local*, 15 December 2021. https://missionlocal.org/2021/12/mayor-breed-wants-to-override-privacy-law-to-increase-police-access-to-surveillance-tech-but-experts-say-she-misread-it/.

Ball, Kirstie, and Kevin D. Haggerty. 'Editorial: Doing Surveillance Studies.' *Surveillance & Society* 3, no. 2/3 (2005): 129–38.

Barnard-Wills, David. *Surveillance and Identity: Discourse, Subjectivity and the State*. New York: Routledge, 2012.

Baudrillard, Jean. *America*. New York: Verso, 2010.

Breed, London. 'A Safer San Francisco.' 14 December 2021. https://londonbreed.medium.com/a-safer-san-francisco-eb40d9d502e4.

Canon, Gabrielle. 'San Francisco Mayor Declares Neighborhood State of Emergency amid Overdose Deaths.' *The Guardian*, 18 December 2021. https://www.theguardian.com/us-news/2021/dec/17/san-francisco-state-of-emergency-drug-overdose-deaths.

Castagnino, Florent. 'Critique des *surveillances studies*. Éléments pour une sociologie de la surveillance.' *Déviance et Société* 42, no. 1 (2018): 9–40.

Chapter 19B: Acquisition of Surveillance Technology Ordinance. https://codelibrary.amlegal.com/codes/san_francisco/latest/sf_admin/0-0-0-47320.

Charles, Jaimie Michael. 'America's Lost Cause.' *Public Interest Law Journal* 18, no. 2 (2009): 315–48.

———. 'Commonwealth v Norman: A Sea Change in Pre-trial Electronic Surveillance.' *Boston Bar Journal* 64, no. 4 (2020). https://bostonbarjournal.com/2020/11/18/commonwealth-v-norman-a-sea-change-in-pre-trial-electronic-surveillance.

Deleuze, Gilles. 'Foucault / Lecture 07.' In *The Deleuze Seminars*. 10 December 1985. https://deleuze.cla.purdue.edu/seminars/foucault/lecture-07.

Deleuze, Gilles, and Félix Guattari. *A Thousand Plateaus: Capitalism and Schizophrenia*. 1980. Translated by Brian Massumi. Minneapolis: University of Minnesota Press, 2005.

Foucault, Michel. *Abnormal: Lectures at the College de France 1974–1975*. Translated by Graham Burchell. New York: Verso, 2003.

———. *The Birth of Biopolitics: Lectures at the Collège de France 1978–1979*. Edited by Michel Senellart. Translated by Graham Burchell. New York: Palgrave Macmillan, 2008.

———. *Discipline and Punish: The Birth of the Prison*. 1975. Translated by Alan Sheridan. London: Penguin Books, 2019.

————. 'Panopticism.' *Race/Ethnicity* 2, no. 1 (2008): 1–12.

Hoeven, Emily. 'California Homeless Crisis Takes on New Urgency.' *Cal Matters*, 18 January 2022. https://calmatters.org/newsletters/whatmatters/2022/01/ california-homeless-crisis-election/.

Holpuch, Amanda. '"I am Beside Myself": Millions in the US Face Evictions amid Looming Crisis.' *The Guardian*, 25 August 2020. https://www.theguardian.com/ world/2020/aug/25/millions-of-americans-face-evictions-crisis.

Humboldt County Civil Grand Jury. *Les Misérables: The Criminalization of the Home-less in the City of Eureka*. Humboldt County Civil Grand Jury Report, 2019. https://humboldtgov.org/DocumentCenter/View/73546/Les-Miserables-The-Criminalization-of-the-Homeless-in-the-City-of-Eureka---Humboldt-County-Civil-Grand-Jury?bidId=.

Hunter, Julie, Paul Linden-Retek, Sirine Shebaya, and Samuel Halpert. *Welcome Home: The Rise of Tent Cities in the United States*. National Law Center on Homelessness & Poverty, Allard K. Lowenstein International Human Rights Clinic, Yale Law School, March 2014. https://homelesslaw.org/wp-content/ uploads/2018/10/WelcomeHome_TentCities.pdf.

Kisely, Steve R., Leslie Anne Campbell, and Neil J. Preston. 'Compulsory Com-munity and Involuntary Outpatient Treatment for People with Severe Mental Disorders'. Cochrane Database of Systematic Reviews, 16 February 2011 (2): CD004408.

Katz, Michael B. *The Undeserving Poor: America's Enduring Confrontation with Poverty*. Oxford: Oxford University Press, 2013.

Leeuwen, Bart van. 'To the Edge of the Urban Landscape: Homelessness and the Politics of Care.' *Political Theory* 46, no. 4 (2018): 586–610.

Levin, Matt. 'California is Scrambling to House the Homeless. Here's How it's Playing Out.' *CalMatters*, 26 March 2020. https://calmatters.org/health/ coronavirus/2020/03/california-coronavirus-covid19-homeless-gavin-newsom/.

Levin, Sam. '1,500 Unhoused LA Residents Died on the Streets during Pandemic, Report Reveals.' *The Guardian*, 1 December 2021. https://www.theguardian. com/us-news/2021/dec/01/1500-unhoused-la-residents-died-on-the-streets-during-pandemic-report-reveals.

————. 'California Proposal Would Force Unhoused People into Treatment.' *The Guardian*, 4 March 2022. https://www.theguardian.com/us-news/2022/ mar/03/california-proposal-forced-unhoused-treatment#:~:text=Governor% 20Gavin%20Newsom%20of,and%20addiction%20disorders%20into%20 treatment.

Lopez, Steve. 'Column: In the Dysfunction of L.A. Homeless Policy, One Cop Tries to Make a Difference.' *Los Angeles Times*, 17 November 2019. https://www.latimes. com/california/story/2019-11-17/l-a-homeless-policy-cop-steve-lopez-column.

Lyon, David. *The Culture of Surveillance: Watching as a Way of Life*. Cambridge: Polity, 2018.

————. 'Editorial. Surveillance Studies: Understanding Visibility, Mobility and the Phonetic Fix.' *Surveillance & Society* 1, no. 1 (2002): 1–7.

————. *Surveillance Studies: An Overview*. Cambridge: Polity, 2007.

Marin, Peter. 'Helping and Hating the Homeless. The Struggle at the Margins of America.' *Harper's Magazine*, January 1987. https://harpers.org/archive/1987/01/helping-and-hating-the-homeless-the-struggle-at-the-margins-of-america/.

Monahan, Torin, and David Murakami Wood. *Surveillance Studies: A Reader*. Oxford: Oxford University Press, 2018.

National Coalition for the Homeless and National Law Center on Homelessness & Poverty. *A Dream Denied: The Criminalization of Homelessness in U.S. Cities*. January 2006. https://www.nationalhomeless.org/publications/crimreport/report.pdf.

National Coalition for the Homeless and National Law Center on Homelessness & Poverty, with the National Homeless Civil Rights Organizing Project. *Illegal to be Homeless: The Criminalization of Homelessness in the United States*. National Coalition for the Homeless and National Law Center on Homelessness & Poverty, and the National Homeless Civil Rights Organizing Project, 2001. https://www.nationalhomeless.org/publications/crimreport/Crim2002.pdf.

National Law Center on Homelessness & Poverty. *Housing Not Handcuffs: A Litigation Manual*. National Law Center on Homelessness & Poverty, 2016, 2017, 2018 and 2019. https://homelesslaw.org/wp-content/uploads/2018/10/Housing-Not-Handcuffs-Litigation-Manual.pdf.

———. *No Safe Place: The Criminalization of Homelessness in U.S. Cities*. National Law Center on Homelessness & Poverty, February 2019. https://homelesslaw.org/wp-content/uploads/2019/02/No_Safe_Place.pdf.

Rogez, Yvonne-Marie. 'Shopping Carts, Property Rights and the Fourth Amendment: Dealing with Homelessness in Contemporary North-America.' In *The Dark Sides of the Law: Perspectives on Law, Literature, and Justice in Common Law Countries*, edited by Géraldine Gadbin-George, Yvonne-Marie Rogez, Armelle Sabatier, and Claire Wrobel, 177–89. Paris: Michel Houdiard Éditeur, 2019.

Rugkåsa, Jorun, John Dawson, and Tom Burns. 'CTOs: What is the State of the Evidence?' *Social Psychiatry and Psychiatric Epidemiology* 49, no. 12 (2014): 1861–71.

San Francisco Police Department. '19B Surveillance Policies.' https://www.sanfranciscopolice.org/your-sfpd/policies/19b-surveillance-technology-policies.

Scott, Anna. 'High Cost of Los Angeles Homeless Camp Raises Eyebrows and Questions.' *NPR*, 25 May 2021. https://www.npr.org/2021/05/25/999969718/high-cost-of-los-angeles-homeless-camp-raises-eyebrows-and-questions.

Southern Legal Counsel. *Jailbirds in the Sunshine State: Defending Crimes of Homelessness*. Southern Legal Counsel, May 2016. https://www.southernlegal.org/application/files/1616/1074/4472/Defending_Crimes_of_Homelessness.pdf.

Tinoco, Matt. 'Government-Run Homeless Camps Could Come to L.A.' *LAist*, 7 May 2020. https://laist.com/news/homeless-coronavirus-carter-settlement-camping.

Wells, Bill. 'Downplaying the Reality of Addiction in the Homeless Community Doesn't Solve Anything.' *Voice of San Diego*, 27 November 2019. https://voiceofsandiego.org/2017/11/27/downplaying-reality-addiction-homeless-community-doesnt-solve-anything/.

Wright, Nancy A. 'Not in Anyone's Backyard: Ending the "Contest of Nonresponsibility" and Implementing Long-Term Solutions to Homelessness.' *Georgetown Journal on Fighting Poverty* 2, no. 2 (1995): 163–241.

13

Gender and Surveillance in Margaret Atwood's Novels, from *Bodily Harm* (1981) to *The Testaments* (2019)

Claire Wrobel

I. Introduction

Surveillance, as has been forcefully demonstrated in earlier chapters, does not apply indiscriminately. As Banita and Joy have argued in their discussions of race, the visual persists at its core, and the question of who is visible to whom is crucial.[1] Similarly, surveillance is never gender blind, and visuality underlies the gendered experience of surveillance as much as it does its racialised exercise. Gendered dimensions of surveillance have nevertheless remained unexamined in the academic field, so much so that the title of a special issue of the *Surveillance & Society* journal published in 2009 claimed that '[s]urveillance studies needs gender and sexuality.'[2] This oversight is often traced back to Foucault's description of the 'modern subject' as a generic 'he' in *Discipline and Punish*.[3] By contrast, the research which has been produced on gender and surveillance tends to focus on the 'subjectivity and the experience of surveillance' and to study 'the local, the discursive, the performative and the embodied'.[4] In a similar vein, van der Meulen and Heynen write that '[g]endering the field involves thinking about surveillance practices as socially located, as embodied and as having differential impacts'.[5] This chapter adopts this proposed shift in perspectives to study gendered surveillance not in sociology but in fiction.[6]

---

[1] See Banita, Chapter 10; Joy, Chapter 11, both in this collection.

[2] Ball et al., 'Surveillance Studies', 352, 355; Koskela, '"You Shouldn't Wear that Body"', 49; Abu-Laban, 'Gendering Surveillance Studies', 45; van der Meulen and Heynen, *Expanding the Gaze*, 4.

[3] See Bartky, 'Foucault, Femininity'.

[4] Ball et al. 'Surveillance Studies', 352, 355.

[5] van der Meulen and Heynen, *Expanding the Gaze*, 4.

Why fiction? Literary fiction, through its instantiation power, offers a privileged means to study surveillance from the perspective suggested above. By focusing on the experience of surveilled subjects, fiction makes salient the surveillance effects which often remain elusive in social life. For instance, while providing a literary representation of databases is arguably quite a challenge, fiction can stage the struggles of individual characters when databases are the primary source of their social identity.[7] Literature gives a perspective 'from below',[8] offering readers a vicarious experience of environments which are exponentially saturated by surveillance – and in particular to observe the interpretative skills one develops in such a context – and drawing their attention to trends which are already present in their own societies. Rather than encouraging a wait-and-see attitude, fiction both stages resistance and develops its own literary modes of subversion, among which satire features prominently. As the chapter will make clear, Atwood is to some extent the heiress of early modern authors such as Swift, and of their textual strategies, highlighted by Tadié in Chapter 3 of this volume.

Why turn to Margaret Atwood's fiction to study the intersection of gender and surveillance? Already in *The Electronic Eye*, David Lyon had identified *The Handmaid's Tale* as a possible source of meaningful metaphors which could offer alternatives to Big Brother and the Panopticon as master tropes.[9] The engagement of Atwood's fiction with surveillance predates its rise to prominence in contemporary literature in the wake of the 9/11 attacks.[10] Moreover, her work has consistently focused on the gendered implications of surveillance over time, as evidenced by the six novels studied here, starting with *Bodily Harm*, her fifth novel, published in 1981 and ending with *The Testaments*, the sequel to *The Handmaid's Tale*, published in 2019.

---

[6] The essays in *Feminist Surveillance Studies*, ed. Dubrofsky and Magnet, leave literature unexplored. For a recent contribution on gendered surveillance in literature specifically, see Thompson, *Gender, Surveillance, and Literature*.

[7] For a discussion of this particular scenario in Atwood's *The Heart Goes Last* (2015), see Wrobel, 'Negotiating Dataveillance', § 16.

[8] Narratological aspects of the question of point of view are studied in Wasihun, *Narrating Surveillance*.

[9] Lyon, *Electronic Eye*, 78.

[10] See for example Ventéjoux, Chapter 8 of this collection. See also Wasihun's work on American and German literature: Wasihun, 'Surveillance Narratives'; Wasihun, *Narrating Surveillance*. Atwood discusses 9/11 in connection with literary dystopia in *In Other Worlds*, 148–9.

Any discussion of gender in Atwood's novels needs to come with a caveat regarding the author's relationship to feminism, a label which she embraces only reluctantly. While she states that *The Handmaid's Tale* was born of her desire to 'try a dystopia from the female point of view', she asserts that 'this does not make [it] a "feminist dystopia", except insofar as giving a woman a voice and an inner life will always be considered "feminist" by those who think women ought not to have these things'.[11] Atwood explains that she writes about women because she finds them interesting, while bearing in mind that 'women' is not 'woman' and avoiding essentialist claims.[12] Does Atwood's fiction simply '[add] women' to the 'existing framework' of surveillance?[13] Not necessarily, as the surveillance mechanisms which screen, control and exclude women, or some categories of women, can be transposed to ethnic, political or religious groups – such as Jews, African Americans and dissident religious groups in *The Handmaid's Tale*.

The first part of this chapter focuses on *Bodily Harm* to show that Atwood consciously locates her novel within discussions of the 'male gaze' while complexifying the latter. The chapter then moves on to *The Handmaid's Tale* and its sequel to show how the surveillance apparatus of Gilead targets women, but not indiscriminately. Yet the two novels highlight how an apparently foolproof system can be subverted, a notion of resistance which, as has been noted with respect to Foucault's panopticism, is often missing in surveillance studies.[14] This theme becomes more prominent in the MaddAddam trilogy, which is the focus of the last section. There, Atwood shows how corporate surveillance is on the side of murderous patriarchy. However, by staging characters who thwart surveillance and drawing on satire to highlight the 'ironic vulnerabilities' of surveillance systems,[15] Atwood puts the question of individual agency back in the centre and reintroduces openness in the self-fulfilling prophecies of pre-scripted narratives.[16]

II. Complexifying the Male Gaze in *Bodily Harm* (1981)

1. Gender Dissymmetry under Surveillance

The six novels under scrutiny take a detour through time and/or space to offer an indirect portrait of contemporary society. The protagonist of *Bodily*

[11] Atwood, *In Other Worlds*, 146.
[12] Atwood, 'If You Can't Say Something Nice'.
[13] 'Incorporating gender into surveillance studies [should mean] more than simply adding women (which is often the default when speaking of gender) to an existing framework.' van der Meulen and Heynen, *Expanding the Gaze*, 4.
[14] See Brunon-Ernst, Chapter 6 of this collection.
[15] Marx, 'Tack in the Shoe', 369.
[16] See Banita, Chapter 10 of this collection.

Harm, Rennie, is a Canadian journalist in her thirties, who sets off to a Caribbean island ostensibly to write a piece for a magazine but also to escape from a personal crisis involving breast cancer and a mastectomy, abandonment by her lover, and the intrusion of an anonymous stalker figure in her apartment – three events which are not unrelated. Reminiscences of Rennie's life in Canada are narrated from the prison cell where she is detained and juxtaposed with her experience in the Caribbean. The detour via the island, where political and personal violence is overt, leads Rennie to reconsider what passes as 'normal' in North America. She finds herself in the position of the 'tourist-journalist' who, according to Atwood, is central to utopian texts from More, Swift and Defoe on.[17] *Bodily Harm* therefore has some affinities with the author's 'ustopias',[18] a view that is confirmed by Rennie's thoughts as, on the plane back to Canada, she reflects that it is as if she had been on a 'space trip' or in a 'time warp'.[19]

In the epigraph to *Bodily Harm*, Atwood directs her readers to John Berger's *Ways of Seeing*: '[a] man's presence suggests what he is capable of doing to you or for you. By contrast, a woman's presence [. . .] defines what can and cannot be done to her.'[20] In Berger's text, being watched and internalising the male gaze is constitutive of being a woman, the latter's psyche incorporating both the surveilling instance and the surveilled. Although Atwood does not refer to Laura Mulvey's essay on 'Visual Pleasure and Narrative Cinema', women's 'to-be-looked-at-ness' and the structure of the male gaze are both theoretical frameworks that underlie *Bodily Harm*. The gender dissymmetry constitutive of watching and being watched is not limited to 1970s artistic criticism. Indeed, Hille Koskela's recent work on CCTV cameras, for instance, shows that surveillance is heavily gendered. In an article on public urban space, Koskela notes that 'most of the persons "behind" the camera are men and most of the persons "under" surveillance are women'.[21] Furthermore, by virtue of 'gendered social practices', '[w]omen are constantly reminded that an invisible observer is a threat': 'In crime prevention advice, for example, women are recommended to keep their curtains tightly closed whenever it might be possible for someone outside to see inside', and '[t]his potential observer is presented as male.'[22]

---

[17] Major representatives of the genre 'all send an emissary from an oppressive contemporary society into the future as a sort of tourist-journalist, to check out improved conditions and report back'. Atwood, *In Other Worlds*, 103.

[18] To describe her own work, Atwood coined the word 'ustopia': 'Ustopia is a word I made up by combining utopia and dystopia – the imagined perfect society and its opposite – because, in my view, each contains a latent version of the other.' Ibid., 85.

[19] Atwood, *Bodily Harm*, 289.

[20] Berger, *Ways of Seeing*, 39–40.

[21] Koskela, 'Video Surveillance', 263.

[22] Ibid., 263.

Moreover, video surveillance may be understood as an instance of 'male policing in the broadest sense', and 'the reproduction of patriarchal power by the
guards and the police who are responsible for the daily routine of surveillance'
leads to mistrust on the part of women.[23] Echoing Mulvey, Koskela notes how
voyeurism is understood as a 'solely male' characteristic.[24]

2. The Stalker Figure

The gendered aspects of surveillance can be brought to the fore by analysing
the opening scene of *Bodily Harm*. On coming home, Rennie hears male
voices in her apartment. Two policemen are waiting inside, to inform her that
her apartment has been entered by an intruder, who is immediately assumed
to be a 'he'. The scene is almost a direct transposition of Koskela's description.
The police officers give Rennie the usual advice about getting safety locks
and ask her whether she closes the curtains when she takes a shower or when
she gets dressed at night. One of them has a patronising attitude, violating
Rennie's privacy by opening her closet 'as if he had every right' and asking
her whether she has a lot of different male visitors.[25] The parallel between the
intruder and the condescending policeman is quite clear.

After the event, Rennie '[can't] shake the feeling that she [is] being
watched, even when she [is] in a room by herself, with the curtains closed'.[26]
She feels she has been studied and interiorises the voyeuristic gaze that has
been cast on her private space: 'She began to see herself from the outside, as if
she was a moving target in someone else's binoculars.'[27] Her behaviour when
she gets to her hotel room in St Antoine – 'clos[ing] the Venetian blinds on
the narrow window', 'turn[ing] off the overhead light' and making sure 'she
isn't reflected anywhere' before she undresses – shows she has internalised the
instructions about making herself invisible.[28]

Surveillance is embodied, albeit elusively, in what Timothy Melley calls 'the
stalker figure', of which the ghostly intruder is only the first manifestation.[29]
Rennie imagines her stalker to be a 'faceless stranger',[30] who has numerous
avatars in the novel. The merging of masculine figures culminates in Rennie's

[23] Ibid., 263.
[24] Ibid., 264. On the affinities between surveillance and voyeurism, see Ventéjoux, Chapter 8
of this collection.
[25] Atwood, *Bodily Harm*, 6.
[26] Ibid., 31.
[27] Ibid.
[28] Ibid., 39.
[29] Melley, *Empire of Conspiracy*, 107.
[30] Atwood, *Bodily Harm*, 32, 31.

recurrent dream, in which '[t]he face keeps changing, eluding her' and 'he's only a shadow, anonymous, familiar'.[31] The generic, anonymous stalker embodies the 'social norms that threaten women' and the violence that stems 'not from single, deviant individuals but from a larger complex of social institutions, narratives, and conditions', including the 'violence involved in the production of "normal" heterosexual relations'.[32]

3. Postcolonial Blindness

As we have seen throughout this volume, the individual and the social body are connected. Rennie's arrival coincides with an imminent election, a context which intensifies political tensions, suspicion and even paranoia. Although the text of *Bodily Harm* is strewn with references to the visual – sunglasses, binoculars, cameras and telescopes – Rennie looks but cannot see, since she does not understand the social and political reality of the island. The tourist's 'function', Rennie notes during a tour on a boat with a glass bottom, is to 'look', but looking is not the same as seeing, as the protagonist understands when observing a couple of tourists fooling with a camera: 'like her they can *look* all they want to, they're under no obligation to *see*, they can take pictures of anything they wish'.[33] The tourist gaze thus entails a form of blindness.

Rennie's identity is not reduced to her gender. Her status as a white woman in a postcolonial space is made clear when she comes across a field with tents set up for people who had lost their homes in a hurricane:

> Across the field, walking away from them, there's a small group of people, white, well dressed. Rennie thinks she recognizes the two German women from the hotel, the old couple from the reef boat, binoculars pointed. That's what she herself must look like: a tourist. A spectator, a voyeur.
>
> Near her, on a mattress that's been dragged out into the sun, a young girl lies nursing a baby.
>
> 'That's a beautiful baby,' Rennie says. In fact it isn't, it's pleated, shrivelled, like a hand too long in water. The girl says nothing. She stares woodenly up at Rennie, as if she's been looked at many times before.[34]

As Banita reminds us, surveillance remains fundamentally visual,[35] and by becoming a voyeur, Rennie casts a gaze which is coded as masculine. The

[31] Ibid., 277.
[32] Melley, *Empire of Conspiracy*, 121, 127, 132.
[33] Atwood, *Bodily Harm*, 79, 175, emphasis added.
[34] Ibid., 117. The stare of mutual incomprehension also appears in *The Handmaid's Tale*, in which Offred remembers being shown films about third-world countries in geography class.
[35] See Banita, Chapter 10 of this collection.

blank stare she gets in return signifies the gap between the white tourist and the young girl.

In *Bodily Harm*, Atwood uses the anonymous stalker figure and her female character's sense of being watched to embody social violence against women. She also articulates the male gaze thus exerted with the postcolonial gaze. *Bodily Harm* suggests that being under surveillance is fundamental to the female experience, with or without an elaborate technological arsenal. That gendered surveillance relies on powerful psychological springs and mobilises ambivalent human desires is also apparent in the ways in which Handmaids subvert the repressive surveillance that targets them in the works studied in the next section.

III. Shifting Perspectives in *The Handmaid's Tale* and *The Testaments*

1. Gendered Surveillance and Totalitarianism

Atwood started writing *The Handmaid's Tale* in Berlin in the spring of 1984, and visited East Berlin, Poland and Czechoslovakia to get 'the flavor of life in a totalitarian – but supposedly utopian – regime'.[36] We encounter here the paradox of surveillance as having a dual and contradictory aspect, a paradox already touched upon in this volume.[37] The journey led Atwood to reflect on Western society, wondering '[h]ow thin is the ice on which supposedly "liberated" modern Western women stand.'[38] She notes that '[a]ll imagined worlds must make some provision for sex' and that 'most totalitarianisms we know about have attempted to control reproduction in one way or another'.[39] As an imagined totalitarian state, the Gilead republic of *The Handmaid's Tale* is no exception. This sexist theocracy relies on a combination of brutal force and surveillance to control the population. The novel is told from the point of view of a Handmaid – a fertile woman forced into surrogacy – with flashbacks to her earlier life. The 2019 sequel alternates between three points of view, including that of the leader of the Aunts, the order in charge of exerting a very specific type of female surveillance.

Gilead is a near future dystopia which uses the Old Testament as its foundational text and is ruled by elite male Commanders. Surveillance mechanisms include a secret police (called The Eyes of God), control at checkpoints and borders, as well as a system of passes. In *The Testaments* the door to the office of

[36] Atwood, *In Other Worlds*, 86–7.
[37] See in particular Sabot, Chapter 2; Tadié, Chapter 3; Poullet, Chapter 4; Rogez, Chapter 12, all in this collection.
[38] Atwood, *In Other Worlds*, 87.
[39] Ibid., 62–3, 87.

Commander Judd, who leads the Eyes, has '[a] large Eye with a real crystal in the pupil' for him to see who is about to knock.[40] Data seems to be collected and stored through a number of devices such as Compuchecks or Compubites. The population is chilled into obedience through the creation of a paranoid atmosphere, evidenced by references to a ubiquitous, shape-shifting 'They' or to the possible presence of microphones or informants.

The regime resorts to social sorting, defined by David Lyon as the 'sort[ing of] people into categories, assigning worth or risk' using factors such as gender, class or race to discriminate and discipline.[41] Gendered social sorting lies at the origin of Gilead. At the time of the coup which overthrew the US government in Atwood's novel, 'real money' had disappeared and the letter with which bank accounts started – M or F according to gender – made it easy to identify and shut down women's accounts. Deprived of financial resources as well as of the possibility of working, women were thus placed 'in economic servitude to men'.[42] *The Testaments* gives more details about how women were classified: Aunt Lydia describes how women in her office were assigned to groups according to their occupation and level of fertility, information which was somehow already known. As she points out, 'There was no point about denying who we were: they already knew.'[43] Even though men too are sorted into different groups in the rigidly stratified Gilead society, they still benefit collectively from the gender dissymmetry, getting their share of the 'patriarchal dividend'.[44]

Peter Marks notes that '[i]t is not simply the fact that they are women that exposes [the Handmaids] to antagonistic observation: Offred is sexually fertile in a near future where fertility is problematic.'[45] It is their role as breeders for the ruling class that defines their identity. Handmaids are renamed after the Commander for whom they are supposed to breed (Offred means 'Of Fred'). They embody the paradoxical situation of women, who are rendered both invisible and hyper-visible.[46] Their outfits make them highly visible because of their red colour ('red is so visible', Offred remarks when she contemplates escape) but also invisible by erasing their identities: 'in those outfits they wear you can hardly see their faces. They all look the same.'[47]

[40] Atwood, *The Testaments*, 63. The motif of the eye was already omnipresent in *The Handmaid's Tale*, e.g. 69, 176.
[41] Lyon, *Surveillance as Social Sorting*, 1.
[42] Marks, *Imagining Surveillance*, 91.
[43] Atwood, *The Testaments*, 68–9.
[44] See Connell, *Masculinities*.
[45] Marks, *Imagining Surveillance*, 87.
[46] van der Meulen and Heynen, *Expanding the Gaze*, 10–11.
[47] Atwood, *The Handmaid's Tale*, 304; Atwood, *The Testaments*, 90.

Surveillance is remarkably low tech. While cameras do appear in *The Testaments*, Gilead does not need them in *The Handmaid's Tale*. The medical monitoring that Handmaids are subjected to consists in tests, the dates of which are determined by their monthly cycles: 'urine, hormones, cancer smear, blood test; the same as before, except that now it's obligatory'.[48] The most powerful apparatus is psychological. The regime has managed to convince Offred that the ritualised rape she has to undergo during the so-called Ceremony is something she chose.[49] In addition to their all-covering outfits, Handmaids wear hats with wings that limit their field of vision. Thus, as she goes through a neighbourhood checkpoint, Offred is aware of the presence of floodlights and pillboxes with armed men, but cannot see them. Handmaids also know what they are supposed to look at, such as the bodies hanging on the Wall: 'We stop, as if on signal, and stand and look at the bodies. It doesn't matter if we look. We're supposed to look.'[50] Like Rennie in *Bodily Harm*, Offred has interiorised the gaze: 'We must look good from a distance [. . .] Soothing to the eye, the eyes, the Eyes, for that's who this show is for.'[51]

These processes of interiorisation lead Offred to monitor her own body – '[e]ach twinge, each murmur of slight pain, ripples of sloughed-off matter, swellings and diminishings of tissue, the droolings of the flesh'. The experience of the fertile female surveilled subject is determined by 'the expectations of others, which have become [her] own', and the surveillant gaze ascribes disproportionate importance to her uterus, which 'glows red within its translucent wrapping'.[52] It is as though her skin had become transparent and the most intimate part of her body visible.

2. *The Separate Spheres of Surveillance*

Gilead relies on peer monitoring and hierarchy. Thus, Handmaids '[c]overtly [. . .] regard each other, sizing up each other's bellies' in the doctor's waiting room and, more generally, denunciation is encouraged.[53] The disciplining of the Handmaids is left in the hands of the Aunts. *The Testaments*, by offering the point of view of Aunt Lydia – the founder and leader of the order – gives insights into the gendered exercise of surveillance and highlights its contradictions. The Aunts' power does not fit within the official binary system of gender and puzzles the young girls of Gilead:

48 Atwood, *The Handmaid's Tale*, 69.
49 Ibid., 105.
50 Ibid., 42.
51 Ibid., 224.
52 Ibid., 83–4.
53 Ibid., 69.

I had begun to wonder how a woman changed into an Aunt. Aunt Estée had said once that you needed to have a calling that told you God wanted you to help women and not just a single family; but how did the Aunts get that calling? How had they received their strength? Did they have special brains, neither female nor male? Were they even women at all underneath their uniforms? Could they possibly be men in disguise?[54]

The organisation of surveillance reproduces the ideology of separate spheres which is explicitly mentioned in the novel.[55] Aunt Lydia is in control of 'the women's side of their enterprise',[56] and commands the Pearl Girls, missionaries who are sent to Canada to try to convert women there but also bring back intelligence. The fact that women are doing espionage work is denied by Commander Judd, who refers to 'women's intuition' or 'intuitive female gleanings'.[57]

The Aunts' and Pearl Girls' positions exemplify the contradictions within the gendered system of Gilead. The men in charge put women under surveillance but also need women to exercise surveillance. Because 'it would seem unseemly for [them] to involve [themselves] in the details of what is essentially women's work', they have no choice but to delegate authority and allow some autonomy.[58] Thus, Aunt Lydia's contradictory position as a female cog in the surveillance machine means that, far from being a mere instrument, she regains agency. Not only does she decide what information she shares with the Commander, but she also monitors the male elite, becoming the very embodiment of surveillance: 'I am everywhere and nowhere: even in the minds of the Commanders I cast an unsettling shadow.'[59] The fact that she can enter anyone's home and listen in on her young recruits inside Ardua Hall enables her to keep an incriminating archive of 'the secret histories of Gilead'.[60] Because she is officially excluded from the sphere of power, she is beyond suspicion, which enables her to sabotage the regime, thereby confirming Gary Marx's suggestion that 'most surveillance systems have inherent contradictions, ambiguities, gaps and blind spots', and that they can be resisted, or even destroyed, from within.[61]

[54] Atwood, *The Testaments*, 156; see also 328.
[55] Ibid., 174–5.
[56] Atwood, *The Handmaid's Tale*, 62.
[57] Atwood, *The Testaments*, 64, 141.
[58] Ibid., 64.
[59] Ibid., 32.
[60] Ibid., 35.
[61] Marx, 'Tack in the Shoe', 372.

3. From the Surveillance Gaze to the Look of Desire

Theories of surveillance built on panoptic premises often understand it as 'exacting inescapable compliance'.[62] By contrast, concepts such as 'post-panopticism' or 'sousveillance' try to complicate the picture.[63] Atwood's novels, which show the possibilities for resistance within the seemingly perfectly oiled machinery of surveillance, perform on the level of fiction the work done by such concepts on the level of analysis. To the totality of a seemingly omniscient system, Atwood opposes the necessarily limited perspective of an individual character who, as enmeshed as she is in the daily exercise of surveillance, takes advantage of the 'ambiguities, gaps and blind spots' highlighted by Marx. Throughout *The Handmaid's Tale*, Offred's acts of resistance – which are not romanticised but motivated by survival instinct – are local, embodied and dependent on the contingencies of human interaction. Nowhere is this more apparent than in her efforts to regain agency and privacy, a concept which although contested remains crucial to discussions of surveillance.[64]

The very first page of *The Handmaid's Tale* shows how the Handmaids find ways to communicate, in 'semi-darkness', 'when the Aunts weren't looking': they 'whisper almost without sound', 'touch each other's hands across space', 'lip-read [. . .] watching each other's mouths'.[65] The Handmaids develop an ability to spot and use even the smallest cracks in the system. Offred and Moira use a 'hole in the woodwork' of the lavatories, which the Aunts do not know about, to have secret conversations.[66] By using what may be the 'legacy of an ancient voyeur', the Handmaids turn voyeurism on its head.[67] Similarly, the hidden corner in the closet of Offred's bedroom where her predecessor has written *'Nolite te bastardes carborundorum'* symbolises the microscopic and yet essential blind spots which the surveilled subjects exploit to regain privacy: 'there it was, in tiny writing, quite fresh it seemed, scratched with a pin or maybe just a fingernail, in the corner where the darkest shadow fell'.[68]

The 'small hole' which enables Offred and Moira to exchange information reappears as a metaphor to refer to moments when Offred subverts surveillance, as when she exchanges forbidden looks with a Guardian: 'It's an event, a small defiance of rule, so small as to be undetectable [. . .] Such moments are possibilities, tiny peepholes.'[69] Offred believes that it is possible, through

---

[62] See Brunon-Ernst, Chapter 6 of this collection.
[63] Ibid.
[64] See Gligorijević, Chapter 5 of this collection.
[65] Atwood, *The Handmaid's Tale*, 13–14.
[66] Ibid., 83.
[67] Ibid., 83.
[68] Ibid., 62.
[69] Ibid., 31.

interpersonal contact, to subvert the surveillant gaze and turn it into a look of desire. 'If only they would look', she remarks of the Angels standing outside the football field.[70] Far from being a paralysing gaze, that look would open a possibility for the Handmaids to regain agency, and take part in a 'deal' or 'trade-off'.[71] When the Commander first invites Offred to spend the evening in his study, she spots an opportunity:

> there must be something he wants, from me. To want is to have a weakness, whatever it is, that entices me. It's like a small crack in a wall, before now impenetrable. If I press my eye to it, this weakness of his, I may be able to see my way clear.[72]

Offred's feeling that there is bound to be 'a black market', 'a grapevine, an underground of sorts', 'resistance' and 'alliances' is confirmed in *The Testaments*, where resistance is just as low tech and microscopic as in *The Handmaid's Tale*.[73] Information is smuggled across the border using the microdot, a technique which, precisely because it has 'fallen into disuse', is likely to remain unnoticed.[74] It is 'so small as to be almost invisible' and provides the means by which Aunt Lydia's 'top-classification crimes files' are smuggled across Canada.[75] The individual body again comes to the fore as the site of counter-surveillance, since the microdot is embedded in a scarified tattoo on Rachel's arm. She becomes a 'carrier pigeon' and her body becomes one with the message.[76]

The ultimate example of invisible embodied information may well be biometrics. And yet, *The Testaments* shows the Pearls fooling the Canadian immigration system by associating Rachel's photograph and biometric information with the registration number of a deceased Aunt.[77] The MaddAddam trilogy, which this chapter now turns to, goes even further by suggesting that even such data can be forged. The advent of biometrics would seem to make surveillance even more embodied, individualised and therefore inescapable but Atwood's more recent fiction, in keeping with earlier works, persists in highlighting the possibilities of resistance and subversion, both on the fictional stage and in the writing itself.

---

[70] Guardians are in charge of keeping order in daily life. Angels are soldiers who fight on the front lines.
[71] Atwood, *The Handmaid's Tale*, 13; see also 32.
[72] Ibid., 146.
[73] Ibid., 24, 63, 115, 139.
[74] Atwood, *The Testaments*, 140.
[75] Ibid., 196.
[76] Ibid., 333, 360.
[77] Ibid., 270.

IV. Staging and Performing Resistance to Surveillance

1. Corporate Surveillance and its Gendered Implications

The last works studied in this chapter belong to the MaddAddam trilogy, which includes *Oryx and Crake* (2003), *The Year of the Flood* (2009) and *MaddAddam* (2013). Several shifts must be noted both in Atwood's writing and in the broader reception of surveillance. Since the first half of the 1990s, when both *Bodily Harm* and *The Handmaid's Tale* appeared, surveillance has become digital, leading to the rise of 'dataveillance'.[78] Atwood's more recent fiction registers and creatively exploits technological advances and the possibilities they open up. Moreover, surveillance's prominence as a literary theme in contemporary fiction goes along with heightened general public awareness. These factors may explain why the treatment of surveillance, including in its gendered implications, is more heavy-handed in the MaddAddam trilogy. While *Bodily Harm* showed how the figure of the stalker made it possible for Rennie to gain better awareness of social practices of gendered surveillance and *The Handmaid's Tale* focused on Offred's strategies to survive in a surveillance-saturated society, later works shed some of that subtlety, as if exponential surveillance called for similarly exponential responses. The characters of the MaddAddam trilogy are much more proactive and their resistance to surveillance moves centre stage, so that the three novels may be read as drawing on readers' fantasies of getting off the grid and thwarting the most intrusive surveillance technologies. Finally, on a metafictional level, the trilogy unleashes fully-fledged satire, which sometimes produces comic effects. Building on Tadié's suggestion that 'satire offers, if only symbolically, means of examining, interrogating and overthrowing dominant forces and modes of control',[79] it may be suggested that Atwood uses it to draw readers' attention to the kinds of surveillance they are already under while pointing out the ways that are open to them of subverting it.

The three novels go back and forth between a post-apocalyptic narrative present, in which almost all of humanity has been wiped out by a man-made plague, and the survivors' earlier lives, in which society was divided between an anarchy (the pleeblands) and a technocracy (the elite living in secured Compounds with extreme levels of surveillance). This dystopic past, which is described through flashbacks, is a satirical depiction of contemporary society. Current trends are exaggerated, especially the unholy alliance between state and corporate surveillance which Shoshana Zuboff exposes in her work on

[78] On dataveillance specifically, see Wrobel, 'Negotiating Dataveillance'.
[79] See Tadié, Chapter 3 of this collection.

Surveillance Capitalism. In the pre-apocalyptic world of the MaddAddam trilogy, surveillance is indeed associated with Corporations which have taken over state responsibilities. *The Year of the Flood* describes how the CorpSeCorps 'started as a private security firm for the Corporations' and then took over from the underfunded police forces, 'sending their tentacles everywhere',[80] with the approval of the population who only saw the economic benefits of the change and failed to see the political danger.

Just like in *Brave New World*, people inside the Compounds are controlled by conditioning and consumption. Having interiorised social norms, they monitor their appearance – and spend money accordingly. Here, Atwood offers a biting satire of capitalism's empty promises and cynicism. *The Year of the Flood* describes the pink realm of the AnooYoo spa, which has a winking eye as a logo, in what is probably a wink at the omnipresent eye of Gilead. The customers of the spa are 'anxious women who [. . .] come, for rest and rejuvenation' and 'to get improvements done to [themselves]'.[81] When they go out again, they are 'buffed and tightened and resurfaced, irradiated and despotted', and very likely to come back soon, as they cannot be made ageing-proof or even immortal.[82] Susan Bordo's analyses on women's 'improvement' may be relevant here, as the spa customers become 'what Foucault calls "docile bodies," – bodies whose forces and energies are habituated to external regulation, subjection, transformation, "improvement"'.[83] However, Atwood makes it clear that both women and men are targeted by such companies. As Paul Hamann notes, in the MaddAddam trilogy, the surveillance society 'no longer discriminates between genders and applies just as much to the novel's male protagonist'.[84]

2. Dodging Patriarchal Surveillance in a Digital World

However, just because male characters are the target of surveillance does not mean that surveillance has suddenly become gender neutral. Patriarchy implies a hierarchy among masculine groups too, and surveillance is one of the tools mobilised to maintain it. The last two volumes of the MaddAddam trilogy focus on characters running away from oppressors who embody almost caricatural forms of patriarchal violence. Thus, Toby has to go into hiding to avoid being killed by her former manager, Blanco, who has a history of wearing

---

[80] Atwood, *The Year of the Flood*, 25.
[81] Ibid., 5, 65.
[82] Ibid., 264.
[83] Bordo, 'Body and the Reproduction of Femininity', 14.
[84] Hamann, 'Under Surveillance', 67.

the female employees he picks as sex slaves to death.[85] Similarly, Zeb is running away from his patriarchal father, a Petrobaptist and leading figure of the Church of PetrOleum called 'the Rev' who bugged his son's room when he was a child and murdered his wife. After he reveals his father's crimes, which also include embezzlement, Zeb knows that 'the giant Rev monster eye' will come looking for him.[86] A continuum links the past acts of brutality to the threatened acts of revenge, which take on a spectral quality. Both Toby and Zeb are being stalked, like Rennie in *Bodily Harm*. The 'faceless stranger' of the first novel discussed in this chapter reappears, for instance when readers are told that '[Toby] could never shake the feeling that someone was sneaking up on her.'[87] The physical stalking evoked in *Bodily Harm* has now also gone digital, making Atwood's characters' efforts to avoid identification and location ever more complex. As Hamann suggests, the 'fear of data surveillance' allowed by 'the advent of credit cards' in *The Handmaid's Tale* is 'radically amplified in the trilogy's digital culture'.[88] Thus, while in hiding, Zeb, who consciously stays away from possible snoops and drones, avoids 'anything [. . .] with an electronic signal'.[89]

Because Toby and Zeb are facing death threats, they need to change their identities and find ways to subvert identification by genetic data. The arsenal of surveillance tools at the hands of the CorpSeCorps includes data collection – of 'iris image', 'fingerscans', 'DNA' and 'dental work'.[90] While genetic data may be supposed to be 'a final marker of identity',[91] in Atwood's world, even genetic data can be modified and commodified, despite 'the fingerprint identity cards now carried by everyone': 'there were people cruising around in those places [the pleeblands] who could forge anything and who might be anybody'.[92] Identity can be refashioned in this black market, including '[g]ender, sexual orientation, height, colour of skin and eyes'.[93] There seem to be no physical boundaries to identity changes: new fingerprints can be secured, skin colour can be changed and it is even possible to get a 'DNA infusion'.[94] Toby gets a new scalp, new voiceprint as well as face recontouring.

---

[85] On sexual exploitation in *Oryx and Crake*, see Tolan, *Margaret Atwood*, 286–93.

[86] Atwood, *MaddAddam*, 283.

[87] Ibid., 242.

[88] Hamann, 'Under Surveillance', 67.

[89] Atwood, *MaddAddam*, 148.

[90] Atwood, *The Year of the Flood*, 115, 267.

[91] Hamann, 'Under Surveillance', 76.

[92] Atwood, *Oryx and Crake*, 33.

[93] Ibid., 289.

[94] Atwood, *The Year of the Flood*, 30, 119.

Countering a sense that surveillance is inevitable and inescapable, or the 'psychic numbing' which according to Zuboff characterises our relation to surveillance capitalism,[95] Atwood's novels stage characters actively resisting a digitally enhanced form of patriarchal surveillance.[96]

3. Literary Modes of Subversion

If the novels present characters who are trying to thwart surveillance on the fictional stage, on a metafictional level, the use of irony and satire produces comic effects which are also a way of undermining surveillance and its gendered effects. As Tadié reminds us in this volume, 'neither surveillance nor its discontents were inventions of the twentieth century',[97] and Atwood may be regarded as the heiress of early eighteenth-century satirists – Swift in particular. This legacy is claimed by the author herself in the epigraphs to *The Handmaid's Tale*, which include a few lines from Swift's *A Modest Proposal*, and *Oryx and Crake*, which feature a passage from *Gulliver's Travels*.[98] Moreover, as already discussed, the trope of the island, which features in Bacon's *New Atlantis*, Swift's *Gulliver's Travels* and Defoe's *Robinson Crusoe*, is taken up in *Bodily Harm*, in which Rennie lands on a Caribbean island, a remote space from which she can better reflect on North America. The opening pages of *Oryx and Crake*, which show Jimmy stranded on the shores of North America, wondering whether he is the sole survivor of the shipwreck which has engulfed humanity, also display an intertextual relation with *Robinson Crusoe*. The literary modes which Atwood chooses to engage with surveillance self-consciously position her within that tradition.

Biting irony defeats the intense surveillance by which the Compounds try to seal themselves off from the pleeblands, identifying cracks in seemingly foolproof borders. The Compounds evoke medieval castles – with moats, watchtowers, ramparts, slits for observation – spliced with the modern tools of political control and oppression – searchlights, videocams, loudspeakers, 'tear-gas nozzles' and 'long-range sprayguns' – combined with biometric means of identification.[99] The heavy monitoring is supposed to protect the Compounds and their elite scientists from 'other companies, other countries, various factions and plotters' and, increasingly, bioterrorist attacks.[100] The

---

[95] Zuboff, *Age of Surveillance Capitalism*, 11.

[96] See the development on 'counter-surveillance' in Wrobel, 'Negotiating Dataveillance'.

[97] See Tadié, Chapter 3; Poullet, Chapter 4, both in this collection.

[98] Atwood offers her reading of *Gulliver's Travels* in 'Of the Madness of Mad Scientists: Jonathan Swift's Grand Academy', in *In Other Worlds*, 194–211.

[99] Atwood, *Oryx and Crake*, 270, 279.

[100] Ibid., 27.

enforcement of heightened surveillance at borders is furthermore gendered, with Jimmy's mother complaining about the guards who 'liked to strip search people, women especially', in a statement reminiscent of Koskela's remarks on male voyeurism.[101] However, as one character drily observes, 'no boat was ever built that didn't spring a leak eventually',[102] and borders prove to be ironically vulnerable. For instance, in *Oryx and Crake*, the smuggling of a man-made virus undermines the inhabitants' belief that '[their] people had [them] sealed up tight as a drum'.[103] The very surveillance devices prove to be liabilities, as the trackers adopted by some of the scientists in fear of being kidnapped also reveal their location to their enemies, becoming 'a means of targeting their bearers and tracking them down'.[104]

Atwood's treatment is not Manichaean, and even the characters who are on the side of resistance may fall victim to ironic developments. Jimmy's mother, who in *Oryx and Crake* manages to escape with stolen data, resurfaces in *The Year of the Flood*. She has gone into hiding and finds temporary shelter with Toby,[105] whose ironic distance deflates the heroic aspirations of defectors: 'Like all Corp defectors, she thought she was the only one ever to have taken the momentous and heretical step of defying a Corp; and like all of them, she desperately wanted to be told what a good person she was.'[106] The very situation itself is ironic, as 'she hadn't told them anything they didn't already know' or, in Toby's words, ended up risking her life to smuggle 'a teaspoonful of stale-dated crap'.[107]

Atwood draws on a wider range of registers in her response to surveillance in the MaddAddam trilogy. She sometimes seems to revel in the creativity allowed by potential technical developments, for instance when she imagines cyborg bee spies, which have 'micro-mechanical systems [. . .] inserted into them'.[108] The whole trilogy is characterised by linguistic creativity, humorous puns and parody, as when the marketing language through which women are literally crooned into monitoring their appearance is mimicked: '*Do it for Yoo*, [. . .] *The Noo Yoo*.'[109] One of Toby's strategies to 'hid[e] out in plain view' involves taking a spurious job which consists in walking the streets dressed up

---

[101] Ibid., 53–4.

[102] Atwood, *The Year of the Flood*, 105.

[103] Atwood, *Oryx and Crake*, 18.

[104] Atwood, *MaddAddam*, 284.

[105] Toby herself has found shelter with an environmentalist cult called 'God's Gardeners', to which Zeb belongs, and which has developed numerous counter-surveillance strategies.

[106] Atwood, *The Year of the Flood*, 248.

[107] Ibid., 248–9.

[108] Ibid., 277.

[109] Ibid., 237, original emphasis.

as a pink duck, wearing a sandwich board that proclaims in bold characters: 'ANOOYOO! DO IT FOR YOO!'[110] The cells of sympathizers who provide the Gardeners with information that enable them to 'monitor' their enemies are comically referred to as 'Truffles', because 'they were underground, rare, and valuable, because you never could tell where they might appear next, and because pigs and dogs were employed to sniff them out'.[111] Grotesque effects are also produced when, for instance, it is stated that 'the internet [. . .] leaked like a prostate cancer patient'.[112] A similar strategy is used by Angela Carter who, in *Nights at the Circus*, deflates the much-dreaded Panopticon by comparing it to a 'doughnut' or '*baba au rhum*'.[113] While monolithic entities such as 'the surveillance society', 'surveillance systems' or indeed the Panopticon may seem to preclude the very possibility of resistance, the mobilisation of satire, humour and irony by writers creates the necessary distance to undermine claims to ubiquity and omnipotence.

V. Conclusion

Questions of surveillance and social control are deeply embedded in Atwood's body of work. Her fiction makes it possible to study the full complexity of gendered surveillance through the individual experience of her characters. It dramatises the tension between internal and external control as well as the paradoxical situation of female subjects who are made invisible *and* hypervisible. It questions the boundary usually set between the private and the public spheres, showing how the personal is indeed the political. It highlights the mechanisms by which female bodies are made 'docile' – social sorting and medical monitoring in the Gilead regime; improvement and self-regulation in *Bodily Harm* and the MaddAddam trilogy. It offers multiple points of view – that of the surveilled (Offred in *The Handmaid's Tale*) and that of the surveilling instance (Aunt Lydia in *The Testaments*) – while showing how both can coexist within one psyche. Although the individual experience of the female surveilled subject may be less prominent in the MaddAddam trilogy, there is little doubt as to the fact that surveillance is on the side of hubristic science and murderous patriarchy, as highlighted by ecofeminist readings of the novels.[114]

Atwood's novels register the evolution in surveillance technologies – from the spooks of *Bodily Harm* to the credit cards and social sorting in *The Handmaid's Tale*. Surveillance cameras and microdots appear in *The Testaments*

---

[110] Ibid., 260.
[111] Ibid., 189–90.
[112] Atwood, *MaddAddam*, 148–9.
[113] Carter, *Nights at the Circus*, 210–11, original emphasis.
[114] See for instance Stein, 'Surviving the Waterless Flood'.

but they seem relatively unsophisticated compared with the devices available to the CorpSeCorps with bugs, drones, algorithmic online tracking and the collection of genetic information. Collectively, they show how gendered surveillance need not be mediated by technology but also how even the most cutting-edge innovations can be defeated, thereby opening the possibility of resistance. Atwood's vision of surveillance is fundamentally embodied and dynamic – oppression is met with resistance, control by avoidance, espionage by counter-espionage.

If, as the Introduction to this volume suggests, being contemporary means not adjusting to the demands of our time, then Atwood's novels provide precisely the distance and clarity that we need. Distance is inherent in 'speculative fiction', which she defines as 'human society and its possible future forms, which are either much better than what we have now or much worse'.[115] Her reworkings of science fiction, dystopia and post-apocalyptic genres hold a critical mirror to contemporary Western society. Individual stories function as a magnifying glass to observe both localised attempts at resistance and surveillance phenomena at work. Atwood's reliance on literary modes of subversion, and satire in particular, locates her within a tradition which harks back to the early modern period and continues to the present day, as evidenced by Dave Eggers' recently published *The Every*. In this sequel to *The Circle*,[116] the endeavours of the female protagonist, Delaney Wells, to sabotage 'the Every' – an ecommerce giant aptly located on 'Treasure Island' in San Francisco Bay – indeed constitutes a vehicle to satirise surveillance capitalism. When it comes to the social critique of surveillance, literature does remain a powerful resource.

VI. Bibliography

Abu-Laban, Yasmeen. 'Gendering Surveillance Studies: The Empirical and Normative Promise of Feminist Methodology.' *Surveillance & Society* 13, no. 1 (2015): 44–56.
Atwood, Margaret. *Bodily Harm*. 1981. New York: Anchor Books, 1998.
———. *The Handmaid's Tale*. 1985. London: Vintage, 1996.
———. 'If You Can't Say Something Nice, Don't Say Anything At All.' *Saturday Night* 6 (13 January 2001). Later published in *Dropped Threads: What We Aren't Told*, edited by Carol Shields and Marjorie Anderson, 133–48. Toronto: Vintage Canada, 2001.
———. *In Other Worlds: SF and the Human Imagination*. London: Virago Press, 2011.
———. *MaddAddam*. London: Virago Press, 2014.
———. *Oryx and Crake*. London: Bloomsbury, 2003.
———. *The Testaments*. London: Chatto & Windus, 2019.

[115] Atwood, *In Other Worlds*, 115.
[116] The film adaptation is discussed in Brunon-Ernst, Chapter 6 of this collection.

————. *The Year of the Flood*. New York: Anchor Books, 2010.

Ball, Kirstie, Nicola Green, Hille Koskela, and David J. Phillips. 'Surveillance Studies Needs Gender and Sexuality.' Editorial. *Surveillance & Society* 6, no. 4 (2009): 352–5.

Bartky, Susan. 'Foucault, Femininity, and the Modernization of Patriarchal Power.' In *Feminism and Foucault: Reflections on Resistance*, edited by Irene Diamond and Lee Quinby, 61–88. Boston: Northeastern University Press, 1988.

Berger, John. *Ways of Seeing*. 1972. London: BBC/Penguin, 2008.

Bordo, Susan. 'The Body and the Reproduction of Femininity: A Feminist Reappropriation of Foucault.' In *Gender/Body/Knowledge: Feminist Reconstructions of Being and Knowing*, edited by Alison M. Jaggar and Susan R. Bordo, 13–33. New Brunswick, NJ: Rutgers University Press.

Carter, Angela. *Nights at the Circus*. London: Chatto & Windus, 1984.

Connell, R.W. *Masculinities*. Sydney: Allen & Unwin, 1996.

Dubrofsky, Rachel E., and Shoshana Amielle Magnet, eds. *Feminist Surveillance Studies*. Durham, NC: Duke University Press, 2015.

Eggers, Dave. *The Every*. New York: Vintage, 2021.

Hamann, Paul. 'Under Surveillance: Genetic Privacy in Margaret Atwood's MaddAddam trilogy.' *Journal of Literature and Science* 12, no. 2 (2019): 62–79.

Koskela, Hille. 'Video Surveillance, Gender, and the Safety of Public Urban Space: "Peeping Tom" Goes High Tech?' *Urban Geography* 23, no. 3 (2002): 257–78.

————. '"You Shouldn't Wear that Body": The Problematic of Surveillance and Gender.' In *The Routledge Handbook of Surveillance Studies*, edited by Kirstie Ball, Kevin D. Haggerty, and David Lyon, 49–56. New York: Routledge, 2012.

Lyon, David. *The Electronic Eye: The Rise of Surveillance Society*. Cambridge: Polity, 1994.

————. *Surveillance as Social Sorting: Privacy, Risk and Digital Discrimination*. New York: Routledge, 2005.

Marks, Peter. *Imagining Surveillance: Eutopian and Dystopian Literature and Film*. Edinburgh: Edinburgh University Press, 2015.

Marx, Gary T. 'A Tack in the Shoe: Neutralizing and Resisting the New Surveillance.' *Journal of Social Issues* 59, no. 2 (2003): 369–90.

Melley, Timothy. *Empire of Conspiracy: The Culture of Paranoia in Postwar America*. Ithaca, NY: Cornell University Press, 2000.

Mulvey, Laura. 'Visual Pleasure and Narrative Cinema.' *Screen* 16, no. 3 (1975): 6–18.

Reburn, Jenny. 'Profiling the City: Urban Space and the Serial Killer Film.' In *Expanding the Gaze: Gender and the Politics of Surveillance*, edited by Emily van der Meulen and Robert Heynen, 103–13. Toronto: University of Toronto Press, 2016.

Stein, Karen. 'Surviving the Waterless Flood: Feminism and Ecofeminism in Margaret Atwood's *The Handmaid's Tale, Oryx and Crake* and *The Year of the Flood*.' In *Critical Insights: Margaret Atwood*, edited by J. Brooks Bouson, 313–33. Ipswich, MA: Salem Press, 2013.

Thompson, Lucy E. *Gender, Surveillance, and Literature in the Romantic Period: 1780–1830*. Abingdon: Routledge, 2021.

Tolan, Fiona. *Margaret Atwood: Feminism and Fiction*. Amsterdam: Rodopi, 2007.

van der Meulen, Emily, and Robert Heynen. *Expanding the Gaze: Gender and the Politics of Surveillance*. Toronto: University of Toronto Press, 2016.

Wasihun, Betiel, ed. *Narrating Surveillance – Überwachen erzählen*. Baden-Baden: Ergon, 2019.

———. 'Surveillance Narratives: Kafka, Orwell, and Ulrich Peltzer's Post-9/11 Novel *Teil der Lösung*.' *Seminar: A Journal of Germanic Studies* 52, no. 4 (2016): 382–406.

Wrobel, Claire. 'Negotiating Dataveillance in the Near Future: Margaret Atwood's Dystopias.' *Commonwealth Essays and Studies* 43, no. 2 (2021). https://journals.openedition.org/ces/7718.

Zuboff, Shoshana. *The Age of Surveillance Capitalism: The Fight for the Future at the New Frontier of Power*. London: Profile Books, 2019.

Index

EU representative:
Easy Access System Europe
Mustamäe tee 50, 10621 Tallinn, Estonia
Gpsr.requests@easproject.com

www.ingramcontent.com/pod-product-compliance
Lightning Source LLC
Chambersburg PA
CBHW070842300326
41935CB00039B/1371